PERSONALITY

Personality Theories and Applications

Robert Hogan
Hogan Assessment Systems

Robert Smither
Rollins College

2008

Hogan Press
2622 E 21st Street Tulsa, OK 74114
www.hoganpress.com

ISBN 978-0-9816457-3-5

ISBN: 978-0-9816457-3-5

5 8 5 0 0

9 780981 645735

BRIEF CONTENTS

ILLUSTRATIONS

Boxes

PREFACE:

Five distinct features set this book apart from the many personality texts currently available. The first of these concerns the historical relationship between personality theory and clinical psychology. Most of the major personality theorists over the past hundred years have been psychiatrists or clinical psychologists, and their theories are generally used to diagnose, explain, and treat psychopathology. In addition, most personality textbooks present their theories from a clinical perspective.

In contrast, this book focuses on what the theories have to say about issues that concern normal people—competence and effectiveness, interpersonal relations, career and life success. We take this perspective for two reasons, one of which is related to an important lesson we have learned from assessment psychology over the past fifty years—namely, that competence and psychiatric problems are often unrelated. In short, well–adjusted people can be incompetent, just as highly successful people can have personal problems. The other reason is that undergraduate students are typically much older today than they were ten years ago—and although a few of them have personal problems, almost all of them will have careers. Accordingly, we focus on the links between personality, competence, and career success—a focus that is unique to this book.

The second feature that distinguishes this book is that it concerns topics rather than theories. Each of the major theorists discussed here was concerned with a particular issue—usually related to his or her personal history—and we attempt to explain why that issue is universally applicable. For example, Freud had difficulty dealing with authority figures, Jung was concerned about the psychological meaning of religious faith, and Erikson had trouble finding his own identity. These problems formed the core of each theorist's ideas about human nature. In our view, the traditional split between textbooks devoted to personality theory and those devoted to research topics is ineffective because every major theory focuses on a particular topic. To demonstrate the relevance of each theory to everyday life, we end each chapter with a practical example that applies the theory to a modern problem.

Third, although we are both familiar with clinical psychology, our research and writing have been primarily devoted to showing how personality psychology is important for understanding everyday life in general and organizational behavior in particular. Indeed, as longtime consultants in business and industry, we have tried to demonstrate how an understanding of personality can and should be used to analyze such important issues as selecting the best employees, helping people achieve at high levels, and identifying who will become leaders. In short, we have applied personality theory and assessment to industrial and organizational—rather than clinical—psychology. (To our knowledge, the only other textbook that shares this emphasis is Ross Stagner's Psychology of Personality, which was written in 1937.)

Fourth, we believe that a small number of "root ideas" form the core of personality theory. These ideas provide a framework for comparing the various topics under discussion; they also contribute to the organizational structure of each chapter. Fifth, and last, we have taken a practical approach to personality theory. Instead of writing a text rich in scholarly detail, we have focused on those topics that we hope students will be able to apply to their own lives.

We enjoyed writing this book; we hope you enjoy reading it.

PART ONE

Introduction to Personality Psychology

PERSONALITY

The Study of Human Nature

- Goals of the Book
- Organization of the Book
- Choice of Topics
- What Is Personality?
- Personality Theory Defined
- The Root Ideas of Personality Theory
- Practical Application: Assessing a Job Applicant's "Fit"

Much of what we do in our lives each day depends on how we think about other people—whether we think they are funny or hateful, whether they can be trusted, whether they will help us when we need them. Within academic psychology, the discipline that studies what people are like is called personality psychology.

Although most of our theories about others are not very clear or detailed, they are what we rely on when we deal with other people. Other academic disciplines, such as anthropology, criminology, economics, history, sociology, and political science, also depend on assumptions about human nature. Economists, for example, assume that people make decisions based on rational self-interest; anthropologists and sociologists assume that human nature is quite flexible and that people are primarily shaped by their cultures; historians and political scientists use ideas about personality to explain the biographies of famous people.

Personality psychology helps us explain the behavior of famous people.
Sources: Joseph Sohm, Chromosohm Inc./Corbis; Sisters of Mercy; Corbis; Mitchell Gerber/Corbis.

The unique role of personality psychology in modern life is that it concerns theories about human nature and tries to evaluate them in an empirical way—an effort in which it is essentially alone. In fact, this emphasis on the empirical study of human nature is what makes personality psychology a unique discipline.

Goals of the Book

This book has three goals. The first is to describe and present the most important theories of human nature. Sigmund Freud, Abraham Maslow, and B. F. Skinner strongly influenced the way we think about history, political behavior, management practices, and social policy, and every educated person should be familiar with these theorists. In contrast with narrow academic specialties, the study of personality influences many fields outside psychology and is an essential part of any liberal education. Ideas have consequences; thus we should be clear about what our ideas are and how we justify them.

A second goal of this book is to evaluate the major theories of human nature. Some of these theories can be evaluated in terms of how well they are supported by empirical research; others can be evaluated in terms of their logical consistency. Such evaluations reveal that every theory of personality—like every theory in science generally—contains some valid points and some critical flaws.

Finally, we hope that you, the reader, will develop some feeling for the spirit of personality psychology. Each of the theorists we discuss offers ideas that help us address the major problems of life. We find these ideas both useful and fascinating, and hope you will come to share our enthusiasm.

Organization of the Book

The organization of this book is different from that of most personality texts. It is based on our understanding that the authors of the major personality theories were concerned about specific questions, and that the theories were designed to answer those questions. Accordingly, each theory is organized around a key issue.

This format characterizes most of the chapters, each of which contains five sections. The first presents a short biography of the theorist and describes the major influences on his or her ideas. The second section describes the core issue with which the theorist was concerned and how he or she analyzed it. The third section outlines the theory's image of human nature in terms of the six "root ideas" that form the conceptual backbone of personality psychology. (These root ideas are defined later in the present chapter.) The fourth section evaluates the theory, describing its unique strengths and shortcomings. And the fifth section applies the theory to a problem or situation that almost everyone faces at one time or another.

The chapters themselves are presented in chronological order, reflecting the development of personality psychology from Freud to the present. We believe that ideas about human nature have evolved over time—in other words, that all personality theorists are influenced by their predecessors (even those they disagreed with) and that all personality theories build on earlier ones.

Chapter 2 provides brief history of personality theory. Chapters 3, 4, and 5 deal with traditional European depth psychology, which is where modern personality theory began. Chapters 6, 7, and 8 describe the American reaction to the European tradition. Chapter 9, on the sociological tradition, is unique to this book; but we believe that an understanding of how sociologists think about human nature is essential for understanding personality. In addition, because the sociological viewpoint criticizes the psychological perspective on human nature, it deserves close attention. Chapters 10, 11, and 12 present possible replies to the sociological challenge.

In Box 1.1 we discuss an innovative approach to understanding personality that was developed by a historian.

BOX 1.1 Personality and the End of History

In a book entitled *The End of History and the Last Man (1992)*, the historian Francis Fukuyama startled his colleagues and the reading public by arguing that history has come to an end. The great German philosopher G.W.F. Hegel (1770–1831) argued that there is a movement and direction to history. The question is, "What drives the movement of history?" Fukuyama, like many social and political theorists before him, based his answer on his theory of human nature.

According to Fukuyama, major writers in the history of Anglo-American political theory—Hobbes, Locke, Madison—didn't understand what drives people. They assumed that people are motivated primarily by reason and self-interest and that history is a sort of random walk as people seek to find that which will serve their self-interest.

On the contrary, Fukuyama argues, people are motivated by *thymos*—a term, borrowed from Plato, that means "desire for recognition." According to Fukuyama, *thymos* is the primary force in history. The possibility of being recognized, he notes, is maximized in modern liberal democracies, since democracy is the form of government that allows the greatest number of people to satisfy *thymos*. With the development of modern democracies, then, history has come to an end— because it has reached a form of government that satisfies the force that drove history in the first place.

Many personality psychologists would disagree with Fukuyama, who, according to Gordon Allport, bases his argument on too "simple and sovereign" a theory of motivation. First, although some people desire fame, others clearly don't—and Fukuyama ignores the problem of individual differences. Second, there is simply more to human motivation than a desire to be famous; Freud might have added that Fukuyama has projected his own primary need on the rest of humankind.

The essential point here is that writers in fields other than psychology necessarily make assumptions about human nature and then develop their own historical, political, or economic arguments based on such assumptions. This book evaluates those assumptions.

Choice of Topics

Some psychologists argue that the major personality theories have been discredited, are out of date, or are too vague to be scientific. They also argue that students should study developments in modern research rather than outdated or empty theories.

The problem with focusing solely on modern research trends, however, is that many of these trends turn out to be fads that last only a short while. The theories of Freud or Skinner, by contrast, still generate interest among researchers and the public. We believe that these and other traditional theories are valuable because they provide a context for understanding modern research problems. In our view, students should have a background in such major theories before they are introduced to modern research. Without this background, they won't fully understand the implications of the new findings.

What Is Personality?

There are almost as many definitions of personality as there are personality theorists. Consequently, it is tempting to conclude that personality can't be defined, that the definition depends on the theory, or that definitions are irrelevant. If we can study biology without defining life, for example, why can't we study people without defining personality? We believe that definitions are important, however, and one way to deal with them is to ask how the word we want to define is used in everyday language. In the case of technical terms, for example, we would ask how they are used among people who work in that technical specialty.

Scholars agree that the English word *personality* comes from the Greek word *persona,* which referred to the large masks used by actors in ancient Greek drama (500 b.c.) and, later (around 100 b.c.), by actors in the Roman theater. The persona, or mask, signified the actor's part in a play—just as your personality reflects the role you play in the everyday drama of your life. The word for an actor's mask quickly took on other meanings. According to Gordon Allport *(1937),* author of one of the first textbooks in personality psychology, the Roman statesman Cicero (106–43 b.c.) used the word *persona* in at least four different ways. Over the years the meaning of *personality* also continued to expand, such that Allport was able to find fifty different definitions by 1937. Today, more than six decades later, there seems to be even less consensus among scholars about the meaning of this word.

Despite the semantic confusion it seems clear that, in ordinary language, the word *personality* is used in two primary ways. On the one hand, *personality* refers to the distinctive impression a person makes on others. When we think of a parent, a friend, a favorite or hated teacher, we think of his or her interpersonal style. The philosopher Charles Horton Cooley used the word in this way: "That which we usually speak of as 'personality' in a somewhat external sense, is a sort of atmosphere, having its source in habitual states of feeling, which each of us unconsciously communicates through facial and vocal expression. We cannot assume or conceal these states of feeling with much success. . . . We impart what we are without effort or consciousness, and rarely impart anything else" *(1902, pp. 106–107).* In short, what we impart becomes our personality from the perspective of the others with whom we interact, and this, in turn, becomes our reputation.

On the other hand, many writers are interested in the inner core of people, and they regard reputations as relatively superficial. These writers are concerned with the deep structure of personality, which they believe is the essence of a person. Morton Prince, an early American personality psychologist, provides an example of how the word personality is used to refer to internal structure: "Personality is the sum-total of all the biological innate dispositions, impulses, tendencies, appetites, and instincts of the individual, and the acquired dispositions and tendencies—acquired by experience" (1924, p. 532). These internal characteristics make up personality from the perspective of the individual.

With regard to these two meanings of personality, the first—personality from the observer's perspective—is easier to study than the second—personality from the individual's perspective. To study the first, we can ask a person's family, friends, and neighbors about his or her characteristic interpersonal style and then evaluate these descriptions in terms of their structure, stability, and consistency with other facts about the person in question.

To study personality from the individual's perspective, however, we must somehow get inside that individual's mind. This normally involves having the person tell us about him- or herself. But personal reports are difficult to analyze in a scientific manner, for two reasons: They are difficult to verify, and many people don't understand themselves very well.

It is also important to ask how the two primary meanings of *personality* are related. We know that they are related statistically; indeed, the stories that individuals tell us about themselves tend to correlate with, and thus can be used to predict, how their friends and colleagues will describe them. Obviously, then, what goes on inside a person's mind must in some way cause or explain his or her unique interpersonal style. So the two forms of personality are related; but to what extent we can't say, nor do we know what the actual links may be.

The distinction between personality "from the outside," or reputation, and personality "from the inside," or a person's self-view, reflects the important distinction between prediction and explanation. Generally speaking, in science our first problem is to be able to predict that something such as thunder will follow something else such as lightning. Our second problem is to explain *why* thunder follows lightning. In the field of personality specifically, we can use a person's reputation to predict how he or she will behave in the future because *the best predictor of future behavior is past behavior*. But once we are able to predict someone's behavior, we must then try to explain why it occurs, and this is where we need a model of personality "from the inside." We use a person's self-view to explain why that person acts as he or she does and thus essentially creates his or her particular reputation.

Although personality psychologists often define *personality* in different ways, they accept the reliability and scientific status of the concept. They agree first that personality exists—that inside each of us is a set of relatively stable structures and recurring processes (however they may be defined) that give unique form and coherence to our actions and, ultimately, to our lives. They also agree that these stable structures and processes can be used to explain, interpret, and understand our behavior as it develops and is expressed over time.

However, some psychologists in other fields have argued that what people do is best explained in terms of factors in the social environment—that is, in terms of "situations" that evoke certain behaviors. In fact, personality psychology is unique among the disciplines of modern psychology in maintaining that there are relatively stable structures inside people that determine what people do. But once again, it is important to note that not all psychologists agree with this belief.

We can summarize our discussion so far as follows. The word *personality* has two primary meanings: (1) the unique impression that a person makes on others and (2) a person's "true" inner nature. The first meaning refers to personality from the observer's viewpoint; the second meaning refers to personality from the individual's viewpoint. Most theories emphasize one or the other of these meanings, but it is important to keep both definitions in mind. Moreover, both definitions rest on the assumption that there is a stable core to personality, and that people's actions can be understood and explained in terms of this stable core.
Box 1.2 presents a chronology of some of the methods that researchers have developed to make judgments about personality.

Personality Theory Defined

A **personality theory** is a set of assumptions and expectations that one has about oneself and other people that guide one's perceptions of, and actions with regard to, oneself and other people. And what do personality theories do? They attempt to answer three major questions:

1. In what ways are all people alike? For example, are humans naturally aggressive?

2. Given that each person's behavior tends to be consistent over time and across situations, yet is often different from the behavior of others, what are the causes and structure of individual differences in human behavior?

3. How can we interpret or explain unusual actions, such as Lee Harvey Oswald's assassination of President John F. Kennedy?

Personality theories differ in terms of how well they deal with these questions; some deal with all three, others do not. (This dimension—breadth—is another criterion for evaluating the theories themselves.)

Many psychology textbooks maintain that theories should be evaluated in terms of how well they are supported by empirical data. In a similar vein, Sir Karl Popper, a British philosopher of science, proposed that theories be evaluated in terms of whether or not they can be refuted. Popper *(1959)* was initially impressed with how well the theories of Freud and of Alfred Adler (his competitor and contemporary) could explain the same behavior. Popper eventually concluded, however, that this was problematic: "I could not think of any human behavior which could not be interpreted in terms of either theory" *(Popper, 1959, p. 35)*. According to Popper, the fact that Freudian and Adlerian theories could explain every human action meant that they are irrefutable and, therefore, not scientific.

BOX 1.2 A Brief History of Methods for Studying Personality

Personality assessment is the primary method for doing personality research. As indicated in the following chronology, the Chinese developed assessment as a method for choosing civil servants about one thousand years ago, and modern personality assessment began with Freud's use of free association as a way of uncovering hidden conflicts.

206	The Chinese (Han Dynasty) develop assessment as a method for choosing civil servants.
1880	Sigmund Freud uses free association to uncover hidden conflicts.
1903	Carl Jung develops the word association test to make free association systematic.
1924	Hermann Rorschach invents the inkblot test to study elements of the Jungian unconscious. The Rorschach is now the most widely used assessment device in the world.
1930	Morton Prince founds the Harvard Psychological Clinic—the first assessment center in the United States. At the time it was used to study maturity in Harvard undergraduates.
1935	Henry Murray develops the Thematic Apperception Test (TAT) as another method to study the unconscious. The TAT is now the second most widely used personality test in the world.
1936–1942	Henry Murray and his colleagues set up two assessment centers designed to select special agents for the Office of Strategic Services, or OSS (the precursor of the Central Intelligence Agency).
1943	Starke Hathaway and J. C. McKinley publish the Minnesota Multiphasic Personality Inventory—the most widely used objective psychiatric screening device in the world.
1948	The Institute of Personality Assessment and Research is established at the University of California–Berkeley for the purpose of studying high-level effectiveness.
1954	Harrison Gough publishes the California Psychological Inventory, the first measure of normal personality designed to predict effectiveness.
1961	Edward Tupes and Raymond Christal publish the monograph that inaugurates the Five-Factor Model.
1962	Isabelle Myers publishes the Myers-Briggs Type Indicator; based on Jungian theory, it becomes the most popular personality test in the world.
1963	Robert Guion and Richard Gottier publish a devastating critique of the validity of personality measurement.
1968	Walter Mischel publishes a devastating critique of personality theory.
1970	Personality psychology enters a period of decline and neglect.
1991	Meta-analytic evidence regarding the validity of personality assessment initiates a rebirth of the discipline.
1996	Robert Hogan and Joyce Hogan publish the Hogan Personality Inventory—the first measure of normal personality, based on the Five-Factor Model, designed to predict effectiveness.

Although it seems reasonable that we should evaluate theories in terms of empirical data and their refutability, the history of science demonstrates that major theories about anything are rarely accepted or rejected on the basis of empirical support *(Kuhn, 1965)*. Consider, for example, Copernicus's ideas about the structure of our solar system. His model, which he proposed in De revolutionibus orbium coelestium in 1543, has been accepted by scientists for over four hundred years. Yet it wasn't until 1851 that Foucault invented his pendulum and provided the first scientific evidence for Copernicus's theory. This scenario is a common one in the history of science *(Burtt, 1954)*.

Another way of looking at the value of empirical support for theories is to realize that scientists don't test a theory, they test the implications of a theory. The process of deriving testable implications requires substantial imagination on the part of the researcher. Accordingly, the fact that a theory has little empirical support may say more about the talent of the people who want to evaluate it than about the merits of the theory itself.

In this book we have evaluated theories not only in terms of their empirical support but also in terms of their originality, their logical consistency, and their fit with common historical experience.

The Root Ideas of Personality Theory

Certain issues form the core of any important theory of personality. These issues are the topics around which the great debates swirl and they are the distinctive subject matter of personality psychology. Just as physical theory must deal with matter, time, and energy, personality theory must deal with the concepts of motivation, personality development, self-knowledge, the unconscious, psychological adjustment, and the relationship between the individual and society. The theories discussed here vary in terms of the way they treat these ideas, providing yet another way for evaluating them. Below we discuss each of the six root ideas of personality psychology. These ideas make up the fourth section of most of the chapters and essentially form the core of the book.

1. ***Motivation.*** Motivation concerns what makes people act – what provides the energy, force, or reasons behind their actions. Motives are the primary explanatory variables in personality psychology. That is, personality psychologists generally use motivational concepts to explain why people do what they do. Although motivational terms vary widely among theorists, they can be categorized in one of two ways.

The first category includes biological or physiological terms such as *drive, need, instinct, passion, and urges*. Theorists who use these terms generally have a biological theory of motivation in mind. However, although motives may be consciously perceived, these perceptions are not motives themselves.

Biological models of motivation—such as Freud's psychoanalytic theory—explain human action in terms of fixed and unchanging motives. According to these models, people are all very much alike in terms of their basic motives. Biological motives are usually described as unconscious or beyond rational control (i.e., they can't be educated) and as harmful or dangerous if they are frustrated or ignored for a long time. According to this view, biological motives such as hunger, thirst, sex, and elimination are insistent; they must be dealt with from time to time or they will cause problems of some sort.

The second motivational category concerns psychological or mental terms such as *values, expectations, attitudes, preferences, and goals*. When theorists use these terms, they have psychological motives in mind. Cognitive social learning theorists, in particular, describe human motivation in terms of a relatively large number of individual motives that they believe are unique to each person. These motives are usually described as conscious, rationally chosen and controlled, and changeable through education and self-reflection. In contrast with biological motives, psychological motives do not drive human action so much as guide and direct it. Consequently, psychological motives—such as the desire for fame, money, revenge, or a college education—are more subtle and not as insistent as biological motives.

These two perspectives on motivation are quite distinct, but they are often confused. Because the word *motive* refers to two very different concepts, it is inherently ambiguous—and discussions of motivation are often complicated by this ambiguity.

 2. ***Personality development***. Personality theories differ considerably in the degree to which they are concerned with personality development. Moreover, there is an important distinction between "stage" and "learning" theories of development. In traditional developmental theory, personality is described as passing through a series of levels or stages; everyone undergoes these stages, which in turn are usually correlated with chronological age. According to this view, the structure of personality changes markedly as a person moves from one stage to the next, such that the needs, talents, and interests of a three-year-old, say, are very different from those of a middle-aged adult. Moreover, movement from one stage to the next is usually irreversible: People rarely move backward in development.

Traditional developmental theory also assumes that earlier experiences influence later development and are more significant. Thus, events in the first year of life have a crucial impact on adult personality. According to this view, adult neurosis begins with bad experiences in infancy and early childhood. Many European writers, including Freud, Jung, and Erikson, adopted this traditional view of personality development.

In contrast with the traditional view, many British and American writers have taken what might be called the "development as learning" view. For these writers—most notably the behavioral theorists B. F. Skinner and Albert Bandura—development is continuous rather than stage-like: No major structural changes take place during development, and an adult is different from a child primarily because he or she has learned more ways to deal with the world. Children are merely inexperienced adults with essentially the same needs, capacities, and interests. From this viewpoint, then, development is related not to age but to experience—the more experience, the more development. Moreover, development is believed to be reversible—moving backward is as easy as moving forward.

Learning theorists also believe that the timing of experience is not important, and that early experiences are usually no more influential than later ones. Experiences are significant because of their frequency or intensity, not because of their timing. The sources of adult neurosis, therefore, do not necessarily lie in a person's childhood but possibly in the current circumstances of that person's life.

3. **Self-knowledge.** Personality theories differ widely in terms of how they deal with the concept of the self. Behaviorists and factor analytic theorists, for example, tend to give this topic a rather skimpy treatment. By contrast, interpersonal and humanistic psychologists see the self as the image that people have of themselves—an image that filters and screens social behavior. In this view, the self is just one aspect of personality, but it is the central and guiding aspect. Still other theorists, following the approach of Gordon Allport and Alfred Adler, see the self as equivalent to personality itself. Finally, Carl Jung regarded the self as the ultimate stage of personality development; for him, attaining selfhood was the goal of life.

There are some interesting puzzles associated with self-knowledge. For example, the image we have of ourselves is the self we know about—the "known self," as it were. But exactly who is it that knows this self? Who reflects back upon and perceives this image? Here we seem to have an unknown knower, a portion of our psyches or minds that records information about us but cannot itself be experienced. For centuries, philosophers have worried about how to understand this unknown knower and the logical problems it raises.

A second puzzle concerns the truthfulness or authenticity of our self–images. Which is more true or correct: the image we have of ourselves or the image that our friends and family have of us? Alternatively, is our "real" self different from the one we know or other people describe? The problem of authentic self-knowledge is especially important for psychoanalytic, existential, and humanistic personality theorists.

A third puzzle concerns the correspondence between our self-images and our ideal selves. Assuming that we can analyze and describe our self-images, how do these compare with our views of ourselves as we would like to be? The match between real and ideal self-images is often regarded as an index of psychological adjustment—an index that theorists such as Carl Rogers and Karen Horney have used to evaluate the effects of psychotherapy.

4. **Unconscious processes.** The idea that we have an unconscious mind operating outside our control and leading us to do things we don't understand is one of the oldest and most interesting notions in psychiatry and popular psychology. Although traditional psychiatric theory accepts on faith the existence of a dynamic unconscious, many psychologists are suspicious of the idea. Not surprisingly, personality theories differ considerably in terms of how important they think unconscious processes might be. Some ignore the issue altogether; others are very much concerned with the ways in which the unconscious can—and should—be analyzed.

5. **Psychological adjustment.** Because the study of psychological adjustment focuses on how and why people break down, and tries to determine what may be done to help them, it overlaps with the earlier topics we have discussed. Indeed, personality development,

motivation, self-knowledge, and unconscious processes are needed to explain why and how people become stressed and unable to manage their lives. Clinical psychology is concerned with this topic in particular.

Another issue relevant to psychological adjustment is maturity: What does a healthy or mature person look like? Models of maturity are used to formulate and guide public policy in education, welfare, and the juvenile court system. To the degree that it can, government should try to create conditions that foster and maintain maturity.

6. ***The individual and society.*** In the nineteenth century, the French philosopher Auguste Comte suggested that the most important question in the social sciences is how people can both create and be the products of their societies. Implicit in this question is the issue of how best to understand the relationship between an individual and his or her society, and the answer changes as we move from psychoanalysis to theories of personality closer to the sociological perspective.

Some theorists maintain that people are the only reality, that society or culture exists primarily inside people's minds, and, most important, that society is something people invent in order to control their normally selfish and aggressive tendencies. According to this view, there is a deep antagonism between the individual and society: Society is necessary for individual survival, but it exists at the cost of individual happiness. Parents and other adults are thus advised to pay close attention to how children are raised in an attempt to ensure that their normal antisocial impulses are brought under control.

TABLE 1.1   Questions Related to the Six Root Ideas of Personality Psychology

Motivation	Should we explain people's actions in terms of unconscious instincts? Or rational goals and plans?
Personality Development	Do people change over time? If so, in what ways? And can those changes be reversed?
Self-knowledge	Socrates said that the most important goal in life is to "know thyself." What is there to know about yourself, and how do you know if what you know is right?
Unconscious Processes	Are there psychological factors that control our behavior but remain outside our awareness? If so, what are they—and what should we do about them?
Psychological Adjustment	What does it mean to be human? Is the goal of life happiness? Self-knowledge? Serving others?
The Individual and Society	Everyone agrees that culture shapes personality. But how? What are the mechanisms or processes involved? And what are the psychological consequences of having been shaped?

Other theorists take the opposite perspective. They maintain that society or culture exists prior to and outside the control of any one person, that there is no universal human nature, and that the content of people's minds reflects the contents of their culture rather than human instincts. In other words, people are what their society makes them. This view holds that children are naturally sociable and that delinquency results from faulty childrearing.

Both of these perspectives maintain that the rules of society replace instincts as the guiding force in human action. The rules of society concern how to dress, what to eat, how to speak, and, more generally, how to behave. The rules are learned, and they override—even conflict with—natural human tendencies as the key factors regulating our behavior.

When we think about the link between the individual and society, a major issue comes to mind: How do the rules of society come to control and direct human action? As an example, consider the normal "selfishness" of babies and small children. How do they become willing to follow social rules? In fact, the changes that normally occur are associated with the socialization process; socialization forges the link between the individual and his or her society.

Table 1.1 offers some questions related to the six root ideas of personality psychology. As noted earlier, these ideas—motivation, personality development, self-knowledge, unconscious processes, psychological adjustment, and the individual and society—form the substance of personality theory. Every theory deals with some or all of these topics, and theories differ primarily in terms of how they handle them. As we have noted before, section four of most of the chapters is organized around these ideas.

A major goal of education from the time of Socrates to the present has been to develop self-knowledge. "Know thyself" was inscribed above the entrance to the temple of the Oracle at Delphi, and the belief that the truth will make you free is a cornerstone of our society. But what will you know when you know yourself, and what is the truth about yourself that will make you free? Presumptuous as it may sound, this is one of the questions that personality psychology tries to answer. The nature of truth at the level of the individual is in fact the overarching theme of this book and the final reference point for each of the theories discussed. As a way of putting these theories into context, however, we will first review the history of the field in Chapter 2.

Practical Application: Assessing a Job Applicant's "Fit"

Almost everyone has had the experience of meeting someone for the first time and knowing immediately that that person would become a good friend. Probably most people have had the opposite experience as well—meeting someone they knew would never become a friend.

When we meet someone for the first time, we are likely to notice the way that person dresses and what he or she talks about. During this interaction, we are making an assessment—usually unconscious—of how well that person will "fit" with our own lifestyle and friends. We use our own personal theory of personality to make judgments about what that person is like.

A similar process occurs when people apply for jobs: Every interviewer has a theory about the kind of person who will be successful at the job in question. Probably the first judgment an interviewer must make is whether an applicant has the ability to do the work. But an important second consideration is how the person compares to other employees and to the interviewer's ideas about the ideal candidate for the job. The interviewer may wonder, for example, if the applicant's values are compatible with the values of the organization. An applicant who stresses the importance of a high salary, for example, may not fit well with workers at a social service agency where salaries tend to be low. Similarly, applicants who have no interest in technology may not fit well with co-workers at an Internet company.

Several studies *(e.g., Caldwell & O'Reilly, 1990; Guthrie & Olian, 1991)* have shown that, in addition to abilities, "fit" affects success on the job. One study in particular *(Rajagopalan & Datta, 1996)* found that the most effective CEOs were those who had been hired on the basis of the similarity between their values and those of the firm—rather than their knowledge of the firm's industry.

Earlier in the chapter we mentioned that most people have their own theories of personality. Although these theories are unconscious, people use them to interpret the behavior of others. Nowhere is this truer than in employment interviews, where a manager or human resource professional must make judgments about qualities other than an applicant's abilities. That is why all guides to successful interviewing advise applicants to create the impression that their personality and values "fit" with those of the company to which they are applying for a job.

Employment interviewers use their own theories of personality when deciding whether a job applicant will fit in with other workers.

Sources: Photodisc.

2

A BRIEF HISTORY

of Personality Psychology

- The Descriptive Tradition
- The Explanatory Tradition
- Practical Application: Who Will Become Violent?

In Chapter 1 we pointed out that the word *personality* has two basic meanings: (1) reputation, or the way other people would describe us; and (2) self-view, or the way we "really are." A major claim of this book is that each of us has a lot to learn about our personality in both senses of the word. To know ourselves means to understand, on the one hand, how other people see us and, on the other hand, why we typically act the way we do.

These two meanings correspond to the two major traditions in personality psychology: the **descriptive tradition** and the explanatory tradition. The descriptive tradition develops taxonomies in order to classify people. Because the first goal of science is to describe the structure of nature, a method for classifying people and their characteristics is the first step in developing a science of personality. But description is *not* explanation; knowing how something is classified doesn't tell us why it belongs in that classification. In personality psychology, it is the other tradition—the explanatory one—that tries to get beneath the surface of personality to explain why people act as they do.

This chapter briefly reviews these two traditions, which are as distinct today as they were 2,000 years ago.

The Descriptive Tradition

The descriptive tradition contains two related approaches to classifying personality—*type theory* and *trait theory*. Type theory involves classifying people in terms of their distinctive characteristics; trait theory involves classifying the characteristics themselves.

Type Theory

Throughout history, type theory has taken a number of forms. Four of these forms are discussed below.

Literary Type Theory. Theophrastus, the founder of botany, described the personality types prominent in Athens during the time of Alexander the Great (356–323 b.c.). These included the Flatterer and the Miser, as well as the Boorish, Loquacious, Pretentious, Arrogant, Cowardly, Mean, and Stupid man. Theophrastus described these types in a detached tone, allowing his characters to reveal their disagreeable qualities in their appearance, speech, and interpersonal style. Although Theophrastus's work is now over 2,000 years old, his types are perfectly recognizable today.

The classification game started by Theophrastus became quite popular in Europe in the seventeenth century. In 1608, Joseph Hall, a fan of Theophrastus, published *Characters of Vertues and Vices*, the first English collection of character types. Unlike Theophrastus, however, Hall used his character types to promote Christian morality. The next landmark in this tradition is John Earle's *Micro-Cosmography* (1628). Whereas Theophrastus simply catalogued personality types, Earle described the hidden motives and darker conflicts beneath the surface of his odd types, including the Down-Right Scholar, the Pretender to Learning, and the Young Raw Preacher.

The best-known seventeenth-century study of types, however, is Samuel Butler's *Genuine Remains,* published in 1759 several years after his death. Butler, who lived during the time of Oliver Cromwell, despised the people who profited from Cromwell's Puritan government. He described nearly 200 politicians, clergymen, physicians, astrologers, and seers prominent at the time, and his language was pungent and often unflattering.

Although the popularity of literary classification died out in the eighteenth century, vestiges of this typology can be seen in the popular psychology of today—"right-brain and left-brain people," "men are from Mars and women are from Venus," and "Type A personality" (see Box 2.1)—suggesting that people enjoy classifying and predicting the behavior of others.

Physiological Type Theory. Based on Empedocles' (495–435 b.c.) notion that the universe is composed of four elements—earth air, fire, and water—Galen (a.d. 130–200) developed a scheme to classify people. Specifically, he proposed that people were composed of four elements, or "humors," that he called black bile, yellow bile, phlegm, and blood. Imbalances in these humors, he said, produce four types of people: Persons with too much black bile are melancholic and depressed; those with too much yellow bile (which supposedly comes from the spleen) are hostile and bad-tempered; those with too much phlegm are lazy and lethargic

BOX 2.1: Type A Behavior

Although type theory traces back to ancient Greece, researchers continue to identify new categories of personality types. One of the most popular recent developments in type theory has been the identification of the Type A personality.

Type As were discovered by a group of cardiologists who noticed that something unusual was happening to the furniture in their waiting room. The upholstery on the chairs was wearing out on the front edge of the seat, but not on the arms or the back. Apparently the patients, mostly people recovering from heart attacks, were sitting forward on the edge of their seats while waiting for their appointments. The physicians concluded that the patients sat that way so they could jump up quickly when the nurse called their name.

The physicians then begin to notice other characteristics among their heart-attack patients; for example, they always seemed to be in a hurry. These patients also spoke rapidly, expressed impatience with anything that interfered with their plans, and had a hostile and competitive attitude toward other people. In addition, they were highly focused on their careers and had a strong need for achievement.

These observations gave rise to a series of studies that, in turn, led to the identification of Type A and Type B personalities (Friedman & Rosenman, 1974). Type As are people who have the characteristics listed above—including, most notably, a sense of time urgency. Type Bs, by contrast, are more relaxed and easygoing. Although these initial studies linked Type A behavior with greater risk for heart disease and stroke, later research suggests that this is the case only for Type As who also exhibit high levels of anger and hostility (Bluen, Barling, & Burns, 1990; Booth-Kewley & Friedman, 1987).

Researchers have identified a lengthy list of behaviors associated with the Type A personality. For example, Type As often speak so rapidly that they have trouble getting their words out clearly. They are always rushing, never have time to get a haircut, and feel compelled to get through intersections after the stoplights have turned yellow. On the positive side, Type As tend to be busy and productive individuals. When these qualities are linked with anger and hostility, however, they can be dangerous.

(i.e., phlegmatic); and those with too much blood have a cheerful, optimistic, sanguine disposition.

Galen's types have been remarkably influential. Immanuel Kant (1724–1804), one of the greatest philosophers in our history, wrote a best-selling guide to living—Anthropology from a Pragmatic Point of View *(1798)*—that was based on Galen's theory. Wilhelm Wundt, the father of modern experimental psychology, used the theory in his original *(1903)* textbook. Ivan Pavlov, a Russian Nobel Prize–winning physician and author of the theory of the conditioned reflex

(Chapter 8), used Galen's types to describe the four kinds of nervous systems that he found in dogs. And Hans Eysenck (1967) proposed a theory of types based on his ideas about levels of neural arousal in the lower brain stem. Figure 2.1 describes the similarities among the type theories of Galen, Wundt, and Eysenck.

Leon Rostan (1824) developed the most influential typology after Galen. He based his approach on physique or body build and defined four types: cerebral (long and thin); muscular (square and athletic); digestive (rotund); and respiratory (a combination of the three previous types). Giovanni Viola (1909), using more sophisticated measurement methods, reduced Rostan's typology to three categories: microsplanchic (skinny), normosplanchic (normal), and macrosplanchic (chubby). Based on Viola's data, Ernst Kretschmer (1925) developed a physique-based type theory that was very popular prior to World War II. He defined three types: aesthenic (emaciated body build), athletic (muscular build), and pyknic (plump build). He also found relationships between the aesthenic build and schizophrenia, and between the pyknic build and manic-depression. W. H. Sheldon (Sheldon, Dupertuis, & McDermott, 1954) developed the most famous of these physique-based typologies. He called them somatotypes; he believed that they reflected underlying genetic factors and were associated with characteristic personality styles. Ectomorphs—tall, thin people—were shy, retiring, and potentially disposed toward schizophrenia. Mesomorphs—square, athletically built people—were aggressive and

FIGURE 2.1 The Views of Galen, Wundt, and Eysenck Concerning Type. This figure shows the convergence between the various type theories that have been advanced between Greek antiquity and the present. The two main axes—Conformity and Sociability—can be used to generate the four types proposed by Galen and Eysenck and the six types proposed by John Holland (who is discussed later in the chapter).

assertive and potentially disposed toward paranoia. And endomorphs—round people—were jolly and fun and potentially disposed toward manic-depression.

Cognitive Type Theory. Cognitive type theory classifies people on the basis of how they think and what they value. Two versions of cognitive type theory are very popular today. The first, based on Jungian theory (Chapter 4), uses the Myers-Briggs Type Indicator *(MBTI; Myers & McCaulley, 1985)* to assign people to one of sixteen types. The MBTI is widely used in business to promote better relations among people who work together. In Jungian theory no one type is preferable to any other; rather, each type has characteristic strengths and shortcomings. Knowledge of one's own type allows a person to draw on his or her strengths and communicate more effectively with others.

The second variety of cognitive type theory, John Holland's *(1985)* theory of vocational types, is frequently used in counseling psychology. Holland's views, which are based on considerable research data, suggest that careers can be organized in terms of six broad types: Realistic, Investigative, Artistic, Social, Enterprising, and Conventional. When choosing a career, individuals should match their own type profile with the type profile associated with a particular occupation, thereby aligning their specific strengths with the psychological demands of that career.

Physiognomic Type Theory. *Physiognomy* is the process of classifying people on the basis of their appearance—especially the face. Look at the faces in Figure 2.2. Which one seems sad and melancholic? Which one seems choleric and full of fight? Which one seems phlegmatic and bored? And which one seems sanguine and naive? It is easy to guess the emotional state of each person from his or her face—a fact that not only illustrates the appeal of physiognomy as a way to classify personality but also demonstrates a link between physiognomy and type theory.

Aristotle appears to have written the first systematic physiognomy. He suggested that we can judge personality by studying posture, gait, and gestures, in addition to facial expressions, and by looking for consistencies among these signs: "You will have more reason for confidence in your conclusions," he said, "when you find several signs all pointing one way." Physiognomy has been popular since the thirteenth century, but today it is practiced only by palm readers and fortune tellers. It became so popular in England that in the eighteenth century the British Parliament passed laws sentencing persons practicing physiognomy to be publicly whipped or sent to houses of correction.

Fortune tellers notwithstanding, there is, as Aristotle noted, some relationship between a person's characteristic facial expression and his or her personality. This relationship is central to the "facial feedback hypothesis" *(Izard, 1971; Tomkins, 1980)*, which states that typical patterns of emotions are associated with typical patterns of thoughts as well as typical facial expressions. In other words, what people usually think about, how they feel, and how they look are all somehow associated. Indeed, the research of Carroll Izard and Sylvan Tomkins illustrates how personality psychology tries to verify, in a scientific way, the insights of artists and philosophers.

Faces According to Galen's Types

Sources (clockwise from upper left): Steve Chenn/Corbis; Edward Holub/Corbis; Rick Rappaport/Corbis; Bettmann/Corbis.

Trait Theory

Trait theory is another popular method of classifying people. In contrast to type theory, trait theory focuses on specific characteristics rather than types of people. Two approaches to trait theory include phrenology and personality assessment.

Phrenology. Aristotle believed that the brain was irrelevant for understanding people's actions, a view that was only seriously challenged by Franz Joseph Gall (1758–1828) in the late eighteenth century. Gall was the greatest brain anatomist of his generation; his early research showed, for example, that the two halves of the brain are interconnected. Gall also examined differences between normal adult human brains and the brains of animals, children, and persons with head injuries. Overall, he found that the larger and more intact the brain, the more flexible and intelligent its owner. Gall, more than any other person in history, was responsible for demonstrating that the brain is the center of higher human mental activity.

Growing up, Gall was annoyed by the fact that some boys whom he considered less intelligent than himself nonetheless outperformed him in school. He decided that these boys had superior memories, as suggested by the fact that their eyes bulged. He concluded that memory was located in the brain, right behind the eyes, and that a large memory would cause one's eyes to bug out.

This "insight" was the basis of *phrenology*, the study of the relationship between individuals' skulls and their personal characteristics. Gall identified groups of people who were distinctive in some way—for example, they were passionate, delinquent, or generous. He assumed that their brains were also distinctive and that this would be seen in the shapes of their skulls. Over time, Gall identified twenty-seven human capacities and developed charts on which skull bumps were depicted as corresponding to these capacities. By measuring the shape of someone's skull, Gall believed that he could assess that individual's personality. Gall's map of the brain appears in Figure 2.2.

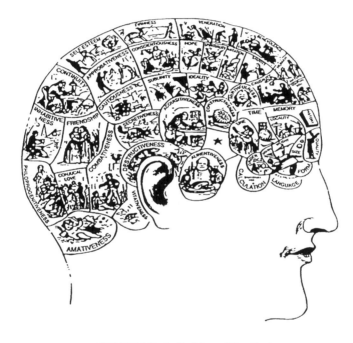

FIGURE 2.2 Gall's Map of the Brain

The notion that bumps on the skull correspond to overdeveloped areas of the brain is, of course, nonsense, and Gall's scientific reputation was badly damaged by his phrenology. Nonetheless, Gall made two important contributions to the study of personality. First, he provided powerful evidence for a link between the mind and the body. Second, whereas other researchers of his time were searching for general laws of the mind, Gall was interested in discovering the dimensions along which people differ and the causes of those differences.

Gall's list of twenty-seven capacities was based on his observations of how people differed from one another. In creating this list, Gall anticipated the work of modern-day factor analysts.

Personality Assessment. Christian Thomasius (1655–1768), a German philosopher and lawyer, appears to have developed the first personality measure—one that consisted of rating scales for "reasonable love," "voluptuousness," "ambition," and "greed" _(Ramul, 1963)_. Thomasius believed that these four dimensions represent the primary ways in which people differ from one another.

Thomasius may have set the stage, but Francis Galton (1822–1911) is widely regarded as the father of _psychometrics, the_ measurement of individual differences. Galton was Charles Darwin's cousin. He was interested in practical measurement, and the book for which he is best known—_Hereditary Genius (1869)_—argues that people inherit cognitive abilities in the same way that they inherit height, eye and hair color, and physical strength.

Galton developed the first questionnaire for psychological measurement and used it to study 104 famous scientists. He published his results in _English Men of Science: Their Nature and Nurture (1874)_, a book that concerns how heredity and environment affect the development of talent. Galton invented the foundation of modern psychometrics, introducing such concepts as the regression line, the correlation coefficient, and regression to the mean; he also pioneered the use of tests to measure psychological differences among people. His work led directly to the development of factor analysis and modern human behavior genetics. Although Galton studied ability rather than personality, his work provided the methods needed to study personality traits.

G. Stanley Hall _(1904)_ used questionnaires in his pioneering personality research with teenagers, but later researchers _(e.g., Goldberg, 1971)_ have argued that modern personality trait research began with the psychiatric symptom checklist developed by the Dutch psychologists Gerard Heymans and Edward Wiersma in 1906. From 1906 until the end of World War II, personality measurement largely entailed identifying the dimensions of psychopathology, or mental illness. Robert Woodworth's Personal Data Sheet _(1918; see Symonds, 1931)_ was the first in a series of tests that culminated in the Minnesota Multiphasic Personality Inventory _(MMPI; Hathaway & McKinley, 1943)_. The MMPI is used for psychiatric diagnosis as well as for evaluating the emotional stability of persons working in jobs where public safety is an issue, such as law enforcement and commercial airlines.

It wasn't until the 1950s that researchers began studying the dimensions of normal personality. This led to the development of such tests as the California Psychological Inventory _(CPI; Gough, 1987)_, the Sixteen Personality Factor Questionnaire _(16PF; Cattell & Stice, 1957)_, and the Guilford-Zimmerman Temperament Survey _(Guilford, Zimmerman, & Guilford, 1976)_.

TABLE 2.1   What Personality Inventories Measure

Dimensions Measured by the Minnesota Multiphasic Personality Inventory	Dimensions Measured by the California psychological Inventory	Dimensions Measured by the Hogan Personality Inventory
Hypochondriasis (physical complaints)	Dominance	Adjustment
Depression	Capacity for status	Intellectance (creativity)
Hysteria (immaturity)	Sociability	Sociability (extraversion)
Psychopathic deviations (conflicts with authority)	Social presence	Likeability (agreeableness)
Masculinity/femininity	Self-acceptance	Prudence (conscientiousness
Paranoia	Independence	
Psychasthenia (anxiety)	Empathy	
Schizophrenia	Responsibility	
Hypomania (elated mood, high energy)	Socialization	
Social introversion (shyness)	Self-control	
	Good impressions	
	Communality	
	Well-being	
	Tolerance	
	Achievement via conformance	
	Achievement via independence	
	Intellectual efficiency	
	Psychological mindedness	
	Flexibility	
	Femininity/masculinity	

The first major scientific personality-assessment instrument was the Minnesota Multiphasic Personality Inventory (MMPI), developed by S. R. Hathaway (a psychologist) and J. C. McKinley in 1943. Its specific purpose is to assist in the diagnosis or assessment of the major mental disorders.

In 1987, Harrison Gough published the California Psychological Inventory (CPI), which was designed to assess personality in normally adjusted individuals. Unlike the MMPI, which evaluates psychological problems, the CPI measures people along dimensions of effectiveness that seem important in every culture.

This table contrasts the basic traits measured by the MMPI, the CPI, and the Hogan Personality Inventory (HPI), a personality measure based on the Five-Factor Model.

In the 1980s, most personality researchers concluded that all the major dimensions of personality—for both normal and psychologically disturbed individuals—could be classified in terms of just five factors. These factors came to be known as the Big Five and are currently the basis for most personality research being done in academic settings.

In the mid-1960s, personality trait research entered a crisis phase because there were so many different tests available, each measuring a different set of traits. In an obscure Air Force technical report, Edward Tupes and Raymond Crystal *(1961)* argued that personality could be described in terms of five broad traits. This argument, which came to be known as the Five-Factor Model, suggests that all existing measures of personality assess the same five dimensions—a viewpoint that is widely, though not universally, accepted by modern personality psychologists *(Block, 1995; Costa & McRae, 1985; Digman, 1990; Goldberg, 1993)*. The search for the structure of personality at the trait level, which began with Gall's twenty-seven capacities, ended with a parsimonious list of five broad dimensions. Table 2.1 contrasts the dimensions measured by the Minnesota Multiphasic Personality Inventory, the California Psychological Inventory, and the Hogan Personality Inventory *(Hogan & Hogan, 1996)*. The latter is a measure of normal personality based on the Five-Factor Model.

In summary, since the time of the Greeks, people have been classified in one of two ways: type theory and trait theory. Type theory classifies people themselves, whereas trait theory classifies the characteristics of people. Both theories are still widely used. Type theory uses either the sixteen Jungian types defined by the Myers-Briggs Type Indicator or the six Holland types; trait theory uses the currently fashionable Five-Factor Model *(Wiggins, 1996)*, which divides all personality characteristics into five broad categories.

The Explanatory Tradition

The descriptive tradition in personality psychology attempts to develop taxonomies of personality characteristics. In contrast, the explanatory tradition concerns efforts to understand what is going on beneath the surface. The descriptive tradition describes themes in people's behavior; the explanatory tradition explains *why* they act that way. This second tradition comes largely from psychiatry.

Hysteria

The ancient Greeks invented the term *hysteria* to describe medical symptoms, primarily in women, that had no obvious physical basis such as blindness, paralysis, and nervous exhaustion. They believed that these problems were caused by the uterus wandering around the body. Galen, the father of Greek medicine, realized that the uterus could not wander and suggested instead that hysterical symptoms were caused by pathogenic vapors rising from the uterus. Although Galen's theory of vapors from the uterus has long been discarded, the concept of hysterical symptoms remains very much in evidence today.

Galen referred patients with hysterical symptoms to the Temples of Asclepius, where they rested and waited for visions that would explain their symptoms. Along with other early non-Christian, non-European thinkers, Galen explained hysterical symptoms in terms of a lack of balance among the various parts of the mind or soul (in Greek, the *psyche*).

The triumph of Christianity in Europe brought a new interpretation of hysterical and other nervous disorders: the notion that they were caused by a devil who had somehow entered the afflicted person's body. Such problems were treated by exorcism, which was intended to drive the demon out. Until the eighteenth century, exorcism was the major method used to treat hysterical neuroses in Europe and the Middle East.

Johann Joseph Gassner (1727–1779), an Austrian country priest, was perhaps the most famous exorcist in history; he cured poor people of their afflictions. When powerful political and religious leaders in Vienna heard about his amazing healing powers, they formed a commission to investigate. One member of the commission, a physician named Franz Anton Mesmer (1734–1815), reproduced Gassner's cures using magnets. Mesmer argued that the secret to Gassner's cures was his unusual "animal magnetism"—the force of his personality—rather than his Christian faith. The hapless Gassner was disgraced and sent to a country parish where he died in obscurity a few years later.

Hypnosis

In his medical school thesis, Mesmer proposed that gravitational energy fills the universe and acts on people through animal magnetism. Mesmer subsequently married a wealthy woman and practiced medicine as a hobby. In 1773, he treated a relative for "hysterical fever"—a collection of symptoms ranging from constipation to temporary blindness. Mesmer gave his relative a medicine containing iron; then he rubbed her body with magnets. She reported feeling a strong force flowing inside her and subsequently fell into a "crisis" that included convulsions and intense pain in the body parts corresponding to her symptoms. When the crisis ended, her symptoms were gone. Mesmer repeated the treatment several times, and the young woman was seemingly cured. Contemporary reports indicate that she went on to live a normal, healthy life *(Ellenberger, 1970)*.

Mesmer used this treatment with other patients, telling them that they would fall into a crisis—which many did. Next, Mesmer began simply passing his hands over his patients and this also seemed to work, leading Mesmer to conclude that his body was full of animal magnetism, making real magnets unnecessary.

Mesmer moved to Paris, a city known for its fads, and set up a practice. Soon he had more patients than he could handle in his usual way. Accordingly, he built a large tub and placed iron bars around the outside and water and iron particles in the bottom. Groups of patients would get into the tub; then Mesmer, dressed in a long robe, would point at them. After one or two entered a crisis state, others would follow. Soon his treatment room was full of writhing, thrashing bodies, and the most extreme of these would be carried into a crisis room to be specially treated. Mesmer is widely regarded as the inventor of hypnosis—originally called mesmerism. (He also made a lot of money through his "cures.")

One of Mesmer's students, the Marquis de Puysegur (1751–1825), disliked the convulsions that occurred during the crisis state. While magnetizing a servant, he convinced the man that a crisis wasn't necessary. The servant fell into a simple trance, during which he responded to Puysegur's suggestions. When he awoke, he performed several actions that Puysegur had suggested, but he had no memory of either the trance or the suggestions. Following up on this experience, Puysegur discovered most of the phenomena associated with modern hypnosis, including posthypnotic amnesia and posthypnotic suggestion: "When you awaken, you won't remember the session but you will feel wonderful." More important, he determined that posthypnotic suggestion is evidence for the existence of unconscious forces—processes that influence one's actions even though they remain outside of awareness and beyond control.

Auguste Liebault (1823–1904), a French country doctor, read about animal magnetism and hypnotism in medical school. Fascinated, he offered his patients the choice of regular treatment for a fee or hypnotic treatment for free. The popularity of his hypnotic treatment rapidly increased and his income declined.

Hippolyte Bernheim (1840–1919), a young doctor from Nancy, heard about Liebault's hypnotic cures and visited him in 1882. He studied for a while with Liebault, then began practicing hypnotherapy full time back in Nancy. After analyzing his patients' responses, he concluded that his most successful cases came from the lower social classes. Contrary to Mesmer, Bernheim proposed in 1886 that hypnotism had little to do with the hypnotist; rather, he argued, the key is individual differences in clients' suggestibility. Specifically, he believed that highly suggestible working-class people are easily hypnotized and that suggestibility is a trait that varies in the normal population.

Jean-Martin Charcot (1825–1893) was, from the 1870s until his death, the best-known psychiatrist in Europe. As director of the enormous Salpetriere Hospital in Paris, Charcot was called the "Napoleon of the Neuroses." He was an inspiring speaker, and his lectures in the 1880s were attended by writers, philosophers, famous actresses, and other notables.

In the 1860s, Charcot studied a variety of neurological diseases, including poliomyelitis, multiple sclerosis, and epilepsy. He believed that, for most such diseases, there is a pure form that reveals the essential characteristics of the disease. In the case of epilepsy, for example, he believed that patients with *grand mal* are the pure type. In the 1870s, Charcot began studying a group of patients who were diagnosed as epileptic but who had a variety of other symptoms and were called hysterics—persons suffering from a variety of symptoms for which no underlying physical cause could be found.

In the late nineteenth century, most physicians believed that hysteria was a female problem and that hysterics faked their symptoms. Charcot disagreed because he found hysterical symptoms in male patients, and because he thought hysterics suffered too much to be faking. Following his method, Charcot identified a class of hysterics who were pure cases; they suffered from what he called *la grande hysterie*. These patients became stars in Charcot's public lectures and celebrities in the hospital. One attractive young woman, Blanche Wittman, became known as the Queen of the Hysterics because she displayed exotic symptoms during Charcot's lectures and treated other patients with haughty disdain.

Charcot believed that hysteria was caused by progressive degeneration of the nervous system, rendering people unable to integrate memories and ideas. Their memories become dissociated, resulting in hysterical symptoms. Charcot further noticed that (1) hypnotic subjects resembled hysterical patients, (2) hysterical symptoms could be induced in hypnotic subjects, (3) some of his patients with *la grande hysterie* were highly hypnotizable, and (4) their symptoms became more dramatic under hypnosis. He concluded that hypnotic effects and hysterical symptoms have the same cause—which he termed "dissociation"—and that hypnotic susceptibility was a symptom of hysteria. In 1882, Charcot presented his theory of grand hypnotisme to the French Academy of Sciences, thereby establishing hypnotism as a legitimate scientific topic and reversing Mesmer's legacy.

In the 1880s, a terrific quarrel broke out between Charcot in Paris and Bernheim in Nancy over the question of whether hypnotic susceptibility was normal. Charcot argued that being hypnotizable was neurotic by definition; Bernheim's belief that hypnotic susceptibility is a normal characteristic gradually prevailed. But of significance for our present purposes is the fact that, during the winter of 1885–1886, a young doctor from Vienna named Sigmund Freud went to Paris to study with Charcot. When Freud returned to Vienna, he began using hypnosis to study hysteria, and his career as a personality researcher was launched. The rest, as they say, is history.

Academic fields are born with the publication of textbooks. Although interest in personality goes back to the ancient Greeks, personality psychology as a formal discipline began in the late 1930s with the publication of Kurt Lewin's *(1935) A Dynamic Theory of Personality*, Gordon Allport's *(1937) Personality: A Psychological Interpretation*, and Ross Stagner's *(1937) Psychology of Personality*. The field has grown steadily since the 1930s; today, personality is one of the most active research areas in all of psychology, and personality psychology has become one of the most popular courses in the undergraduate curriculum.

The descriptive and explanatory traditions in personality psychology have arisen from very different intellectual motives. The descriptive tradition reflects the ancient human need to organize the world by sorting it into categories. The explanatory tradition is motivated by a need to understand mental illness.

As it was in the beginning, so it is today. Personality psychologists who do research in psychometrics and assessment are typically uninterested in theories of human nature or models of mental illness, whereas those largely concerned with understanding mental illness have little interest in measurement and statistics. Much personality research today is generated by trait and type theories. And psychologists who speculate on human nature tend not to be involved in research on mental illness—and vice versa. As a result, personality psychology looks a lot like the world in general: It encompasses many separate tribes, each of which has its own status hierarchy, communicates only along the borders, and rarely unites with the others except when confronted by a common threat.

Practical Application: Who Will Become Violent?

Assuming you knew nothing about the boys whose photographs appear on page 38, what judgments would you make about their personalities? Would you guess that they were part of a circle of friends, earned top grades, worked at a pizza restaurant, and even participated in a bowling team every day at 6:15 a.m.? Would you also have predicted that they would walk into their high school and murder twelve other students and a teacher and then kill themselves?

Although psychologists have studied violent people for many years, predicting who will become violent has become an increasingly urgent issue. In addition to shootings at schools, more than 1,000 people are murdered in the United States each year at their jobs; this makes murder the number-one cause of death for female workers and the number-two cause for male workers *(Smither, 1998)*. Healthcare and social service agencies are particularly dangerous places in terms of workplace violence.

Eric Harris and Dylan Klebold. Based on the appearance of these two individuals, what personality traits would you list to describe them?
Source: AFP/Corbis

Researchers have used a variety of approaches in an effort to identify not only who will become violent *(prediction)* but also what causes violent behavior *(explanation)*. Some have studied biological factors such as hormones or chemical imbalances. Others have studied factors in a person's home life and upbringing or personality characteristics in adulthood. Still others believe that environmental factors cause violent behavior. One model of workplace violence, for example, suggests that violence is especially likely in situations where people are mistreated and supervisors (or teachers) model aggressive behavior, reward intense competition, and create a stressful environment *(O'Leary-Kelly, Griffin, & Glew, 1996)*.

With respect to personal characteristics, researchers agree that younger males with a history of violence are the group most likely to behave violently. Other characteristics often associated with violent behavior are anger, depression, paranoid delusions, and loner status *(Johnson & Indivik, 1994)*. Behaviors associated with violence at work include frequent lateness or absenteeism from work, excessive complaining to supervisors, recurrent accidents, poor relations with co-workers, deterioration in hygiene, and evidence of drug or alcohol abuse *(Waxman, 1995)*.

Unfortunately, none of these approaches have been particularly successful in either explaining the causes of violent behavior or predicting who will become violent. Psychologists can identify many of the predictors that appear to lead to violent behavior, but not everyone who matches the predictors becomes violent. In the case of the Columbine High School murderers, for example, their fascination with violence was seemingly offset by conscientious parents and a promising future.

Contradictions like these add to the difficulty of identifying violent individuals and preventing violence. Given the importance of this topic, however, we can be certain that personality researchers will continue to study violent behavior.

PART TWO

Classical Psychodynamic Theories

3

SIGMUND FREUD
and Psychoanalytic Theory

- The Life of Freud
- Core Problem: Relations with Authority
- The Psychoanalytic View of Human Nature
- Evaluating Psychoanalytic Theory
- Practical Application: Freud's Views on Leadership

Through his development of psychoanalytic theory, Sigmund Freud became one of the most important social theorists of the twentieth century. His ideas have been so influential that some people think all of psychology is little more than Freudian theory. Although Freud's influence has declined somewhat in the United States and England, he is still highly regarded in other parts of the world, especially France, Italy, and South America. Freud had an enormous impact on modern culture, and every educated person should know something about psychoanalysis.

Freud was one of the most original writers in the history of personality theory—and, indeed, every major personality theorist since Freud has used his theory as a starting point. Freud's contributions to scientific psychology are less important today, but many of his insights into human nature are still valid. In a sense, Freud has the same relationship to modern psychology as Ptolemy does to modern astronomy. Ptolemy (ca. a.d. 127 to 151) wrote a textbook, the Almagest, that remained the standard work in astronomy until 1543, when Copernicus showed that it was wrong—because Ptolemy assumed that the earth is the center of the universe. Nonetheless, if you wanted to sail a boat from Boston to Buenos Aires, you would use Ptolemaic astronomy to get there, because it is still useful for practical navigation. Similarly, although much of Freud's theory is not literally true, it can be a perceptive guide to everyday life.

The Life of Freud

Freud was a private man who didn't want people prying into his personal affairs or writing his biography; in 1885, for example, he destroyed all of his notes and manuscripts and burned his diaries. Nonetheless, Ernest Jones published a three-volume biography of Freud in 1953, and a great deal has been written about him since. Peter Gay's (1988) book, based on Freud's surviving letters, is probably the most accurate and best-written account of Freud's life.

Sigmund Freud.
Source: Mary Evans/Sigmund Freud Copyrights, Wivenhoe/Bettmann/Corbis.

Childhood and Family Relations. Freud was born on May 6, 1856, in Freiburg, Moravia, a small town northeast of Vienna. His parents moved to Vienna when he was four. Freud's father, an unsuccessful wool merchant, was a warm, generous man who doted on young Sigmund. Freud's mother—an energetic and domineering woman twenty-one years younger than his father—doted on him, too. Sigmund was her first and favorite child, and Freud's special relationship with his mother had a lasting effect on him. He later wrote: "A man who has been the indisputable favorite of his mother keeps for life the feeling of a conqueror, that confidence of success that often induces real success" *(quoted in Jones, 1953, p. ix).*

In his letters Freud mentions two childhood incidents that seem especially important. The first was a story his father told him about how, one day in Freiburg, a Christian deliberately knocked off his hat because he was Jewish. His father merely picked up the hat and wiped it off. Freud vowed to avenge this insult, and his desire for revenge probably fed his ambition. The second incident concerned an occasion when Freud urinated in his parents' bedroom in their presence. Freud's father became angry at this insolent gesture and remarked that his son would never amount to anything. The remark haunted Freud for years—and also fanned his need for success.

Freud was a bright child and adults often predicted that he would become famous. As the oldest boy, he was also expected by his family to be successful. Family pressures, combined with his desire to prove himself to his father and the world, made him intensely ambitious; in his thirties and forties he constantly fantasized about becoming wealthy and famous *(Gay, 1988)*.

For seven years Freud was the best student in his class at the Gymnasium, from which he graduated with distinction in 1873. He had a talent for languages—including Latin, Greek, French, English, Italian, Spanish, and Hebrew—and won a number of writing prizes in school. As early as age sixteen Freud became keenly interested in psychology *(Gay, 1988)*. Later in his life he reported that he went into medicine not because he wanted to help others but because, in this way, he could do psychological research while supporting his family. At the end of his life he remarked that he had always been fascinated by "cultural problems" and that his career in medicine had been "a detour."

University Education and Influence. In 1873, at the age of seventeen, Freud entered the University of Vienna to study medicine. Although the medical degree normally required five years, Freud spent eight, graduating in 1881 when he was twenty-five. This outcome was partly due to Freud's lack of interest in medicine: He spent his first year studying "humanistic subjects" and always argued that a medical education was too narrow. But his interest in research also delayed his graduation. He initially worked for the great German anatomist Carl Claus, in whose laboratory he studied eel gonads. Then, between 1876 and 1882, he worked for Ernst Brucke, perhaps the best-known physiologist of the time, in whose laboratory Freud studied the nervous system.

Three experiences at the university shaped the development of psychoanalytic theory. First, Freud was impressed by the philosopher Ludwig Feuerbach, a critic of theology and other philosophical systems, who taught his students to pay attention only to facts or "reality." Feuerbach's best-known work, The Essence of Christianity *(1841)*, argued that religion is an illusion, a mask designed to disguise less attractive human tendencies. Feuerbach taught Freud to look behind the mask of polite social behavior in order to see people as they really are.

The second major influence on young Freud was evolutionary theory as stated in Charles Darwin's book, Origin of Species *(1858)*. Darwin challenged the widely held religious belief that animal life suddenly came into being by an act of God and that people are unique in the animal kingdom, suggesting instead that people share a set of core instincts with lower animals and that all living creatures are the products of a long line of development stretching back into prehistory. Because Freud's teachers applied the Darwinian perspective to medical research, they were seen as radical, daring, and perhaps even dangerous. Freud was fascinated by these ideas, and his letters often refer to "the great Darwin" whose influence is particularly apparent in Freud's writings on social theory *(e.g., Totem and Taboo, published in 1913)*.

Finally, Freud was influenced by Ernst Brucke the man. Brucke was a gifted painter and a political liberal who despised the anti-Semitism of Vienna. He was the opposite of Freud's father—world famous and very demanding; Freud described him as "the greatest authority that worked upon me" *(Gay, 1988)*.

Brucke criticized theory-making and speculation, insisting that empirical research is the only way to acquire dependable knowledge. This view is known as positivism; developed by the philosopher Auguste Comte (1798–1857), it reflected the French enthusiasm for science. Ernst Brucke and three other brilliant young physiologists—Emile du Bois-Reymond, Carl Ludwig, and Herman von Helmholtz—were swept up by this new view and invented a radical mechanistic biology that was consistent with positivist principles.

The premier scientists at the University of Vienna medical school—including Brucke—had been brought to Vienna to teach this new gospel of positivism. They argued that people are like machines and, hence, are best understood in purely mechanical and biochemical terms. Freud adopted this approach. He believed that every mental impulse is determined in a law-like fashion, that even the most trivial thoughts, gestures, and statements are meaningful, and their causes can be analyzed. Moreover, in the spirit of positivism, Freud believed that human nature can be studied as scientifically as physics, but only if one gives up religion and philosophy and concentrates on empirical facts.

Career. Freud finished his medical degree in 1881 but continued to work in Brucke's laboratory because he hoped to have a career in medical research. Although Freud did excellent work, Brucke encouraged him to go into private practice. In the summer of 1882, Freud became engaged to Martha Bernays; her family had serious doubts about his ability to provide for a wife while working as a medical researcher. Freud then followed Brucke's advice, taking a junior position at Vienna's General Hospital and starting a private practice in neurology—the treatment of "nervous disorders."

Freud soon noticed that many of his patients suffered from hysterical disorders (described in Chapter 2). To better understand hysteria, he went to Paris in 1885 to study with the celebrated French psychiatrist Jean Martin Charcot. Freud was captivated by Charcot, a charismatic and spellbinding lecturer, and thereafter imitated his lecture style. As noted earlier, Freud learned hypnosis from Charcot and took it back to Vienna. Freud also learned from Charcot that hysterical patients become emotionally attached to their physicians, and that this attachment can become a part of the cure. Finally, Freud learned from Charcot to pay close attention to what patients say, and to avoid prejudging their symptoms and ignoring their complaints.

While working with Brucke, Freud met Josef Breuer, a prominent and wealthy physician twelve years older than Freud. Breuer became Freud's patron, giving him money, friendship, encouragement, and patients for several years. Using Charcot's methods, Freud and Breuer experimented with hypnosis as a treatment for hysteria. In 1895, they published Studies on Hysteria, the first statement of psychoanalytic theory. Five years later, in 1900, Freud published Interpretation of Dreams; although the book sold only 351 copies in the first six years, it is regarded today as Freud's most important work.

In the fall of 1902, Freud organized the Wednesday Psychological Society, which met weekly to discuss his ideas. The society steadily attracted more members, and by 1907 visitors were coming from Hungary, Germany, and Switzerland to attend meetings—including a young Swiss psychiatrist named Carl Jung.

In 1909, G. Stanley Hall, who founded the first laboratory of experimental psychology in the United States at Johns Hopkins University and later became president of Clark University, invited Freud to Clark to receive an honorary degree. This was Freud's only trip to the United States. At Clark he gave five lectures (in German) that were well received. He also toured New York City and met William James, the Harvard philosopher who wrote the first American textbook in psychology (James, 1892). Freud described his honorary degree as the first official recognition of his ideas; on returning to Europe, he said it was the first time he had been able to speak publicly about his work. The trip to Clark was a major "ego boost" for Freud.

In 1911, Freud founded the International Psychoanalytic Society and appointed Carl Jung as its president. During his active career, from 1895 to 1938, Freud spent his time seeing patients and promoting psychoanalysis. He also wrote twenty-eight volumes of papers, three of which—*Totem and Taboo* (1913), *The Ego and the Id* (1923), and *Civilization and Its Discontents* (1930)—are among the most interesting essays in all of psychology.

Freud was remarkably self-disciplined and hardworking. He rose each morning at 7:00, saw patients until lunch, and then, after a short break, saw patients until dinner. After dinner, he would go to his study and write until 1 or 2 a.m. His one indulgence was cigars, which he smoked almost constantly during his adult life. In the spring of 1923, he developed cancer of the mouth and underwent the first of several operations. During the last sixteen years of his life, Freud lived in increasing pain; he nonetheless remained intellectually active to the end. Freud lived and worked in Vienna until the Nazi invasion of 1938. He then moved to London, where he died on September 23, 1939.

Although Freud was insightful about human nature in general, he was a poor judge of individuals. Over the years, he went through a series of ill-advised friendships, each ending in a bitter quarrel and a permanent break. In addition, like many nineteenth-century writers, Freud was a chauvinist who believed women were inherently inferior to men. Although he seems to have been a good father and husband and a charming conversationalist, Freud treated his family, students, and followers in an authoritarian way, and those who didn't respect his rules and opinions were dismissed from his company.

Core Problem: Relations with Authority

People normally associate Freud with the idea that sex is the major force in everyday life. Sex is an important topic in clinical psychology. In our view, however, Freud was even more concerned with the problem of authority—specifically, the role of authority in the development of personality and in the structure of society. Authority is symbolized by the rules of one's family, religion, and government, and it is personally represented by parents, police, teachers, and others responsible for training and controlling young people and those who tend to be disobedient (to authority). Good attitudes toward authority are associated with conformity and good citizenship; bad attitudes toward authority are associated with nonconformity and delinquency. Disregard for authority creates serious social problems.

Freud is also associated with a method for treating hysterical neuroses. In fact, he studied hysterical neuroses for about twenty-five years—for sound strategic reasons. Thanks to Charcot, hysteria had become a popular topic, and analyzing it was a useful way to earn a living and establish a reputation. Nonetheless, there are three reasons why we think authority is the crucial theme in psychoanalysis. First, Freud argued that too much respect for authority is the cause of hysterical neuroses; second, Freud believed that respect for authority is the cornerstone of civilization; and third, Freud himself had problems with authority throughout his life.

Authority and Neurosis. Freud argued that neurosis is caused by repressed sexuality—a radical view at the time. But if sexuality is a normal part of biology, why would people repress it? Freud's answer was that their conscience, or superego, makes them feel guilty about sexual impulses. The superego develops out of a child's relations with his or her parents. Once developed, it prevents sexual impulses from being recognized or expressed. These impulses may then reappear as hysterical symptoms. So, according to Freud, a child's attitudes toward parental authority are as important as sexual instincts in the development of neurosis.

Authority and Society. In his controversial book Totem and Taboo *(1913)*, Freud argued that society develops out of the human need for authority—specifically, the need to be dominated by a powerful figure such as a god or a king. Freud thought Totem and Taboo was his most important book: In a letter to Sandor Ferenczi dated May 4, 1913, he wrote, "I am working on the Totem with the feeling that it is my greatest, my best, perhaps my last good thing." He repeated the argument of Totem and Taboo in two more books: Group Psychology and the Analysis of the Ego *(1921)* and Moses and Monotheism *(1938)*, his last major work. At the end of his life, Freud said that he had always been more interested in "cultural problems" than in medicine. And, indeed, he argues in Totem and Taboo that culture is caused by unconscious attitudes toward authority. Clearly, then, relations with authority were a central issue in Freudian theory. Freud's own biography shows this even more definitively.

Freud's Problems with Authority. Freud was the oldest of seven children. Gay describes him as "an attentive but somewhat authoritarian brother, helping his brothers and sisters with their lessons and lecturing at them about the world... The family accepted Freud's boyish imperiousness with equanimity and fostered his sense of being exceptional" *(1988, p. 14)*. Apparently, Freud's authoritarian personality was evident even in childhood.

Throughout his life, Freud developed intense relationships with older men from whom he received emotional support and encouragement. The first of these relationships was with his father, which seems normal. But Freud was neurotically depressed for years after his father's death, which suggests an unusually strong dependency. Freud's letters suggest that he also developed an adoring dependency on Ernst Brucke at the University of Vienna.

After graduation, Freud transferred his dependency to Josef Breuer, the physician whom he met in Brucke's lab: "Freud adopted Breuer as one in a succession of fatherly figures, and became a regular in the Breuer household" *(Gay, 1988, p. 32)*. Next on the scene, after Freud broke with Breuer, came Wilhelm Fliess. The two men met in 1887 and maintained an unusually intense relationship for ten years. Even Freud's most enthusiastic supporters *(e.g.,*

Rieff, 1959) have been embarrassed by his long and neurotic dependency on Fliess—a quack who believed that people's lives are governed by their noses, according to an eccentric theory of biorhythms. Using this theory, Fliess treated hysterical symptoms by operating on people's noses.

After Fliess, Freud apparently became dependent on a younger man, Carl Jung; but Jung could not accept Freud's major ideas, and they inevitably quarreled and broke apart. When his father died, Freud became quite depressed and embarked on a self-analysis. During this period he discovered the meaning of his various dependent attachments and concluded that he had transferred his unanalyzed feelings toward his father to a series of older men, including Fliess.

In sum, authority is the core issue in psychoanalytic theory. According to Freud, the manner in which children adjust themselves to the authority of their parents determines their personality in adulthood; thus authority is not only the organizing theme in psychoanalysis but also the primary factor underlying the major institutions—religion, business, military—of adult society. But finally, modern research on personality shows that attitudes toward authority are, after cognitive ability, the single most important predictor of occupational and career success *(see Ones, Visweswaran, & Schmidt, 1993)*. Box 3.1 describes two famous psychological studies that demonstrate how even simulated authority affects behavior.

The Psychoanalytic View of Human Nature

Motivation. Motivation concerns the internal causes of human action. Freud changed his motivational theory several times during his career, but each version assumed that (1) human behavior is unconsciously determined by biological instincts and (2) these unconscious instincts are contradictory so that human motivation is always conflicted. In his early theory *(i.e., The Interpretation of Dreams, 1900)*, Freud talked about instincts for self-preservation and self-respect, which motivate us to stay out of trouble, and sexual instincts, which motivate us to seek pleasure and immediate gratification. Freud believed that these instincts are in conflict, which in turn generates "neuroses"—physical symptoms and complaints that have no underlying neurological or physiological basis.

Sex and Aggression. In his later writing, Freud argued that the two primary human motives are eros and thanatos—more commonly known as sex and aggression *(see Civilization and Its Discontents, 1930)*. The sexual instinct—which Freud called libido—draws people together; the aggressive instinct drives them apart. These instincts are unconscious, unchanging, and insistent. Like a fire under a boiler, they create a constant instinctual pressure that must be released sooner or later; indeed, a major problem in life is to find acceptable ways to relieve this pressure. Little children express sexual and aggressive instincts openly; they are often surprisingly cruel in the way they treat insects, little animals, and younger siblings. Freud also described children as "polymorphously perverse;" that is, they are sexually uninhibited and able to find sexual pleasure in a surprising variety of ways. In Freud's time, such ideas were shocking because parents did not wish to think of their babies as little libidinal beasts.

As noted, the sexual instinct draws people into groups; it is the glue that holds them together.

BOX 3.1 Authority and Obedience

Freud was not the only researcher interested in the impact that authority has on personality. Over the years, a number of experiments have demonstrated just how powerfully authority can impact behavior. Two classic studies in this area are Zimbardo's (1972) prison study and Milgram's (1974) study of obedience to authority.

Becoming an Authority. Researcher Philip Zimbardo was interested in studying the dynamics of prison life—an environment that encourages the most extreme examples of obedience and authority. Zimbardo recruited college students as participants and constructed a simulated prison in the basement of the Psychology Department at Stanford University. Volunteers for the experiment were randomly assigned the role of "guard" or "prisoner." Guards were provided with uniforms, billy clubs, and whistles. Prisoners were locked in cells and forced to wear uniforms.

By the second day of the experiment, participants had radically changed their behavior. The guards enforced cruel and degrading activities on the prisoners, who, in turn, rebelled, broke down, or became hysterical. The experiment was designed to last two weeks, but after only six days Zimbardo closed the prison. Onlookers were shocked at how quickly normal college students had accepted the role of cruel prison guards—and at how quickly others had fallen into the role of servile prisoners at the mercy of the guards' commands.

Being Obedient to Authority. In another famous experiment, Stanley Milgram set out to study the relationship between authority, conscience, and behavior. Volunteers were told that Milgram's experiment concerned the effects of punishment on learning. One volunteer would serve as the "learner," whose job was to answer questions; another volunteer would serve as the "teacher," whose job was to administer an electric shock each time the learner gave an incorrect answer.

Unbeknownst to the teacher, the learner was a confederate of the experimenter and intentionally gave incorrect answers. In response to these errors, the teacher was required to give shocks ranging from "Slight" (15 volts) to "Danger: Severe Shock" (435–450 volts). During the experiment, the learner only grunted at shocks up to 105 volts, but at 150 volts, he asked the teacher to let him out of the experiment because of the pain. At 270 volts, the learner screamed in agony, and at 330 volts, he fell silent.

Before performing the experiment, Milgram asked groups of students, adults, and psychiatrists to state what they thought was the average level of shock a teacher would be willing to administer. Whereas all three groups predicted that the teacher would not administer shocks beyond 135 volts, twenty-five of the forty participants in the experiment went all the way to 450. Despite screams of agony and ominous silence from the learner after 330 volts, these teachers were willing to continue administering increasingly severe shocks.

In reality, of course, the learner was not receiving any shocks since Milgram was actually interested in how far people would go in obedience to a perceived authority figure. The finding that people would not hesitate to follow directions even if they believed they were putting someone's life in danger greatly disturbed social scientists. Particularly unsettling was the fact that people could so quickly slip into the role of dangerous obedience without questioning the directions of the authority figure.

Aggression, on the other hand, drives them apart. According to Freud, because the targets of sexual and aggressive impulses are other people, all human relationships are inherently ambivalent. Every personal relationship contains a mixture of these two instincts. At an unconscious level, then, love is always mixed with hatred, and loathing or disgust is mixed with attraction.

How Instincts Are Expressed. Freud described the instincts as "biological fictions" that are never observed directly. What we can observe, he said, are mental images that appear in dreams, fantasy, and creative works. These images have sexual and aggressive themes. Sometimes they are vivid and explicit; at other times they are highly disguised. The key point, however, is that mental life—the conscious and unconscious content of the mind—is caused by and reflects, in a somewhat mechanical way, the pressure of the underlying instincts.

Freud believed that sex and aggression must be controlled if society is to survive. He also believed that the conflict between these instincts and the demands of society stimulates our psychological development as we learn how to gratify the instincts without getting into trouble. People avoid expressing their instinctual urges directly because other people will disapprove of them. They usually repress these urges and drive them into the unconscious part of the mind; if the urges reappear in social behavior, they must be disguised. Freud believed that the medical symptoms of his hysterical patients expressed or symbolized repressed impulses. What this means more generally is that our bodies have a language of their own that includes physical symptoms as well as slips of the tongue, memory lapses, and other accidents. These symptoms, errors, and accidents often symbolize and express unconscious wishes and desires. Nothing happens by chance; careless mistakes reveal underlying desires.

Before leaving this topic, we should note two questions regarding Freud's theory of motivation: First, was Freud correct in saying that human motivation is rooted in biology? And second, was he correct in saying that sex and aggression are the major components of human motivation? The answer to the first question is probably yes, and the answer to the second one is probably no. For example, the urge to play in childhood is very important but probably has nothing to do with sex or aggression—although play can certainly take a sexual or aggressive turn. Nonetheless, we must also ask what the American public wants most in their movies and TV programs. Overwhelmingly the answer is sex and violence—an answer that corresponds to Freud's views on human motivation.

Personality Development

According to Freud, the survival of each person, and of society in general, depends on control over sexual and aggressive instincts. Most people develop this control naturally during childhood. According to Freud's theory of development, psychic structures known as the id, the ego, and the superego evolve as part of an effort to control the instincts. Each of these structures develops at a different time and serves a different purpose; together they promote the survival of the individual and society.

The Id. The part of the mind known as the id is present at birth. The id is like a reservoir in which psychic energy produced by the sexual and aggressive instincts is bottled up and then demands to be released. Children younger than two years are completely dominated by the id. When they want something, they want it now. They express impulses directly and spontaneously. They hit or kick people, animals, or objects when they are angry, and they relieve themselves when they feel the urge. And they do these things with no regard for the wishes and feelings of others. (Immature adults also behave this way.)

The id pushes us to gratify sexual and aggressive needs in direct, explicit, and sometimes bizarre ways, leading to all forms of sex and aggression including incest and cannibalism. In short, it obeys what Freud called the pleasure principle. Because pleasure is the id's only aim, it pays no attention to the demands of reality or morality. Its motto would be "If it feels good, do it."

The impulses of the id are usually unconscious. However, if these impulses appear in consciousness, they become part of primary process thought, a primitive way of thinking that consists of fantasies, images of immediate gratification, dreams, and other creative products. Freud might have said that the lyrics of some rock and rap music resemble primary process thought.

Stages of Psychosexual Development. As a child develops, id impulses pass through five stages, each of which is defined both by the manner in which the instincts are gratified during that time and by the kinds of conflicts the child experiences in relation to adult authority. The first stage, which spans the first year and a half of life, is known as the oral stage. During this period, children find sexual and aggressive gratification in nursing and other oral activities (such as biting). Weaning eventually becomes a problem because children want to continue nursing on demand, contrary to the mother's interests.

The second stage, which extends from eighteen months to three years of age, is known as the anal stage because children experience instinctual satisfaction in the elimination processes at this time. As in the oral stage, the impulses of the id conflict with parental wishes: Children's desire for spontaneous bowel activity conflicts with the parents' desire for their children to become toilet trained, and the children must control their bowel movements in order to maintain the parents' approval.

The phallic stage is next. Defined by the beginnings of sexual curiosity, it lasts from age three to age five or six. During this time, parents and children conflict over modesty training—

children want to play naked and adults want to cover them up. Children's basic sexual orientations also begin to develop during the phallic stage as they ask, in various ways, "Am I a boy or a girl?" The phallic stage ends with the Oedipus conflict, which involves gender identity and self-control. We will discuss the Oedipus conflict later in more detail.

After the Oedipus conflict has ended, the child enters the latency phase, and the id becomes quiet. Somewhat later, at the onset of adolescence, the young person enters the final period of psychosexual development, which Freud called the genital stage. During the genital stage, the id becomes active and the person experiences the sexual desires of adulthood. The manner in which these desires are expressed depends on what happened during the Oedipal crisis.

Fixation and Personality Style. This pattern of change in how the instincts are expressed is known as Freud's theory of psychosexual development, which Freud used to explain how certain types of personalities are formed in childhood. Too much gratification or frustration at each stage will cause a "fixation" that shapes a child's personality. For example, according to Freud, children who are weaned in an indulgent manner tend to develop great self-confidence and self-esteem; they also tend to be "orally aggressive"—sarcastic and critical of others. Their sarcasm is a kind of symbolic biting because, said Freud, children who are weaned too late begin to bite. By contrast, children who are weaned too early tend to become "orally dependent"; they are self-doubting and depressed, and they manipulate others for praise and support. In some cases, people express unconscious oral-dependent feelings symbolically through thumb sucking, fingernail biting, cigarette smoking, and excessive use of alcohol.

According to Freud, children who are toilet trained in a relaxed and leisurely manner develop into "anal expulsives," becoming careless, slovenly, and untidy. They waste their money—a symbol of fecal matter—and they enjoy activities where they can get dirty, such as pottery making, auto repair, or gardening. Conversely, children who are toilet trained in a strict way become "anal retentives." As adults they are neat, tidy, careful about details, and thrifty. They are often stubborn, and they prefer detail-oriented activities such as mathematics, accounting, computer programming, and collecting. These activities reflect their fear of getting "dirty" or "messy"—fears that might have been caused by their toilet training.

Freud's ideas about fixation during psychosexual development are intriguing, and the personality types he describes seem quite familiar. But research has not found clear links between the manner in which children are raised and their specific adult personalities (see Sears, Maccoby, & Lewin, 1958). On the other hand, Freud made two general points about childhood and psychological development that may be valid. First, he argued that children must learn to control their impulses in order to become members of their communities; children don't "automatically" become socialized, as some writers tell us. Second, he suggested that forcing children to exercise self-control has a lasting impact on how they deal with problems later in life. Both of these points seem reasonable.

Box 3.2 describes a Freudian interpretation of how psychological problems in adulthood may be influenced by a person's character.

BOX 3.2 Character and Neurosis

One of the most intriguing questions in psychoanalysis concerns a person's "choice of neurosis": What causes a person to choose a particular set of behaviors to express a neurotic problem? Early psychoanalysts traced neurotic behaviors such as compulsive handwashing or hysterical paralysis to a specific drive and stage of psychosexual development. Later psychoanalysts advanced an alternative theory. In their view, neurotic individuals developed a certain character or style of functioning, then chose symptoms that fit well with their character. In such cases, it is more important to analyze a person's "neurotic style," defined as his or her characteristic way of functioning, than the specific symptom.

Psychoanalyst David Shapiro *(1965)* identified four major neurotic styles that many psychotherapists and researchers have cited in their efforts to understand the relationship between character and neurosis.

1. People with the *obsessive-compulsive* style show a rigidity in their thinking that causes them to disregard information that contradicts what they already believe. Instead, they use their sharp powers of concentration to look for facts and evidence that support their point of view. In addition, obsessive-compulsive people treat everything they do, including relaxing, as a goal that must be completed successfully. For them, life is an endless list of tasks that require their attention: Dress neatly, work in the yard, read the current bestseller, schedule and plan a vacation, and so forth. In psychoanalytic terms, obsessive-compulsives suffer from an overly punitive superego.

2. People who exhibit the *paranoid* style believe that suspicious activity is going on in the world around them. Like obsessive-compulsives, paranoid individuals scan the environment, looking only for clues that confirm what they already believe. Others who try to persuade such individuals to look at alternative viewpoints often become objects of suspicion themselves. Paranoid people quickly notice anything out of the ordinary and try to discover the "meaning" of the unexpected. In addition, they rarely laugh; even when they act as if they are laughing, they do not seem to be genuinely amused.

3. In contrast to the sharp focus on details associated with the paranoid style, the *hysterical* style is characterized by an emotional, impressionistic approach to the world. Hysterical individuals seem incapable of persistent concentration; they are easily distracted, and their reactions are based on emotions, not facts. Hysterical people ignore information and seem genuinely surprised at outcomes that were obvious to everyone around them. They believe that everything will turn out right and typically cling to nostalgic and romantic views of their parents and childhood. In addition, hysterics tend to be dramatic and theatrical in their behavior.

4. People who have the *impulsive* style seem disconnected from normal feelings of planning and intentionality. Their lives are characterized by impulses or whims that get them into

trouble. Unlike most people, impulsives feel they must act on the ideas that occur to them, whatever the outcome: an alcoholic binge, a sexual adventure, or gambling at the race track. Interestingly, although impulsive people can be charming and socially self-confident, they are usually uninterested in anyone or anything outside themselves. Finally, impulsive individuals tend to focus their attention on the present, seeing life as a series of opportunities, temptations, and experiences without consequences.

The Ego. The id motivates us to seek instinctual pleasure with no regard for self-preservation; to survive, however, a child must learn to exercise self-control, even if only briefly. The ego is the part of the psyche that is responsible for self-preservation and for dealing with the demands of reality. Abilities such as memory, problem solving, and hand-eye coordination depend on the ego. According to Freud (1930), the ego develops out of the id. Indeed, it gets its energy from the id, using this energy to explore the world, face reality, and survive. The ego thus becomes the center of personal experience.

The ego begins developing at approximately the time children begin to move about by themselves. By controlling their instinctual desires in the short run, they are often able to satisfy the id more completely. For example, if a child hits the cat now, his mother will spank him; if he waits until she leaves the room, he can give the cat a terrific whack. Nevertheless, the ego begins as, and always remains, the servant of the id. If the ego is unable to satisfy the id, it begins to lose energy and weakens—and the id again comes to the surface, as in the case of children who are tired and cranky or adults who drink too much or take drugs.

The primary job of the ego, according to Freud, is to satisfy the id in an efficient and dependable manner. By making satisfaction dependable, the ego replaces the pleasure principle of the id with its own reality principle; it also replaces primary process thought with secondary process thought. Thus the reality principle allows us to distinguish the unrealistic demands of the id from the demands of reality, and secondary process thought involves understanding that if we put off immediate gratification, we can usually experience greater satisfaction later.

Repression and Anxiety. The ego controls the id primarily through repression and anxiety (Freud, 1930). In circumstances involving repression, the ego simply drives id impulses out of awareness and then concentrates on thoughts that are incompatible with the repressed impulse. In the case of aggression, for example, the ego might go through the following unconscious process: "If I am aggressive, people won't like me; so I am not going to be aggressive, I am going to be very nice." According to Freud, excessively nice people are usually repressing aggression.

Repression is closely related to **anxiety**, the second mechanism that prompts the ego to control the id. When a sexual or aggressive impulse threatens to break into consciousness, the superego directs a jolt of aggressive energy from the id to the ego, causing us to feel anxious or guilty. These feelings of anxiety or guilt warn us that we are about to get in trouble. The ego then represses the impulse along with any thoughts of satisfaction. Indeed, according to Freud, our very survival depends on the ego's control over impulses from the id—a control that is brought about through repression and anxiety.

The Superego. The ego promotes survival, but children with a well–developed ego can be a threat to the rest of society. Even if they follow the reality principle and control their sexual and aggressive impulses, they are amoral if they exercise self-control only for the moment in order to gain greater satisfaction later. Such children care nothing about right and wrong. With the development of the superego, however, children begin to control the id in ways that meet with society's approval. Once the superego develops, it acts as a judge or critic of the ego. The superego is the voice of conscience, and it encompasses the rules, values, and demands of a child's parents. Freud *(1930)* described the emergence of the superego as the most important event in human development—both for the individual and for society.

We argued earlier that psychoanalysis is primarily concerned with understanding the causes and consequences of people's orientations to authority; Freud's analysis concerns the development of the superego. Superego development begins with the process of identification. According to Freud *(1923)*, there are three types of identification. Anaclitic identification is an emotional bond with another person based on respect and affection. It is the earliest and most primitive emotional tie between children and their parents. Defensive identification occurs when a person feels threatened by someone else and tries to imitate that other individual. Here the threatened person says symbolically: "I am just like you; if you hurt me you'll only be hurting yourself." Communal identification refers to the bonds that develop among people when they work together toward a common goal; these emotional ties are sometimes referred to as "morale." According to Freud, morale or group identification symbolically expresses unconscious homosexual desires.

The superego depends on these three kinds of identification. The manner in which the superego develops, however, is different for boys and girls. Small boys are normally tied to both parents through anaclitic identification, or respect and affection. As they enter the phallic stage, however, boys begin to feel sexual desires toward their mother; they also begin to compete with their father for their mother's attention. (Freud chose the term Oedipus complex to describe this process because, in Sophocles' ancient Greek tragedy by the same name, Oedipus unwittingly kills his father and marries his mother.) Boys' sexual desires are not, of course, expressed in terms of adult sexual behavior, but their feelings toward their mother are clearly erotic.

Boys in the phallic stage want their mother's exclusive attention and become increasingly jealous of their father. Because they also admire and respect their father, this creates a tension that gets worse when they realize that their father can hurt them if he wishes. Finally, boys begin to think that their father intends to castrate them for demanding their mother's attention—a scenario that releases a flood of castration anxiety. In order to escape this anxiety, the boys identify with the aggressor—their father.

The process of defensive identification causes boys to internalize the image of their father—so that they think of themselves as small versions of their father. By identifying with their father, they come to believe that "Dad and I are one," thus avoiding the threat of castration. After all,

Dad would never hurt himself. Furthermore, identification with their father indirectly satisfies the original problem—a sexual relationship with their mother. Most important, the internalized image of their father becomes the core of their superego or conscience; boys with a well-developed superego can never escape their father's supervision. Should they do something—or even think of doing something—that their father would disapprove of, their superego will punish their ego with an aggressive energy that causes feelings of guilt.

The Oedipus conflict unfolds differently for girls. According to Freud, little girls are initially tied to both parents, but especially to their mother, through anaclitic identification. As they enter the phallic stage, however, they begin to feel incestuous desires toward their father and resentment toward their mother. The resentment begins when they realize they lack a penis, causing penis envy, and they blame their mothers for this "misfortune." Daughters turn even more strongly toward their father, increasing the tension between them and their mother. The tension grows until a crisis point is reached.

Fearing that their mother will reject them, little girls repress their desire for their father, internalize an image of their mother, and displace their desire for their father onto the men they meet later in life. As a result, the internalized image of their mother becomes their superego. However, because girls experience no castration anxiety, a girl's Oedipus complex is resolved less decisively than a boy's. Accordingly, Freud believed that women have a weaker conscience—and are less firm, strict, and duty bound—than men.

Box 3.3 describes some more recent theorizing about the effects of early childhood on personality.

Consequences of Superego Formation. Freud's description of the Oedipus complex raises two questions. First, are there sex differences in the structure of conscience? And second, if there are differences, did Freud describe them correctly? Modern research suggests that there are indeed sex differences in conscience, but that it is women, not men, who are more likely to be rigid, duty bound, and strict (Gilligan, 1984). For example, women consistently receive higher scores than men on measures of socialization, positive attitudes toward authority, prudence, and proneness to guilt. Such tendencies suggest that Freud was wrong on this point. (In Chapter 5 we discuss sex differences in personality in more detail.)

Superego development has several important consequences. First, after the superego develops, sexual and aggressive impulses are never again expressed directly and openly. Moreover, a child with a well-developed superego needs little adult supervision because the "supervisor" has been internalized. Second, prior to the development of the superego, children are bisexual, but afterward, boys behave in a typically masculine manner and girls in a typically feminine manner. Third, the superego is the means by which culture is transmitted from parents to children. The Oedipus complex explains, for example, why most people have the same political and religious affiliations as their parents and tend to raise their children in the same way they were raised. Fourth, any deviations from the "normal" family structure—for example, a boy raised by his mother—will disturb superego development and sex-role identification. And fifth, the superego reflects a child's view of his or her parents at an early age. Consequently, the superego tends to be harsh, punitive, and judgmental. According

BOX 3.3 Psychoanalysis Since Freud: Object Relations

Just as some people mistakenly believe that psychology is chiefly concerned with mental health, others believe that psychoanalysis concerns only the theories of Freud. Although Freud did not tolerate deviation from his theories during his lifetime, since his death many psychoanalysts have modified his views. For example, many modern psychoanalysts deemphasize the role of sexual and aggressive drives in human motivation and reject the idea that the Oedipal conflict is the most significant event in personality development.

Among these psychoanalysts are object relations theorists, who believe that the quality of the relationship between infant and caretaker (the "object" of the child's emotions) in the first years of life is the key to personality development. According to these theorists, babies who experience this first relationship in life as adequate—such that their needs for food, warmth, and love are met—will grow into normal, healthy adults. By contrast, children whose caretaking is inadequate will have problems with self-esteem and interpersonal relationships throughout their lives. Three major object relations theorists are Margaret Mahler *(Mahler, Pine, & Bergman, 1975)*, W.R.D. Fairbairn *(1952)*, and D. W. Winnicott *(1962)*.

Object relations theorists deviate from Freud in two crucial respects. First, they believe that our relationship with our mother (the primary caretaker in almost all cases) is more important than our relationship with our father. Second, they believe that events in the first year of life—the oral stage—are more important for personality development than events during the phallic stage. Had he been alive during the period when object relations analysts were developing their theories, Freud almost certainly would have rejected this approach.

Interestingly, modern research in developmental psychology is much more supportive of the object relations view of personality development than of Freud's view. Researchers in the area of attachment theory, in particular *(Ainsworth, 1979; Bowlby, 1969)*, have presented strong evidence indicating that disruptions in the mother-child relationship have important consequences for development later. Although few psychoanalysts entirely reject the concept of the Oedipal conflict, almost all now recognize the enduring significance of the child's relationship with the mother.

to Freud, this primitive conscience prevents most people from developing adult sexuality. Persons with "too much" superego treat their sexual partners with too much respect and too little passion; in effect, they feel guilty about sex and are psychologically frigid or impotent. Conversely, persons with "too little" superego tend to be promiscuous; they treat their partners with little respect and are unable to form enduring relationships.

After the Superego. At about age six, after the Oedipus complex is resolved, children enter a latency phase in which the id is quiet. Then, when adolescence begins, the id reawakens and sexual and aggressive impulses reappear. The outcome of the Oedipus complex determines how sexual and aggressive desires are expressed in adolescence and adulthood. According to Freud, individuals who develop an inadequate superego will be unable to control their sexual and aggressive impulses in adulthood and will seem antisocial or delinquent, whereas those whose superego develops normally will overcontrol their sexual and aggressive impulses and possibly experience neurotic symptoms. In short, all adults will have problems of one sort or another—problems that trace back to the superego. These problems can be resolved only by reworking the Oedipus complex, which is unconscious.

Freud's theory of personality development can be summarized as follows. Personality is the product of the competing demands of our instincts and society—the demands of our id and our parents. Because conflict is inevitable, psychological development is always difficult for children; it is a road paved with anger and frustration. The experiences of childhood have a lasting impact and determine our reactions to authority throughout the rest of our lives. Most of the issues that concern us in adulthood can be traced to our childhood development. Adult neuroses, in particular, can often be traced back to childhood events that involved the Oedipus complex.

Unconscious Processes

Although philosophers and other scholars before Freud had recognized that all individuals have an unconscious that affects their behavior, Freud was the first to make the unconscious the center of his theory. In Freud's view, the unconscious manifests itself in four major ways: through dreams, errors, creativity, and hysterical symptoms.
Freud compared the mind to an iceberg. Only about one-tenth of an iceberg rises above the surface of the ocean—and consciousness is the tip of the psychological iceberg. Most of what goes on in the mind is unconscious.

What exactly is the unconscious? It is composed of the id, the activities of the ego, and the thoughts, memories, and desires that were repressed when the superego developed.
We study the unconscious by finding and analyzing traces of it in consciousness. Consider Freud's assumptions in this context: First, instinctual desires that aren't satisfied in reality will be satisfied in fantasy (thus, hungry people dream of food, lonely people dream of love, and people who have been wronged dream of revenge); and second, unconscious thoughts may become conscious when the superego relaxes. This latter process happens most often when we dream. Freud *(1900)* called dreams the "royal road to the unconscious," and his method for understanding the meaning of dreams, as described in The Interpretation of Dreams *(1900)*, is also his method for understanding the meaning of neurotic symptoms.

Dreams. Freud believed that dreams express unconscious desires, and that these desires can be discovered by analyzing the manifest content of a dream. The manifest content is what the dreamer remembers about his or her dream. Beneath the manifest content is the latent content—the wish or desire that caused the dream in the first place. Dream analysis involves tracing the manifest content back to the latent content. The latent content of every dream, Freud argued, expresses sexual or aggressive desires. Dreams allow sexual and aggressive impulses to be satisfied, but in a way that doesn't upset the superego.

When we sleep, said Freud, the superego relaxes. Instinctual impulses come into the conscious part of our minds, but they are anxiety-provoking even when we sleep. Through a process called dreamwork, unconscious desires are remodeled, disguised, repackaged, and then experienced as a dream.

Dreamwork consists of two additional processes: condensation and displacement. Both processes disguise instinctual impulses from the superego. During condensation, several latent meanings are combined into a single image or word. For example, in a dream, a gun might represent both sexual and aggressive impulses since it is both a phallic symbol and an instrument of destruction. Displacement separates an impulse from its original aim and directs it toward other objects. For example, a student might dream of shooting his teacher as a disguised way of expressing anger toward his father. As a result of displacement, the most important part of the latent dream may appear in the insignificant details of the manifest dream.

Condensation and displacement provide a way to interpret the meaning of a dream. Assume, for example, that one part of a person's latent dream concerns hostility toward her father. The hostility might be displaced onto another male authority figure, or onto some object associated with the father himself—his glasses, his nose, or his tropical fish. This hostility may then be condensed into an image that expresses both fondness and hostility, such as a fishing pole—companionship with father, death for the fish. There is never a single interpretation of a dream; rather, interpreting a dream is like unraveling a ball of yarn in which the interpretation of each strand leads further into the unconscious core of a person's character.

To interpret a dream, Freud asked his patients to free-associate. Free association requires that people relax, think about a piece of a dream, and then say whatever comes into their minds. They are asked to relate anything that occurs to them, and not to censor their thoughts no matter how embarrassing, stupid, or irrelevant they may seem. By reconciling his patients various associations with his theory of dreamwork, Freud often arrived at stunning interpretations of their dreams.

Although Freud may have been correct in saying that dreams contain clues to unconscious wishes and motives, many people object to his interpretations of specific dream symbols. In fact, Freud had a "dictionary" for dream interpretation in which he translated the meaning of common themes; for example, the act of flying in a dream symbolized sexual arousal. By contrast, other theorists, such as Carl Jung (Chapter 4), believed that the meaning of a dream depends on the dreamer's free associations to the dream image. The fact that different theorists have disagreed about what it means to dream of flying suggests that Freud's method of interpretation is somewhat arbitrary. Freud thought otherwise; he insisted that his interpretations were correct because he, the first psychoanalyst, said so.

The Psychopathology of Everyday Life. Freud turned from the study of dreams to an analysis of slips of the tongue and errors of memory, which he referred to as "the psychopathology of everyday life"—also the title of an influential book he wrote in 1939. These small errors usually seem trivial: So what if you suddenly can't remember the name of your best friend from high school? However, Freud thought nothing in the psyche happens by accident. His 1939 book contains many brilliant demonstrations of this point. Consider the following example.

While traveling in Italy, Freud met a young scholar. The man complained to Freud that his career wasn't going well, and he blamed his problem on anti-Semitism. He vowed revenge, trying to emphasize his point with a quote from Virgil's Aeneid in which Dido curses Aeneas for abandoning her—Exoriare aliquis nostris ex ossibus ultor ("Let an avenger arise from my bones")—except that he couldn't remember the word aliquis. When Freud gave him the missing word, the young man pointed out that, according to Freud, such lapses of memory were supposed to have a meaning. Freud replied that he could analyze the meaning of the error if the young man would provide some free associations. The young man agreed and began: "There springs to mind the ridiculous notion of dividing the word aliquis like this: a and liquis." The next association was reliquiem (the Latin word for relic); this was followed by "liquefying . . . fluidity, fluid." Then the associations changed directions. "I am now thinking of Simon of Trent, whose relics I saw two years ago in a church at Trent. I am thinking of the accusation of ritual blood-sacrifice which is being brought against the Jews just now. . . . " (Simon of Trent was a two-and-a-half-year-old boy whom the Jews in the fifteenth century had been accused of killing as part of a blood ritual. Under torture, the Jews confessed to the crime, and Simon was declared a martyr and a saint. Centuries later, the Catholic Church exonerated the Jews.) The young man's next free association concerned an Italian newspaper article entitled "What St. Augustine Thinks of Women." And then: "I am thinking of a fine old gentleman I met on my travels last week. He was a real original, with all the appearance of a huge bird of prey. His name was Benedict."

Freud interrupted to point out that "here are a row of saints and fathers of the church: St. Simon, St. Augustine, St. Benedict, and the church father, Origen."

Continuing to free associate, the young man reported that he was thinking of "St. Januarius and the miracle of his blood."

Freud again interrupted: "Just a moment: St. Januarius and St. Augustine both have to do with the calendar. But won't you remind me about the miracle of his blood?"

The young man explained: "They keep the blood of St. Januarius in a phial inside the Church of Naples, and on a particular holiday it miraculously liquefies. The people attach great importance to this miracle and get very excited if it is delayed as happened once at a time when the French were occupying the town. So the general in command . . . took the [priest in charge of the church] aside and gave him to understand with an unmistakable gesture towards the soldiers posted outside that he hoped that the miracle would take place very soon. And in fact it did take place."

Then the young man stopped, seeming troubled. "Why do you pause?" Freud asked. "Well, something has come into my mind," the young man stated, "but it's too intimate to pass on. . . . Besides, I don't see any connection, or any necessity for saying it."
But Freud already knew the meaning of the young man's memory lapse: "Of course I can't force you to talk about something you find distasteful; but then you mustn't insist on learning from me how you came to forget your aliquis."

The young man reluctantly continued: "I have suddenly thought of a lady from whom I might easily hear a piece of news that would be very awkward for both of us." Freud said, "That her periods have stopped?" The young man was stunned: "How could you guess that?"

Freud answered: "That's not difficult any longer. . . . Think of the calendar saints; the blood that starts to flow on a particular day; the disturbance when the event fails to take place; the open threats that the miracle must be vouchsafed or else. . . . In fact, you have made use of the miracle of St. Januarius to manufacture a brilliant allusion to women's periods." Freud then went on to say that the Latin prefix a means "no" and liquis means "liquid," and that in forgetting aliquis the young man was trying to repress the idea "a liquis"—no liquid, that is, no menstruation. In other words, his friend was pregnant! Moreover, the young man had already begun to feel guilty about a solution to his problem other than marriage—namely, abortion, symbolized by Simon of Trent, who had been sacrificed as a child.

At this point, the young man asked Freud to stop and wondered how Freud had been so lucky with his analysis *(Freud, 1939, pp. 41–44)*.

There are two lessons to be learned from this example. First, the processes that produce a memory lapse are identical to those that produce a dream: An unconscious thought moves toward conscious awareness. The thought is repressed, condensed, displaced, and then expressed in symbolic form—in this case, as a lapse of memory. The second lesson concerns the principle of psychic determinism. Once again, according to Freud, there are no accidental mental events; everything, without exception, has a cause.

Artistic Creativity. Freud next analyzed works of art, especially novels, by searching for the unconscious wishes that they expressed. Novelists, he argued, are like everyone else: They want money, fame, and romance. If they can't get these in reality, they turn to fantasy. Accordingly, the process of writing a novel closely resembles the way dreams are formed. The artist's unconscious sexual and aggressive impulses threaten to become conscious, but they are detected by the artist's superego and then repressed. Because the impulses continue to seek expression, they are condensed, displaced, mixed with fragments of the artist's earlier experience, and then expressed as a novel—or poem, painting, movie, or play. Art is like a public dream; dreams are like private art.

In the case of artistic creation, antisocial sexual and aggressive drives are expressed as socially acceptable—even desirable—products. This process is known as sublimation, which Freud called "the only socially useful perversion." (He regarded every indirect expression of sexual impulses as unnatural.) In short, sublimation allows the important work of society to get done.

By today's standards, the scientific status of Freud's theory of dreams is mixed. Virtually all mammals dream, and when they dream, their brains enter a state defined by characteristic electrical waves. Like humans, animals that are allowed to sleep but not to dream become irritable and disoriented, suggesting that dreams refresh both humans and animals in some physiological sense. Although most researchers reject the specifics of Freud's theory of dream interpretation, recent studies *(e.g., Flanagan, 2000)* have shown that dreams are linked to emotions, just as Freud hypothesized. Freud may also have been right when he argued that works of art as well as mental errors—slips of the tongue, lapses in memory—can be interpreted in terms of desires and intentions that people might prefer to keep to themselves.

Hysterical Symptoms. As we noted earlier, patients with hysterical disorders complain about medical problems for which there are no detectable neurological or physical causes. In the psychoanalytic literature, the best-known example of how hysterical symptoms are formed is the case of Dora, a bright and attractive sixteen year old with a hysterical cough. Upon examining her, Freud discovered that, as a child, she had experienced a severe illness and a cough; however, these had long since passed. Through Dora's free associations, Freud concluded that her cough reflected guilt over masturbation; she had developed a slight vaginal infection and, by coughing, she was symbolically removing the watery discharge.

Probing somewhat deeper, Freud deduced that Dora's cough reflected incestuous desires from her still-unresolved Oedipus complex. Dora was in love, as it were, with her father, who was having an affair with a married woman, "Frau K." On those occasions when Dora's father prepared to visit Frau K., Dora would have a coughing attack, which was unconsciously intended to persuade her father to stay home.

Freud then decided that Dora's cough was also related to more ordinary sexual desires. Herr K., the husband of Dora's father's mistress, had begun to pay romantic attention to Dora. Although Dora stated that she found him repugnant, Freud suggested that she was actually attracted to Herr K. and that her cough was a symbolic expression of this sexual desire. Freud argued that Dora had unconscious erotic fantasies about Herr K., and that these fantasies produced pleasurable feelings that were consciously frightening. The pleasurable feelings turned into feelings of disgust: The cough symbolized gagging. Dora disagreed, but Freud pointed out that her coughing spells often took place when Herr K. was out of town, precisely when she would be most prone to have romantic daydreams. Finally, Freud presented an elaborate argument to the effect that Dora's cough was related to homosexual longings for Frau K., her father's mistress! Here Freud thought he had finally arrived at the core of Dora's problem; but at this point, Dora left treatment.

Dora's case illustrates several important implications of psychoanalytic theory, some of which we have already discussed.

First, her symptoms can be interpreted in the same way that one would interpret a dream. The cough (the manifest content) was a symbolic expression of several underlying impulses (the latent content). The ego used physical symptoms to resolve the conflict between the superego and the id's demand to express instinctual desires. And the symptoms provided some relief from the pressure of the id. (Such relief is called primary gain.)

Second, Dora's symptoms had a manipulative intent. In addition to expressing unconscious desires, she used the coughing spells to persuade her father to stay at home with her. (The use of medical symptoms to control others is known as secondary gain.)

Third, Dora's symptoms allowed her to avoid recognizing at least some of her sexual desires. Freud (1900) defined neurosis as an inability to face reality, a turning away from the world and escaping into fantasy. A goal of psychoanalysis, therefore, is to persuade people to face reality and, at the personal level, to recognize the truth about their motives.

Fourth, everything we do has a symbolic meaning; virtually any action can be given a psychoanalytic interpretation.

Self-Knowledge

Freud popularized the view that we never make important decisions, such as choosing our mates or our vocations, for rational reasons. This view highlights the problem of self-awareness: People often don't understand the "real" motives for their actions—motives that can be discovered only after considerable effort.

Barriers to Self-Knowledge. In Chapter 1 we made a distinction between the you that you know and the you that your friends and family know—but what about the you that nobody knows? According to Freud, the you that you know is hardly worth knowing. Each of us, he said, is a stranger to ourselves, and the most important problem in life is acquiring self-knowledge.

What is it that you will know when you know yourself, from a Freudian perspective? That your primary motives are selfish and disagreeable, and that they largely concern having your way with, exploiting, dominating, or destroying other people. But because we don't like to think of ourselves in these terms, we invent elaborate excuses for our actions (e.g., "I spank my child because he needs it, not because I resent him"), and we typically become defensive when others point out the true meaning of our actions. Freud called this defensiveness resistance; he considered it to be perfectly normal but something we need to outgrow. Because we are so very good at lying to ourselves, we usually need professional help to gain self–knowledge, according to Freud.

Benefits of Self-Knowledge. If self-knowledge is so hard to acquire, then why should we pursue it? Freud suggests two reasons. First, the superego is unconscious and makes people self-critical, guilt-ridden, anxious, and unhappy. Gaining insight into the superego permits normal sexual adjustment. And having a normal sex life allows a person to get on with the rest of life—to go about earning a living, say—because psychic energy is not tied up in repressed sexuality.

The second reason one should pursue self-knowledge is intellectual honesty. Freud believed that people should have the courage to face unpleasant truths about themselves, and that each of us has a significant number of such truths to confront.

How valid is Freud's analysis of the problem of self-knowledge? To answer this question, we must address two others. First, are people often motivated by selfish and immoral impulses that they try to justify and explain away? Everyday experience suggests that the answer is yes. Second, do our selfish and immoral actions and desires always reflect sex and aggression? Based on everyday experience, the answer is probably no.

Psychological Adjustment

According to Freud, once the superego develops, it prevents us from directly recognizing or expressing sexual and aggressive desires. The superego controls these impulses by punishing the ego with guilt. But the id is relentless and demands satisfaction. To resolve the tension between the id and the superego, the ego forms a kind of compromise by disguising sexual and aggressive desires, and then allowing the disguised impulses to come into awareness. Dreams are one way in which this happens. But the most important way the ego disguises the instincts is through hysterical symptoms.

Defense Mechanisms. According to Freud, the primary means by which we conceal our intentions from ourselves is through defense mechanisms. These are techniques that the ego uses to manage id impulses in order to avoid being punished by the superego. Freud considered two defense mechanisms particularly important.

1. Projection involves blaming others for one's own sexual and aggressive desires. For example, because we don't like to think of ourselves as hostile, we may project our hostility onto others, as when "I hate him" becomes transformed into "He hates me."

2. Reaction formation turns id impulses into their opposite. If we are unable to admit our feelings of affection, the unconscious thought "I love him" may be expressed consciously as "I hate him." Reaction formation often leads to behavior that denies the id impulse while, at the same time, allowing the impulse to be gratified. For example, a person who crusades against pornography might volunteer for a committee that reviews obscene movies. Similarly, a person who hates dirt may spend a great deal of time around dirt while cleaning his or her house.

Note that all the defense mechanisms involve repression, which consists of driving an impulse into the unconscious and then forgetting the act of repression itself.

Table 3.1 lists several other defense mechanisms that people often use in everyday life.

Maturity. What is Freud's definition of maturity? Maturity involves being able to recognize or acknowledge the sexual and aggressive intentions behind our actions, then get beyond them. In Freud's terms, we need to replace repression with an understanding of why we behave as we do. Immature people can't admit they have selfish, libidinal, and aggressive impulses; not only are mature people are not only capable of admitting they have such impulses but they can control them. In doing so, they are able to get past their childhood history (e.g., anger toward their parents) and get on with their lives. Toward the end of his career, Freud offered a simple but insightful definition of maturity: It is, he said, the ability zu lieben und zu arbeiten—to love and to work.

The Individual and Society

Freud always said that he was more interested in cultural phenomena than in neurosis, and he developed a theory about the origins of society that he first outlined in *Totem and Taboo* (1913). He started with the Oedipus complex, which he believed is universal in all societies

Table 3.1 Additional Defense Mechanisms

Displacement	When people cannot express their true feelings toward a specific person, they sometimes direct those feelings toward someone else. For example, a worker may silently endure his boss's criticism all day long, then go home and yell at his wife and family.
Denial	Sometimes situations are just too painful to face, so people try to ignore what is actually happening. They drink too much or their romantic partner is absent for long periods without a good explanation, but they convince themselves that nothing out of the ordinary is happening.
Rationalization	This defense mechanism arises when people look for reasons to justify their behavior. A person who chooses to party the night before an important exam, for example, may rationalize her behavior by telling herself that the exam will be easy, that she's already studied enough, or that a party will help her relax and perform well on the exam.
Somaticization	Sometimes people use physical complaints to justify their behavior. Catching a cold before an important family event or being injured before an important sports event may be a way to avoid what could be an unpleasant situation.
Sublimation	Sometimes we cannot get what we want, so we find a substitute. Instead of having sex, for example, a person may play sports, watch movies that have a sexual theme, or gratify himself by overeating. Sublimation may keep him out of trouble, but, as Freud pointed out, it is never as enjoyable as the real thing.

One of the cornerstones of psychoanalytic theory is the idea that people push painful memories into their unconscious, a process known as repression. Freud's daughter Anna, herself a psychoanalyst, extended her father's ideas by describing other ways that people avoid dealing with knowledge that makes them anxious. These methods are called defense mechanisms. Two defense mechanisms—projection and reaction formation—are discussed in the text. Some additional ones are listed here.

and a problem that every child must face. But why is the Oedipus complex universal? His argument is clever, and some scholars interested in the social implications of psychoanalysis believe that *Totem and Taboo* is Freud's most important book *(see Marcuse, 1955; Rieff, 1959; Roazen, 1968)*.

Primitive Religion. In the nineteenth century, anthropologists believed that all primitive societies were based on two themes: incest taboos (rules against incest that are brutally enforced) and rules against harming the tribe's totem animal. Totem animals—the American eagle, the British lion, the Russian bear (all modern examples of totems)—symbolize the spiritual ancestors and protectors of a tribe; they are the gods to whom tribe members look for guidance, luck, and help during times of trouble. On certain holy days and during major religious festivals, according to Donald Frazer *(1911)*, primitive tribes conduct a ceremony that involves sacrificing and eating the totem animal. The Thanksgiving turkey is a modern American example of this process; the Christian ritual of communion can also be seen as an example of a totem ritual.

Freud assumed that universal themes in culture reflect universal themes in the human unconscious; he concluded that the totem animal is a symbolic father figure and that a desire to murder the father is a universal feature of the human unconscious. To support this conclusion, Freud noted the ambivalence with which people treat their leaders, who are symbolic father figures. We think our leaders have unusual powers, and we regard them with both affection and hostility. Consider, for example, how people react to a visit by the American president, the Pope, or any other major leader: Many people are respectful, but a few have murderous intentions. For Freud, this ambivalence reflects an important feature of human nature.

The Primal Horde. Where do these universal features of culture—incest taboos, ritual worship and sacrifice of totem animals (i.e., religion), ambivalence toward leaders, and the Oedipus complex—come from? Drawing on Darwin *(1871)*, Freud proposed that, in human prehistory—for hundreds of thousands of years—people lived in a certain kind of family structure. Specifically, prehistoric human societies were organized into hordes or small family groups, each dominated by the primal father—a brutal, tyrannical despot who ruled the family with an iron hand and controlled the women and "other supplies." Male children, upon reaching puberty, were castrated, killed, or driven out of the horde. This was the universal fate of male children in prehistory.

The sons of a primal father who escaped and survived gathered together in a band, united by homosexual bonds and common hatred of their father—which we earlier described as communal identification. The sons stalked their father, wanting to replace him. At some point in the history of each horde, the sons rushed into the family compound, killed their father, and ate him in order to gain his power. They then engaged in an orgy of incest.

When the frenzy subsided, the sons were overcome with guilt and remorse, and for good reason. They were faced with anarchy because each son wanted to be the next primal father. They were also in danger because they had killed the most competent member of the tribe, who knew how to find food and protect the family. But most important, they began to miss their father's domination, which, according to Freud, they actually needed. To solve these problems, they brought their father back in symbolic form by making him the tribal god. They then made a religion of his rules—including his rule against incest—and they worshipped him through the ritualized sacrifice of his symbolic substitute, the totem animal.

What are the modern consequences of the primal horde? According to Freud, this series of events happened over and over during human prehistory and, after hundreds of thousands of years or more, somehow became stored in the human unconscious. He argued that unconscious memories of life in the primal horde explain a number of important psychological phenomena today—for example, why the Oedipus complex is universal and why each male child is destined to compete with his father. (Freud's myth predicts that conflict between boys and their fathers is inevitable, and that there is nothing fathers can do to avoid being criticized and resented by their sons.) These memories also explain the development of totemism and, therefore, the development of religion—an important cultural universal.

In addition, the myth of the primal horde contains a theory of political leadership. According to Freud, successful politicians are throwbacks to the primal father: They are domineering, narcissistic, self-aggrandizing, psychopathic, and interested in others only insofar as they can use them. Politicians are able to dominate their followers because they arouse in them unconscious memories of the primal father.

In *The Future of an Illusion* (1927), Freud analyzed the relationship between politics and religion. He argued that gods are projections of one's own father into the heavens. This projection allows people to believe that someone will take care of them when their own parents are gone. The idea of a god is also a way to control people's instincts; if they fear being punished for disobeying God's rules against open displays of sex and aggression, they are more likely to be good citizens. In this way, religion becomes a substitute for the superego. Freud further argued that political leaders use religion to persuade their followers to ignore their daily problems and to believe that they will be rewarded in an afterlife. Through religion, then, political leaders keep people in a fantasy world; religion relieves their suffering in the short run but maintains their leaders' political domination in the long run.

Nonetheless, the history of every society consists of one revolution after another, as each generation of sons tries to slay the primal father. Every revolution is fought in the name of certain lofty ideals—freedom, equality, and justice—but every revolution is also followed by further oppression, because the true goal of revolutionary leaders is to become primal fathers themselves. In Box 3.4 we discuss some modern "primal fathers."

Finally, Freud's myth predicts that democratic governments are ultimately unstable because they don't satisfy people's unconscious needs to be dominated. The major virtue of democracy, according to Freud, is that it allows more would-be primal fathers to gain access to power.

How accurate is Freud's primal horde theory? As it turns out, although a number of his predictions about society seem consistent with the historical record, Totem and Taboo has been widely criticized for several reasons. First, modern biology tells us that the experience of the primal horde could not have been encoded in our memories. This idea, known as the "inheritance of acquired characteristics," was widely accepted in Freud's time but is rejected by biologists today. Second, it is unlikely that early human groups were organized in the way that Freud described. Current research suggests, instead, that early human groups included several adult males who were needed to protect the group from large animals and other human tribes. Third, evidence indicates that the leaders of existing hunter-gatherer groups are not tyrannical. Rather, they become leaders because of their superior moral qualities, interpersonal skills, and skill as hunters.

Despite these criticisms, charismatic figures do occasionally spring up and establish strange social groups that exist for a while and then fail—often at great human cost. The murderous and paranoid Joseph Stalin, for example, was one of the best-loved leaders in Russian history. Consider also the Ayatollah Khomeini, the inspirational Iranian leader who persuaded his followers to reject modernity and adopt a strict and punitive social system based on teachings from the thirteenth century. Freud's social theory is especially interesting given that, for the most part, modern psychological research cannot explain the extraordinary influence that Stalin, the Ayatollah, and other leaders have exerted over their followers.

Evaluating Psychoanalytic Theory

Problems with Psychoanalysis. In American academic psychology today psychoanalysis is regarded as outdated, disproved, and mildly amusing. It is not clear, however, that the theory is always criticized for the most important reasons. In our view, there are four major problems with psychoanalysis that raise serious questions about its scientific status.

The first problem concerns the narrowness of the motivational theory. There is obviously more to human motivation than sex and aggression. For example, people also need a sense of control, a feeling that they can manage their own lives, even if only in very small ways, and they suffer psychologically when that need is frustrated *(Abramson, Seligman, & Teasdale, 1978)*. Moreover, both common sense and evolutionary theory suggest that people are naturally sociable as well as selfish, altruistic as well as egocentric *(Campbell, 1965)*. Finally, Freud himself admitted that his theory was better designed to understand the motivation of men than of women, and toward the end of his life he wrote that he had not sufficiently dealt with women and their motivations. On these grounds, Freud's motivational theory is simply too limited.

Second, the concept of repression is illogical—a serious problem given that it is central to Freudian theory because it explains how the ego controls the id. On the one hand, repression involves not only repressing id impulses but also repressing the act of repressing such impulses. However, in order for that repression to be unconscious, we must repress the act of repressing the act of repressing the id impulses. And this sequence is an infinite regression. On the other hand, it is not clear why repression must occur in the first place—because there is no part of the psyche from which the repressed id impulse must be hidden. It is not hidden from the id because that's where the impulse starts. It is not hidden from the ego because the ego knows what it is repressing. And it is not hidden from the superego because the superego is the reason for the repression in the first place. The concept of repression, which Freud called the "keystone of the psychoanalytic arch," is thus logically incoherent.

Third, although psychoanalysis is designed to explain the origins of hysterical symptoms, the record suggests that few of Freud's patients got better *(Gay, 1988)*. This discrepancy can be interpreted in two ways: (1) Freud might not have been a very effective therapist, and (2) the theory itself may be incorrect as an explanation for the causes of hysteria.

Finally, psychoanalysis is not a scientific theory because many of its key concepts—including castration anxiety and penis envy—cannot be measured. Freud privately recognized this problem; in a letter to Wilhelm Fliess, he described himself as "actually not at all a man of science, not an observer, not an experimenter, not a thinker. I am by temperament nothing but a conquistador, an adventurer . . . with all the inquisitiveness, daring, and tenacity characteristic of such a man" *(Schur, 1972, p. 201)*.

Insights from Psychoanalysis. Despite the problems with psychoanalysis, the theory contains many useful insights that are worthy of further investigation and may even be true. Following are five examples.

First, Freud argued that a particular set of family conditions are necessary for normal childhood development (i.e., two parents, a warm or nurturant mother, a father who sets limits), and that variations from these conditions can create problems in personality development. This point is important and probably true *(see Hardesty, Wenk, & Morgan, 1995; Maccoby, 1992)*.

Second, Freud believed that an unconscious biological substrate gives a distinctive flavor to each individual's personality. This substrate may be defined in terms of activity levels in the lower brain stem or in terms of hormone levels and genetic predispositions; either definition supports Freud's view that personality is built on a biological foundation. Moreover, this view has received substantial support from modern researchers *(see Buss, 1999; Buss & Plomin, 1975)*.

Third, Freud maintained that we often deceive ourselves about the meaning and intent of our actions, and that these deceptions are generally self-serving. This point, too, has received widespread support *(e.g., Greenwald, 1992)*. In a similar vein, Freud believed that we should get beyond our self-deceptions both for mental health and for intellectual honesty; he proposed a kind of war against the unconscious that was justified by medical and moral considerations. The implication here is that those persons who are least self-deceived will do better in their lives. This suggestion has largely been ignored by personality researchers.

Fourth, according to Freud, our public behavior can and will be interpreted by others, and we sometimes send messages to others without realizing what we are doing. Research on nonverbal communication *(Ekman et al., 1987)* suggests that he was correct on this point.

Finally, Freud suggested that an understanding of personality requires that we consider the evolutionary context in which homo sapiens evolved. Personality psychology, he said, should begin with evolutionary theory and is properly understood only in that context *(Wilson, 1975)*. This perspective is gradually gaining ground in modern psychology *(see Simpson & Kenrick, 1997)*—but here Freud was clearly ahead of his time.

Some Freudian Advice. Modern society seems wedded to the belief that technology will inevitably bring progress and that everyone has a right to be happy, to be healthy, and to seek personally satisfying ways to express themselves. In contrast, Freud adhered to the ancient Greek view that life is hard and that we must simply endure as best we can. He believed that the structure of society is such that most people will be prevented from achieving even the beginnings of self-realization. Freud's perspective, though harsh, may actually be kinder in the long run. Consider his advice to his patient Dora: The goal of psychoanalysis is not to make you happy; the goal is to persuade you to exchange your neurotic unhappiness for the common misery of mankind. With a clear view of reality and few illusions, you may be better armed against that misery.

Box 3.5 applies a psychoanalytic interpretation to some of the events in the life of Nobel Prize–winning author Ernest Hemingway.

BOX 3.5 Biography: Ernest Hemingway

The American writer Ernest Hemingway was born in 1899 in the affluent Chicago suburb of Oak Park, Illinois. In 1961, he shot himself in Ketchum, Idaho. Many people consider Hemingway the greatest American writer since Henry James; he received a Pulitzer prize in 1953 for his novel The Old Man and the Sea and a Nobel Prize in 1954 for a lifetime of literary achievement.

Despite his importance as a writer, Hemingway is perhaps even better known for his lifestyle. He was an extraordinarily colorful personality: charming and self-centered, self-disciplined and hard drinking, compulsively unfaithful to his several wives, and outrageously self-dramatizing. But most of all, he was the ultimate macho male.

Hemingway worked hard at his writing, but he was an equally diligent drinker, fisherman, hunter, gourmandizer, fighter, and womanizer. During the summer of 1935, for example, while living on the island of Bimini, Hemingway offered $100 to anyone there who could survive three rounds of boxing with him. There were four challengers, and he knocked them all unconscious. Nine years later, in Africa, Hemingway was a passenger in a small plane that crashed during takeoff. The plane caught fire and Hemingway was trapped in the back. Although he could have gone out through the cockpit, he escaped by butting open a jammed door with his head; the results included a concussion and crushed vertebrae. Cerebro-spinal fluid dripped down his face at the press conference that followed.

Relative to most literary people, professional athletes, or soldiers of fortune, Hemingway was an amazing risk taker. How would Freud have explained Hemingway's need to court danger and demonstrate over and over again his courage and "grace under pressure"? Most likely, Freud's answer would have involved the Oedipus complex.

Hemingway's father, Ed, had been a big, powerful, vigorous man devoted to the outdoors and to such traditional masculine pursuits as hunting and fishing. He was also a manic-depressive, with moods that alternated between joyous enthusiasm and dark rage. In 1929, at the age of fifty-six, he shot himself.

Hemingway's mother, Grace, was aggressive, ambitious, and self-centered. She dominated her husband and seemed to enjoy humiliating him. She was also willful and unconventional and, according to Kenneth Lynn (1987), was involved in a lesbian relationship during the time that Hemingway was in high school. Early on, Grace Hemingway dressed her son Ernest like a girl and made him act as if he and his older sister Marcelline were twins. This elaborate charade, during which Ernest was forced to wear long hair and dresses, went on for years.

Freud would probably have argued that Hemingway only partially resolved his Oedipus complex. Because his mother was the dominant figure in his home, and because she made him pretend to be a girl, Hemingway internalized an image of his mother along with an image of his father at the end of the Oedipal period. As a result, he entered adolescence burdened with serious doubts about his masculinity and considerable hostility toward authority as represented by his mother. He dealt with these doubts and challenged his mother with outrageous public displays of drinking, fighting, and risk taking.

The strongest evidence for the idea that Hemingway was uncertain about his sexual identity can be found in his unpublished novel The Garden of Eden *(see Lynn, 1987, pp. 540–544)*: Wishes that are blocked in reality, Freud wrote, will inevitably be expressed in dreams and other fantasy materials such as creative writing. Although Hemingway consciously resisted his mother's authority, he may unconsciously have yielded to it—in effect, becoming Marcelline's psychological sister.

Practical Application: Freud's Views on Leadership

More words have been written about leadership than about any other topic in business and management science, and for a good reason—leadership is a subject that affects everyone. Good leadership allows organizations and societies to prosper and flourish, but bad leadership ruins organizations and can cause death, destruction, and misery of horrific proportions, as the examples of Hitler in Germany, Stalin in Russia, and, more recently, Slobodan Milosevic in Serbia have shown. Despite the enormous volume of work on this subject, there is little consensus in modern psychology regarding the personality characteristics of effective leaders *(see Hughes, Ginnett, & Curphy, 1999)*. In fact, the topic of leadership is often ignored in textbooks because there seems to have been so little progress in leadership research.

Freud was keenly interested in the dynamics of leadership and the personalities of leaders; it was a topic he returned to again and again, beginning with Totem and Taboo *(1913)* and ending with Moses and Monotheism *(1938)*. Freud argued that there are two kinds of people in the world, each with their own psychology: those who follow and those who lead. The first category comprises most of us. And, indeed, traditional psychoanalysis, as described in this chapter, concerns our everyday psychology. The key feature of this everyday psychology was first described in Totem and Taboo. Here, Freud argued that memories of life in the primal horde are stored deep in the unconscious of most people, and that one component of these memories is a need for authority—a need to be mastered, dominated, and ruled. On one level, this need leads people to crave religious instruction and authority—they want to be told, by a great and powerful authority, what to believe and how to behave.

On another level, the same need prepares them to accept the dictates of worldly authority. According to Freud, then, the majority of people need to be dominated by a powerful external authority, and they become anxious and nervous when this need is not met.
The second and much rarer kind of person, Freud said, is the potential primal father. These people have their own psychology: As noted earlier, they are arrogant, self-centered,

manipulative, impulsive, ruthless, exploitative, overbearing, and interested in others only insofar as others are willing to serve them. However, they have the capacity to captivate and fascinate normal people who, once again, at a deep, unconscious level, need to be controlled and dominated.

All of this becomes especially interesting when we consider such cases as the Jonestown massacre in 1977 *(Conway & Siegelman, 1979)*. James Jones was a dynamic, charismatic, and exceptionally engaging religious leader from the San Francisco area who founded a religious retreat in Guyana. The term massacre refers to the fact that Jones persuaded 912 of his followers to commit suicide by drinking cyanide. As bizarre as this event may seem, it is not particularly unusual.

In 1993, in Waco, Texas, eighty-five members of the Branch Davidian religious community, a splinter group of the Seven Day Adventists, died in a pointless confrontation with federal authorities. Some perished in a fire that started mysteriously and consumed the compound's buildings; others were shot in the head. Twenty-five of the dead Branch Davidians were children. The key to this disaster was the leader of the community, David Koresh, who was described as intelligent, charismatic, temperamental, violent, and controlling. The events surrounding the Waco disaster were carefully scrutinized in the press *(Samples et al., 1994)*; the general conclusion was that it could not be explained. Four years later, in 1997, thirty-nine members of the Heaven's Gate religious community near San Diego committed mass suicide at the urging of their magnetic leader—again, to the astonishment of the news reporting establishment.

Our point here is that from time to time, strangely charismatic leaders appear on the scene, build a community of followers, and then lead them to destruction. In each of the cases described above, both the popular press and academic psychology were at a loss to explain what happened. But Freud provided a clear and explicit answer in Totem and Taboo. People may not like the answer, but it fits the facts; and in the absence of a better one, perhaps Freud deserves some credit for analyzing this socially significant consequence of charismatic leadership.

C. G. JUNG

and Analytic Psychology

- The Life of Jung
- Core Problem: Individuation and Life's Meaning
- Jung's View of Human Nature
- Evaluating Jung
- Practical Application: Using Psychological Type to Resolve Conflict

Early in his career as a psychiatrist, Carl Jung treated a withdrawn -eighteen-year-old girl who had suffered from severe delusions for two years. Her delusions began after she was seduced by her brother and sexually abused by a schoolmate. When she finally spoke to Jung, she told him that she lived with a group of people on the moon. The men there hid their wives and children in an underground cave to protect them from a vampire who would fly down from the mountains and kidnap them.

The girl said that she had decided to help the moon people by killing the vampire. One night she waited for him with a sacrificial knife hidden in her gown. When the vampire appeared, he resembled a great black bird with several pairs of wings, but when the wings opened, a man of unearthly beauty stood before her. The man wrapped her in his wings so tightly that she could not use her knife, then flew with her into the mountains.
At this point, the girl became angry and accused Jung of trying to prevent her from returning to the moon. "My life on Earth is empty," she said, "but my life on the moon is full of meaning."

The girl became violently psychotic and had to be hospitalized. Eventually, however, she improved enough to leave the hospital and become a nurse in a sanitarium. When a doctor later made a sexual advance toward her, she shot him. She resumed treatment with Jung and steadily improved. At their last meeting, she gave Jung her gun and said that she had planned to shoot him if her therapy failed. The girl later married and had several children. Her symptoms never returned.

Jung believed that the girl's delusions about life on the moon were caused by a powerful unconscious myth. Throughout human history, incest has been taboo except among gods and royalty. After the girl was seduced by her brother, a memory of the ancient incest taboo emerged from her unconscious, causing her to think she was no longer human. She

Carl Gustav Jung.
Source: National Library of Medicine.

fantasized that she lived with a vampire god on the moon where incest was permitted. The young woman then transferred her feelings about the vampire onto Jung, whom she also saw as beautiful, but whom she nonetheless planned to kill if he didn't rescue her. Jung believed that when she transferred her feelings from the vampire to him, she began to get better.

This case *(Jung, 1965)* illustrates several key themes from Jung's theory of personality. Jung believed that our unconscious contains fragments of ancient myths and legends that affect our behavior in the modern world. He also believed that when we lose touch with our unconscious past and become absorbed in the unimportant details of everyday life, problems inevitably occur. And finally, Jung argued that the ultimate goal of life is to find a sense of personal meaning, which requires integrating the primeval contents of the unconscious into consciousness.

Unlike most personality theorists, Jung believed that religious practice is one of the most effective ways to integrate the unconscious into everyday life. Because of his interest in religion, some psychologists dismiss Jung's ideas as mystical and unscientific. However, with the rise of cognitive psychology and the decline of behaviorist approaches to personality, many of Jung's ideas have been rediscovered by modern psychologists. These include the word association test; the concepts of introversion, extraversion, and psychological androgyny; the notion of a "self" at the center of personality; and the idea that self-realization and discovering meaning are the main goals of life.

Jung's concept of types also plays a significant role today, especially in education and business. Two psychological measures inspired by Jungian theory—the Myers Briggs Type Indicator and the Rorschach Inkblot Test—are among the most widely used personality tests in the world. Although Jung's writings sometimes have a mystical tone, he nonetheless developed significant insights about human nature.

The Life of Jung

Jung was born in Kesswil, Switzerland, on July 26, 1875, the son of a poor country pastor and the nephew of eight other parsons. His grandfather, Carl Gustav Jung (1794–1864), a legendary figure in the Swiss city of Basel, was reputed to be an illegitimate son of the great German writer and scientist Goethe. Jung's father, Paul, had once been an accomplished classical scholar, but he seemed to have run out of energy. Jung suspected that his father had lost his religious faith and was depressed. Jung's relationship with his father was strained; he was closer to his mother, a strange woman who talked to animals and attracted poltergeists who supposedly caused dishes to move and showers of stones to fall on the house. Jung's mother was hospitalized for several months with a nervous disorder while he was a child.

Jung was a sickly but thoughtful boy who spent much time alone and had a number of unusual experiences. For example, as a young boy, he carved a little manikin out of wood and placed it in a pencil box, then took an oblong black stone from the Rhine river, painted it in two halves, and placed it in the box with the little man. He hid the box in the attic, and when he felt misunderstood by his parents, he would comfort himself by thinking about the little man. Much later, Jung read that stones found in prehistoric caves in Europe and magical stones used by Australian aborigines were oblong, black, and painted in two halves. This discovery led him to conclude that we all inherit archaic psychic components from previous generations.

In school, Jung was a mediocre student; on one occasion, when he wrote a good paper, his teacher accused him of cheating. He was unpopular with the other children and his school years were mostly unhappy. As a teenager, Jung read philosophy and science, and he noted in his autobiography that he was strongly influenced by the German philosophers Kant and Schopenhauer. He was especially impressed by Kant's view, described in the *Critique of Pure Reason (1781)*, that knowledge comes from experience but experience becomes meaningful only after it is placed in categories that are innate in the mind. In other words, experience brings knowledge only when the mind has some way of organizing the experience to make it meaningful.

Reflecting Kant's influence, Jung's concept of an **archetype** (discussed below) concerns innate patterns of thought and perception that help people organize their experience. In addition, Jung believed that people think about the world in different ways, and that the ways in which they think can be classified into sixteen types. For example, "thinking" types evaluate experience logically, whereas "feeling" types evaluate experience in terms of what it means to them. Jung's type theory, discussed later in the chapter, is the most popular part of his theory today.

Jung seems to have been even more influenced by Arthur Schopenhauer's book, *The World as Will and Idea (1818)*. Schopenhauer (1788–1860) argued that the dominant force in the universe is "Will," a blind energy source that also appears in the unconscious minds of individuals and guides their behavior. Although Will is neither good nor evil, it causes life's miseries. Schopenhauer believed that life is suffering, but that devoting oneself to art, developing sympathy for other people, and practicing religious asceticism (which leads to an understanding of the unity of the world) can make life bearable.

Jung believed that Schopenhauer's Will referred to God and concluded that God doesn't send us war, famine, disease, and other natural disasters; indeed, he was convinced that God pays no attention either to people or to these events, which people must simply endure. Jung extended this idea to psychology, arguing that personal fulfillment is found not in the external world but within one's self. This is the cornerstone of Jungian thought.

Jung became a physician, but he believed that academic medicine ignores the larger issues in life, ultimately deciding to pursue a career outside the mainstream of science. Jung argued that the scientific emphasis on rationality and its hostility toward religion create problems for many people. Scientists, for example, often lose touch with their intuitions and feelings, and like Jung's father, they then lose their sense of meaning in life. Jung also believed that the existence of God is a question for philosophers, not psychologists; but he conceded that people need the comfort and meaning that religion provides.

Jung read Freud's *The Interpretation of Dreams* and was greatly impressed. At the University of Zurich, he taught classes on psychoanalysis, the psychology of primitives, and Charcot's ideas about hypnotism. He also set up a laboratory for experimental psychology and developed the word association test, which is described in Box 4.1. In 1906, Jung sent Freud a copy of his book, *Studies in Word Association*. After exchanging letters, the two met in Vienna in March 1907. Freud disliked small talk and immediately asked Jung to tell him about one of his dreams. Thus commenced a thirteen-hour conversation, after which Freud began to refer to Jung as his scientific heir.

In 1908, Jung helped Freud organize the first International Congress of Psychoanalysis in Salzburg. Jung's research on word associations had been very well received, and he was invited, along with Freud, to the psychoanalytic conference at Clark University in 1909. Jung and Freud crossed the Atlantic together on a ship and passed the time analyzing each other's dreams. According to Jung, Freud disagreed with Jung's interpretations of his own dreams. Moreover, when Jung asked Freud to free-associate to elements in his (Freud's) dreams, Freud refused, saying he could not risk his authority as leader of the psychoanalytic movement. Jung took this as a sign of intellectual dishonesty.

In contrast to Freud, Jung believed that dreams contain information that may be hard to understand but is not intentionally disguised. Jung also doubted that repressed sexual impulses cause neurosis. Finally, Jung didn't believe that the Oedipus complex is universal because he couldn't remember any incestuous feelings toward his mother. Freud complained that Jung was deviating from standard psychoanalytic theory. Jung responded in a letter in which he accused Freud of failing to appreciate other people's ideas, of treating his followers

BOX 4.1 The Word Association Test

As you think of each item in the list below, what word comes to mind?

> Violin
> Automobile
> Father
> Desk
> Personality
> Breast
> Suicide
> Mother

Although Jung is largely remembered today for his view that myths, religions, and other ancient belief systems dramatically impact modern personality, it is important to remember that he began his career as an experimental researcher. Early in his career, Jung *(1910)* developed the word association test after being persuaded of the power of the unconscious as described in Freud's Interpretation of Dreams.

Word association is a projective measure of personality. In other words, both the stimulus presented to the test taker and the possible responses are ambiguous, such that the word association is designed to reflect, or "project," the internal state of the test taker. The test administrator states a word; then the test taker says the first word that comes into his or her mind. Since there are no right or wrong answers, responses are believed to reveal possible concerns and areas of conflict within individuals.

Although the logic of the word association test is clear, scientific studies of word association techniques have not been very promising. As with all projective tests, responses are so personal and individual that it is hard to establish validity or reliability. Some clinicians still use word association, but most have moved to using tests that have stronger scientific support.

in an authoritarian manner, and of refusing to admit his own shortcomings. In reply, Freud suggested in 1913 that they end their relationship.

Jung was quite upset by his break with Freud. Between 1913 and 1918, he underwent an intense self-analysis in which he became so self-absorbed and distracted that he seemed psychotic. His disorientation began to fade in 1918–1920. Directed by unconscious forces, each day Jung sketched a circular figure known as a mandala. Jung believed that these mandala sketches reflected his changing inner psychological state—an experience that convinced him the goal of life is the discovery of the self.

In 1921, Jung published his most influential book, *Psychological Types*. Nine years later, in 1930, his study of alchemy, the medieval form of chemistry related to astrology, convinced him that alchemy contains symbols found in ancient myths and in modern schizophrenic delusions, suggesting that the alchemical symbols are still active in the unconscious of modern people. In 1944, he published *Psychology and Alchemy*, which describes the similarities between alchemy and his analytic psychology.

Jung had a heart attack later that same year. During the heart attack he experienced a vision in which his soul left his body and traveled far above the earth; he then saw a Hindu temple floating in the sky. Jung sensed that the temple contained the meaning of life. Just as he was about to enter it, a voice from Earth told him to return. The vision then evaporated. Jung was depressed for months afterward because he had not entered the temple.

Jung never fully recovered from his heart attack. He spent his later years corresponding with clergy, and he popularized his ideas through interviews and less technical books such as Man and His Symbols. Despite these efforts, his psychology never attracted as much attention as psychoanalysis did—an outcome that keenly disappointed him.

In 1948, the C. G. Jung Institute was founded in Zurich. Although Jung wanted the Institute to sponsor the study of dreams, mythology, and experimental psychology, it became a center for training Jungian analysts. Jung died in 1961.

Core Problem: Individuation and Life's Meaning

Freud argued that the unconscious is composed of repressed memories and desires that must be controlled. Jung disagreed; he believed that controlling the unconscious was undesirable—not to mention impossible—and that psychological health depends on the ability of people to integrate unconscious material into their daily lives. This integration, in turn, leads to the discovery of a person's truest nature—a process Jung referred to as individuation (see the section on motivation below). Individuation gives meaning to life, and for most people, the easiest way to integrate the unconscious into consciousness is through religious practice.

Freud believed that persons who are concerned about the meaning of their lives are, by definition, neurotic. In sharp contrast, Jung believed that the need for meaning in life is the fundamental human motive, and that persons who are not concerned about it (such as Freud) are neurotic. People achieve meaning, Jung said, by exploring the unconscious and discovering their true selves. Although the idea of learning about ourselves by exploring our unconscious may seem odd to many modern people, primitive peoples have always recognized the importance of getting in touch with psychological forces outside consciousness. Australian aborigines, for example, go on "walkabouts," which are voyages of self-discovery, and American Plains Indians underwent "vision quests" to find their special signs in nature. According to Jung, people who do not experience individuation find life meaningless; it is individuation that allows us to find meaning beyond the everyday cares of the world.

Jung's View of Human Nature

Motivation

Jung described motivation in terms of a complex energy system that he called libido, but Jungian libido includes more than the sexual and aggressive instincts of Freudian theory.

Psychic Energy. According to Jung, libido consists of two types of energy: physical processes and psychic energy. Physical processes are the biological instincts that sustain life. **Psychic energy**, on the other hand, results from the individuation process and promotes psychological development.

Jung believed that when psychic energy leaves one psychological area, it reappears in another; he referred to this phenomenon as the **principle of equivalence**. For example, if love for one's mother declines over the years, it will be replaced by an equally intense love for something or someone else. Similarly, psychological symptoms that disappear will reappear later in another form.

Psychic energy changes according to what Jung called the **principle of entropy**: Energy that is absorbed by psychological conflicts will gradually leak away and be followed by feelings of equilibrium. Jung noted, for example, that the "storms of youth" give way to the "tranquillity of age" *(1960, p. 27)*. People also invest psychic energy in and withdraw it from various topics in a process that Jung called progression and regression. Progression involves adapting to the world, whereas regression involves withdrawing from the world and adapting to oneself. Freud thought regression was immature; Jung believed that psychological development depends on occasionally withdrawing from society and concentrating on one's inner life, which is a form of regression.

Enantiodromia. Psychic energy also changes through the **principle of enantiodromia**, a concept originally proposed by the Greek philosopher Heraclitus, according to which everything eventually turns into its opposite. Jung *(1921)* believed that conscious wishes and desires have their opposite in the unconscious and that during healthy psychological development, psychic energy flows freely between these two regions. People should develop all aspects of their psyches, he said—not just the rational side, as Freud recommended.

Individuation. Psychic energy is controlled by what Jung called "age-old and endlessly complicated" hereditary factors; at an unconscious level, psychic energy pushes people to understand themselves and their relationship with the world. Jung referred to the search for self-understanding as **individuation**: "Individuation means becoming an individual, and, in so far as individuality embraces our innermost, last, and incomparable uniqueness, it also implies becoming one's own self. We could therefore translate individuation as coming to selfhood or self-realization" *(Jung, 1953b, p. 173)*.

The process of individuation is a lifelong search, but it does not lead to nirvana, enlightenment, or worldly transcendence. Rather, individuation helps people understand themselves and the meaning of their lives. According to Jung, individuation involves integrating conscious knowledge, repressed memories, and unconscious knowledge from our ancestral past. Although Jungian analysis is not essential for individuation, it usually facilitates the process.

Personality Development

Jung had no interest in the sexual problems of children, and he did not believe that childhood experiences strongly influence adult personality. He was primarily interested in how consciousness develops and how people think about the world. Jung's views on personality development contrast sharply with those of Freud; Box 4.2 compares these two approaches.

Childhood Through Old Age. Jung referred to the period from birth to puberty as childhood; during this time the child's personality reflects the psychic atmosphere of the parents, and the child's behavior is controlled largely by instincts. It is unusual for serious problems to arise during childhood. When problems do occur, they generally bother the adults who have to live with the children rather than the children themselves. Jung also noted that parents are often blamed unfairly for the problems of their children.

Jung *(1960)* was one of the first theorists to recognize the importance of the mother-child relationship in personality development: "The mother-child relationship is certainly the deepest and most poignant one we know. . . . [I]t is the absolute experience of our species, an organic truth." This view contrasts with Freud's notion that the father is the more important parent.

In addition, Jung believed that during the period of *youth*, which lasts from late adolescence to about forty years of age, people should come to terms with the issues of marriage, establishing a career, and having children. Those who have had a normal childhood, he said, will adapt easily to the problems of youth.

People begin adulthood sometime around forty, according to Jung. At this point, the need for individuation and meaning becomes important. People who are not ready for the transition to adulthood cling to the memories and lifestyle of their youth. This, of course, is psychologically unhealthy. Adulthood involves a period of introspection necessary for individuation and preparation for old age. Introspection changes people's normal thought patterns and creates the so-called midlife crisis that is part of the popular culture. During this period, some people become open to new ideas, whereas others become rigid and even fanatical in their beliefs. Some people avoid introspection by becoming overly involved in their careers or their illnesses, or by being obsessed with the past. In principle, however, this third stage should fulfill the individuation process.

Jung also believed that during the final stage of life—*old age*—people should be satisfied with their accomplishments and respected by younger persons. In primitive societies, older people are honored as the guardians of the mysteries and laws. However, as older people have no such role in modern society, many feel unappreciated and regret how they have lived their lives. Religion can be especially helpful at this point by suggesting that eternal life will compensate for worldly disappointments. In old age, people may once again become

BOX 4.2 Personality Development: Freud Versus Jung

One of the most interesting aspects of personality psychology is the fact that the major theorists, all highly intelligent and gifted individuals, could look at the same aspect of personality and come up with such different explanations for why or how it occurs. Nowhere is this more evident than in the disparity between Freud's and Jung's ideas about personality development.

As you may recall, Freud believed that personality develops as a function of the sexual instinct, which, over time, is directed toward different parts of the body. This process, which results in significant psychological trauma to the child, starts at birth and is virtually complete by age five when the phallic period ends. For the rest of the person's life, everything else of psychological importance reflects events that occurred during this brief period.

In contrast, Jung felt that the sexual instinct was not particularly important in personality development, and that psychological development continues throughout a person's lifespan. Indeed, Jung considered childhood a relatively insignificant part of life and, for most people, not at all traumatic. According to analytic psychology, real personality development does not begin until around the age of forty as people increasingly turn their attention to the process of individuation. (One indication of Jung's lack of interest in children is his autobiography, where he and Freud are the main characters and his own children are barely mentioned.)

Because theories of personality deal with the psychological development of humans, researchers have not yet found scientific ways to test most of the theorists' hypotheses. So, in many cases, theories are evaluated based on their plausibility rather than on modern standards of acceptable psychological research. At this stage in our knowledge, we have no way to confirm or deny conclusively either Freud's or Jung's ideas on development.

At the beginning of this book we argued that each personality theory reflects a personal concern of its creator. In the present context we might also argue that each theory that attracts followers may reflect the personal concerns of those individuals. According to this view, people who are concerned about their childhood probably find Freud's views more convincing, whereas those who are interested in self-realization are probably more attracted to Jung.

a problem for others; nonetheless, this stage can also be highly rewarding if the important questions from youth and adulthood have been answered.

Psychological Types. As noted earlier, Jung *(1921)* argued that people perceive and think about the world in different ways and that these differences produce the characteristic features of their personalities. According to Jung, people can be sorted into types based on such differences; his classification of personality types is the best-known part of his theory. Jung's theory of types is also widely used today in schools, organizations, and businesses as a way of helping people work together.

Types are formed from combinations of unconscious "attitudes" and "functions." **Extraversion** and **introversion**, for example, are unconscious attitudes that refer to where a person habitually directs his or her attention—to the external or the internal world. If one attitude dominates in consciousness, the other dominates in the unconscious; hence introversion dominates the unconscious of an extravert and extraversion dominates the unconscious of an introvert. Individuation requires recognizing the opposite side of one's personality, usually by allowing unconscious material to enter consciousness.

Jung argued that extraverted and introverted types cut across racial, sexual, and social class lines; seem to be distributed randomly in the population; and have a genetic base. In Jung's terms, extraverts are attracted to objects in the world and introverts are stimulated by their own minds. Today, introversion and extraversion refer to shyness and sociability, but these were not Jung's original meanings. For Jung, extraverts need not be particularly social and introverts are not necessarily quiet and shy; rather, the distinction concerns where they focus their attention.

In addition to the attitude types, Jung identified four function types. Thinking and feeling are rational functions, and sensation and intuiting are irrational functions. The one rational and one irrational function that dominate consciousness are called the **superior functions**, whereas the one rational and one irrational function that dominate the unconscious are called the **inferior functions**.

The irrational functions of **sensing** and **intuiting** concern how a person takes in information. Sensing individuals pay attention to facts and empirical data. Sensing types are likely to enjoy good food and athletic activities. In contrast, intuiting individuals filter information through their unconscious, searching for possibilities, connections, and associations. Intuiting people enjoy activities that require deduction and anticipating the future.

The rational functions of **thinking** and **feeling** concern how people evaluate information. Thinking types value objective data, logic, and facts, and they evaluate facts in terms of how true they are. Jung described businessmen as extraverted thinking types and philosophers as introverted thinking types. In contrast, feeling types are interested not in facts themselves but in the implications of facts. Feeling types evaluate events in terms of their personal significance rather than as a function of objective truth or error, and they are often interested in art, literature, and music.

In summary, introversion and extraversion refer to whether a person focuses his or her attention inward or outward. Sensing and intuiting refer to how a person takes in information; thinking and feeling refer to how a person evaluates that information. The superior functions dominate consciousness, and the inferior functions dominate the unconscious. The inferior functions are the key to individuation because if they become conscious, a person can change how he or she processes information. Finally, each of the attitudes and functions is independent; they combine to form the psychological types.

Isabel Myers *(1962)* developed a personality inventory called the Myers–Briggs Type Indicator (MBTI), which assesses people on the basis of Jung's psychological types. Box 4.3 discusses the Jungian foundation of the MBTI along with that of the Rorschach Inkblot Test, another important Jungian measure of personality.

Unconscious Processes

Like Freud, Jung believed that everything of importance in the psyche takes place in the unconscious and that the contents of consciousness are often relatively trivial. But unlike Freud, Jung did not think the unconscious should (or could) be controlled; rather, Jung said, the individuation process requires adapting to and learning to use the power of the unconscious. Jung distinguished between the personal unconscious, with which Freud was primarily concerned, and the collective unconscious, with which Jung himself was primarily concerned.

The Personal Unconscious. The personal unconscious contains memories that have been repressed. These repressed memories form complexes, which are clusters of thoughts, emotions, and memories concerning a particular topic. Individuals may have complexes about their mothers or fathers, their childhood acquaintances, their weight and general appearance, or virtually any other aspect of their lives. In Jung's view, the Oedipus complex is just one of many complexes that children can develop. The contents of the personal unconscious are based on individual experience; because psychoanalysis analyzes only the personal unconscious, Jung thought its benefits were limited. Nonetheless, problems in the personal unconscious must be resolved before individuation can begin.

The Collective Unconscious. Lying below the personal unconscious is the impersonal and genetically based layer of memories and response tendencies that Jung called the collective unconscious. The contents of the collective unconscious are not based on an individual's experience; instead, they are inherited, universal, and belong to all people everywhere.

Early in his career, Jung decided that the delusions of schizophrenics are meaningful for the person who experiences them. From his study of alchemy, world literature, folktales, and other exotic topics, Jung *(1912)* concluded that hallucinations often contain elements from the myths of earlier, even prehistoric, peoples and resemble the visions of people from ancient Mithraic, Cretan, and Aztec civilizations.

Archaic memories arising from the collective unconscious affect adults in many ways. Jung believed that the modern preoccupation with the supernatural—UFOs, angels, ghosts, werewolves, vampires, zombies, and so forth—reflects universal unconscious thought patterns. UFOs, for example, are simply a modern version of the belief that gods come down from the sky to intervene in life on Earth. Jung believed that the supernatural topics that fascinate us today are versions of ancient thought patterns that have been with us since prehistory.

The Archetypes. Anthropologists tell us that certain ideas occur in all cultures. These include laws of ownership and inheritance; rules governing courtship, marriage, and adultery; taboos relating to food and incest; initiation ceremonies for young men; associations of men that exclude women; gambling; athletics; trade; the manufacture of weapons and tools; rules of

BOX 4.3 Jungian Approaches to Personality Assessment

One measure of the usefulness of a psychological theory is the degree to which it can be tested scientifically. Unfortunately, most theorists failed to provide methods for testing their ideas. Ironically, analytic psychology, though often regarded as the most esoteric theory, is the basis for the two most widely used measures of personality—the Rorschach Inkblot Test and the Myers-Briggs Type Indicator. Jung's influence on these two measures is discussed below.

The Rorschach Inkblot Test. Hermann Rorschach (1885–1922) was a Swiss psychiatrist who studied with Jung's mentor, Eugen Bleuler, and attended Jung's lectures at the University of Zurich Medical School in 1907–1908. Although he did not directly attribute his work to Jung in Psychodiagnostik (1949), his major work, it is certain that he was influenced by Jung's ideas of a collective unconscious (McCully, 1987).

Rorschach's test consists of ten inkblots chosen to elicit unconscious material when presented to individuals. The inkblots themselves have no meaning; the responses given are simply the projections of the respondent. From these responses, the administrator looks for both universal and individual themes. The Rorschach is especially popular among psychologists who are interested in unconscious processes.

The Myers-Briggs Type Indicator. Isabel Myers was a remarkable woman who was profoundly affected by World War I and wanted to do something to help people understand one another better. Her mother (Katharine Briggs) had an interest in Jung's ideas, and from their conversations, Isabel, too, became interested in psychological types. In the 1940s, with no formal training in psychology or statistics, she began to develop a personality inventory to identify Jungian types.

Over the years, Myers developed a pool of questionnaire items and studied statistics in order to make her measure psychometrically sound. To further her research, she tested students, friends, and anyone else she could find. Not surprisingly, many academic psychologists dismissed Myers's work. Eventually, however, the president of Educational Testing Service, the country's largest test publisher, began to distribute the Myers-Briggs Type Indicator. Although initial interest was slight, supportive evidence for the type concept—and for the MBTI itself—eventually began to appear in psychological journals.

By the 1970s, the Myers-Briggs Type Indicator had became one of the most popular measures of personality in North America. In 1975, the Center for the Applications of Psychological Type was founded to further research in this area.

The MBTI consists of 126 forced-choice items that ask about a person's interests, attitudes toward other people, and ways of thinking. From the responses, an individual's four-letter code is derived, based on the dimensions of extraversion versus introversion, sensing versus intuiting, thinking versus feeling, and judging versus perceiving.

Below are two items from the Myers-Briggs.

Is it higher praise to say someone has
(A) vision, or
(B) common sense?

Out of all the good resolutions you may have made, are there
(A) some you have kept to this day, or
(B) none that have really lasted?

etiquette governing forms of greeting, modes of address, use of personal names, visiting, feasting, hospitality, and funeral rites; status differentiation based on a social hierarchy; belief in the supernatural; religious rituals and a concept of the soul; myths and legends; dancing; homicide; suicide; homosexuality; mental illness; faith healing; the interpretation of dreams; medicine; and meteorology *(Fox, 1975; Murdock, 1945)*.

Jung suggested that these cultural universals reflect archetypes, which he defined as biological predispositions to respond to the world in certain ways. How a person responds depends on his or her culture. In a sense, archetypes create a kind of mental outline that a person fills in based on his or her personal experience. For example, Christ is the archetype of the self for Christians (as discussed below), whereas Mohammed represents the self for Muslims.

Although archetypes make up a large part of the collective unconscious, we never perceive them directly; they appear primarily in dreams, myths, fairy tales, and religious practices. Modern people have the same archetypes as early humans and their behavior is influenced in much the same way. The archetypes become particularly active during times of stress or when science or reason cannot provide a satisfactory solution to an important problem. The fact that millions of people look for advice in the astrology columns of newspapers each day is an example of an archaic belief system arising from the collective unconscious.

Although the number of archetypes is unknown, some are more important than others. The most important include the persona, the shadow, the anima or animus, the hero, and the self. Individuation depends on understanding these archetypes, an understanding that allows a person to see that his or her particular experience is universal.

1. **The Persona.** People in every culture understand that, in order to live in society, we must often disguise how we really feel. For example, when people ask us how we are, we say "fine" regardless of how we actually feel; when meeting new people we try to appear friendly and interested rather than hostile and bored. Our concern about social approval is controlled by the persona archetype. The persona drives us, in an unconscious and compulsive way, to seek status and prestige. Although the persona seems to impart a sense of individuality and uniqueness, in actuality it is a mask that hides our real selves.

Thus, to the degree that we are concerned with social approval, we are controlled by the persona and the collective unconscious, and the individuation process is blocked.

2. **The Shadow.** The horrors of World War I led Freud to propose the existence of a death instinct, but they led Jung to conclude that our capacity for mass murder reflects the operation of an archetype. Just below the persona lies the opposite archetype, the shadow. The persona causes us to be concerned about social approval, but the shadow is primarily involved with evil impulses *(Jung, 1959)*. As one Jungian analyst observed, that which we most dislike, hate, and despise in others is a projection of our own shadow:

> It is relatively easy to arouse the shadow: If a person is known to be prejudiced, for example, simply ask him what it is that he dislikes about the racial or ethnic group that he dislikes. If a person claims not to be prejudiced, then ask him to talk about the kind of person he most dislikes. Either way, the person will quickly reveal the key themes in his shadow *(Stevens, 1983, p. 215)*.

The shadow is symbolized by the Devil, and by literary characters such as Captain Ahab (*Moby Dick*), Inspector Javert (*Les Miserables*), and Iago (*Othello*). Individuation or selfhood depends on recognizing and accepting one's capacity for evil, as controlled by the shadow.

3. **The Anima or Animus.** Jung believed that masculinity and femininity are more complex than most psychologists realize. The collective unconscious contains archetypes representing the opposite sex, such that men have an anima archetype with feminine characteristics and women have an animus archetype with masculine characteristics.

In Jung's view, the contrast between assertiveness, rationality, and career aspirations, on the one hand, and passiveness, emotionality, and family orientation, on the other, has nothing to do with gender. Everyone, he said, is born with both sets of tendencies. Society, however, requires men and women to repress the tendencies that seem inappropriate to their gender. Historically, women have suppressed their needs for worldly success and men have repressed their needs to nurture and care for others. These feelings were long ago pushed into the unconscious and became the anima and animus *(Jung, 1953a)*.

The anima and animus help us understand the opposite sex. Fathers are models of how to deal with the world, whereas mothers are models of how to use the unconscious. Mothers arouse the anima in men, and fathers arouse the animus in women. Later in life, we project the contents of the anima or animus onto our husbands or wives.

The anima and animus are in the unconscious of both women and men. Men are attracted to women who resemble the most active aspect of their anima, just as women are attracted to men who resemble the most active aspect of their animus. And sometimes both men and women try to transform their partners into their strongest animus figure. Box 4.4 discusses some of the forms that the anima and animus may take.

4. The Hero. Every culture has its heroes. In Jung's view, people use heroic myths to justify their aspirations and inspire them in difficult times. The hero myths of different cultures are remarkably similar, despite the lack of contact among the cultures themselves. The stories of Oedipus, Moses, Jesus, King Arthur, Hercules, Roland, Mohammed, Buddha, and others all contain common themes.

In many such myths, for example, the hero's mother is a royal virgin and his father is a king who is related to his mother. The circumstances of the king's birth are unusual, and the hero is said to be a son of a god. The hero's father tries to kill him at birth, but the hero is hidden and raised by substitute parents in a far-off country. After a series of victories over giants, wild beasts, or the existing king, he becomes the king himself and marries a princess. All goes well for a while, but eventually the hero-king loses favor with either the gods or his people and is driven from his throne and city. He then meets with a mysterious death, often at the top of a hill. His children, if any, do not succeed him and his body is not buried *(Samuels, 1985)*.

Jung believed that the hero archetype tells us how to handle adversity and gives us strength for facing the challenges of life. The hero archetype also provides a model for development across the lifespan.

5. The Self. The archetype of the self, which Jung often referred to as the soul, represents psychological maturity. For Jung, however, the self is an empirical rather than a philosophical or theological concept *(Samuels, Shorter, & Plaut, 1987)*. In Jungian terms, the self is achieved by integrating all aspects of personality: "The self is not only the center, but also the whole circumference which embraces both conscious and unconscious; it is the center of this totality, just as the ego is the center of the conscious mind" *(Jung, 1953a)*.

Although we can never fully know the self, the process of discovering it is a kind of enlightenment in which people come to understand who they are at the deepest level. Achieving selfhood, in Jung's view, is both a biological drive and a moral responsibility. Jung also believed that modern society's emphasis on rational and technological knowledge alienates us from our true selves. For example, he believed that psychoanalysis is hostile to religion and that academic psychology is preoccupied with objective behavior and rationality. Both ignore the archetypes and, as a result, do little to help people get back in touch with themselves. The solution to this modern alienation, according to Jung, is to find a way to give the archetypes symbolic expression.

The Transcendent Function. The transcendent function is an unconscious psychological process that brings together the conscious and unconscious portions of the mind and permits individuation. It is transcendent because it allows a person to avoid being overwhelmed by either the extreme rationality of consciousness or the irrationality of the unconscious. People energize the transcendent function when they study dreams, slips of the tongue, memory lapses, spontaneous fantasies and daydreams, sketches and drawings, or even automatic writing. As they do so, the collective unconscious begins to creep into consciousness and can be detected if they remain alert to the signs. Although it may be possible to achieve the transcendent function on one's own, professional assistance is usually necessary. Indeed,

BOX 4.4 The Anima and the Animus

One of Jung's most significant contributions to psychology is his concept of the anima and animus. These archetypes, which represent aspects of the female in the male unconscious and aspects of the male in the female unconscious, are related to the modern concept of psychological androgyny. According to some researchers (e.g., Bem, 1974), the ability to exhibit behaviors associated with the opposite sex is a criterion of mental health. Interestingly, modern androgyny researchers rarely credit Jung with this particular insight.

Jung observed that there are at least four types of anima, representing the ways that men think about women. The first type, the *Earth Mother,* represents abundance, love, understanding, and the need to take care of a man's needs. When this form of the anima is activated in a man, he will search for a woman who fits this description.

A second type of anima is the *Love Goddess*, represented by Helen of Troy, Aphrodite, or Cleopatra. Men see this type of woman as being mostly interested in seducing rather than nurturing them. The Love Goddess offers sexual pleasures but can also lure men into danger.

Mary, Queen of Angels, the third type of anima, represents women who are saintly and devout. The opposite of the Love Goddess, Mary represents virginity, piety, and sexual abstinence. Finally, *Sophia* symbolizes feminine wisdom. When this form of the anima is activated, men search for women who are serious, intelligent, and wise in ways that other women are not.

Jung's associate Toni Wolff (1956) later added two more forms of the anima. The *Amazon* is a powerful woman who approaches the world in a "masculine" manner. She focuses on power, achievement, and accomplishing her goals. Amazons do not put themselves in secondary or servile positions. The *Medium* represents the feminine capacity for clairvoyance and intuition. Men who are strongly influenced by the Medium form of the anima often seek women who are fortune tellers, psychics, or psychotherapists—or they choose these occupations for themselves.

Although Jung did not analyze the animus in detail, later Jungian researchers (e.g., Moreau, 1991) have identified several forms that the animus may take in men. As with men and the anima, when a particular form of the animus is activated, women will search for a man who fits that description.

The *Senex*, or wise old man, represents intelligence and judgment. The Senex is worldly and can provide women with security and material comforts. The opposite of the Senex is the *Puer Aeternus*, who symbolizes eternal adolescence. This form of the animus represents youth, immaturity, virility, and an unwillingness to face adult responsibility. The Puer Aeternus often needs someone to take care of him.

The *Warrior* represents a man with a cause. He struggles valiantly to accomplish his mission in life, whether it be getting through medical school, fighting for gun control, writing a novel, or making a fortune in real estate. Women who are attracted to the Warrior need to play a supportive role in helping him accomplish his goals.

Finally, the *Shaman* symbolizes otherworldliness. Shamans reject materialism, preferring to focus on gathering spiritual knowledge.

As noted, Jung believed that men and women are attracted to members of the opposite sex who reflect the form of the anima or animus that is active in their own unconscious. When such a person is not available, they may try to transform their partner or someone else into the anima or animus figure that attracts them. In general, this is a poor strategy for maintaining a relationship.

those people who have typically ignored the unconscious may be overwhelmed when they begin to explore it.

Self-Knowledge

As noted earlier, the problem of meaning is the core of Jungian psychology. We find meaning by understanding our personal psychology in relation to the collective unconscious as represented by the archetypes. Although we can learn some general things about the collective unconscious by studying religions and myths, it is difficult to explore our own unconscious. Because so many important psychological processes are unconscious, coming to know ourselves through self-analysis is hard work. Moreover, even with the best intentions, we are likely to deceive ourselves about our true motives, aspirations, and personal qualities. Because the problems of growing up, establishing a career, and starting a family leave little time for self-reflection, very few people can become individuated without the help of a professional analyst.

Jung agreed with Freud that the unconscious affects everyday life to a large degree, but Jung believed that we need to learn to understand and express—rather than control—the unconscious. In fact, the collective unconscious is too powerful to be controlled. The solution, he said, is to find a way to symbolize the unconscious so as to release its power—but not to surrender ourselves to it.

Although the collective unconscious can be explored through dreams, one can also use **active imagination**, a sequence of fantasies that we produce through deliberate concentration. Active imagination involves thinking about a fragment of a dream or vision and using that fragment to construct a fantasy. Through this process, archetypal material can be brought into consciousness. Jung warned, however, that this technique may produce intense self-absorption and a loss of interest in reality.

A third path to self-knowledge is through art. Jung recommended painting, sketching, and sculpture as ways to explore the collective unconscious. Jung *(1959)* thought the mandala (Sanskrit for "circle") was particularly useful for representing and symbolizing unconscious psychological activity. Box 4.5 discusses the significance of the mandala.

Jung believed that the mandala, or magic circle, represents the self. Although there are formal rules about its construction—for example, three circles of black or dark blue characterize many Tibetan mandalas—he claimed that it provides a view of the psychological state of its creator. Mandalas, he said, appear in dreams—particularly during periods of psychological stress.

In Jung's view, the form of the mandala reflects an effort to impose order on chaos. Specifically, the mandala represents "an attempt at self-healing on the part of Nature, which does not spring from conscious reflection but from an instinctive impulse" *(1959, p. 388)*. As you may recall, Jung used mandalas as a gauge of his emotional health during his self-analysis in 1918–1920.

The two mandalas pictured in Figure 4.1 are discussed in Jung's *The Archetypes and the Collective Unconscious*. The poorly formed mandala on the left was drawn by a middle-aged female patient. Jung interpreted this mandala of a snake inside a maze looking for a square as representing the unconscious of the dreamer in search of the self.

The mandala on the right was rendered by another middle-aged female patient. The phases of the individuation process are represented by the depiction of herself being as caught in a tangle of roots at the bottom of the mandala, as contemplating a book (i.e., using her mind) in the center, and as receiving illumination from a heavenly sphere that frees the personality at the top. Jung commented that this mandala also illustrates the fact that, for individuation to occur, the personality needs to be extended both upward and downward.

Psychological Adjustment

Jung thought that neuroses are caused either by unresolved problems in the personal unconscious or by loss of contact with the collective unconscious. Unlike Freud, Jung was sympathetic to neurosis because he believed it could stimulate a person to pursue individuation. The process of overcoming a neurosis—or even a psychosis—consists of outgrowing the persona and then understanding the shadow, the anima or animus, and the hero archetypes. This journey involves studying dreams, myths, and legends.

Although the idea of exploring the collective unconscious may seem exotic, Jung was often commonsensical when analyzing a person's problems. For example, he was influential in the founding of Alcoholics Anonymous, and Box 4.6 gives a brief account of some correspondence between Jung and one of the founders of AA.

Toward the end of the twentieth century, many Americans became interested in the role of myths as a way to enrich their everyday lives. Jung would have considered this interest in mythical knowledge a positive development. In his view, science and traditional religion cannot answer the problem of meaning; people will always need their myths, and it is a psychological mistake to ignore them.

Humans have practiced religion for perhaps a million years, but they have practiced science

FIGURE 4.1 Two Mandalas

for only about three hundred years. For this reason, Jung believed, religion is emotionally more important to us than science. Whether or not God exists is a question he thought psychologists could not answer. But he also believed that religion speaks to something very old and deep in the human soul and that psychological health depends on coming to terms with it. The power of religion is so great, Jung argued, that even an atheist like Freud found it necessary to turn psychoanalysis into a kind of religion—to give meaning to his life.

Jung maintained that religion has little to do with the rules and practices dictated by religious elites or clergies. In fact, he believed that organized religions were partially responsible for widespread unhappiness in modern societies—especially organized religions that focus only on God's goodness. According to Jung, the orthodox church no longer helps many people find meaning in their lives; consequently, people look elsewhere—to Islam, Eastern religions, or even paganism—for meaning. Jung claimed that religious practices are the most efficient way to symbolize the collective unconscious—because such practices reflect virtually all the archetypes. Again, for Jung the point of religion was not to provide evidence for the existence of God but to help find meaning in life.

The Individual and Society

In the 1930s, Nazi and Marxist theory provided many Germans with an answer to the problem of meaning, but that answer had sinister consequences. Jung disliked both the fascist and the communist movements for the same reason: The Nazi and Marxist myths were poor

BOX 4.6 Jung and the Founding of Alcoholics Anonymous

Shortly before his death in 1961, Jung received a letter from William Wilson, one of the founders of Alcoholics Anonymous. Wilson was writing to describe Jung's influence on a former patient, Roland H., another important person in the founding of AA.

According to Wilson, Jung treated Roland H. for alcoholism in 1931. Roland H. left treatment when he considered himself cured, but he soon began drinking again and returned to Jung as his last hope. Jung spoke to him frankly, stating that his situation was hopeless—that no medical or psychiatric treatment could actually cure him of his drinking. Profoundly moved by Jung's statement, Roland H. asked if there were any other hope for him. Jung replied that sometimes a spiritual or religious experience motivated alcoholics to change, but such instances were rare. Jung's final advice to Roland H. was to place himself in a religious atmosphere and hope for the best.

Roland H. subsequently joined the Oxford Group, a religious movement that encouraged introspection, confession, restitution, service to others, meditation, and prayer. He was able to stop drinking, and he returned to New York to work with the group of ex-alcoholics who later founded AA.

In his letter to Jung, Wilson explained his own sobriety in terms of a religious conversion:

> In utter despair, I cried out, "If there be a God, will He show Himself." There immediately came to me an illumination of enormous impact and dimension, something which I have since tried to describe in the book Alcoholics Anonymous and also in AA Comes of Age.

> In the wake of my spiritual experience, there came a vision of a society of alcoholics, each identifying with and transmitting his experience to the next—chain-style. If each sufferer were to carry the news of the scientific hopelessness of alcoholism to each new prospect, he might be able to lay every newcomer wide open to a transforming spiritual experience. This concept proved to be the foundation of such success as Alcoholic Anonymous has since achieved.

Jung's reply to Wilson explained the case of Roland H. further. Jung was under attack for his ideas while he was seeing Roland H., and he wanted to be careful about his comments. In his view, Roland H.'s craving for alcohol was a spiritual thirst for wholeness, or what had historically been called union with God. Jung pointed out that the Latin word for alcohol was "spiritus," adding that alcohol is just one of the many dangers to which people without faith can fall prey:

> I am strongly convinced that the evil principle in this world leads the unrecognized spiritual need into perdition if it is not counteracted either by real religious insight or by the protective wall of human community. An ordinary man, not protected by an action from above and isolated in society, cannot resist the power of evil, which is called very aptly the Devil. But the use of such words arouses so many mistakes that one can only keep aloof from them as much as possible.

substitutes for religion. Jung felt that individuation cannot be achieved through political allegiances, and he agreed with Freud that, because politics is a mass movement, political involvement is not the way to find either happiness or a meaning in one's life.

Jung disagreed with Freud about the relationship between the individual and society, and the reason concerns their views of the unconscious. Freud maintained that the unconscious is relentlessly antisocial and that life in society requires suppressing the instincts; superego development may be traumatic for the individual, but it is crucial for the survival of society. In contrast, Jung argued that society is a function of the human soul—that the process of learning to live in society is relatively effortless—because the goals of the unconscious and the ends of society are independent. We must learn to play our social roles, Jung said, because individuation depends on our being able to live comfortably in society. What also helps us to do so is the persona, our unconscious tendency to seek praise and status.

In Freud's view, the superego is an alien intrusion; in Jung's, conscience is a natural development. According to Freud, the instincts (sex and aggression) are antisocial; according to Jung, the "instincts" (such as the persona) prepare us for life in society. Freud believed that parents must vigorously correct a child's naturally antisocial tendencies, whereas Jung believed that parents need not worry about the development of their child's conscience. Finally, Freud argued that society is always (and necessarily) repressive and rebellion is, in a sense, always justified—because authority tends to be corrupt. Jung, on the other hand, believed that a person's rebellion is rarely justifiable because it implies that this person has adopted a political ideology as a religion. In addition, Jung argued that individuation depends on being adjusted to one's society so that one has time for self-analysis.

Evaluating Jung

In his later life Jung was disappointed by the lack of recognition his theory received. Psychoanalysis became increasingly influential over the years, but Jungian theory slowly declined. Since Jung's death, however, the popularity of his psychology has grown dramatically as academics and many others have rediscovered his ideas. In the context of this new popularity, it is important to point out both the criticisms and the contributions of Jung's theory.

Criticisms. One of the most problematic aspects of Jungian psychology is the way it mixes science and moral philosophy. According to Jung, people have both a biological need and a moral duty to find meaning in their lives. However, the existence of a moral obligation cannot, in principle, be established empirically; Jungian psychology often seems to confuse the values of its founder with the laws of nature.

Second, the problem of meaning is obviously more important for some people than for others. It may have relevance for educated people who have the time and money to pursue the individuation process; but for persons born in difficult social conditions or forced to live under economic or political oppression, the idea that they should ignore their social circumstances and, instead, find life's meaning inside themselves may seem irrelevant or impossible. Jung's income and social status allowed him time to travel, read, study art, and explore his own psyche, but most people cannot devote their lives to the pursuit of selfhood. In this respect, Jungian psychology seems best suited for the economically advantaged.

Third, although Jung was concerned about how internal psychological processes unfold, he paid little attention to how society affects individual development. No personality psychologist today would agree that social factors are irrelevant for personality development.
Fourth, Jung was clearly wrong in his view that childhood is unimportant for adult development. This remarkable claim is at odds with virtually all research in developmental psychology, and even many Jungian analysts disagree with it. Experiences in the first years of life do strongly affect personality, so Jung's dismissal of childhood is a serious shortcoming in his theory.

A fifth difficulty with analytic psychology is one that it shares with psychoanalysis and virtually every other theory discussed in this book: Much of Jung's theory is simply untestable. Because analytic psychology relies so heavily on assumptions about unconscious processes— for example, archetypes and the transcendent function—there appears to be no way to evaluate the theory in a scientific manner. Thus, analytic psychology is more an interesting set of speculations than a set of testable scientific propositions. This was not what Jung had in mind; he began his career as a serious researcher, and he established the C. G. Jung Institute to evaluate analytic psychology in an empirical way. To date, however, most of analytic psychology remains untested and perhaps untestable scientifically.

Perhaps the most serious problem with Jungian psychology, finally, is its defense of the status quo. According to Jung, the archetypes organize experience, and ignoring the archetypes leads to neurosis and unhappiness. Nevertheless, many of the archetypes themselves cause human misery. For example, males have dominated females for over a million years. From a Jungian perspective, one might argue that this is a "natural" state of affairs that legislation and a few decades of discussion about equal rights for women will not easily overturn. Similarly, since warriors are a privileged class in every society, one might argue that it is natural for warriors to dominate societies. Although some New Age writers consider Jung to be a voice for progress in human affairs, we believe that Jungian theory supports the status quo and criticizes progressive social agendas.

Contributions. Although many of Jung's ideas, like many of Freud's, are not well supported from a research perspective—indeed, some are clearly unscientific—Jung's theory remains a rich source of insights and hypotheses. Moreover, a number of Jung's ideas have become part of mainstream psychology. The word association test and the Myers-Briggs Type Indicator are currently in wide use, and psychological types, androgyny, self–realization, and introversion and extraversion remain standard notions. Although Jung is often dismissed as a mystic, his ideas have had a major influence on modern psychology.

The part of Jungian theory that is most relevant to psychology today is its emphasis on the role of information processing as a foundation for personality. Academic psychologists are particularly interested in thinking, memory, and decision making and the way these faculties affect behavior. More than any other theorist except George Kelly (Chapter 7), Jung believed that an individual's personality reflects the way he or she takes in and evaluates information about the world—a view that is in line with recent research in cognitive psychology. In addition, Jungian archetypes closely resemble the modern psychological concept of schemas, cognitive structures that the human brain uses to categorize experiences *(Galotti, 1999)*.

A final contribution is Jung's emphasis on the role of religion in personality development. Although Jung was largely uninterested in how society influences personality, he believed that religion is a critical aspect of human existence. This view contrasts sharply with that of many American psychologists, who seem to regard religion as an insignificant factor in the lives of most people—when in fact religion is a powerful force in human affairs.

Conflicts in the Middle East, Northern Ireland, the Balkans, Sri Lanka, Tibet, and Africa are based at least partly on religious differences. After actively repressing religion for over sixty years, the Soviet government loosened its control of the church in 1988, in response to the will of the people, and religion has made a powerful comeback in Russia. And in the United States, millions of Americans believe that God created the world in seven days and that wrongdoers go to hell when they die.

For personality psychologists, the truth or falsity of religious beliefs is less important than the fact that religious motives dramatically affect human behavior. Although these psychologists typically assume that humans are rational decision makers and problem solvers, hundreds of experiments in social and cognitive psychology show that this is not so. On the contrary, people are naturally disposed toward superstitious and magical thinking, and Jung was absolutely correct in recognizing the importance of religion in human affairs.

In sum, Jungian theory anticipated many important ideas in modern psychology and pointed to other issues that cannot be ignored. On the other hand, much of Jungian theory is mere speculation; although Jung's ideas are quite interesting, his theory lacks much empirical support.

Box 4.7 interprets the life of Tolstoy from a Jungian perspective.

Practical Application: Using Psychological Type to Resolve Conflict

When conflict occurs, people sometimes blame it on poor communication. Those engaged in a conflict often cannot hear another person's point of view or understand why that person believes as he or she does. When this happens at work, disaster can result: People may make poor decisions, waste company resources, and create an environment most people want to avoid.

Many organizations use Jung's theory of psychological types to address communication problems between workers. In one study, for example, researchers *(Kilman & Thomas, 1975)* studied the relationship between psychological type and each of five methods for handling conflict—competition, avoidance, compromise, collaboration, or accommodation. The results suggested that extraverts had a preference for collaboration, whereas introverts preferred to avoid conflict if possible. Along the same lines, thinking types were more likely to compete and feeling types were more likely to accommodate.

BOX 4.7 Biography: Lev Nikolayevich Tolstoy

The life of Lev Nikolayevich Tolstoy, Russia's best-known novelist, vividly illustrates the importance of meaning in individual lives. Tolstoy, born in 1828, was the son of Princess Marie Volkonsy and Count Nicolas Tolstoy. After his mother died when he was eighteen months old, Tolstoy's family destroyed all her papers and portraits, leaving him to wonder about his mother his entire life. Tolstoy's father died when he was nine, and he and his three brothers and sister were raised by his Aunt Tatiana on his family's estate south of Moscow.

The members of Tolstoy's family belonged to the Greek Orthodox Church, and religious pilgrims often visited them during his childhood. Russian tradition required that these visitors be treated respectfully. Tolstoy recalled:

> *Many of them passed through our house, and I was taught to look upon them with great respect, for which I am deeply thankful to my elders. Even if hypocrites were amongst them, or if in their lives there were periods of weakness and insincerity, nevertheless the aim of their lives, though practically absurd, was so high that I rejoice that from my very childhood I unconsciously learnt to appreciate the loftiness of their purpose.*

Tolstoy attended college in Moscow. A poor student, he ignored subjects that did not interest him and spent his time dancing, attending theater performances, and socializing. He left college without graduating and moved to St. Petersburg, where for a while he lived a rather wild and worldly life. Tolstoy eventually joined the army and was stationed in the Caucasus. During this time he felt his first spiritual yearning. In Jungian terms, Tolstoy began to feel the need for meaning that leads to an awakening of the self:

> *I scarcely slept the whole of last night; after having written a little in my diary, I began to pray. I cannot express the feeling of bliss during that period. I repeated my usual prayers, "Our Father," "To the Virgin Mary," "To the Trinity," "The Gates of Mercy," and "Appeal to the Guardian Angel," and then I still remained in prayer. If praying means to petition or to thank, I did not pray. I longed for something high and good, but what—I cannot convey, though I clearly felt, what I desired. I longed to be absorbed in the all-enfolding Being.*

Tolstoy finished his military service and then traveled around Europe; he returned to Moscow in 1859 and resumed a dilettante lifestyle. In 1862 he married the daughter of the tsar's physician and settled down to manage his family estate. Although Tolstoy had already written many short stories and travel sketches, it was during this period that he wrote *War and Peace* (1864) and *Anna Karenina* (1873), the two novels that made him world-famous.

By the 1870s Tolstoy was wealthy and internationally acclaimed; nonetheless, he entered a profound spiritual crisis: "Life stood still and grew sinister," he wrote in his diary. In 1878, at the age of fifty, Tolstoy concluded that all his possessions, fame, and accomplishments were meaningless because he had been pursuing the wrong goals: "Is life perhaps evil and meaningless because I am living wrongly? That is to say, is my life evil and meaningless—my life and that of all those of my circle who, like myself, do not see any meaning in life?"

Tolstoy turned to the Greek Orthodox Church for a sense of meaning but soon became skeptical of the answers it provided. Studying the Bible, Tolstoy developed his own system of religious beliefs. Among these were two core principles: that wealth and worldly possessions are wrong and that meaning in life comes from simple work. He devised a schedule whereby he spent the first part of each day writing, the second part in hard physical labor, the third in light manual labor, and the fourth in socializing with others. Tolstoy also gave up alcohol, tobacco, meat, and other "impurities." He chopped his own wood, carried his own water, and even made his own boots. He organized his life in terms of five rules: Do not be angry, do not be lustful, do not swear oaths, do not resist evil persons, and be good to both just and unjust persons. Tolstoy also decided that private property was a form of theft and tried to give away his land and money. When his family objected, however, he gave them the rights to his estate. Against his wishes, his wife also gained the rights to his literary works.

After 1880 Tolstoy wrote many books and articles describing his religious and social views, including *An Examination of Dogmatic Theology* (1880), *What I Believe* (1884), and *The Kingdom of God Is Within You* (1893). In this last work, Tolstoy argued that the rich control most governments and use their powers to oppress and murder the poor. Tolstoy's writings about the meaning of life were banned in Russia but published elsewhere. They attracted international attention, and he developed a small group of followers. During the famine of 1891, Tolstoy and his followers organized over two hundred shelters to feed and care for the needy.

Tolstoy continued to challenge traditional religious authority, and in March 1901 he was excommunicated from the Greek Orthodox Church. He subsequently remarked that this did not matter because no worldly power could sever his relationship with God. Despite his problems with the church and the Russian government, Tolstoy's fame continued to grow, and on his eightieth birthday he was honored throughout Russia.

In 1910, Tolstoy wrote his wife a letter explaining that he could no longer live in the luxury of the family estate, and that he was leaving for an undisclosed destination. Tolstoy intended to travel south until he found a place where he could live out the rest of his days. On the trip, however, he fell ill and died in a rural railroad station.

Tolstoy's life is an example of what Jung believed was the basic human motivation—individuation and the search for meaning. Despite his great wealth and fame, Tolstoy felt that his life was empty until he developed and began to live in accordance with a personal philosophy. At the age of fifty, Tolstoy concluded that the first half of his life had been meaningless. At tremendous personal cost, he spent the last thirty-two years of his life searching for his own meaning.

This work was extended in a study involving 199 engineers, architects, and other technical personnel *(Mills, Robey, & Smith, 1985)*. The researchers found that among these groups, thinking types preferred assertive, distributive (i.e., giving more than they take), and competitive conflict-handling styles, and disliked cooperative and accommodating (trying to satisfy the concerns of others) styles. They also observed that the great majority of these technical workers were STJs—sensing, thinking, judging types.

In a similar study *(Chanin & Schneer, 1984)*, feeling types were found to be more inclined to smooth over differences (accommodating style), to give more than they take (distributive style), and to try to satisfy the concerns of others (cooperating style). Thinking types, by contrast, preferred to compete, take more than they give, assert themselves without hesitation, and act immediately to attain their goals.

Studies such as these suggest that knowing a person's Jungian type can improve our own effectiveness. For example, if we know that someone is a thinking type, we know that this person is inclined to be competitive and possibly resistant to our ideas. The person is also likely to take more than he or she gives, to act without lengthy discussion, and to state opinions openly. Feeling types, on the other hand, are more accommodating, open to compromise, and considerate of the wishes of others. Having this information, we can plan our argument or develop a strategy that is more likely to persuade the person we are trying to influence.

Although some questions about the reliability and validity of the Myers-Briggs Type Indicator remain, many organizations have found the instrument to be extremely useful in establishing work teams, dealing with conflict in the workplace, and managing change *(Hirsch, 1984; Provost, 1985)*. Experts estimate that over two million people take the MBTI each year, making it the most popular objective measure of personality currently in use.

5

KAREN HORNEY

and the Psychology of Women

- The Life of Horney
- Core Problem: Living a Life of One's Own
- Horney's View of Human Nature
- Evaluating Horney
- Practical Application: Women and Work

Throughout his life, Freud tolerated no deviance from his theories and psychoanalysts who disagreed with him were usually banned from the psychoanalytic movement. Although Jung and Alfred Adler criticized Freud and developed alternative theories, others tried to modify psychoanalysis while remaining loyal to Freud's general framework.

Karen Horney (1885–1952) was one of the most interesting of these psychoanalytic revisionists; she based her theory on the view that psychoanalysis ignores the psychology of women. When Horney published her first paper on female psychology in 1922, Freud invited her to visit him in Vienna to discuss her ideas. Throughout her life, Horney was very independent and resentful of male authority, so it is not surprising that she ignored Freud's invitation when she was young.

Today, many psychologists believe that all traditional personality psychology ignores women. This is so because, with the exception of Horney, all the major personality theorists have been men. Compounding the problem has been the longtime assumption that research findings from studies based on male participants can automatically be generalized to women. Although psychological researchers have become more aware of sex differences in recent years, Karen Horney pointed out this latter problem in 1922.

This chapter describes Horney's theory of personality and her ideas about the psychology of women. It also presents some more recent ideas about women and personality based on new developments in cognitive psychology and psychoanalysis.

The Life of Horney

Karen Danielsen Horney was born in a small town near Hamburg, Germany, on September 15, 1885. Her father was a Norwegian sea captain who became the commodore of the North German Lloyd shipping company. He was a stern and deeply religious man who was often

Karen Horney.
Source: National Library of Medicine.

out at sea. When he was home, the captain made his wife and children miserable by reading the Bible for hours and then bursting into rages; the children referred to him as "the Bible thrower." As a girl, Karen went to sea several times with her father, and as an adult she loved to travel and often dressed like a merchant sailor.

Karen's mother was Dutch; she was also beautiful and free-thinking. She seems to have favored Karen's older brother, and Karen reported feeling unwanted as a child. Nonetheless, her mother supported and encouraged her, especially in matters concerning her education and her career.

Horney was bright, attractive, and ambitious, as well as an excellent student who decided at age twelve that she wanted to be a physician. Although her father vigorously opposed this career choice, he eventually paid for her education. To prepare for her medical studies, Karen entered a Gymnasium at the age of sixteen—as of then, the only girl in Germany to do so. In 1906 she began college in Freiburg, Germany, at one of the few schools that would accept women. She lived a bohemian lifestyle in college, frequently shocking her mother and brother. In 1909, she married Oskar Horney, a handsome but authoritarian graduate student who resembled her father; they later had three daughters. Karen Horney was one of the first women in Germany to attend medical school; in 1915 she graduated from the University of Berlin, where she studied psychoanalysis and specialized in psychiatry. She published her first psychoanalytic paper in 1917.

Oskar Horney became a successful lawyer and Karen had a private practice; they maintained an elegant lifestyle in Berlin for several years. Then, in 1923, Oskar's firm went bankrupt and he contracted a severe case of meningitis. He became emotionally withdrawn, relations between the couple deteriorated, and they separated in 1924. Horney divorced her husband in 1939. She never remarried, and she raised her three daughters alone.

Karen Horney was trained in orthodox psychoanalysis, and although she disagreed with aspects of psychoanalysis, she always regarded herself as part of the Freudian mainstream. Nonetheless, she felt that Freud's theories had failed to do justice to the psychology of women. Freud's views on the psychological development of women appear in three papers: "Some Psychical Consequences of Differences Between the Sexes" (1925); "Female Sexuality" (1931); and "Femininity" (1933). In the last of these, Freud remarked that he only partially understood women:

> That is all I had to say to you about femininity. It is certainly incomplete and fragmentary and does not always sound friendly. . . . If you want to know more about femininity, inquire from your own experiences of life, or turn to the poets, or wait until science can give you deeper and more coherent information. (1933, p. 135)

When Horney began to doubt Freud's view of female development, she started searching for alternative perspectives. Georg Simmel (1858–1918), whose lectures she attended in Berlin, provided one such perspective. Simmel, a founder of modern sociology, was brilliant and remarkably creative. He was also the quintessential interdisciplinary scholar, writing and lecturing on an unusual range of topics including Rembrandt, Rodin, the Alps, the philosophy of money, shame, and the nature of society. Horney found Simmel's ideas about women especially interesting. Simmel maintained that men experience the world differently from women, but women's experiences are not treated equally because male culture dominates most areas of life. Simmel further suggested that the dominant male culture causes most people to ignore female experience, and that there is a female "continent of culture" where "a different form of knowledge is based on a different mode of being" (Simmel, 1984). Simmel's views are cited throughout Horney's works.

Horney joined the Berlin Psychoanalytic Institute in 1918 and began a training analysis with Karl Abraham, a founding member of the Institute and one of Freud's favorites. She was also analyzed by Hans Sachs, a Freudian fanatic who made his patients lie on a couch and stare at a bust of Freud while they free associated. It was during her analysis with Sachs that Horney began to doubt Freud's ideas about the psychological development of women, and she later described her two analyses as useless (Quinn, 1987). Nonetheless, Horney was invited to join the teaching staff of the Institute in 1920.

Between 1924 and 1930, Horney published many papers and began developing ideas somewhat outside the mainstream of orthodox psychoanalysis. Her reputation grew rapidly and she left Berlin in 1932 to become the associate director of the Chicago Psychoanalytic

Institute. There she met Margaret Mead, H. S. Sullivan, and Erich Fromm, all of whom were brilliant, influential, and famous for linking psychoanalysis with sociology and anthropology. In 1934 she joined the New York Psychoanalytic Institute, taught at the New School for Social Research, and further developed her relationships with Fromm and Sullivan.

In *New Ways in Psychoanalysis* (1939) and several other works, Horney criticized Freud's view that repressed sexuality is the major cause of neurosis, arguing that cultural factors can also cause emotional problems—especially for women. This view was not well received at the New York Institute. The Institute first rejected the theses of some of her graduate students; then the board persuaded the major psychoanalytic journals to ignore her books. Finally, in 1941, the board disqualified her as a training analyst on the grounds that she had deviated so far from Freud that she was no longer practicing psychoanalysis.

Horney resigned from the New York Institute and, with Fromm and Sullivan, founded the American Institute for Psychoanalysis. She subsequently quarreled and broke with them as well. In her later years, she saw fewer patients and spent more time writing. At the end of her life, Horney became interested in Zen Buddhism and traveled to Japan with Daisetz Suzuki, the man who introduced Zen to North America. Horney died of cancer in New York in 1952.

Horney was bright, attractive, charming, and charismatic, but she was also a private person with few close friends. Throughout her life, she challenged male authority, bringing herself into conflict with her family, her husband, her male colleagues, and the entire psychoanalytic establishment. Nonetheless, she was a perceptive writer—the first major psychologist to analyze the problems of women and to argue that society, not just repressed instincts, can cause neurosis.

Core Problem: Living a Life of One's Own

Men repeatedly disappointed Horney: She had unhappy relationships with her father, her husband, Freud, Abraham, Sachs, and Fromm (with whom she was romantically involved). In addition, she conducted her career in the face of persistent conflict, constantly opposed by the men of the psychoanalytic establishment. Horney thought Simmel's view that culture is essentially "masculine" was more important for understanding women than Freud's notions about penis envy.

According to Horney, each person has a unique set of values, goals, and aspirations, and healthy development hinges on the ability to realize them. But most people are frustrated in two ways. First, disturbed relations with their parents cause people to develop ways of dealing with others that distort their own view of reality. These disturbed relations generate anxiety, leading people to devise theories of life that protect them from the anxiety but prevent them from developing lives of their own. Second, the dominant trends of society block development. In Western cultures especially, people try to compete and achieve at the expense of developing cordial relations with other people. Thus, culture, too, can prevent people from living their own lives.

According to Horney, women must deal with the same problems as men, but they must also deal with the difficulties of being women in a society that devalues their unique experiences. Horney remarked about the tendency of psychologists to ignore the importance of women's experiences:

> At this point I, as a woman, ask in amazement, and what about motherhood? And the blissful consciousness of bearing a new life within oneself? And the ineffable happiness of the increasing expectation of the appearance of this new being? And the joy when it finally makes its appearance and one holds it for the first time in one's arms? And the deep pleasurable feeling of satisfaction in suckling it and the happiness of the whole period when the infant needs her care? *(1967, p. 60)*

According to Horney, therefore, the core problem in personality development—and in life—is how to transcend the biases of one's family and culture and pursue one's own values and goals. Implicit in Horney's analysis are two interesting claims. The first is obvious: It is harder for women than men to live a life of their own. But the second claim is less so: Horney suggests that any single way of living one's life is as valuable as any other. This was quite a radical claim in Horney's day; indeed, it challenged the mainstream of developmental theory and anticipated the modern interest in diversity and respect for differences.

Horney herself obviously anticipated the modern feminist argument that the psychology of women is different from the psychology of men, and that research based on male samples, or interpreted by males and turned into universal principles, can lead to biased and faulty conclusions. As she asked, "How far has the evolution of women . . . been measured by masculine standards and how far therefore does this picture fail to present quite accurately the real nature of women?" *(Horney, 1926)*. Freud's ideas about women are an obvious example of this kind of misinterpretation, but even today feminist scholars argue that many psychologists still don't appreciate how the experience of being female affects the development of personality.

Box 5.1 summarizes Horney's views on several women's issues.

Horney's View of Human Nature

Motivation. Horney didn't spell out her motivational assumptions, but they are easy to identify. In general terms, she adopted a self-realization model of motivation similar to that proposed by the humanistic psychologists twenty years later (Chapter 10): "[M]an has the capacity as well as the desire to develop his potentialities and become a decent human being, and . . . these [potentialities] deteriorate if his relationship to others . . . [is] disturbed" *(Horney, 1945, p. 19)*.

More specifically, Horney believed that people are motivated by two unconscious needs. The first is a need for affection, acceptance, and respect from the people with whom they interact, and, at the same time, avoidance of criticism and rejection. Second, people need order and predictability in their relationships and, indeed, find lack of order distressing: "Man is ruled . . . by two guiding principles: safety and satisfaction" *(Horney, 1939, p. 73)*. Over time, these two unconscious desires turn into needs for social recognition, power, and so forth; but most

BOX 5.1 Horney's Views on Women's Issues

Although courses in the psychology of women are commonplace today, few psychologists were interested in women's issues during the time Horney was alive. Below are Horney's views—usually developed within a psychoanalytic framework—on five topics related to the psychology of women.

Premenstrual Tension. Horney was one of the first psychologists to recognize the significant psychological basis of premenstrual discomfort. Some psychologists believe that the near onset of menstruation brings about an increase in libido, and that women who fulfill themselves sexually during this period feel less tension. According to Horney, however, the cause of premenstrual tension is its psychological connection with pregnancy. Menstruation, she said, arouses unconscious conflicts about childbearing, and only those women who are conflicted about motherhood have severe premenstrual tension.

Marriage. Horney thought that many women enter unhappy marriages because they choose their mates on the basis of unsatisfied childhood needs. For example, some women who are ambitious choose ambitious men and live their lives vicariously through them. Then, because they resent their own lack of opportunity, they create conditions conducive to their husbands' failure. Other ambitious women choose gentle husbands and then despise them for being weak. Horney also believed that men tend to choose women who resemble their mothers; that just as boys like to escape from their mothers' rules, men use sports, clubs, or even the military to escape from women; and that men have strangely dichotomous views about women—seeing them as either saints or harlots.

Finally, Horney observed that some men attempt to undermine their wives' self-confidence. This behavior, she argued, is based on a boy's Oedipal fear of being unable to satisfy his mother sexually. Accordingly, a major task in puberty for boys is to outgrow incestuous desires and to master their fear of women.

Monogamy. Horney believed that monogamous marriages are rare. Peoples' attitudes toward marriage are based on their relationships with their parents; but as these relations from childhood do not concern marital fidelity, monogamy is not a deeply ingrained value. Horney also rejected the notion that men are naturally more promiscuous than women; she described this belief as "a tendentious confabulation in favor of the man" (1967, p. 95). Women are more monogamous simply because men control the economic and physical means of punishing promiscuity, and they have promoted—for their own purposes—the idea that their brides must be virgins.

Another reason for the greater monogamy among women concerns the Oedipal conflict. According to Horney, castration anxiety causes little boys to renounce their sexual feelings for their mothers completely, thus making all other women potential love objects. But little girls do not renounce their sexual feelings for their fathers quite so completely; traces of these feelings remain active throughout their lives. In a sense, then, the Oedipal conflict prepares women for a life of loyalty to one man.

Maternal Conflicts. Psychoanalysis assumes that sexuality begins at birth, and that sexual conflict occurs between all family members. According to Horney, women are conflicted by unconscious sexual attractions to their sons, which she thought was a transfer of affection that the women originally feel toward their fathers.

A second conflict for mothers is competition with their daughters, which is based in their earlier competition with their own mothers for the affection of their fathers during the Oedipal period. A third conflict concerns women who have a masculinity complex, feel unfulfilled, then dominate their children. Such women interfere in their children's lives and tend to be overprotective. Horney also described a widespread problem in America—fear of being an inadequate parent. Parents who are obsessively concerned with their relationship with their child are trying to relive their relationships with their own parents and to compensate for the shortcomings of their own childhood.

The Neurotic Need for Love. Horney believed that certain women have an overwhelming need for love. Their obsession with being loved, or being in a relationship, is caused by years of criticism. Our male-centered culture tends to denigrate female values; consequently, for many women, self-esteem depends on being romantically involved with a man.

Beyond growing up in a male-dominated culture, Horney thought that the most important cause of the neurotic need for love is an intimidating older sister who competes for the father's or brother's attention. When this happens, younger sisters come to see themselves as unable to attract the attention of men. Not surprisingly, these women as adults feel intense feelings of rivalry toward other women.

Horney suggested that women with a neurotic need for love have problems as they grow older:

> With increasing years, say in about the thirties, continued failure in love comes to be regarded as a fatality, while gradually at the same time the possibilities of a satisfactory relationship become more hopeless, chiefly for internal reasons: increasing insecurity, retardation of general development, and therefore failure to develop the charms characteristic of mature years. Furthermore, the lack of economic independence gradually becomes more of a burden. . . . They think that they can be happy through love, whereas, constituted as they are, they can never be, while on the other hand they have an ever-diminishing faith in the worth of their abilities. (1967, p. 212)

important, people require positive social relations and some order and predictability in those relations.

Horney also believed that children inevitably experience a sense of powerlessness when dealing with their parents. Many parents, distracted by their own problems, neglect, indulge, overcontrol, or reject their children. The children then develop basic hostility toward their parents, but quickly repress it. In addition, "the child does not develop a feeling of belonging . . . but instead a profound insecurity and vague apprehensiveness, for which I use the term basic anxiety" (1950, p. 18). Horney defined basic anxiety as "a feeling of being small, insignificant, helpless, deserted, endangered, in a world that is out to abuse, cheat, attack, humiliate, betray, envy" *(Horney, 1937)*. She believed that all children experience some degree of basic hostility and basic anxiety because no parents can be perfect.

In summary, Horney proposed that people are primarily motivated by a need for positive and predictable interpersonal relations. The likelihood that this need will be met, however, depends on the quality of the relationship between a child and its parents. Horney's ideas about motivation were more fully developed by later psychoanalysts—particularly by object relations and attachment theorists (see Box 3.3, p. 64 in Chapter 3).

Personality Development

Horney believed that two major forces drive personality development. The first is children's need for positive relations with their parents and, later, with peers, teachers, and other people. This need for positive relations means that children must also deal with the basic hostility and anxiety that result from unpleasant experiences with their parents—a process that promotes development from within.

The second major force is cultural, and not necessarily helpful. Western culture promotes the notion that people should care for one another, but it also encourages people to pursue economic success, normally at the expense of others—and these are conflicting requirements. Moreover, although society urges us to pursue success, we can never have enough—a circumstance that creates additional unhappiness. Society also teaches children that everyone can be successful, but life circumstances prevent many children from achieving this goal. Finally, Horney believed that society values masculine attributes (e.g., competitiveness and independence) over feminine attributes (e.g., warmth and nurturance), thus putting girls at a disadvantage. These cultural forces shape development from the outside. Box 5.2 describes some other ways of thinking about the psychological development of women.

Both sets of problems—how to get along with others and how to respond to the demands of society—must be resolved by dealing with other people. When interacting with others, children have three options. They can conform, as Horney did when she was young; they can rebel, as Horney did in college; or they can withdraw, as Horney did as an adult. Over time, people specialize in one of these three methods, and, from Horney's perspective, the style a person uses to deal with others is the basis of his or her personality. (These three styles of dealing with others are discussed more fully below.)

Self-Knowledge

According to Horney, people's beliefs about themselves influence their behavior in important ways. Horney distinguished between two versions of the self concept—the real self and the ideal self. The real self reflects the "clarity and depth of his own feelings, thoughts, wishes, interests; the ability to tap his own resources, the strength of his will power, the special capacities and gifts he may have; the faculty to express himself, and to relate to others with his spontaneous feelings" *(Horney, 1950, p. 17)*.

BOX 5.2 Other Views on Women's Development: Nancy Chodorow and Carol Gilligan

Even during Freud's lifetime, some psychoanalysts rejected his ideas about female development and attempted to develop alternative explanations for the childhood experiences of girls and how they affect personality. One of the most popular modern psychoanalytic theories was developed by Nancy Chodorow (1978, 1989), who acknowledges her intellectual debt to Horney.

According to Chodorow, it is mothering—rather than the father-centered Oedipal conflict—that shapes personality. In her view, the primary task for an infant is to recognize its uniqueness and to develop a sense of self. Unfortunately, however, mothers sometimes block their daughters' independence: At an unconscious level, they reexperience their own mother-daughter relationship and want to discourage their daughters' separation from them.

Because mothers don't identify with their sons in the same way as with their daughters, they encourage their boys' separation. Thus boys are taught from infancy to be independent and less concerned with relationships. By contrast, girls are kept in a close relationship, and they grow up wanting stronger ties to other people. In short, men's experience with their mothers teaches them to be independent, whereas women learn to emphasize relationships.

Carol Gilligan, though not a psychoanalyst, has developed another popular theory of women's development. Like Horney and Chodorow, Gilligan believes that sex differences in values and attitudes reflect the ways boys and girls have been raised (Gilligan, 1982). For boys, psychological development involves becoming different from their mothers, and not becoming different hinders the development of their masculinity. For girls, on the other hand, psychological development does not depend on becoming different from their mothers; rather, closeness promotes the development of femininity.

Gilligan also believes that males tend to avoid intimacy because it threatens their independence, whereas females seek intimacy and often avoid independence. Because our culture values independence over relationships, women often seem insecure because of their greater concern with relationships. If the culture placed a higher value on relationships, Gilligan argues, then men would seem insecure—because they are primarily concerned with competition and independence. In Gilligan's view, being concerned with achievement and independence and fearing intimacy creates hostility in some men. If our culture valued relationships more than achievement, there would be far less aggression in society.

Gilligan (1987) further argues that adolescence is particularly difficult for girls because they must increasingly deal with boys, and that the relationships they had with parents and teachers in childhood are inappropriate. In order to get along with boys, girls try to be nurturant and dependent, and they also downplay their intellectual abilities, their assertiveness, and their decisiveness (Brown & Gilligan, 1992). As their relationships with males become more important, women tend to suppress themselves even further, because many women perceive a disrupted relationship as a loss of self.

In summary, Gilligan, like Horney, believes that psychology has largely misunderstood women. Whereas most men are motivated to compete, most women are motivated to maintain a network of social relationships. Because our culture, like many others, values achievement over relationships, women—to the degree that they pursue relationships rather than achievement— seem weak and indecisive. But this would not be true if society had different values.

The ideal self is identical to Alfred Adler's concept of striving for superiority (see Box 5.3). People use their ideal selves to compensate for the feelings of inadequacy, unworthiness, or incompetence that often develop in childhood. Ideal selves take three forms, each of which is unrealistic. A person may see him- or herself as (1) charming and attractive, (2) talented and successful, or (3) independent and self-sufficient. Moreover, when people try to live up to the demands of their ideal selves, they become alienated from their "true" or real selves and become prisoners of a false agenda. Horney noted that her concept of the ideal self was not original—Freud called it the ego ideal and Adler called it striving for superiority (Horney, 1945, p. 99)—but, she argued, the importance of the concept has not been fully appreciated. Horney described the idealized image of her patient "Z":

> He was domineering and inclined to exploit. Driven by a devouring ambition, he pushed ruthlessly ahead. He could plan, organize, fight, and adhered consciously to an unmitigated jungle philosophy. . . . He kept strict guard, though, not to get involved in any personal relationship nor to let himself enjoy anything to which people were essential contributors. . . . And there were underlying puritanical standards, used chiefly as a whip over others—but which of course he could not help applying to himself—that clashed headlong with his jungle philosophy. . . . In his idealized image he was the knight in shining armor, the crusader with wide and unfailing vision, ever pursuing the right. *(1945, pp. 107–108)*

According to Horney *(1950, pp. 64–65)*, the idealized self creates the *tyranny of the should,* the belief that we should excel at whatever we do. This includes always loving one's parents and families, never feeling hurt, always enjoying life, never being tired or ill, solving every problem, and completing in one hour tasks that require three. Finally, and most important, the tyranny of the should makes people self-critical. When we are not pleasant, helpful, polite, and productive, for example, we feel guilty—an emotional state that disturbs our relations with others.

Unconscious Processes

The Freudians criticized Horney for deviating from orthodox psychoanalysis, but she considered herself a true psychoanalyst because she studied the unconscious conflicts of her patients and used dream analysis to understand them. Whereas Freud believed the unconscious contains repressed sexual and aggressive impulses, Horney believed the unconscious contains a person's strategies for overcoming feelings of inferiority. Despite this difference, however, Horney agreed with Freud that most people have unconscious conflicts that cause psychological problems.

According to Horney, incompetent parents make their children hostile, but they quickly repress the hostility. Parental incompetence also creates feelings of worthlessness, and children develop ideal selves to compensate for these feelings. The ideal self—or, more precisely, one end of the ideal self—is unconscious. A person who overtly appears to care about pleasing others may be deeply selfish at the unconscious level, just as a person who seems overtly confident and successful may be quite insecure at the unconscious level. Moreover, at the unconscious level people dislike their ideal selves.

In short, Horney believed that the unconscious contains repressed hostility toward one's parents, repressed anxiety (as a result of feeling unwanted by one's parents), and a repressed and disliked ideal self that compensates for the anxiety. The unconscious also contains one's real self—one's real interests, values, goals, wishes, and aspirations. Finally, there is an unconscious conflict between the real and the ideal self.

What we have just described might be called Horney's theory of the personal unconscious. Horney, like her associate Erich Fromm, believed in the power of the sociological unconscious, which consists of the norms, values, and expectations of the culture that parents pass on to their children. (Fromm's Marxist approach to personality is summarized in Box 5.4.) Among the many unconscious sociocultural values that affect personality, Horney was particularly interested in rules about sex-appropriate behavior; specifically, she believed that most people are unaware of how their unconscious views about the proper behavior of men and women control their own behavior.

Psychological Adjustment

Horney, best known today for her detailed description of neurotic styles of interpersonal behavior, defined neurosis in a very specific way. She believed that people are neurotic to the degree that they are unable to express the values, goals, and aspirations that constitute their real selves. As we noted earlier, many parents are occasionally neglectful, and some are routinely indulgent, overprotective, demanding, rejecting, or abusive. Children depend on their parents for survival, and, according to Horney, their response to being neglected is basic anxiety. They then behave in ways that protect them from anxiety but that also prevent them from expressing their real selves.

Furthermore, regardless of how children are treated by their parents, if the culture in which they are raised doesn't value their unique characteristics, they will be forced to suppress their real selves. Horney believed that Freud ignored the way culture shapes development and, therefore, did not understand the true cause of many people's problems or the forces that actually motivate their behavior.

Horney identified ten patterns of interpersonal behavior that depend on or reflect neurotic needs:

1. *The neurotic need for affection and approval* causes some people to try to be liked by everyone. As a result, they comply with every request, even if the request goes against their principles, and they are extremely sensitive to any sign of disapproval.

2. *The neurotic need for a "partner" who will control their lives* causes some people to search for others who can solve their problems and give their lives meaning. Unfortunately, people with this need are not very discriminating and often get involved with people who are as neurotic as they are.

3. *The neurotic need to restrict their lives within narrow borders* leads some people to avoid

BOX 5.3 Adler's individual psychology

Many textbooks recognize that Horney's views resemble the ideas of the Viennese physician Alfred Adler (1870–1937), who also developed an important theory of personality. Although Horney never met Adler, she acknowledged that parts of her theory reflect his influence.

Adler was one of the first members of Freud's inner circle, joining the psychoanalytic movement in 1902. Eventually, however, he rejected Freud's ideas and left in 1911 to develop his own theory—known as individual psychology. In particular, Adler objected to the idea that sexuality and aggression are the major human motives, arguing instead that social influences have an important impact on personality development. Adler's theory of personality is summarized in terms of the six root ideas below.

Motivation. Unlike Freud, Adler believed people are inherently social and need to be understood in terms of the social environment in which they live. People are motivated by a striving for perfection, which is the need to develop and express their abilities completely. But they also have feelings of inferiority, which trace back to the helplessness and dependency experienced in the first years of life. In order to deal with feelings of inferiority, people develop a lifestyle—a pattern of behavior that helps them manage these feelings and reach their goals.

Personality Development. Adler accepted Freud's view that personality largely develops in the first five years of life and does not change much after that unless a person makes a conscious effort to change. During the first five years of life, children develop methods to help them cope with their feelings of inferiority.

If development during the first five years is normal, children acquire social interest, which Adler defined as responsiveness to and concern about other people. Social interest is the basis for friendship, love, and maturity; people who lack social interest become selfish and self-centered.

Adler was married to an avid feminist who helped him understand that children are taught sex roles during the first five years of life, and that most cultures teach that the female role is inferior to the male role. Some women struggle against the way society devaluates women; Adler called this struggle masculine protest.

Unconscious Processes. Like most psychoanalysts, Adler believed that most of the important aspects of psychic life are unconscious. He did not believe, however, that we repress unpleasant thoughts; rather, he maintained that we simply avoid thinking about them. In short, he believed that it is always possible to gain access to the contents of the unconscious. Adler also argued that all people have an idealized self-image in their unconscious and that they organize their lifestyle around trying to achieve that image.

Self-Knowledge. In direct contrast with orthodox psychoanalysis, Adler, along with Horney, believed that people can explore their own unconscious without the help of a psychotherapist.

However, self-analysis requires an unusual degree of intellectual honesty, which many people don't have.

Psychological Adjustment. Adler (like Horney) was particularly interested in understanding how neurosis develops. He believed that all well-adjusted people have social interest but that neurotics are caught in a dilemma in which, because they feel inferior, they compulsively strive for superiority. These strivings for superiority cause a great deal of anxiety. Eventually, neurotics realize that most of their strivings end in failure, at which point they develop an arrangement, which is an intellectual justification for their failure.

Adler also introduced the idea of organ inferiority, which refers to the fact that most people consider a particular part of their body to be inferior to other parts. This body part—such as a nose that they believe is too big—can be the basis for an inferiority complex and further neurosis. The Individual and Society. According to Adler, societies exist because people balance their personal needs with the demands of society. Psychological health consists in striving for superiority in ways that enhance society, but neurotic people strive for superiority in selfish ways. One of the many negative ways to strive for superiority is through criminal behavior, which Adler believed is an attempt to overcome feelings of inferiority.

situations where they may look bad. Consequently, they attempt to be inconspicuous, avoid unfamiliar activities, and make their lives as predictable as possible.

4. *The neurotic need for power* causes some people to seek status and success in order not to feel weak or inferior. Such people attempt to control basic anxiety by dominating others, or by avoiding situations in which they might appear weak.

5. *The neurotic need to exploit* others leads some people to take advantage of others, then to fear that those others will take advantage of them. These people feel that no one can be trusted.

6. *The neurotic need for social recognition and prestige* causes some people to evaluate themselves in terms of what others think. People with this need tend to choose their friends and careers based on whether they will impress others.

7. *The neurotic need for personal admiration* causes some people to believe that they are perfect and that everyone admires them. Although these people deny they have any personal flaws, they doubt their own worth on an unconscious level.

8. *The neurotic need for personal achievement* causes some people to want to be the best at everything. They strive constantly to be the smartest, the most attractive, and the most successful members of their social circle. They are so concerned with success that they can't appreciate what they have accomplished because they fear someone may be gaining on them.

9. *The neurotic need for self-sufficiency and independence* causes some people to avoid others. They assume an attitude of superiority, withdraw from interaction, and keep social

BOX 5.4 Fromm's Sociopsychoanalytic Theory

Horney met Erich Fromm (1900–1980), the founder of sociopsychoanalytic theory, while she was at the Berlin Psychoanalytic Institute. They met again in Chicago and later, when they were both at the New York Psychoanalytic Institute, they developed an intimate relationship. Fromm was trained in psychoanalysis, but he often remarked that Karl Marx had influenced him more than Freud. According to Fromm, personality is primarily shaped by the social system into which a person is born. In his view, capitalist societies have a particularly negative effect on personality development because they emphasize competition and success rather than the development of genuine human relationships.

Fromm's book *Escape from Freedom* (1941) was enormously popular at the time and is still read today. The book argues that most people are afraid of the isolation and responsibility associated with true freedom, so they escape in one of three ways. Some people choose *authoritarianism*; they identify with and submit themselves to political or religious causes, and they admire power and despise anything that seems weak. Other people escape from freedom through destructiveness; they try to destroy anyone they perceive as different from themselves. Still other people choose *automaton* conformity; they accept society's rules and values so as not to have to think for themselves. This is the most popular means of escaping freedom; conformists sacrifice their own values for those of society.

Fromm also developed the idea of a *personality market,* whereby people adopt the behaviors that seem to be in fashion. When it is fashionable to be religious, for example, people act religious; but when this trend goes out of style, they stop being religious. Along the same lines, when it is fashionable to be known as someone who drinks a lot, they adopt this behavior, then discard it when drinking is no longer fashionable. Fromm believed that the personality market is a major source of anxiety for most people because they can never be certain they have the "right" personality style.

Like Horney and Adler, Fromm believed the unconscious encompasses a sociological unconscious as well as memories of repressed personal experiences. The sociological unconscious, in turn, encompasses the values, beliefs, and attitudes that parents teach their children and the children accept as true without ever evaluating them. Each society has a unique set of values that it passes on to its younger members, and these values, beliefs, and attitudes greatly affect personality.

Fromm was particularly interested in understanding how political systems influence personality; indeed, his ideas are better known today among economists, political scientists, and sociologists than among psychologists. Nonetheless, Fromm and Horney strongly influenced each other's thinking and their ideas overlap in two major ways. First, they both believed that culture influences personality, often in unpleasant ways. Second, they both thought about adult personality in terms of three broad types—that is, in terms of general orientations that involve conforming to, dominating, or ignoring others.

contact at a minimum. By refusing to depend on others, they can maintain the illusion that they are self-sufficient.

10. *The neurotic need for perfection and unassailability* causes some people to adopt standards of virtue and morality that are impossible to maintain. When they are unable to meet these standards, they feel even more guilty.

Horney *(1945)* later combined these ten needs into three styles of interpersonal interaction that she called moving toward people, moving away from people, and moving against people. These tendencies are described below.

1. Moving toward people (compliance). People who adopt this strategy for dealing with anxiety have a strong need for affection. They want to be liked, accepted, welcomed, appreciated, helped, and protected. As a result, they work hard to meet the needs of others. Horney described the person who moves toward others as follows:

> He tends to subordinate himself, takes second place, leaving the limelight to others; he will be appeasing, conciliatory, and—at least consciously—bears no grudge. Any wish for vengeance or triumph is so profoundly repressed that he himself often wonders at his being so easily reconciled and at his never harboring resentment for long. Important in this context is his tendency automatically to shoulder blame. *(1945, p. 52)*

Although persons who move toward others seem virtuous and maintain a facade of social conformity, they occasionally have outbursts of anger and resentment. Despite their public submissiveness, they are privately arrogant and hostile. Nevertheless, this type believes that the solution to his or her problems is to be loved by someone.

2. Moving against people (aggression). People who move against others see them as hostile and believe that life is a struggle of all against all:

> His needs stem fundamentally from his feeling that the world is an arena where, in the Darwinian sense, only the fittest survive and the strong annihilate the weak. What contributes most to survival depends largely on the civilization in which the person lives; but in any case, a callous pursuit of self-interest is the paramount law. Hence his primary need becomes one of control over others. *(1945, p. 64)*

People who adopt this strategy seek success and power to compensate for their anxiety. They try to exploit and outsmart others; they choose their mates for financial gain rather than love; and they are cynical and suspicious, constantly evaluating the competency and power of their competitors. Aggressive people may be good employees because they usually seem self-confident and their honesty, directness, and enthusiasm make them seem highly effective. Not surprisingly, aggressive people are attracted to compliant people because they fulfill each other's needs. Finally, although aggressive people appear to be ambitious, shrewd, and energetic, these characteristics hide their basic anxiety.

3. Moving away from people (withdrawal). Everyone needs some time alone, but people

BOX 5.5 Studying Differences Between Boys and Girls

Virtually every researcher recognizes that influences on personality differ for boys and girls. Some of these influences are biological, but most result from the ways that parents interact with their children. Although boys and girls are more alike than they are different, it is hard to imagine that these differences in biology and parental interaction do not influence personality development.

One of the most interesting biological differences between boys and girls is that girls come into the world much more physiologically robust than boys: Girls are actually tougher than boys. Miscarriages and prenatal death rates are higher for males, and almost one-third more boys die in the first year of life than girls *(National Center for Health Statistics, 1992)*. In addition, girls are born more physiologically mature than boys *(Tanner, 1978)*, and newborn girls maintain eye contact for longer periods than boys.

In terms of interactions with parents, psychological research clearly demonstrates that parents respond differently to newborns on the basis of sex *(Karraker, Vogel, & Lake, 1995)*. In general, new parents of daughters see their children as smaller, less attentive, and more finely textured than new parents of sons *(Rubin, Provenzano, & Luria, 1974)*—even when the babies are comparable in size. Evidence also suggests that mothers talk about emotions more frequently with daughters, and that daughters use emotional vocabulary more often than sons *(Dunn, Bretherton, & Munn, 1987)*.

Another study *(Haviland, 1977)* revealed that mothers responded more actively when daughters expressed pain and less sympathetically when they expressed anger, but responded more actively when boys expressed anger than when they expressed pain. Mothers pay more attention to boys during feeding than they do to girls *(Walraven, 1974)*. Finally, boys get more physical stimulation such as being held or tossed up and down, whereas girls are looked at and talked to more *(Fitzgerald, 1977)*.

Still, there are difficulties associated with research into the origin of sex differences. Although researchers—and parents—recognize sex differences in behavior, it is often difficult to determine whether these differences are the result of instinct or interaction. Horney would probably have argued that cultural forces—that is, patterns of interaction—are the major influence on the personality development of women.

who move away from others both withdraw from them and, in a sense, withdraw from themselves. They get along well with others in a superficial way, but they never allow anyone to become close or to know them well. They conform to the accepted rules of social behavior because they want to avoid trouble, but inwardly they reject those rules. Above all, they want to be independent and self-sufficient. Beneath their facade of competency and independence, however, they want others to care for them; yet they think that no one can or will. According to Horney, this interpersonal orientation may be more maladaptive than the first two:

> [I]n contradistinction to the other two, whose predominant trends are directed toward
> positive goals—affection, intimacy, love in the one; survival, domination, success in the

BOX 5.6 Social Constructivism

Another perspective on the psychological development of women involves analysis of how people interpret information about the world. Historically, psychologists have believed that personality arises through the influence of biology and environment—a view that might be described as "reality constructs the person" *(Unger, 1989)*. An alternative view, however, is that "the person constructs reality"—in other words, that people have different views of life, and reality depends on a person's experiences. For example, the degree to which a person is attractive, aggressive, or friendly depends on who makes the judgment.

Most psychological research is based on the empirical tradition—a tradition that assumes reality is stable and can be discovered if the proper research methods are used *(Gergen, 1982; Sampson, 1985)*. Constructivism challenges the empirical tradition, maintaining that scientific research is not an objective search for truth but, rather, is often driven by personal agendas. For example, government scientists can make discoveries that support certain political views, suggesting that even scientific "truth" is relative.

The constructivist position is popular among some feminist scholars and others interested in the psychology of women. Indeed, constructivists often argue that women have a "collectivist," as opposed to "isolated," view of the self whereby other people are seen as a part of their selves rather than independent or separate from them *(Markus & Oyserman, 1989)*.

These views of the self as either inherently connected to others or separate from them influence everyday social behavior. People who see themselves as connected—usually women—tend to be sensitive and responsive to the needs of others, and they become skilled in interpersonal relations. In contrast, people who see themselves as separate—usually men—tend to act alone and pursue individual goals.

One group of researchers *(Belenky et al., 1986)* studied the ways that women "know" things. Starting with the assumption that men base their knowledge on evidence and rationality, they wondered whether women base their knowledge on other factors. To answer this question they interviewed over one hundred women and identified five different ways that women "know." One group of women seemed not to know anything for themselves; they had few opinions and largely obeyed the authority figures in their lives. A second group of women based their knowledge on the opinions of parents, teachers, or other authority figures. A third group relied on subjective knowledge, in which they trusted an inner voice or personal experience more than authority figures to inform them.

A fourth group used procedural knowledge: They believed that truth must be discovered through reason and the evaluation of different viewpoints. And the last group used constructed knowledge, integrating what they learned from others with what they personally knew to be true. These constructivist women knew that "[a]ll knowledge is constructed and the knower is an intimate part of the known" *(Belenky et al., 1986, p. 137)*.

others—his goals are negative: he wants not to be involved, not to need anybody, not to allow others to intrude on or influence him. There is a general tendency to suppress all feeling, even to deny its existence. (1945, pp. 81–82)

Horney's discussion of neurotic styles anticipated the study of personality disorders, a major development in modern psychology. Personality disorders are more subtle and less disruptive than traditional neurosis, although they may turn into neurosis. People whom Horney described as moving toward others closely resemble what the latest edition of the Diagnostic and Statistical Manual of the American Psychiatric Association (DSM-IV) calls the dependent personality; those who move against others resemble what DSM-IV calls narcissistic, histrionic, and antisocial personalities; and those who move away from others resemble schizoid, schizotypal, and avoidant personalities. Indeed, Horney's three types capture the underlying structure of the modern personality disorders.

According to Horney, compliant people need to recognize their selfishness, aggressive people need to recognize their feelings of inferiority, and withdrawn people need to recognize their dependency so that the growth process can begin.

The Individual and Society

Horney is often called a social psychoanalyst because she emphasized the ways in which society shapes personality. Many social psychoanalysts think that society has a positive effect on personality, but Horney felt that most societies ignore women's values and push them into subordinate roles, which causes problems for everyone. From her clinical work, Horney concluded that some men would like to be more nurturant (and feminine) but repress such impulses in order to seem dominant and "manly."

Box 5.5 describes some of the difficulties involved in studying differences between boys and girls.

Freud believed that society is a necessary evil, an alien force, and a primary source of suffering in life, and that people other than our parents are only marginally important in psychological development. Horney believed that society teaches children harmful values, but that people nonetheless find meaning for their lives in their relationships with others—a point that Freud, and also Jung, missed. People who cannot establish meaningful relationships are, according to Horney, neurotic in the sense that they are unable to live their own lives because they are still concerned with avoiding basic anxiety.

Evaluating Horney

Karen Horney is unique in the history of personality psychology in that she was the first woman to develop an original theory, and she is the only major personality theorist to write about issues that specifically concern women. Textbooks typically describe Horney as merely repackaging the ideas of Freud and Adler, but we think she is much more important than that. Fortunately, her contributions have been rediscovered. Her ideas about the self were adopted by later psychoanalytic writers including Erik Erikson (Chapter 11) and the object relations

BOX 5.7 Biography: Simone de Beauvoir

"Representation of the world, like the world itself, is the work of men; they describe from their own point of view, which they confuse with absolute truth" *(Beauvoir, 1949, p. 161).* Simone de Beauvoir was a teacher, an existentialist philosopher, and one of the most influential feminist writers of the twentieth century. Her book *The Second Sex (1949)* influenced generations of feminists who followed her. Beauvoir was born into a genteel but impoverished family in Paris in 1908. Her mother, a devout Roman Catholic, sent Simone to a Catholic school where mothers attended classes to supervise their children's behavior and ensure that teachers didn't deviate from Catholic dogma. Madame de Beauvoir was greatly concerned about appearances; although her husband, a journalist and salesman, had a meager income, she struggled to maintain the appearance of an upper-class lifestyle.

Beauvoir was brilliant; she excelled in school and was the center of attention at home. Although she had a good relationship with her mother in childhood, they did not get along well during Beauvoir's adolescence. Speaking of her mother, she commented:

> She was very hostile toward me, really unbearable, during my entire adolescence. My relationship with her, from the time I was about ten or eleven, was one of conflict. After that, we began to have a good relationship again, but it was very distant because we could not get along at all. Gradually, I came to understand that my mother held dear all those bourgeois, Catholic, pious, well-thinking ideas which I was learning to detest. She absolutely did not like my ideas. I could not speak to her about anything that mattered to me. She disapproved of everything. *(Quoted in Bain, 1990, p. 55.)*

Beauvoir's father frequently commented that Simone and her sister would never marry because they had no dowry. Nonetheless, he applauded Beauvoir's schoolwork, explaining her success by saying, "Simone thinks like a man!" Beauvoir felt much closer to her father than to her mother, and identified more strongly with him. Monsieur de Beauvoir was an atheist, and Simone eventually rejected Catholicism as well. Although her father wanted her to become a civil servant, Beauvoir preferred to study philosophy—an honored male activity in France. They compromised by agreeing that Beauvoir would become a teacher of philosophy—rather than a philosopher in her own right.

At the elite Ecole Normale Superieure in Paris, Beauvoir became friends with Maurice Merleau-Ponty, Claude Levi-Strauss, and Jean-Paul Sartre—all of whom would become famous. Beauvoir formed an intimate relationship with Sartre that lasted fifty years; although they considered marriage, neither wanted children or the restrictions on personal freedom that they felt marriage would bring. In 1934, Sartre began to develop the existential philosophy for which he is best known, and he and Beauvoir spent a great deal of time discussing these ideas. Through the years, Beauvoir played a key role in reading, editing, and commenting on Sartre's writing.

Beauvoir, too, liked to write. During 1938–1941, as the Germans overran France, she authored her first novel, *The Guest*, which was published in 1943. In 1941, Sartre proposed that they form a clandestine group to support the French Resistance. Although this plan never materialized, members of the Resistance asked Sartre to write about his impressions of the liberation of Paris in 1944. A series of articles appeared under Sartre's name, but they were actually written by Beauvoir *(Bain, 1990)*.

After the war, Beauvoir became well known for her novels and philosophical writings, and in 1947, she was invited on a lecture tour in the United States. During this trip, she met the American writer Nelson Algren, with whom she developed a romantic relationship that continued for almost ten years. Beauvoir resolved to write her autobiography but decided, first, to analyze the condition of women in general. Her life had been an untraditional one for a woman—she was a successful writer and a famous intellectual who had engaged in romantic relationships with two men—and she concluded that she knew little about the problems most women face. She was also influenced by Algren's suggestion that the position of women of the 1940s was similar to that of American Blacks—a group of people living in a prejudiced society about whom White men knew very little.

A major point of Beauvoir's *The Second Sex* is that all existing theories of human nature are biased because they ignore the psychology of women. The book appeared in France in 1949 and was published in the United States in 1953. Two weeks after its publication, it became a best-seller; thereafter, it went into many editions and was translated into several languages, making Beauvoir internationally famous. In 1954, her novel The Mandarins won the prestigious Prix Goncourt in France.

From 1957 to 1972, Beauvoir wrote her autobiography in four volumes: *Memoirs of a Dutiful Daughter (1958)*, *The Prime of Life (1960)*, *Force of Circumstance (1963)*, and *All Said and Done (1972)*. In 1970, a feminist group asked Beauvoir to speak about an abortion bill that was about to be presented in the British parliament. This was the first time any group had asked for her support on her own and not because of her connection to Sartre. From then until her death in 1986, Beauvoir frequently spoke on women's issues. Although almost all of her writings concern feminist topics, she did not become active in the women's movement until 1970.

From the time of the French Resistance in World War II until her death, Beauvoir was also involved in leftist politics. She believed that women could gain power only through mass action, and she doubted that a revolutionary movement directed by men could or would address women's issues adequately:

> *Men were always telling [women] that the needs of the revolution came first and their turn as women came later. . . . [A]nd so I realized that women would have to take care of their problems in ways that were personal, direct, and immediate. They could no longer sit waiting patiently for men to change the society for them because it would never happen unless they did it themselves. (Bain, 1990, p. 555)*

Beauvoir read Karen Horney, cited her in *The Second Sex*, and spent a large part of her life developing the point that Horney made in 1922—that the experiences of women are different from those of men, and that we know little about the psychology of women. This is less true today than it was when The Second Sex was published in 1949, but obviously a great deal of research remains to be completed.

theorists (Chapter 3), as well as by the interpersonal theorists (Chapter 7) and the humanistic psychologists (Chapter 10).

Horney expanded psychoanalytic theory by recognizing the importance of social motivation, which is a standard view today. Most modern theorists have adopted her idea that a child's relations with its parents—outside the Oedipal conflict—are a major influence on personality development. And Horney's view that women see the world differently from men is popular among most modern feminist scholars; much feminist research today concerns understanding how women construct reality. Box 5.6 describes a constructivist approach to women's psychological development.

Horney also believed that the mother-child relationship is more important than the father-child relationship, and many modern theorists agree. Moreover, Horney was concerned about how culture affects personality twenty-five years before other psychologists began to take the problem seriously. But most important, Horney's typology of interpersonal behavior—moving toward, against, and away from others—anticipated the modern study of personality disorders, currently one of the "hottest" topics in clinical research. All these contributions make us wonder why Horney is regarded as a minor Freudian revisionist. The mainstream of personality psychology has absorbed many of her ideas without recognizing their original source, and as a result there has been virtually no modern research on Horney's theory.

The primary problem with Horney's theory, in our judgment, concerns her indifference to biology. Like all theorists who emphasize the role of culture in shaping personality—and this includes sociologists, economists, anthropologists, and behaviorists—Horney's theory pays little attention to the biological factors that inevitably underlie personality. For example, the schizoid tendencies that parallel the interpersonal style she described as "moving away from others" have a well-defined genetic base *(Siever, 1992)*. Children's needs for attention and care are also biological in nature. Most researchers would argue that individual differences in these areas are bound to have an impact on personality development.

Box 5.7 looks at the life of the feminist writer Simone de Beauvoir from the perspective of Horney's theory.

Practical Application: Women and Work

Although women currently comprise about 50 percent of the workforce, some people would argue that work is an area where the values, experiences, and contributions of women have only just begun to be taken into consideration. One problem is the small number of women at the highest levels of organizational leadership. Although many women now hold managerial positions, very few ever reach the position of CEO or chairman of the board. Among the numerous possible explanations for this phenomenon is the suggestion that psychological factors operating in the workplace affect women's career progress.

For example, women are often perceived as being less dedicated to their careers than men. One group of researchers *(Heilman et al., 1989)* asked a group of male managers to choose adjectives that describe male and female managers. Words chosen to describe males included leadership ability, self-confidence, assertiveness, logic, and emotional stability. Words chosen to describe females included curiosity, helpfulness, intuition, creativity, understanding, and neatness—qualities not generally associated with higher leadership positions. Another study *(Ohlott, Ruderman, & McCauley, 1994)* revealed that when jobs carried significant responsibility, men were more likely to be picked than women.

Another important issue for women is salary: As of 1996, women were earning only 75.5 cents for every dollar men earned *(Belknap, 1996)*. Although both men and women regard salary as important, women appear to have lower expectations in this area than men. In a study of university workers, for example, one group of researchers *(Hollenbeck et al., 1987)* found that women were more likely to apply for lower-paying jobs regardless of their qualifications. And in a study of salary expectations among engineering students *(Jackson, Gardner, & Sullivan, 1992)*, researchers found that women's estimate of the amount they would be earning at the peak of their career was $35,000 less than that of their male counterparts.

The results of these studies would not have surprised Horney, who believed that the devaluation of women and their experiences had an important impact on all aspects of their lives. Like psychoanalysis, work has historically been a "man's world"; hence the sex differences in career achievement, salaries, and even level of aspiration.

Horney would probably have been gratified, however, at the recent development of "family-responsive" work environments, which involve issues traditionally relegated to women. In one study *(Grover & Crooker, 1995)*, for example, researchers found that policies such as parental leave, flexible schedules, and childcare increased employee commitment to the organization and lowered intentions to quit. Perhaps not surprisingly, results from another study *(Goodstein, 1994)* suggested that companies with higher percentages of female workers were most likely to adopt such policies. Although these are small steps toward developing a full understanding of women's experiences and values, Horney would likely have considered them signs of progress.

PART THREE

Traditional American Theories

6

GORDON ALLPORT AND HENRY MURRAY

Trait Theory and the Psychology of Uniqueness

- The Life of Allport
- Core Problem: Understanding Individual Uniqueness
- Allport's View of Human Nature
- Evaluating Allport
- The Life of Murray
- Core Problem: Understanding Lives
- Murray's View of Human Nature
- Evaluating Murray
- Practical Application: Assessment Centers

Until the 1930s, most personality theorists were Europeans. Then, in the late 1930s, two Harvard professors published textbooks that established personality psychology as an academic discipline in North America. Gordon Allport's *Personality: A Psychological Interpretation (1937)* and Henry Murray's *Explorations in Personality (1938)* defined personality psychology for subsequent generations of researchers. Although the two were colleagues at Harvard, they were not personally close: Allport was a prudish, introverted academic who despised psychoanalysis; Murray was a fun-loving dilettante and socialite who promoted psychoanalysis.

Despite their differences, there are several reasons why they belong in the same chapter. First, Allport and Murray founded personality psychology in North America. Second, both were dedicated to the notion that personality psychology involves the detailed evaluation of an individual life history, which is referred to as personology. Third, they thought that understanding a person requires clarifying that person's motives, and they had similar views about motivation. Fourth, they were both influenced by their brilliant Harvard colleague, William McDougall, one of the best-known psychologists in America during the 1920s and 1930s.

Finally, Allport and Murray were literary humanists who celebrated the uniqueness of individuals and often seemed more interested in art than in science *(see Maddi & Costa, 1972)*. Allport stated that he had no talent for science, and Murray spent his life working on an unpublished study of Herman Melville, the author of *Moby Dick*. Their influence on modern personality psychology has diminished somewhat, but many of their ideas are worth remembering today.

• • •

Gordon Allport is often called the father of trait theory, which is the view that personality can be defined in terms of a small number of statistically defined dimensions of individual differences. It is curious to note, then, that Allport was quite critical of traditional trait theory as well as of psychoanalysis and behaviorism (Chapter 8). The problem with all three perspectives, according to Allport, is that they reduce people to abstract categories invented by psychologists. He believed that people can be understood only in terms of their own unique motives.

The Life of Allport

Gordon Allport was born in 1897 in Montezuma, Indiana, the youngest of four brothers. His father was a doctor who turned the family home into a hospital, and it was here that Allport learned about the virtues of cleanliness and the dangers of infection. His mother was a pious former schoolteacher who taught her boys "the importance of searching for ultimate religious answers" *(Allport, 1961, p. 202)*. Home life was characterized by "plain Protestant piety and hard work."

Allport grew up in Cleveland, where he was a bright loner, a social misfit, and an indifferent student. He followed his older brother Floyd—one of the best-known social psychologists of his generation—to Harvard where, after a rocky start, he became an excellent student. Allport had no talent for science or mathematics; instead, he studied psychology, helped his brother with his research, ran a boys' club, worked as a probation officer, assisted foreign students, and was active in social service—an eclectic pattern that he followed for the rest of his life. Allport became interested in personality psychology because he thought it could be used to help normal people.

Allport graduated from Harvard in 1919; in 1920 he taught English and sociology in Constantinople (Istanbul) and traveled around Europe. He visited Freud in Vienna that year and the visit had "the character of a traumatic developmental episode" *(Allport, 1968, p. 384; we will return shortly to that famous visit)*. Allport received his Ph.D. in psychology from Harvard in 1922. He studied in Germany for two more years, then taught at Dartmouth College from 1926 to 1930. He was married in 1925 and had one son. In 1930 he returned to Harvard, where he remained until his death in 1967.

Allport had an unusually successful academic career. In 1926 he developed and taught the first course in personality psychology in the United States. His 1937 book, *Personality: A Psychological Interpretation,* made him famous. He ultimately published a dozen books, many journal articles, and two personality inventories. He edited the major journal in his field,

Gordon Allport.
Source: Bettman/Corbis.

was elected president of the American Psychological Association (APA) in 1937, served as the first Richard Cabot Professor of Social Ethics at Harvard in 1967, and received the APA Distinguished Scientific Contribution award in 1964.

Allport was a self-professed eclectic—that is, he stitched ideas together from various sources rather than developing a systematic theoretical model. A prolific writer and a spirited debater, he was unusually thoughtful about the core issues in personality psychology. Although he is not as well known as Freud or Jung, many of his ideas are quite pertinent today. For example, his definition of personality appears in most contemporary textbooks: "Personality is the dynamic organization within the individual of those psychophysical systems that determine his unique adjustments to his environment" *(1937, p. 48)*. In addition, many important younger psychologists today *(Emmons, 1989; Funder, 1991; Little, 1972; McCrae, 1992; Runyan, 1994)* regard Allport as their model.

Allport's best-known idea is that each person is unique. Some authors *(e.g., Atwood & Tomkins, 1976)* suggest that his devotion to the principle of uniqueness might have been a reaction to his dependence on his older brother Floyd, with whom he was very competitive. Allport's passion for uniqueness may also have been influenced by Hugo Munsterberg. Recruited to Harvard from Germany by William James, Munsterberg was a pioneer of industrial psychology. He regarded people as interchangeable parts, and comparable to pumps, widgets, and other manufacturing instruments. Allport described Munsterberg's lectures as "chilling" and his view of people as repellent. Allport's ideas about personal uniqueness may well be a reaction to Munsterberg's views.

As we will see in the next section, Allport's one meeting with Freud also seems to have had a dramatic impact on his entire intellectual agenda (Freud had that kind of effect on people!). But that meeting aside, Allport was also opposed to the model of human nature implied by psychoanalytic theory—the notion that people are controlled by unconscious instincts to which they can only react.

A third major influence on Allport's thinking was German phenomenology—in particular, Gestalt psychology *(Kohler, 1929)*, *Verstehen* psychology *(Spranger, 1928)*, and personalistic psychology *(Stern, 1921)*, which are all similar in their emphasis on how individuals perceive reality. For example, they all criticize Munsterberg, Freud, and American behaviorism, arguing that the goal of psychology is to understand (verstehen) single individuals, and that psychology should study the whole person rather than "part processes" such as perception, memory, and learning. In his biography, Allport says he found German psychology to be a "liberation," an alternative to traditional American psychology, and a way of thinking about people that was congenial with his humanistic inclinations.

Some textbooks argue that Allport was also influenced by William James. We don't know for certain, but it appears that Allport was strongly influenced by William McDougall, the brilliant though largely forgotten psychologist who was recruited from England to fill James's chair after he retired. Allport knew McDougall, and there is a clear similarity in their views on how the self develops and on how people are motivated by their goals and intentions; in their concepts of attitudes and sentiments, cardinal traits and dominant motives; and in their criticisms of psychoanalysis and behaviorism.

Allport revealed little about his personal or intellectual development, so our comments are somewhat speculative. Nonetheless, he seems clearly to have been influenced by his competition with his older brother, his dislike of "scientific psychology," his exposure to German phenomenology, his acquaintance with William McDougall, and his meeting with Freud in 1920.

Core Problem: Understanding Individual Uniqueness

After graduating from college, Allport traveled in Europe and visited a brother in Vienna. While in Vienna, he decided to try to meet Freud, one of the most famous citizens of Vienna and the best-known psychologist in the world. As noted, this meeting had a powerful impact on Allport. Forty-eight years later, he described the meeting as follows: "With a callow forwardness characteristic of age twenty-two, I wrote to Freud announcing that I was in Vienna and implied that no doubt he would be glad to make my acquaintance. I received a kind reply in his own handwriting inviting me to come to his office at a certain time" *(1968)*. Freud invited young Allport into his inner office, and then sat quietly, expecting Allport to describe the problem that had brought him there.

Allport didn't know what to do next. "I was not prepared for silence and had to think fast to find a suitable conversational gambit. I told him of an episode on the tram car on my way to his office. A small boy about four years of age had displayed a conspicuous dirt phobia. He kept saying to his mother, 'I don't want to sit there. . . . [D]on't let that dirty man sit beside me.' To him everything was *schmutzig* [filthy]" *(1968)*. Allport described the boy's mother as a dominant, controlling, and "well-starched *Hausfrau*," and he thought the point of his story was obvious—namely, that sons of overbearing mothers fear dirt.

> When I finished my story Freud fixed his kindly therapeutic eyes upon me and said, 'And was that little boy you?' Flabbergasted and feeling a bit guilty, I contrived to change the subject. . . . This experience taught me that depth psychology, for all its merits, may plunge too deep, and psychologists would do well to give full recognition to manifest motives before probing the unconscious." *(1968, pp. 383–384)*

Allport believed that he was simply trying to make conversation and that Freud was obsessed with unconscious motives and hidden meanings. Allport obviously overreacted; Freud would never offer a serious psychoanalytic interpretation on the basis of one short story, and he probably was teasing the nervous young American. But Freud was also very insightful: Allport was a prissy, uptight young man who, having grown up in a house converted to a hospital, was obsessed with cleanliness, and Freud's remark cut him to the bone.

Allport spent the rest of his career arguing that Freud's interpretation of the dirt phobia story was wrong. He told the story in every class he taught, and he repeated it in his biography at the end of his career. Allport's reaction to Freud's comment may have been defensive, but his point challenges the most fundamental belief of depth psychology. For Allport, normal people know what they are doing and why; this view directly contradicts Freud's claim that the reasons for our actions are usually unconscious and that we typically become defensive when they are pointed out to us.

The core problem for Allport was whether people's actions should be explained in terms of general categories or unique motives. He stated repeatedly that the key question in personality psychology is "How shall a psychological life history be written? What processes and what structures must a full-bodied account of personality include? How can one detect unifying threads in a life, if they exist?" *(1968, p. 377)*.

Allport's answer to this question is a rebuttal of Freud in three major ways. First, Freud wanted to define the *general* laws of motivation, development, and unconscious thought that affect everyone everywhere; in contrast, Allport argued that the goal of personality psychology is to explain and understand each person's individual life, one at a time. Second, Freud maintained that each life follows the same developmental progression—id, ego, Oedipus complex, superego, subsequent neurosis—and that lives differ only in terms of superficial details. In contrast, Allport thought that the important features of each person's life (including the cause of a his or her neurosis) could be explained only in the specific context of that person's development. Finally, Allport disagreed with Freud about how childhood events influence the development of adult personality. Freud believed that our lives are shaped by unconscious memories of traumatic childhood events, whereas Allport thought this was true only for neurotics; normal adults, he said, are motivated by their future goals rather than by their past memories.

These three disagreements arose directly from Allport's meeting with Freud. Freud's response to Allport's story about the little boy with a dirt phobia suggested that he thought there was more to their interaction than polite conversation. Allport insisted that the reason for his visit was simply a desire to meet a famous psychologist. In reality, both men were probably right. As Freud deduced, Allport was a compulsive man with a dirt phobia, but that did not necessarily explain his desire to meet Freud. Returning to the primary theme of this section: Freud believed that beneath the surface, people all share the same motives; Allport, on the other hand, believed that each person's motives are unique.

Allport's View of Human Nature

Motivation

Freud and Jung believed that human motivation consists of a few unconscious instincts. Allport called such views "simple and sovereign theories"; in fact, his own theory is quite complex and detailed. According to Allport, each person has a unique set of motives that are conscious and constantly changing. Furthermore, he said, we don't need a psychoanalyst to discover a person's motives—we need only ask the person about them.

Like Freud, Allport understood that the concept of motivation is the most important part of any theory of personality. Although he constantly criticized Freud's instinct theory, Allport understood that physiological drives such as hunger and thirst must be satisfied if a person is to survive. But he also felt that normal people "are more concerned with what Goldstein (1947) calls 'self-actualization'—a term that covers the main interest systems of adulthood" (1961, p. 212).

An adequate theory of motivation, Allport argued, must meet four requirements. First, it must focus on the present. Freud believed we are motivated by unconscious sexual and aggressive impulses from the id, but Allport believed we are motivated by what is on our minds when we act. Second, a proper theory of motivation must include motives of many types including instincts, passions, values, goals, and intentions. Some of these motives are temporary, others are persistent; some are conscious, others are unconscious; some reduce tension, others increase it.

Third, according to Allport, an adequate theory must recognize the motivational value of interests and intentions. Freud believed that interests and intentions come from the id and are not important in themselves; Allport believed that intentions are independent of instincts and have comparable motivational power. Finally, Allport argued that motives are specific, concrete, and unique (e.g., Sam works hard because he wants to be a pediatrician) as opposed to abstract and general (e.g., Sam works hard because he is sublimating sexual energy).

We pointed out in Chapter 1 that the word *motive* can refer either to biological instincts or to goals and intentions. We also noted that it is important to keep these two meanings distinct. Despite Allport's fascination with word origins, he ignored this distinction (i.e., instincts vs. intentions) and compared the two meanings in terms of their explanatory power. This is much like trying to compare apples and aardvarks; instincts and intentions are altogether different concepts.

Allport noted quite reasonably that people are motivated by that which interests them, and, indeed, he defined motivation in terms of interests. But he also used several other terms as synonyms for interests, including values, sentiments, and, most important, traits. A trait, according to Allport, is "a neuropsychic structure having the capacity to render many stimuli functionally equivalent and to initiate and guide equivalent (meaningfully consistent) forms of adaptive and expressive behavior" (1963, p. 347). Allport believed that traits are the fundamental units of motivation and the building blocks of personality—which is why many textbooks describe Allport as the father of trait theory. However, this title is not fair to Allport; for modern psychologists, traits are general properties of groups of people and are used to compare people with one another. Although Allport thought it was sometimes useful to compare people, he defined traits as unique characteristics of specific individuals—and individuals, he said, should be compared with themselves, not with one another: "Scarcely anyone questions the existence of traits as the fundamental units of personality. Common speech presupposes them. This man, we say, is gruff and shy, but a hard worker; that woman is fastidious, talkative, and stingy. Psychologists, too, talk in these terms " (1961, p. 332).

Allport was right; we *do* use trait words to describe other people. Suppose we describe someone as assertive. Does this mean that he or she has a trait of assertiveness? On what grounds might we infer that a trait of assertiveness actually exists? Allport proposed three criteria: the frequency with which a person behaves assertively, the range of situations in which the person is assertive, and the intensity with which the person displays his or her assertiveness. Notice, however, that we never see the trait itself; we see only indicators and infer the existence of a trait based on these indicators. Despite the inferential nature of traits, Allport thought they really exist, inside our heads, as a pattern of neural connections. As noted, he defined a trait as a "neuropsychic structure," by which he meant a network of neurological connections somewhere in the brain—a popular view among some psychologists today (e.g., Funder, 1991).

Allport used the distinction between "idiographic and nomothetic science," terms he borrowed from the German philosopher W. Windelband, to elaborate his theory of traits. **Nomothetic science** is concerned with developing general laws; **idiographic science** is concerned with understanding an individual case. Based on these concepts, Allport drew a distinction between "common traits" and "personal dispositions." **Common traits** are nomothetic concepts; they are terms we use to describe other people and they are also the categories measured by standardized tests of personality. **Personal dispositions**, on the other hand, are idiographic concepts, the unique properties of specific individuals. In other words, they are the traits that people actually have.

According to Allport, we use common traits to describe or classify other people. However, to understand what motivates someone, we must discover that person's unique set of personal dispositions—the set of goals, values, and interests that give order and consistency to his or her personality and social behavior: Personal dispositions can only be discovered by "studying exhaustively" a single life (Allport, 1961, p. 364). Therefore, argued Allport, personality psychologists should study single lives using whatever methods are available in order to discover the unifying themes in that person's life. And how many personal dispositions are necessary to characterize an individual personality? Allport *(1961, p. 366)* suggested that even the most complex person can be understood in terms of no more than eight personal dispositions.

Allport also suggested that personal dispositions can be classified in terms of their importance. The most important of these he called **cardinal dispositions**; these traits are so influential that virtually everything a person does can be traced back to them. The Russian novelist Tolstoy, for example, talked constantly about the importance of simplifying his life. Allport would describe Tolstoy's need for simplicity as a cardinal disposition. **Central dispositions** are what one would mention when one writes a careful letter of recommendation for someone. Finally, **secondary dispositions** are idiosyncratic features of a person's behavior that set him or her apart from others but are not crucial features of their lives. Freud, for example, was addicted to cigars; but this fact is only an interesting piece of Freudian trivia. Personal dispositions—conscious patterns of interests, values, goals, and aspirations—are the fundamental units of personality, according to Allport. They are also his motivational concepts. Box 6.1 describes an exercise that illustrates the way we use traits to describe ourselves.

Personality Development

Allport believed that people change in fundamental ways over time, and that most of the changes are positive. For example, in *Pattern and Growth in Personality (1961)*, he described the young child as "an unsocialized horror." Children are demanding, impulsive, and slaves to their bodily needs. Adults, on the other hand, are independent, self-sufficient, able to control their impulses, and master of their bodily needs. How does someone change from an impulse-driven little monster to a self-contained person who cares for others?

In the same work, Allport pointed out that many writers *(e.g., Adler, 1927; Maslow, 1954; White, 1959; and especially Goldstein, 1940)* assume that people are born with a very general drive toward psychological growth. Watch small children when they are not hungry or tired, Allport suggested, and you will see that they constantly try to explore, climb, imitate, and interact. These activities make the children more competent, more effective, and more able to deal with the world, and this general drive toward psychological growth is what explains development.

Development, Allport argued, is defined in terms of changes in one's motives: "[S]ince motives are the dynamos of personality we must expect motives also to grow and to change" *(1961, p. 219)*. Allport proposed a general law of development that he called functional autonomy, designed to explain individual uniqueness. In particular, he believed that the motives for people's actions change over time. Consider, for example, a young person who, early on, worked in the garden in order to be with his or her father. The concept of functional autonomy suggests that, in time, this person may have come to enjoy gardening for its own sake: "The pursuit of literature, the development of good taste in clothes, the use of cosmetics, strolls in the public park or a winter in Miami may first serve . . . the interests of sex. But every one of

BOX 6.1 Who Are You?

Allport believed that traits are both shorthand descriptions of how a person behaves and neuro-psychic structures in the brain. Not all personality psychologists concur with the trait approach to understanding human nature, but one of the most powerful arguments in favor of traits is that everyone understands and uses trait terms.

As suggested earlier, Allport believed that most people could be accurately described in terms of about seven traits. The exercise below is designed to help you identify the traits that you feel are most descriptive of your personality.

1. From the list below, choose seven traits that you feel describe you.

Achieving	Friendly	Pleasure seeking
Adventurous	Family-oriented	Powerful
Affectionate	Honest	Private
Artistic	Independent	Pure
Competent	Influential	Religious
Competitive	Intelligent	Responsible
Cooperative	Leader	Serene
Creative	Loyal	Sophisticated
Decisive	Money-oriented	Truthful
Effective	Nature loving	Wealthy
Efficient	Orderly and predictable	Wise
Ethical	Loner	Hardworking
Fun loving	Sociable	Neurotic
Free spirited	Persevering	Cultured

2. From the list of seven, eliminate the three traits that are least like you.

3. From the remaining four, eliminate the one trait that is least like you.

4. From the remaining three, eliminate the one trait that is least like you.

5. From the remaining two, choose the one trait that you feel best represents your personality.
   [Adapted from Senge, 1994, p. 209.]

In the first chapter, we discussed the two meanings of the word personality: reputation and inner core. The trait you chose obviously represents what you believe to be your most fundamental personality characteristic. But in Chapter 1 we also pointed out that our beliefs about our inner core do not necessarily agree with how others see us. Is the trait you chose to represent your personality the same one your friends would choose? Is it the same one your parents would choose? Your boss? If not, you must be making an impression that doesn't reflect who you believe you are. How do you explain this?

these 'instrumental' activities may become an interest in itself, held for a lifetime, even after they no longer serve the erotic motive" *(1961, p. 228)*.

Freud was once asked why he smoked cigars, a well-known phallic symbol. He replied that there are times when a cigar is just a cigar—which nicely illustrates Allport's point. Functional autonomy is the cornerstone of Allport's theory of development and his criterion of maturity. He argued that some interests or motives become functionally autonomous over time and that this process is the most important feature of human development; even more important, people are mature to the degree that their motives are functionally autonomous.

Self-Knowledge

Allport distinguished between self-awareness and the nature of the self, regarding the latter as a philosophical rather than empirical problem. Psychologists, he argued, should study how self-awareness develops over time. Drawing on a paper by Theodore Sarbin *(1954; see also Chapter 9)*, Allport suggested that self-awareness evolves through seven stages, and that the way people think about themselves depends on what happens at each of the stages.

1. Bodily Self. It seems reasonable to suppose that self-awareness begins with an awareness of one's body. Indeed, as a result of bumping into things (walls, floors, other people), infants realize that there is a point where they end and the rest of the world begins. The sense of the bodily self, therefore, grows out of frustrations imposed by the world, such as hot water, cold air, late dinner, and barking dogs. Throughout life this bodily sense is the anchor for self-awareness, the essential ground of our identity.

2. Self-Recognition. We normally believe that the persons we are now are the same persons we were last week or last year—though in a literal sense, we are not, because the physical molecules of which we are made constantly change. Allport suggested that the development of language in the first year of life makes self-recognition possible. As his parents talk about the baby's ball, the baby's bath, and the baby's shoes, the baby comes to see himself as a common theme in a wide range of activities. Learning his own name further enhances this sense of self-recognition.

3. Self-Esteem. Most personality psychologists today use the term self-esteem to mean positive self-evaluation and self-confidence. But Allport, curiously, used the term to mean egoism and self-centeredness, the third form of self-awareness. Egoistic tendencies, Allport observed, first appear around eighteen months of age as the child enters the age of negativism. During this universally recognized developmental period—the Germans call it trotz alter—children want to do things for themselves and often balk at what their parents want them to do. These so-called "terrible twos" normally end around age four.

Self-esteem (egoism) takes on a second form when a child enters school. Specifically, in our Western culture it turns into competitiveness. "Getting ahead" and "beating the competition" are egoistic impulses that are central to the middle-class lifestyle of Western (and Westernized) culture.

4. The Extension of Self. When children enter school at age five or six, they tend to be egocentric because they have not been required to think about themselves from another's perspective or to consider the rights of others as compared to their own rights. Following McDougall *(1908)*, Allport noted that, after starting school, children gradually come to see persons and objects outside themselves—their pets, toys, families, and even friends—as being important to themselves. They gradually invest egoistic feelings in the other persons and things so that the welfare of these other objects becomes important to them, too. Thus they come to feel protective about their pets, family, and friends. This capacity for self-extension is Allport's fourth form of self-awareness.

5. The Self-Image. Sometime after age four, children begin to understand what their parents expect of them and to compare these expectations with their own behavior. In this way they come to think of themselves in certain ways—for example, as a "good" girl or a "naughty" boy. This awareness of how one is seen by others is the opposite of childish egocentrism, whereby children are unable to understand how others perceive them. Self-image is the foundation for conscience in adulthood.

6. The Self as Rational Coper. Going to school and playing with others leads children to realize that they have certain skills and capacities—that they can do things, solve problems, and achieve certain goals. Children's awareness that they possess certain competencies is the sixth form of self-awareness.

7. Propriate Striving. Citing Erik Erikson (Chapter 11), Allport noted that a primary problem for late adolescents is to choose an occupation or a life goal. Indeed, along with the existentialists (Chapter 10), Allport argued that adult personality is primarily organized around a life task or overarching goal. Adolescents who reach adulthood without a sense of purpose are, according to Allport, relatively immature.

Allport united these seven aspects of self-awareness under a single name—the **proprium**. The proprium refers to all the elements of our lives that we feel to be personally relevant and meaningful. Our names, values, interests, and goals—as well as our fears and aversions—are all aspects of the proprium.

Unconscious Processes

Allport also believed that conscious intentions are the primary motivating force and integrating factor in personality. Conscious intentions, he said, are not based on unconscious desires or motives. "But since the range of consciousness at any given moment is so slender, we have no alternative but to say that much of what goes on in our personalities belongs in some way to an unconscious stratum" *(Allport, 1961, p. 140)*.

The problem for personality psychology, according to Allport, is to determine the correct relationship between conscious and unconscious influences in life. In particular, the question is whether the conscious layer of personality is autonomous or, as Freud suggested, serves the unconscious layer. If both the conscious and the unconscious layers are important, then under what conditions is each important and to what degree?

Allport argued that the issue of conscious/unconscious domination is a matter of degree, and he borrowed Freud's early distinction among the conscious, preconscious, and unconscious strata of the mind. In this model, preconsciousness is a sort of holding pen where unconscious impulses are stored before they appear in consciousness, if they ever do. With this model in mind, Allport *(1961)* proposed that people can be placed on a continuum that ranges from normality to normal creativity to neurotic creativity to insanity. Across this continuum, people vary systematically in terms of the degree to which their consciousness controls their psyches: The thinking of normal people is characterized by conscious dominance, the thinking of creative people is characterized by preconscious dominance, and the thinking of neurotic people is characterized by unconscious dominance and distortion.

Allport's point was that, to the degree that Freud was correct about how unconscious processes dominate everyday thought, Freud was talking about people who are mentally ill— not about normal people. Moreover, Allport argued that the continuum between normalcy and mental illness is not really a continuum: There is a qualitative difference, he said, between normalcy and neuroticism, and the difference is so great that neurotics and normals appear to inhabit different worlds.

In summary, Allport believed that unconscious mental processes exist, and that normal people can discover them simply by thinking about them. Freud's theory of the unconscious, according to Allport, applies only to neurotics; normal people can talk about their impulses and motives. Self-knowledge, therefore, is not difficult to achieve. Whereas Freud believed that we are all, in a sense, strangers to ourselves, Allport believed that normal people can understand themselves through simple introspection.

Psychological Adjustment

As we have seen, Allport drew a strong distinction between neurosis and normalcy. Neurotic behavior is compulsive, rigid, inflexible, and dominated by unconscious impulses. However, the core element of neurosis, according to Allport, is selfishness: "The truest and most general statement about the neuroses seems to be that they are a reflection of uncontrolled self-centeredness. Someone has said that the neurotic will do anything to be loved except to make himself (herself) lovable" *(1961, p. 151)*. This self-centeredness is caused by what Allport called "poor mental hygiene"—bad relations with parents and not evaluating whether one's needs, impulses, and desires are realistic.

Allport was not particularly interested in the origins of neurosis; he was primarily concerned with maturity, which he analyzed in detail. He reviewed the empirical literature, then proposed the following six criteria for maturity *(1961, pp. 283–295)*:

1. ***Extension of the Sense of Self.*** Immature people are self-absorbed and egocentric; mature people, in contrast, care about other people as much as they care about themselves. This capacity for involvement in others is a central aspect of maturity.

2. ***Warm Relating of Self to Others***. Mature people can be intimately involved with other people without being possessive, jealous, or controlling. They accept other people for who

they are without placing bonds or obligations on them.

3. **Emotional Security.** Immature people seem at the mercy of their drives, desires, and appetites, and they overreact to threats and disappointments. Mature people, on the other hand, can control their appetites and emotions, and they take life's inevitable disappointments in stride. They have, as Allport noted, a sense of proportion.

4. **Realistic Perception of Skills.** Immature people see the world in self-serving ways—for example, they take credit for accomplishments that are not their own. They also pursue goals that are unrealistic relative to their talents. Mature people, in contrast, are usually accurate in their appraisals of others, understand their own strengths and limitations, and choose goals that are proportional to their talents, skills, and capacities.

5. **Self-Insight.** Maturity also depends on what Allport called self-insight, which concerns the relationship between how individuals see themselves and how they are seen by others. Accurate self–insight means that one's self-view largely corresponds to how one is seen by others. Mature individuals also have a sense of humor. Most people think they have a sense of humor, but in many cases that turns out be untrue: A sense of humor requires a lack of defensiveness and the ability to laugh at oneself. Allport *(1961)* pointed out that psychologists haven't been very successful in their efforts to study either insight or humor.

6. **The Unifying Philosophy of Life.** "Maturity requires, in addition to humor, a clear comprehension of life's purpose in terms of an intelligible theory. Or, in brief, some form of a unifying philosophy of life" *(Allport, 1961, p. 294)*. According to Allport, the unifying philosophy of life might be religious, but not necessarily. It can also be a commitment to a cause, a quest, a search, or a goal. In short, Allport believed that mature people have something beyond themselves that they live for.

Box 6.2 contrasts Allport's views on psychological health with the views of theorists who studied psychological illness.

The Individual and Society

Allport was well-read in philosophy and social theory and believed that everything of importance in personality is correlated with social class *(1961, p. 174)*: He clearly understood that culture shapes personality. Moreover, he believed that training children for a role in society is one of the most important problems parents must face. Nonetheless, given his commitment to individual uniqueness, his theory of personality largely concerns how people differ from one another.

In *Personality: A Psychological Interpretation*, Allport presented a detailed but not very original analysis of the relationship between the individual and society. He noted, first, that children grow up in a culture that provides ready-made solutions to many of life's problems. In the process, children learn elements of the culture such as hygiene habits, dietary preferences, and clothing styles, and these elements become part of their personalities. This is why there

BOX 6.2 Allport's View of Mental Health

Unlike Freud, Jung, and Horney, Gordon Allport developed his theory of personality outside a clinical setting: He had no background or training in treating mental illness, he did not see clients, and he reported no exotic cases such as Dora, the girl who lived on the moon, or Mr. Z. For the most part, Allport focused on normal people, and his theory of personality is clearly directed toward explaining behavior in everyday life.

Nonetheless, Allport did develop a distinctive criterion for mental health that differs sharply from the ideas of Freud, Jung, and Horney on this topic. As you may recall, Freud believed that mental health entails the development of a strong ego that keeps sexual and aggressive impulses from the id and superego under control. In his view, mental health has nothing to do with happiness, and the most a person can hope for is a productive life.

Jung, in turn, believed that people achieve mental health by integrating the irrational into their lives: Rather than keeping the unconscious under control, people benefit by accessing and using archetypal material that lies in the collective unconscious. The easiest way to do this, Jung believed, is through religious practice.

For her part, Horney argued that mental health is a function of strong interpersonal relations. Unfortunately, if we do not overcome the basic anxiety that comes with infancy, or if our ideal self differs too much from our real self, we may develop neurotic needs that make interpersonal relations difficult.

Allport's ideas about mental health—which were based on his review of psychological research done by others rather than on the study of neurotic people—reflect the notion that mental health is really a kind of maturity. In his view, mature people have the following six qualities: They care about things outside themselves, accept other people and don't try to control them, feel emotionally secure and don't overreact to disappointments, have realistic goals, hold a view of themselves that resembles the view other people have of them, and possess a sense of humor and a philosophy of life.

Although Allport's ideas are appealing, they are based more on speculation or moral philosophy than on scientific data. In contrast, Freud, Jung, and Horney used personal experiences with real people to develop their ideas on mental health. But even though their theories are more "hands-on," they were limited by the fact that their subjects were people who came to psychotherapy because they had problems in their lives.

This difference in approach illustrates a continuing question in personality psychology: Which is more valuable—a theory of human nature based on the lives of people with problems or speculations about the lives of normal people? Although theories based on normal people may seem more appealing, the history of science illustrates that exceptional cases are sometimes more valuable in advancing knowledge. In medicine, for example, our knowledge of health is almost entirely based on the study of disease.

In recent years, personality psychologists have moved away from the clinical approach and relied more on scientific research, but the clinical approach continues to be a rich source of hypotheses about human nature.

are characteristic differences in personality among the members of various ethnic or cultural groups.

Second, Allport (borrowing from Piaget, 1964) noted that children's adaptation to society's rules, values, and requirements undergoes three regular phases. During the first stage, which extends roughly from ages one to three, they largely ignore family and cultural rules. From age four to about ten, however, they obey the rules of their culture in a rigid and dogmatic manner—a pattern that corresponds to the psychoanalytic theory of superego development. Finally, according to Allport, there is a period of adolescent revolt at the end of which individuals blend the elements of culture with their personality and comply with certain social rules because such rules are seen as a natural part of life.

The foregoing is a useful description, but Allport never explored the topic at a deeper level. For example, he didn't ask whether these three stages occur in children across all cultures (and if so, why)—probably because he was not particularly interested in moral development.

Evaluating Allport

Allport had a strong empirical bent. He believed that theories should be supported by data, and he contributed in substantive ways to several important research traditions. For example, a considerable part of modern trait research is based on work that Allport started in the early 1930s. In particular, he noted that language develops in response to social reality, and that aspects of reality, including personality, are most likely reflected in language: "[I]t is obvious that trait-names bear some relation to the underlying structural units of personality, and it is our duty to discover, if we can, what this relation is" (1961, p. 3).

In 1936, Allport and his associate H. S. Odbert compiled an exhaustive list of the trait terms that exist in the English language. There are about 18,000 of these terms, and Allport believed that they represent the basic text or language of personality. The challenge, however, was to translate that language into usable terms. Allport noted that if we disregard trait terms that are purely evaluative (e.g., *adorable*), trait terms that are metaphorical (e.g., *alive*), and trait terms that reflect temporary states of mind (e.g., *frantic*), the list can be reduced to about 4,500 terms. This is where Allport left the discussion, but his list of traits forms the basis for most modern research on the structure of personality.

Later researchers (e.g., Norman, 1963; Wiggins, 1973) proposed that Allport's 4,500 common traits could be reduced to five broad themes or primary dimensions—the components of what later became known as the Five-Factor Model (Chapter 12). Subsequent research has shown that the Allport/Odbert trait list can, in fact, be reduced to somewhere between three and seven dimensions, although individual researchers disagree as to precisely how many (see Wiggins, 1996). Regardless of the disagreement, the key point here is that we can now say with some confidence that the words we use to describe other people (common traits) have an orderly structure, that each person's personality can be described in terms of a small number (three to seven) of dimensions, and that we can do so because of a line of research initiated by Allport over fifty years ago.

The research topic that seemed to interest Allport most was "expressive behaviors," which we refer to today as "nonverbal cues." For example, Allport noted that when we listen to a lecture, we unconsciously make inferences about the speaker's personality on the basis of his or her expressions—and we can't help doing so. Expressive behaviors are important, he added, because "[p]eople develop highly characteristic styles of writing, talking, walking, sitting, gesturing, laughing, and shaking hands" *(1963, p. 473)* that provide clues to their personalities: "[E]very person has one or two leading expressive features which reveal his true nature" *(p. 469)*. His best-known work on the subject, *Studies in Expressive Movement (1933)*, co-written by Phillip Vernon, showed that individual people are remarkably consistent across all forms of expressive behaviors; for example, large handwriting often corresponds to an expansive style. Allport was drawn to the study of expressive behavior because it allowed him to capture individual uniqueness.

Allport is an icon of modern psychology, so it is with some reluctance that we discuss what we see as shortcomings in his theory of personality. Nonetheless, there are three features of Allport's approach that we find troubling. The first problem concerns the concept of functional autonomy, perhaps the single most important idea in Allport's system. Functional autonomy defines his concept of development, drives his analysis of motivation, and serves as his criterion of maturity. However, the concept of functional autonomy is circular. Allport argues that people's motives, in normal circumstances, become functionally autonomous over time—they become independent of their original sources and become motivating in and of themselves. The question is, How can we tell if a motive is functionally autonomous? Consider, for example, the members of Richard Nixon's White House staff who were imprisoned after the Watergate scandal and then experienced religious conversions. Were their prison-based religious beliefs self-serving or functionally autonomous? According to Allport *(1961)*, a motive is functionally autonomous if it is functionally autonomous, and it is not if it is not. Because there is no independent way to verify whether a motive is functionally autonomous, the concept is circular.

A second problem concerns Allport's eclecticism. Eclectics build a theory from ideas on various topics that they find persuasive or credible. This process allows eclectic theorists to stay close to the ongoing research in their field, but it also leads to a theoretical jumble. A good example of this jumble is Allport's discussion of motivation. As we noted above, he argues that an adequate theory of motivation includes motives of all types: instinctual, intentional, short-term, long-term, conscious, unconscious, and so on. This may be the position of an eclectic theorist, but another possible implication is that Allport couldn't make up his mind.

A third problem concerns Allport's view that the goal of personality psychology is to preserve the uniqueness of individuals. In a famous passage in *The Varieties of Religious Experience*, William James *(1902)* suggested that philosophers can be placed along a continuum ranging from "tough-minded" at one end to "tender-minded" at the other. The tough-minded are oriented toward science; the tender-minded are more sympathetic to mysticism. In the terms of James's book, Freud is tough-minded whereas Allport, along with other humanistic psychologists, is tender-minded. But the problem with defining the goal of personality psychology as the study of individual uniqueness is that such a process makes generalization impossible. And in the absence of generalization, there can be no accumulation of knowledge and therefore no science. Being indifferent to the accumulation of knowledge is what one would expect of a tender-minded theorist.

Allport is important more because of his dramatization of the key issues in the field than because of the answers he gave to those issues. This dramatization was indeed useful, especially in combination with three specific contributions. First, his spirited and thoughtful defense of the trait concept seems as sensible today as it did in 1961. It is not clear that anyone has advanced the conceptual analysis of the theory of traits past where Allport left it. Every modern researcher can read Allport on this topic and profit from the experience. Second, Allport's efforts to classify the domain of English trait terms was a direct precursor of what is known today as the Five-Factor Model, which most researchers regard as a major contribution to personality systematics. And finally, Allport's analysis of maturity—in particular, his insistence that maturity is defined by a commitment to long-term goals rather than by an absence of anxiety—is consistent with the best modern thinking in health psychology *(see Friedman et al., 1995).*

Box 6.3 describes Allport's biographical study of Jenny Masterson.

• • •

Like Gordon Allport, Henry Murray believed that the goal of personality psychology is to explain the life of a single person, and that the explanation should be in terms of each person's unique set of motives. As we noted, their two books launched personality psychology as an academic discipline in the United States in the late 1930s, both were influenced by William McDougall, and both were eclectic synthesizers who tried to build models of personality based on the best work of other people. Yet they also differed in important ways. Allport stated that he had no talent for science; Murray was one of the best-trained scientists in the history of personality psychology. Allport, after meeting Freud, spent his life trying to show that he was not out of touch with his unconscious. Murray, after meeting Jung, spent the rest of his life trying to explore the unconscious.

The Life of Murray

Henry A. Murray was born in New York City on May 13, 1893. He was the second of three children of a Scottish immigrant who had married the heiress to an insurance fortune. Murray genuinely liked his father, whom he described as "jolly." But he felt rejected by his mother, who preferred his older sister and younger brother. This rejection left him with "a marrow of misery and melancholy repressed by pride and practically extinguished in everyday life by a counteracting disposition of sanguine and expansive buoyancy, . . . an affinity for the darker, blinder strata of feeling, . . . [and] the conviction that I could get along well enough with a

BOX 6.3 Biography: Jenny Masterson

As we have noted, Allport was fascinated by the problem of how to capture individuality. One key to studying individuality in a standardized way is to use personal documents, such as letters, diaries, or autobiographies. In 1942 Allport wrote a monograph describing how to use personal documents to understand individual cases. He defined a personal document as "any self-revealing record that intentionally or unintentionally yields information regarding the structure, dynamics, and functioning of the author's mental life" *(1942, p. xii)*. He understood that these documents could be deceptive and self-promoting, but he thought psychologists should also be interested in the question of why they are deceptive or self-promoting.

One of Allport's best-known works, *Letters from Jenny (1965)*, is an example of what Allport thought personality psychology should be; it is also a crucial test of his point of view. The letters tell the story of a mother-son relationship from the mother's perspective. In this context, Allport notes that "the principal fascination of the letters lies in their challenge to the reader . . . to 'explain' Jenny—if he can. Why does an intelligent lady behave so persistently in a self-defeating manner? When and how might she have averted the tragedy of her life?" *(p. viii)*.

Jenny Gove Masterson was born in Ireland in 1868. Her Protestant parents moved to Montreal in 1873. She was the oldest of seven children, and at eighteen years of age when her father died, she went to work as a telegrapher to support the family. Jenny quarreled constantly with her siblings, and by the time she was twenty-seven the family had fallen apart. Jenny married an American, Henry Masterson, a middle-manager in the railroad business who had previously been married; her marriage further alienated her traditional Irish family.

The Mastersons moved to Chicago. During the next two years they quarreled over Jenny's desire to go to work. Henry Masterson died in 1897 when Jenny was twenty-nine; a month later her son Ross was born. Jenny returned to work to support herself and over the next seventeen years she devoted herself to her boy. Her family in Montreal complained that she seriously spoiled Ross, and disagreements over how he should be raised further alienated Jenny from them.

At seventeen, Ross left home for college. His mother continued to work to support him and his lifestyle. When the United States entered World War I, Ross, who was a sophomore at the time, enlisted in the U.S. Army ambulance corps. When Ross returned from France in 1919, he seemed changed. Although he managed to finish college, he was much less concerned with his mother's approval. For the next few years, his life comprised a series of personal and business failures and a secret marriage. Jenny was furious about all of this.

At this point Jenny began a correspondence with "Glenn" (in reality Gordon Allport), who had been Ross's college roommate and had remained in contact with Ross. Jenny wrote to Glenn as a way of maintaining some contact with her son. In 1929, Ross had surgery for what appears to have been a brain tumor, and two months later he died. Jenny lived for another eight years.

The letters to Glenn, 301 in all, began in March 1926 and continued until Jenny died in October 1937. They cover all aspects of Jenny's life—reflections on her parents and family, her work life, and her concerns about Ross. Many of them reveal bitterness at her family's lack of gratitude, fury over her son's erratic behavior, and depression. The following example is typical: "My father dropped dead one day. . . . Not one in the house capable of earning a penny. It was my salary that kept the house going. . . . [A]nd when I dared to marry the man I had been in love with for years but dreaded to take my money out of their house . . . they said I was like the cow that gave the milk and then kicked the pail" *(Allport, 1965, p. 27).*

One question remained: How should Jenny Masterson's life story be written? Allport asked thirty-six judges to read the letters and then describe Jenny. They used a total of 198 trait names to describe her, and Allport grouped them into nine categories that include, in order of decreasing frequency, suspiciousness, self-centeredness, autonomy, self-dramatization, aggressiveness, pessimism, and sentimentality *(Allport, 1965, p. 194).*

And that is all there is to Allport's biography of Jenny Masterson. He characterized her in terms of a list of trait terms derived from studying her correspondence, but he says little about why her life unfolded as it did or what caused her to be so disagreeable. Freud would have suggested Oedipal problems that led to an overidentification with her father, a marriage to an older man, and an overidentification with her son. Horney would have maintained that Ross was spoiled and certain to disappoint his overindulgent mother when he was grown, and that Jenny's feelings of inferiority (caused by her difficult life in late adolescence) caused her to overindulge her son. But Freud's and Horney's remarks would have been based on ideas about people in general, whereas Allport wanted to preserve Jenny's uniqueness.

Allport's theory is certainly more commonsensical and closer to the available data than Freud's—and, indeed, Allport's many criticisms of Freud were often well-taken. Nonetheless, Allport's analysis of the life of Jenny Masterson reveals the degree to which his theory, when compared to psychoanalysis, is also superficial.

minimum amount of aid, support, appreciation, recognition, or consolation from others" *(1967, p. 300).*

Murray was cross-eyed; a bungled eye operation had left him unable to focus both eyes on the same object. He later developed a bad stutter. His vision prevented him from playing baseball and tennis, so he compensated by becoming a skilled boxer.

Murray studied history at Harvard, where he was a mediocre student but served as captain of the Harvard rowing crew. He graduated in 1915 and married the next year. At Columbia—where he was first in his class—Murray received a medical degree in 1919 and an M.A. in biology in 1920. He finished a two-year surgical internship in 1926, then studied embryology at the Rockefeller Institute for four years. He also studied biochemistry at Cambridge in England, where he received a Ph.D. in 1926. Between 1919 and 1928, he published twenty-one articles on embryology and medicine.

Murray read Jung's Psychological Types in 1923. Shortly thereafter, he met Christiana Morgan, a wealthy Jungian enthusiast with whom he began an affair that lasted until her death in 1967. Murray initially felt guilty about the affair; in 1926, he went to Zurich and met with Carl Jung for a month. The meeting transformed Murray's life (Jung, too, had that effect on people!). Murray also read Freud and Adler, and decided to become a psychologist. In 1927, Morton Prince, a well-known psychiatrist of the period, invited Murray to become assistant director of the Harvard Psychological Clinic—which Prince had founded—and Murray joined the Harvard faculty. Murray said that he was intrigued by the possibility of integrating "current academic and psychoanalytic theories to accord with a large collection of reasonably solid facts obtained by the multiform method of assessment" (1959, p. 13).

The phrase *multiform method of assessment* refers to the fact that, at Harvard, Murray organized the first personality assessment center in the United States. Assessment centers (discussed in detail below) serve as a method for studying a single person in depth using a variety of procedures, including tests, interviews, experiments, and creative productions. Invented by German military psychologists after World War I, this method is still the single best way to study personality. Murray liked the assessment center because it yielded so much information about a single case. During the 1930s, Murray and Morgan also developed the Thematic Apperception Test (TAT), which consists of a series of pictures in response to which people tell stories that reveal important personality features (especially needs). Over the years, the TAT became one of the most widely used psychological tests in the world. In 1935, Murray completed a training analysis and became a psychoanalyst.

During World War II, Murray served as a lieutenant colonel in the Office of Strategic Services (OSS)—the precursor of the Central Intelligence Agency. Murray introduced the assessment center to the army, and after the war, assessment centers became a mainstay in American business as a method of selecting people for high-level jobs. Published in 1948, Murray's book *The Assessment of Men* describes his work with the OSS. In the same year, at age fifty-five and world-famous, he was awarded tenure at Harvard. Murray was a founding member of the Boston Psychoanalytic Society; his enthusiasm for psychoanalysis was the reason he had been denied tenure for so many years. He received a Distinguished Scientific Contribution Award from the American Psychological Association in 1961, retired from Harvard in 1962, and died in 1988 at the age of ninety-five.

Because Murray knew virtually every important British and American intellectual of the 1930s, 1940s, and 1950s, the question of who, precisely, influenced him the most is a somewhat arbitrary one. Nonetheless, certain themes seem clear. Murray was well trained in laboratory science and experimental medicine, and these disciplines, of course, influenced his intellectual development. Then, once he entered psychology, three other influences became important. The first was his meeting with Jung; toward the end of his career he still recalled that meeting in words that trembled with excitement. He met several times later with Jung and eventually came to regard him as somewhat rigid and unscientific. Nonetheless, it was Jung's *Psychological Types* that first brought Murray into psychology.

The second influence was Freud and psychoanalysis. Murray completed a training analysis with Franz Alexander—a member of Freud's original Vienna Circle; Murray (1967) reported that

Henry Murray.
Source: Bettman/Corbis.

the most interesting part of the analysis was his brief flirtation with Alexander's wife. Although he then became a founding member of the Boston Psychoanalytic Society and practiced psychoanalysis for several years, he never became a "true believer."

Finally, Murray, like Allport, was influenced by William McDougall, the Scottish psychiatrist who filled William James's chair at Harvard. He proposed a theory of personality based on unconscious instincts and is best known today for his efforts to classify those instincts. Similarly, Murray is best known today for his classification of "needs," which Murray acknowledged was an extension of the classification system that McDougall proposed in his 1908 book *Social Psychology*.

Core Problem: Understanding Lives

Murray had a wide range of interests and an enormous enthusiasm for personality psychology, but he was not a systematic thinker—a fact he cheerfully acknowledged. The one consistent theme in his writing is that personality psychology concerns the study of individual lives. According to Murray, the unit of analysis in personality psychology is an entire life: "[T]he life cycle of a single individual should be taken as a unit, the long unit for psychology. . . . The life history of the organism is the organism. This proposition calls for biographical studies" *(1938, p. 39).*

In understanding an individual life, Murray wanted to explain three kinds of phenomena: (1) why people do specific things at particular times (e.g., insult their roommates); (2) why there are certain patterns in people's behavior (e.g., frequent quarrels with friends); and (3) why people live their lives as they do. Although he was a practicing psychoanalyst, Murray, like Allport, was primarily interested in normal people. Unlike Allport, however, he thought that most normal people have a "dark side" that contains the key to his or her individuality. Murray was fond of quoting William James on this point: "Individuality is founded in feeling; and in the recesses of feeling, the darker, blinder strata of character are the only places in the world in which we catch real facts in the making, and directly perceive how events happen and how work is actually done" *(James, 1902, p. 501).*

Murray's View of Human Nature

Motivation

Murray, like Allport, thought that we can best explain the actions of others in terms of their motives, and that a theory of personality is essentially a theory of motivation. Murray's analysis of motivation is the most important part of his theory. He believed that we must ultimately explain behavior in terms of **regnancies**—"mutually dependent processes" that form "dominant configurations" in the brain. These dominant (regnant) processes in the brain are, in a fundamental sense, personality. Murray argued, therefore, that personality is represented by mental processes—that personality reflects what people have on their minds, either consciously or unconsciously. This is essentially what Allport said.

Where do regnancies come from? They reflect underlying needs—which, according to Murray, are the building blocks of personality. In *Explorations in Personality* (1938) he defined a **need** as a "hypothetical entity" that reflects a tendency for a person to respond in certain ways in certain conditions. A "need" may be expressed in a single action or in "a more or less consistent trait of personality"; it may also be expressed as a fantasy. Murray suggested that we think of a need as a force in the brain that excites a flow of images, which, in turn, primarily refer to whatever will satisfy the needs. In addition, Murray argued that all needs are directed at "hedonic" ends; it feels good when they are satisfied. Note that Murray also defined pleasure in the same way as Plato, Kant, and Freud—as the absence of tension. Needs, he said, create tension and motivate us to seek release from that tension.

Murray's concept of a need is nearly identical to Allport's concept of a trait. Unlike Allport, however, Murray emphasized the importance of unconscious needs. Needs can create specific desires or vague feelings of tension, and needs that are inconsistent with a person's self-image will be denied. Moreover, needs are periodic rather than constant, and the tensions they create vary over time. According to Murray, the methods we use to deal with our needs can fuse such that certain behaviors may satisfy more than one need (here Murray appears to have borrowed Freud's notion of "overdetermination"). Needs themselves may also fuse and thereafter occur together.

Consistent with our comments on motivation in Chapter 1, Murray distinguished between primary or **viscerogenic needs** and secondary or psychogenic needs. The viscerogenic needs concern physical satisfaction and include the need for air, water, food, sex, urination, and defecation; the need for avoidance of harm; and the need for sensuous gratification.

TABLE 6.1 Murray's List of Needs

Abasement	The need to submit passively to external force
Achievement	To accomplish something difficult
Affiliation	To draw near and enjoyably cooperate or reciprocate with an allied other (an other who resembles the subject or who likes the subject)
Aggression	To overcome opposition forcefully
Autonomy	To get free, shake off restraint, break out of confinement
Counteraction	To master or make up for a failure by restriving
Defendance	To defend the self against assault, criticism, and blame
Deference	To admire and support a superior
Dominance	To control one's human environment
Exhibition	To make an impression
Harm avoidance	To avoid pain, physical injury, illness, and death
Infavoidance	To avoid humiliation
Nurturance	To give sympathy and gratify the needs of a helpless object: an infant or any other being who is weak, disabled, tired, inexperienced, infirm, defeated, humiliated, lonely, dejected, sick, or mentally confused
Order	To put things in order
Play	To act for "fun" without further purpose
Rejection	To separate oneself from a negatively cathected object
Sentience	To seek and enjoy sensuous impressions
Sex	To form and further an erotic relationship
Succorance	To have one's needs gratified by the sympathetic aid of an allied object
Understanding	To ask or answer general questions

Murray's List of Needs. Murray believed that people have two kinds of needs: *viserogenic needs*, which concern physiological processes such as the need for food, warmth, and sex, and *psychogenic needs*, twenty of which are listed above. One of the major determinants of personality, according to Murray, is the strength of each need within an individual.

Murray noted that some of these needs can be further broken down, and that some are more important than others.

The secondary or **psychogenic needs** are based in the primary needs; some may be innate, but they are not fundamental biological drives. Murray carefully defined twenty-five psychogenic needs (see Table 6.1). One group of five concerns doing things to inanimate objects. A second group reflects ambition, the desire for status, or the need to avoid losing status. A third group concerns dominating or submitting to others. The fourth major group of needs involves seeking, giving, or withholding affection.

Because specific abilities are required to meet various needs, our abilities determine the needs to which we primarily attend. Over time, certain objects become associated with the satisfaction of certain needs; these objects—security blankets, favorite sweaters, old friends—are **cathected**. Murray observed that we can understand an individual's personality if we study the objects that he or she has cathected—that is, the things he or she values or detests. People also develop certain behavior patterns that allow them to satisfy their needs. For example, we behave in certain ways in order to please (or not annoy) our parents and friends. Certain needs, cathected objects, and behaviors become linked and then represented in the brain. Murray called these mental clusters of needs, objects, and behaviors **complexes**, an idea that closely resembles Jung's notion of a complex.

Complexes "explain" the consistencies in a person's behavior and the uniqueness of his or her personality. Complexes that are expressed in overt behavior are called **manifest complexes**; complexes that do not appear in overt behavior are called **latent complexes**. Latent complexes are expressed primarily in fantasies and vicarious identifications with others—people we know or characters in novels, movies, and plays. An adequate description of a person, therefore, requires describing his or her complexes—both manifest and latent.

Murray's classification of needs and analysis of complexes is the best-known part of his theory of motivation. In his later writing, however, he added the notion of a **serial**: Whereas complexes provide the energy for action, serials provide the direction. Thus, like Allport, Murray argued that serials or long-range goals are as important as complexes for understanding a person's motivation and uniqueness. Finally, to return to a word introduced at the beginning of this section, complexes and serials are regnancies.

Personality Development

Murray studied embryology before taking up psychology, and his early research strongly shaped his views about development: "[I]n the embryo . . . the organism as a system [is] characterized by perpetually changing states of equilibria, states that move in an irreversible direction" (1959, p. 17). Similarly, he believed that people are constantly changing and developing their whole lives.

Murray agreed with Freud that developmental experiences are important, that early events are more influential than later events, and that the effects of developmental experiences last for a long time. Specifically, Murray (1938, pp. 363–385) identified five stages in childhood that he believed influence adult personality. Each stage is associated with a particular form of pleasure, each stage ends when adults intervene, the manner in which each stage ends may create a complex, and every person must go through all five stages.

The first stage is typified by the security of the womb. If being born is traumatic, a person may (a) seek the security of small, dark, warm, private places (e.g., live in a monastery); (b) fear open spaces, change, and novelty; or (c) become claustrophobic and fear closed spaces.

The second stage is typified by the bliss of nursing and being held. If weaning is traumatic, then a person may (a) constantly seek love, support, protection, and sympathy; (b) be excessively aggressive in an oral manner; or (c) have an aversion to putting things in his or her mouth, be afraid of kissing, or become bulimic.

The third stage involves the pleasure of uninhibited defecation. If toilet training is traumatic, a person may (a) become dirty, disorganized, and aggressive; or (b) become excessively neat, clean, and thrifty.

Murray's fourth stage is unique. If toilet training of urination is traumatic, the result may be bedwetting, inflated self-esteem, exhibitionism, or excessive ambition. A specific version of this last outcome, known as the Icarus complex, combines ambition and self-destruction. In the Greek myth, Icarus is given a pair of wings and cautioned not to fly too high. Ignoring the warning, Icarus soars toward the sun. The wax in his wings melts, and he plunges to his death in the sea, thus illustrating the idea that soaring ambition is self-destructive.

The final stage of development concerns modesty training. If this training is too severe, the result may be a fear of sexual mutilation.

The foregoing description is our effort to interpret Murray's developmental speculations, and it captures the flavor of Murray's thinking.

Murray believed that development is continuous rather than timed according to specific developmental events such as the Oedipus complex. In a related vein, he believed that personality is in constant flux and not necessarily stable: "[C]reativity—the transformation of new and consequential entities and new and consequential patterns of activity—is a central determining capacity of nature, more especially of human nature" (1959, p. 36).

Self-Knowledge

The concept of the self is not important in Murray's writings. The word *self* rarely occurs in the index of *Explorations in Personality* (his most important book) or in that of his later works. Like Freud and Jung, Murray believed that unconscious forces influence our behavior to such a degree that the contents of consciousness are almost superficial. Moreover, unlike Allport, all three believed that we can learn very little about ourselves by simply thinking about ourselves.

Along with Freud and Jung, Murray also believed that the primary goal of life is self-development—that other people are important only insofar as they help us develop and, thus, that there is little point in being concerned about how we are perceived by others. None of these men seemed to understand Horney's concept of social involvement and how the self-concept is a reflection of social feedback.

Unconscious Processes

When Murray visited Jung in 1923, he was a charming, confident, and successful man with famous friends and a bright career ahead of him. Wealthy, talented, and well-educated, Murray seemed not to have a care in life. Yet he reported that his talks with Jung produced an eruption of unexpected emotion that he found astonishing and almost incapacitating. He was particularly surprised to discover the degree to which he resented being rejected by his mother, and how he had worked since perhaps age four to make himself emotionally untouchable.

Later, at the Harvard Psychological Clinic, Murray *(1938)* noted, "[W]e became less interested as time went on in conscious overt behavior . . . and increasingly absorbed in the exploration of unconscious complexes. . . . [M]any people do not know what they 'really' need for their own well–being. They recognize it only when they find it, after much fumbling about or after being shown by someone else." It is easy to suppose that Murray was describing himself here, which is not to say that he was wrong.

Murray's experience with Jung stimulated his ideas about the unconscious. Each of us, he argued, is born with more or less the same biologically based needs. These needs periodically require satisfaction and give rise to images. To some of these images we can attach words and thereby recognize and talk about them and perhaps the underlying needs as well. But for other need-based images there are no words, because the images are unconscious. Over time, various needs and images cluster together and form complexes. Complexes are the units or building blocks of the unconscious, the "darker, blinder strata of character" that William James believed are the key to understanding why people act as they do. Complexes, which manifest as "regnant processes" in the brain, are unconscious but can become conscious in the right circumstances. However, according to Murray:

> There are other unconscious processes . . . which seem to be debarred from consciousness. . . . [O]n the "deepest level" we must consider traces of the racial past and the early infantile past which lack adequate verbal associations. . . . Then, on a "higher level," we have the inhibited, once verbalized tendencies, many of which are infantile. Finally, we have processes that "pass," as it were, in and out of consciousness; as well as those that have become mechanized (habits and automatisms) which can, but rarely do, enter consciousness. *(1959, p. 136)*

As the foregoing suggests, Murray wasn't altogether consistent in his views. Nonetheless, he identified four forms of the unconscious. First are the complexes that can be made conscious, usually through analysis. Then there are three other layers of the unconscious that are much harder to know. These include memories from our ancestral past (as Jung suggested), repressed memories from childhood (as Freud suggested), and habits (as William James suggested). Finally, Murray believed that most of what is important in personality lies in the unconscious.

Psychological Adjustment

Although Murray was a practicing psychoanalyst, he was more interested in healthy people than in neurotics. Nonetheless, he believed that even the best adjusted of us periodically experience unhappiness, and that the unhappiness arises from unresolved unconscious issues from infancy and childhood.

Psychological health, he argued, requires that unconscious complexes be made conscious so they can be analyzed and dealt with. They need not be expressed directly or overtly, but they must be symbolized and acknowledged; otherwise they will cause us problems. In particular, our unconscious complexes must be aligned with our long-term life goals, which are not necessarily associated with the satisfaction of biological needs. In perhaps his most cogent single description of maturity, Murray stated that "[t]he chief over-all function of personality, then, is to create a design for living which permits the periodic and harmonious appeasement of most of its needs as well as gradual progressions toward distant goals. At the highest level of integration, a design of this sort is equivalent to a philosophy of life." Murray's emphasis on the importance of a philosophy of life as a criterion of maturity is essentially the same as Allport's view of maturity.

The Individual and Society

Murray's perspective on the relationship between the individual and society is quite similar to Freud's. Murray accepted Darwin's notion that group-living tendencies are part of human biology and, thus, that the relationship between people and their culture is built into their genes: "Here again I have been influenced by Darwin, specifically by the theory that the group more than the individual has been the evolutionary unit. . . . I have come to think that no theoretical system constructed on the psychological level will be adequate until it has been embraced by and intermeshed with a cultural-sociological system" (1959, p. 43).

Although people are, in a sense, programmed to live in groups, they are not programmed to live in any particular group; thus each group (i.e., family or society) has its own rules and each child must be taught them. These rules concern how to live in the group—what to eat and when, what to wear and when, whom to respect and when, and so forth. Social rules, together with our innate biological tendencies, tie us to our societies. Indeed, the survival of society depends on the allegiance of its members. Children, therefore, must internalize the rules of society, which are imposed on children by a variety of methods. It follows that, from the perspective of a child, culture is a set of rules dictated by adult authority, and most of the rules concern ways to satisfy society's needs. A child typically obeys social rules through fear of punishment or loss of parental love.

In the course of development, Murray suggested, social rules are internalized and become an unconscious superego system. This system, in turn, inhibits behaviors that are contrary to the interests of a person's society. Children—along with well-socialized adults—not only believe they should obey the rules of their society; they believe that these rules are truly "right" in a moral sense, that the rules are justified by the religious deities of their society.

Murray also analyzed the links between the individual and society at the level of a particular social interaction. In order to explain what a person does on any occasion, we need to know the "situation" in which the person is located and the motives that are active at the time. Murray referred to situations as **press**, explaining that there is press as it objectively exists and press as people perceive it. But, as Murray himself argued, the problem with saying that people's actions are partly determined by situations is that we have no way to classify situations. He suggested, instead, that we "classify an *environment* in terms of the kinds of benefits . . . and the kinds of harms . . . which it provides" *(1938, p. 185; emphasis added).* It is worth noting that the field of personality psychology in the 1970s and 1980s was paralyzed by endless discussions of the relative merits of "traits" versus "situations" as explanations of social behavior. From the perspective of Murray's *(1938)* book, however, the entire trait/situation debate was pointless, inasmuch as what we do at any given time is a function of both who and where we are—that is, a function of both "traits" and "situations."

Freud argued that people must give up instinctual satisfactions for the sake of society, thereby condemning themselves to a life of tension and unhappiness; indeed, unhappiness is the price that they must pay for the benefits of living in society. In contrast, Murray argued that the price of living in society is sometimes too high—and that when it is, people should criticize society's rules. Freud regarded this criticism as a sign of an unresolved Oedipus complex; Murray regarded it as a natural human tendency.

Evaluating Murray

Murray, like Allport, was an eclectic, rather than systematic, theorist; his theory is a collection of the ideas of others that he liked best. Thus, Murray was not a particularly original thinker, especially when compared to Freud and Jung—an ironic fact given how much Murray valued creativity. In addition, there is a sense of deliberate incompleteness about Murray's theory. Perhaps Murray was unusually self-critical or modest; he described everything he wrote as a beginning, a preliminary sketch, a provisional scaffold, or an outline, and whatever it was, it needed much further attention. He was a slow writer who never really finished anything.

These stylistic oddities notwithstanding, Murray made four contributions that ensure his continued relevance to personality psychology. First, he acutely analyzed the shortcomings of standard psychological research methods and got to the heart of issues that seemed to elude many other psychologists. For example, the tedious debate in personality psychology during the 1970s and 1980s about whether traits or situations determine people's behavior ended on a less sophisticated note than that of Murray's *(1938)* discussion of needs, press, and unity themes. Murray's writing in this context is a treasure trove of methodological insights that, although not particularly interesting to new students, are very important for practicing researchers. Second, in his 1938 book, Murray developed a system for classifying needs. Virtually every new investigation of the structure of human motivation in the last fifty years has begun with Murray's list. Murray regarded his need system as one of his two most important contributions and the modern consensus is that he was right. Third, Murray not only introduced the modern assessment center (further described below), which many researchers consider the ideal way to study personality, but also invented the Thematic Apperception Test (TAT), one of the most widely used personality tests in the world. With the assessment center and the TAT, Murray gave personality psychologists two of their most powerful research tools.

Finally, Murray was probably the most influential person in the history of personality psychology in the United States, inasmuch as he attracted many bright and imaginative researchers to the study of personality, gave them a vision of what the study of personality could be, and provided a methodology for following through. Murray's introduction to *Explorations in Personality* is a great rallying cry for the founding of the new discipline of

In 1961, psychologist David McClelland published his landmark book *The Achieving Society*, which argued that accomplishments are affected by the levels of need for achievement among a society's members. According to McClelland, societies in which literature stresses achievement themes—such as the United States—enjoy greater economic prosperity than societies where the literature stresses themes such as family or religion.

Building on Murray's list, McClelland and other researchers *(McClelland & Boyatzis, 1982; McClelland & Burnham, 1976)* later identified a configuration of three needs—achievement, affiliation, and power—that are found in successful leaders. Need for achievement is particularly important for entrepreneurs and people who are starting businesses. However, as the businesses get larger, need for achievement often becomes less important.

The reason is as follows. With larger size comes the necessity for more employees. The business leaders end up spending more time interacting with these additional people and directing them to do the work than doing the work themselves. Because successful interaction requires an enjoyment of people, need for affiliation becomes more important than need for achievement as the organization grows larger.

The third quality important for successful leadership is need for power. But as McClelland and other researchers have pointed out, this quality is best employed to influence rather than dominate others. Successful leaders use their power not for personal aggrandizement but to influence others to work for the good of the organization.

Thus the most successful leaders have high levels of need for affiliation and power, and moderate levels of need for achievement.

personology, and the people who worked with Murray over the years—Erik Erikson, Nevitt Sanford, Donald MacKinnon, Silvan Tomkins, Brewster Smith, R. W. White, Morris Stein, Clyde Kluckhohn, and Edwin Shneiderman—were and are among the most distinguished scholars and researchers of the 1950s through the 1970s. Allport's 1937 textbook legitimized the field of personality psychology, but Murray subsequently recruited a cohort of researchers and invented what is still the field's most potent methodology.

Practical Application: Assessment Centers

In 1942, Congress created the Office of Strategic Services to recruit spies and saboteurs to operate behind enemy lines in World War II. In its first year of operation, the OSS, which later became the CIA, chose people to be spies without any special screening. Unfortunately, many of the people selected could not handle the stress of the job, so the OSS eventually instituted a three-day screening program.

The goal of this screening program was to predict who would be successful as a secret agent. Applicants had to complete a detailed personal history form and health questionnaire, as well as tests that measured vocabulary, observation and memory, mechanical comprehension, and map reading and teaching skills. What made this approach to assessment unusual was that psychologists and psychiatrists observed the applicants—as they completed their tests and participated in various group activities—in order to make a judgment about qualities such as emotional stability, anxiety, and social skills.

One activity required an applicant to direct two other men in assembling a wooden cube. Although the applicants believed the activity focused on leadership skills, it was actually a test of emotional stability. Unknown to the applicants, one of the men had been told to act lazy and the other was told to be aggressive and critical; only one of the applicants finished the cube on time. In another activity, applicants were given twelve minutes to make up a story to explain their being caught going through secret government files. Three hostile and abusive interrogators then questioned the applicants about their story.

The OSS screening program was such a success that it led to the widespread use of employment testing after World War II. In one of the most famous applications, AT&T used the realistic approach of the OSS procedure to screen candidates for executive positions. In the modern assessment center, candidates are evaluated on aptitudes, abilities, interests, and personality factors that are relevant to handling situations that managers face. Candidates complete assessment instruments and participate in leaderless group discussions, in-basket exercises, and other activities while being observed by assessors from higher levels in the organization. After two or three days of such activities, the assessors select the persons they feel will most likely succeed in a management position.

The modern assessment center is clearly derived from the program designed by the OSS during World War II—a program that both Allport and Murray played a role in developing. Some of the current methods used to select executives also reflect their ideas about needs, traits, and the importance of using a variety of methods for studying personality. As mentioned earlier in this chapter, the assessment center method—whether used for research or for selecting spies or executives—remains one of the best ways to study personality.

7

GEORGE KELLY AND H. S. SULLIVAN

Interpersonal Theory

- The Life of Kelly
- Core Problem: Solving Life's Problems
- Kelly's View of Human Nature
- Evaluating Kelly
- The Life of Sullivan
- Core Problem: The Origins and Consequences of Anxiety
- Sullivan's View of Human Nature
- Evaluating Sullivan
- Practical Application: The FIRO Awareness Scales

With the exception of Karen Horney, the personality theorists discussed so far in this book share a common feature—they all analyzed personality in *intrapsychic* terms. That is, they focused on the contents of a person's mind in an effort to understand how the person developed those contents and how the contents could be studied and changed. The theorists used different terms to describe the contents—*id, archetype, ideal self, need, trait,* and so forth—but their aim was to explain how individuals are influenced by the contents of their minds.

All the theories covered so far are also *individualistic.* That is, they treat other people as objects in the external world who are important only insofar as they influence our welfare. Other people can feed, teach, shelter, or injure us, but they are no more special than other objects in the world. In terms of their influence, they are essentially indistinguishable from pets, characters in a movie, or even plants.

In contrast, the interpersonal theorists covered in this chapter believed that people are primarily oriented toward other people and that personality arises from, is modified by, and expresses itself in social interaction. In this regard they directly extend Karen Horney's thinking. But these theorists are also distinctive because of their contributions to personality assessment. George Kelly invented a novel measurement procedure called the Role Construct Repertory Test—or "Rep Test," as it is known—and Harry Stack Sullivan invented a model for the structure of interpersonal behavior that has been brilliantly extended in recent years by a number of researchers (e.g., Wiggins & Trapnell, 1996).

The interpersonal theorists stimulated a great deal of high-quality and converging research over the years. We begin with George Kelly because his ideas formed a transition in North American psychology from the individualism of Allport and Murray to pure interpersonal theory. Kelly is often regarded as the founder of the cognitive approach to psychotherapy (e.g., Meichenbaum, 1977), but we believe that he is more properly considered an interpersonal theorist (Kelly believed this, too.)

We then turn to H. S. Sullivan, who was a friend of Karen Horney's and laid the foundation for modern interpersonal theory. Although people rarely think of Kelly and Sullivan in the same intellectual context, there are many important parallels in their thinking. Perhaps the easiest way to compare them is to note that Kelly is Sullivan without the emotion, and Sullivan is Kelly with emotion. Kelly ignored emotion, whereas Sullivan focused on anxiety.

• • •

The Life of Kelly

George Kelly was born in 1905 on a farm thirty-five miles south of Wichita, Kansas. His father was a Presbyterian minister and his mother was a schoolteacher. Both were well educated and taught their son until he was thirteen, when they sent him to live and attend high school in Wichita. Kelly remained away from home from then on. He spent three years at Friends University in Wichita and one year at Park College in Parkville, Missouri (both are religious schools), where he majored in math and physics.

After college, Kelly traveled around the Midwest, working at a variety of jobs, including speech and drama instruction and aeronautical engineering. He received a master's degree in educational sociology at the University of Kansas, another education degree from the University of Edinburgh in Scotland, and a Ph.D. in communicative disorders in 1931 from the State University of Iowa. In 1932, in the depths of the Great Depression, he joined the faculty of Fort Hays Kansas State College, where he taught physiological psychology. Kelly eventually decided that helping people was more important than pondering synaptic connections, and he became a psychotherapist. He persuaded the state legislature to support a traveling psychological clinic, and he and his students provided counseling services to depression-ridden young people throughout Kansas until the outbreak of World War II.

Kelly served as an aviation psychologist in the navy during the war and, afterward, spent one year at the University of Maryland. In 1946, he moved to Ohio State University to be the director of the Counseling Center; there he became quite famous after the publication of his major work, *The Psychology of Personal Constructs*, in 1955. Kelly was a founding member of the American Board of Examiners for Professional Psychology, a member of the Special Advisory Group for the Veterans Administration, and a member of the Training Committee of the National Institute for Mental Health and National Institutes of Health from 1958 to 1967—which is to say that he was influential in setting policy for psychologists at the national

George Kelly.
Source: National Library of Medicine.

level for many years. In 1965, Kelly joined the faculty of Brandeis University; he died in 1967. Kelly differs from the theorists discussed earlier in this book in that he grew up in rural areas far from any urban centers, did not attend elite universities, seems to have been largely self-educated, worked primarily with troubled young people, and didn't write much about his ideas. Despite (or perhaps because of) his intellectual isolation and nontraditional educational background, he developed a highly original, distinctive, and influential viewpoint on personality.

Core Problem: Solving Life's Problems

Kelly developed his ideas while working in Kansas, helping young people who were having problems in school. Recall that Kelly had a background in science and engineering. Scientists develop and test theories in order to solve problems, and the problems are usually technical. But ordinary life is also full of problems, and ordinary people have been known to develop theories about the world in order to solve such problems. (Obviously, some solutions are better than others, and some people are better problem solvers than others.) For Kelly, there was no sharp distinction between problem solving in science and problem solving in ordinary life. He believed that people have persistent problems in their lives because they have bad theories, but if they can develop more adequate theories, their problems will be better resolved, if not actually fixed.

Kelly's theory of personality entails learning to analyze how people with problems think about the world and helping those people develop better theories. As Kelly himself put it, his theory is about analyzing the laws of thought. And for him, most problems could be fixed easily—if they were analyzed correctly. He argued that personality is like a suit of clothes: If you don't like the one you have, you can get another one fairly quickly. Because the personality you have reflects the way you think about the world now, if you change your way of thinking, you will change your personality.

Though written in somewhat idiosyncratic language, *The Psychology of Personal Constructs* is commonsensical, having been designed to provide a counselor with the tools necessary to help a person solve life's problems. The theory is organized in terms of one major postulate and eleven corollaries. The fundamental postulate is Kelly's first rule of thought and the basis for the entire theory: "A person's processes are psychologically channelized by the ways in which he [or she] anticipates events" *(Kelly, 1955, p. 46)*. In other words, people's behavior reflects the manner in which they predict the future: What they do depends on what is on their mind and what they expect will happen to them.

Kelly referred to units of thought as **constructs**, his word for concepts. People use constructs to anticipate and predict what will happen next. They form them by "construing" reality—by imposing an interpretation on the world. In particular, they compare and contrast how something in the world is like some things and different from others. In addition, all constructs are bipolar—although what is at the other end of a given construct depends on the person. For example, if a person frequently thinks other people are aggressive, Kelly would wonder what the opposite of aggressive is for that person, and the answer would depend on the person. People are different from one another, Kelly said, because they construe the world differently. What makes sense for one person may not make sense for another, but that doesn't matter because each person's construct system is all he or she has to make sense of the world. Constructs can be revised with experience, but they differ in terms of their permeability: Some are easier to change than others.

At the heart of Kelly's system is the sociality corollary: "To the extent that one person construes the construction processes of another, he [or she] may play a role in the social process involving the other person" *(Kelly, 1955, p. 95)*. That is, in order for people to interact, they must construe (think about) how other people think about them.

Kelly's system of corollaries is described in Table 7.1.

Kelly introduced two critical ideas in his theory—role constructs and roles. A **role construct** is what we think another person expects we will do when we interact with him or her, and a **role** is what we do based on that role construct. Roles are the fundamental unit of analysis in social interaction (roles are what we do), and role constructs are the units of explanation (role constructs explain why we do what we do). Kelly considered calling his perspective "Role Theory" but decided instead to call it "Personal Constructs Theory." Our key point here is that the interpersonal aspects of Kelly's theory involve analyzing people's ideas about what others expect of them during social interaction, and that people's problems are caused by faulty ideas about the expectations of others.

TABLE 7.1 Kelly's Corollaries

1. Fundamental Postulate

A person's processes are psychologically channelized by the ways in which he anticipates events.
In other words, our behavior is based on what we expect in the future.

2. Construction Corollary

A person anticipates events by construing their replications.
We make sense of what happens to us by comparing our situation to what has happened before.

3. Individuality Corollary

Persons differ from each other in their construction of events.
The main differences between people result from their viewpoints.

4. Organization Corollary

Each person characteristically evolves, for his convenience in anticipating events, a construction system embracing ordinal relationships between constructs.
Each person develops a hierarchy of constructs in which some beliefs are more important than others.

5. Dichotomy Corollary

A person's construction system is composed of a finite number of dichotomous constructs.
Constructs differ from each other, and people make choices based on these differences.

6. Choice Corollary

A person chooses for himself that alternative expressed in the dichotomy construct through which he anticipates the greater possibility for extension and definition of his system.
People compare the differences between constructs, then make choices based on what they consider the most beneficial outcome.

7. Range Corollary

A construct is convenient for the anticipation of a finite range of events only.
Because no construct can cover all possible situations, each construct is relevant only to a range of situations.

8. Experience Corollary

A person's construct system varies as he successively construes the replication of events.
People modify their constructs through experience.

9. Modulation Corollary

The variation in a person's construction system is limited by the permeability of the constructs wit whose range of convenience the variants lie.
Some constructs are more permeable than others.

10. Fragmentation Corollary

A person may successively employ a variety of construction subsystems that are inferentially incompatible with each other.
Because people are not always logical, they may hold constructs that are contradictory.

11. Commonality Corollary

To the extent that one person employs a construction of experience which is similar to that employed by another, his psychological processes are similar to those of the other person.
People may have different experiences, but if their experiences lead them to the same constructs, they will tend to hold similar viewpoints.

12. Sociality Corollary

To the extent that one person construes the construction processes of another, he may play a role in a social process involving the other person.
To communicate successfully with others, a person needs some understanding of the others' constructs.

Kelly's View of Human Nature

Motivation

Kelly seems to have been determined to stake out a position for himself that was as original as possible. This is most obvious in his views on motivation, which he set out in a famous essay in 1958. Kelly was a serious critic of the concept of motivation, which is the foundation of all traditional theories of personality. Kelly objected to the concept for three reasons.

First, he argued, motivational concepts are used primarily to explain why people are active—but if we assume that people are *inherently* active, motivation becomes a redundant and unnecessary concept. This is an interesting position that resembles the discussion in seventeenth–century physics about the nature of gravitational attraction. How to conceptualize gravitation was one of the oldest problems in physics; Isaac Newton advised that people consider gravity a mathematical constant and end the discussion altogether. Newton's critics warned that doing so would set physics back 500 years, but Newton was clearly right. And this seems to be Kelly's point about motivation: Consider it a constant and forget about it.

Kelly's second objection to the concept of motivation relates to the context of trying to help people. What, Kelly asked, can you do for someone once you assign him a motive? To call him lazy is to say that he lacks motivation, but what do you do for him after you decide that he is lazy? Kelly's point is that the concept of motivation is not useful when trying to help people with their problems because it doesn't lead to a plan of action.

Third, Kelly noted that motivational terms are dangerous because they can be used unfairly to stigmatize other people. Here Kelly anticipated what is called **labeling theory**. Labeling theory holds that if a psychologist assigns a label such as delinquent, retarded, or schizophrenic to a person and others learn about the label, they may treat her as if she is delinquent, retarded, or schizophrenic. Then, she herself may notice this treatment and begin to respond to others' expectations, acting as if she is, in fact, delinquent, retarded, or schizophrenic. This outcome, in turn, reinforces the label and sets off a spiral of dysfunctional behavior.

Along with Kelly's notion that personality is like a suit of clothes that we can change, his critique of the concept of motivation is the most distinctive and original part of his theory.

Personality Development

Kelly thought about development in terms of the steady expansion of the scope, accuracy, and complexity of construct systems—that is, personal theories of how the social world operates. Over time and with experience, these construct systems become more comprehensive, allowing people to predict and understand a greater variety of phenomena. At the same time, because they can comprehend a greater range of issues, the possibilities in their lives gradually expand, thereby freeing them to make choices in the sense that they are no longer captives of a narrow and primitive theory of the world. A particularly important aspect of the construct system is the self-construct, which is described in the next section.

But Kelly's views differ from traditional developmental models in two ways. First, unlike Freud, Jung, and Allport, Kelly postulated no defined endpoint to development. Both the manner in which each person's constructs evolve and their final form are idiosyncratic, bounded only by the relatively loose constraints of reality. Second, in a very real sense, development didn't matter to Kelly. His theory is completely ahistorical: We are not victims of our childhood histories, he said (contrary to what Freud would have argued). Rather, we are prisoners of our own construct systems, which we can change at any time.

Self-Knowledge

Kelly believed that we form theories about ourselves—self-constructs—in much the same way that we form any other constructs. That is, we compare ourselves to others and decide how we are like them and how we are different. Our self-construct reflects these comparisons and contrasts. But our self-construct is a particularly important part of our overall construct system because, once formed, it serves as the reference point for our interactions with others. Recall that our role construct is what we think others expect of us during an interaction; thus our role constructs are developed in reference to our self-construct, once it is formed.

People who have not developed a self-construct lack an anchor for their social behavior; consequently, they seem impulsive and erratic. In addition, because they do not think about the expectations of other people during social interactions, they give the impression of being egocentric, self-centered, inconsiderate, and rude. However, when they develop a self-construct, all of this changes because they now have a reference point for their role construct and will begin to guide their behavior based on what they think others expect of them.

Unconscious Processes

Kelly had a great deal of experience helping people with their problems, and, as a result, he recognized that people are often unaware of the reasons for their actions. For Kelly, this meant that people's actions are sometimes guided by unconscious constructs. But how do constructs become unconscious? Kelly suggested that they become unconscious in two ways. The first concerns the fact that all constructs are bipolar. For example, if you call a person deceitful, the implication is that you think about others in terms of a construct, one end of which is deceitful and the other end is not yet defined.

Imagine that a person uses a construct to understand others and focuses intensely on one end of the construct while never acknowledging the other end. For example, he might describe others as "loving" even though others constantly take advantage of him. This might mean that, for this person, (a) deceitful is the opposite of loving and (b) the term deceitful is not consciously available to this person when he thinks about others. Thus, the construct of deceitful would be unconscious. This version of how a construct becomes unconscious resembles the Freudian concept of repression.

The second way that a construct becomes unconscious has to do with the fact that normal people constantly modify their construct systems in response to new experiences. It seems reasonable to suppose that small children develop constructs—expectations about the behavior of others—before they develop language. Constructs developed before language has developed would be effectively unconscious because the child could not think about them in words.

Psychological Adjustment

For Kelly, psychological adjustment is a function of a person's construct system. Specifically, mature people have three characteristics in common. First, they have enough role constructs available that they can understand and interact appropriately with a wide range of people; persons who are less mature can interact only with a small number of people. Second, mature people have appropriate roles available—that is, patterns of interpersonal behavior—such that their social behavior is consistent with other people's expectations. Other people know what to expect when dealing with them, and usually approve of their behavior. And third, mature people have permeable role constructs, which means that they will listen to negative feedback from others and adjust their role constructs based on that feedback. In contrast, immature people ignore feedback and cannot adjust their constructs even when others react badly to their behavior.

Although there has not been much research evaluating this aspect of Kelly's theory, his views regarding the determinants of maturity seem sensible. In particular, it is plausible to conclude that people who can accurately interpret the intentions of others, and then act in ways that are appropriate to the expectations of others, tend to be effective in their social behavior. In short, Kelly seems to have identified the determinants of social skill.

Kelly also invented a novel method for helping people gain some perspective on their construct systems, a technique that he called fixed role therapy. Assume, for example, that a client of Kelly's had a problem being sufficiently assertive and that her lack of assertiveness was caused by the manner in which she construed others' expectations. Kelly would have asked her to practice being assertive while dealing with him, and to continue doing so until she was comfortable being assertive in that context. Then Kelly would have encouraged her to be assertive when dealing with other important people in her life and to pay careful attention to their reactions. In this way the client would, in principle, have become capable of testing the validity of her construct system for predicting the expectations of others regarding assertive behavior.

The Individual and Society

Freud thought carefully about how people are linked to their societies, the psychological processes that are involved in forming the linkages, and the costs and benefits of life in society. These topics, however, do not come up in Kelly's writing; he was exclusively interested in how we deal with other people, one person at a time, and did not comment on the nature of people's relations to society as a whole. In short, Kelly had nothing to say about the topic of moral development, other than to note that delinquents typically lack a self-construct.

Evaluating Kelly

George Kelly was very much a maverick in academic psychology. He not only criticized psychoanalysis, behaviorism, and Gordon Allport's ideas about traits but also tried to develop a model of personality that was as different from these mainstream views as possible. To a substantial degree he was successful; the result was a unique, creative, and distinctive view of personality that attracted a great deal of interest during his lifetime. Kelly's ideas, though still popular and influential in the United Kingdom, are much less so in North America, despite the interesting issues he raised. Perhaps his ideas have been absorbed into the mainstream of cognitive social learning theory (Chapter 8). In our judgment, at any rate, one of Kelly's most important contributions was his sheer originality—as contrasted, for example, with the derivative eclecticism of Allport and Murray.

A second contribution was his analysis of social skill, a topic of importance for training sales and managerial personnel and, indeed, for enhancing interpersonal effectiveness in general. No other personality psychologist has provided a better analysis of how people interact. A third and closely related contribution was his invention of fixed role therapy as a technique for training social skills. Behavioral modeling *(Latham & Saari, 1979)*, today the most popular and effective modern method for management and sales training, appears to be closely related to fixed role therapy.

Fourth, and on a more technical note, Kelly was a key figure in introducing the "cognitive revolution" into modern personality psychology. Kelly was cognitive before it became trendy, and Albert Bandura *(1977)* and Walter Mischel's *(1973; Chapter 8)* intellectual roots are planted squarely in Kelly's 1955 book.

There are, however, two important problems with Kelly's theory. First, as noted, he had nothing to say about the moral dimension in personality; the manner in which people are linked to their societies seems not to have interested him. Given that crimes—murder, homicide, theft, illegal drug use—are among the most important social problems of our time, Kelly's indifference to the issue is an important, and surprising, omission.

A second problem is that Kelly's views about motivation are self–refuting: Despite Kelly's claim that the concept of motivation is unimportant, his theory crucially depends on certain unacknowledged motivational assumptions. Consider, for example, his metaphor of Man the Scientist. With this metaphor, Kelly assumed that people are fundamentally motivated to understand and predict the world around them—especially the social world. But without intellectual curiosity as a motive, neither the metaphor nor the theory is workable. In short, Kelly was simply wrong to argue that the topic of motivation is unimportant—a viewpoint he was unable to sustain.

Consider as well the concepts of role constructs and roles, the key ideas in his theory. Kelly argued that a role construct is our view of what we think others expect of us during social interaction, and a role is what we do given what we think others expect. But the concept of a role construct implies that we are motivated to understand what others expect of us, and the concept of a role implies that, once we know what others expect, we are motivated to act in accordance with that knowledge. Therefore, the two most important ideas in Kelly's theory rest on the unacknowledged motivational assumption that we need to know what others expect of us and that we feel compelled to comply with those expectations.

These two problems notwithstanding, George Kelly developed an interesting and very influential way of thinking about personality. In terms of originality alone, Kelly deserves at least the same level of recognition normally given to Allport and Murray.

Box 7.1 interprets the life of Malcolm X in terms of personal constructs theory.

· · ·

The Life of Sullivan

Harry Stack Sullivan's biography is full of gaps and inconsistencies *(see Perry, 1982)* and is, overall, a sad story. His Irish Catholic parents had moved to the small, rural Protestant community of Norwich, New York, where he was born on an isolated farm on February 21, 1892. He was the third of three boys and the only one who lived. As a result, his mother coddled and overprotected him. A depressed semi-invalid who disappeared for more than a year when he was thirty months old, she was the dominant figure in his development. Periodically hospitalized for her "disturbances," she despised her husband and poisoned her son's relations with him. Sullivan was a small, shy, sensitive, lonely child. He was the only Catholic in his school, where he was abused and rejected by the other children because of his religion, his Irish accent, and his strangeness.

Sullivan was also very bright. In 1908, at the age of sixteen, he graduated from high school as the class valedictorian and won a scholarship to Cornell. Precocious, awkward, and friendless, he failed all his classes in college, got into legal trouble after being set up by some older boys, was expelled, and disappeared for two years. Some writers (e.g., Perry, 1982) have suggested that he had a schizophrenic break, but no one knows for certain.

In 1911, Sullivan entered the Chicago College of Medicine and Surgery, a branch of Valparaiso University, where he was a mediocre student. He finished his studies in 1915 but did not receive his degree until 1917 when he finished paying his tuition. What Sullivan did between 1915 and 1921 is not clear, but records indicate that he served as a medical officer in the U.S. Army during World War I. In 1921, with no formal training in psychiatry, Sullivan joined the staff at St. Elizabeth's Hospital in Washington, D.C., as a liaison between the government and the hospital. At St. Elizabeth's, "Sullivan learned psychiatry from the most reliable of teachers, the patients. He was fascinated by the patients he saw on the wards of St. Elizabeth's, especially the schizophrenics, and this absorption remained with him for the rest of his life" (Chapman, 1976, p. 37). At the same hospital, he worked with William Alanson White, the best-known American psychiatrist of his day.

In 1922 Sullivan joined the Sheppard and Enoch Pratt psychiatric hospital in Baltimore and quickly acquired a national reputation as a near-wizard for his success in treating male schizophrenics. His radical new treatment method utilized the relationship between a therapist and a patient to bring about a "cure."

Sullivan was homosexual and never married. In 1927, he adopted a -fifteen-year-old boy who was found in a catatonic state on a Baltimore street. The boy, James Inscoe, lived with Sullivan for the rest of his life, serving as his secretary and traveling companion. Although Sullivan never legally adopted Inscoe, he considered him his son.

In 1930, Sullivan moved to New York City to start a private practice. He also entered psychoanalysis and became friends with Erich Fromm and Karen Horney. Through Fromm and Horney, he met the great University of Chicago sociologists G. H. Mead, R. E. Park, and W. I. Thomas, the anthropologist Edward Sapir, and the political scientist Harold Lasswell. These men were among the most distinguished and important thinkers in the history of American social science, and Sullivan's association with them, despite his inferior education, indicates how bright and engaging he must have been.

In 1933 Sullivan, along with Sapir and Lasswell, established the William Alanson White Psychiatric Foundation in Washington, D.C. Sullivan also founded the journal Psychiatry, which featured articles by psychiatrists focusing on interpersonal relations. In 1941 he became an honorary member of Karen Horney's American Institute for Psychoanalysis.

In 1943, psychoanalyst Otto Fenichel wrote a scathing review of Erich Fromm's Escape from Freedom, and on the basis of this review, the Institute arbitrarily expelled Fromm for deviating from Freud's ideas (see Box 5.4 in Chapter 5, p. 132). Sullivan resigned from the Institute

BOX 7.1 Biography: Malcolm X

The dramatic events in the life of the Black leader Malcolm X fit well with Kelly's ideas about how our lives are guided by personal constructs. Malcolm X was born Malcolm Little in Omaha, Nebraska, in 1925. His father was a Baptist minister and an organizer for Marcus Garvey's Universal Negro Improvement Association, a "back-to-Africa" group of the 1920s. Members of this association had a theory of the world that included the belief that they would have to take control of their own lives, since they could expect little help from the dominant White majority of American society.

Malcolm grew up on a farm near Lansing, Michigan. The family, though poor, was self-sufficient until Reverend Little died in 1931. Malcolm's mother suffered a nervous breakdown in 1937, and the children became wards of the state. At thirteen, Malcolm was sent to the Michigan State Detention Home, where he became a favorite of the home's White operators.

Malcolm was an outstanding student and very popular with his schoolmates, but his world fell apart in the eighth grade. When he told his English teacher he would like to be a lawyer, his teacher replied that becoming a lawyer was not a realistic goal for a an African American. He advised Malcolm to consider instead becoming a carpenter—an occupation that was more in keeping with what society expected of his race. After that conversation, Malcolm realized that society judged him on the basis of his color rather than his capabilities, and that there was little he could do to achieve his occupational goals. Malcolm's construct that society would reward his achievements in the same way it rewarded the achievements of White people was shattered.

This incident with his teacher was a turning point in Malcolm's life. He became a behavior problem and was sent to live with his sister Ella. Ella, who belonged to the Black elite of Boston, soon discovered that her brother was more interested in street life than in respectability. On the streets, Malcolm learned how to sell liquor and marijuana, to gamble, and to find prostitutes for White businessmen. After being arrested and convicted of robbery, he was sentenced to ten years in prison.

In 1948, while Malcolm was still in prison, his brother Reginald visited him and told him about the teachings of Elijah Muhammad, the founder of the Black Muslims, a separatist group that believed White people are evil. This information dramatically changed the way Malcolm saw the world. He joined the Nation of Islam, dropped the "slave name" Little, and took "X" as a last name to represent his unknown family name in Africa.

Paroled in 1952, Malcolm went to Chicago and served under Elijah Muhammed. In 1953, he organized a Black Muslim temple in Boston, and another in Philadelphia the following year. As a reward, Elijah Muhammed made him minister of the Temple in Harlem. However, as Malcolm became increasingly famous as a critic of White society, Elijah Muhammed became jealous of his popularity. At the same time, Malcolm discovered that Elijah Muhammed had been committing adultery, behavior that Malcolm regarded as particularly unfitting for the head of a religious group. Eventually, Malcolm left the Black Muslims and founded his own organization in Harlem—Muslim Mosque, Inc.

In 1964, Malcolm made a pilgrimage to Mecca with funds provided by his sister Ella, who had become a Black Muslim as well. During the journey, Malcolm realized that it was not "whiteness" that made people evil; rather, it was the bigoted attitudes and behaviors of White people that were evil. Malcolm concluded that people of all races could be united under Islam. This was the third and final shift in his construct system. On his return from Mecca, he received a celebrity's treatment in several Middle Eastern and African countries.

At a meeting in Harlem on February 21, 1965, while Malcolm was speaking, a fight broke out in the audience. During the confusion, three gunmen shot Malcolm several times. The men, two of them Black Muslims, were captured and convicted of murder. Although some people are convinced that the assassination of Malcolm X was part of a government conspiracy, most believe that he was murdered by the Nation of Islam.

This biography of Malcolm X illustrates how constructs affect personality—and how changing constructs can change behavior. Born the son of a minister, Malcolm returned to religion after a life of crime and debauchery. Just as his father had worked for the improvement of the lives of Black people, Malcolm himself dedicated his life to serving Blacks. Despite his intellectual gifts, society—represented by his White English teacher—expected him to accept a lesser role regarded as appropriate for his race. When Malcolm rejected that role, he became an outcast of society.

At the end of his life, Malcolm X grew more tolerant of White society. He began to reach out to more moderate Black leaders, and he dreamed of uniting people of all races under Islam. Over the years, Malcolm X had changed his beliefs about society on the basis of his experiences. And some of these changes were the result of encountering the personal constructs of other people, such as his English teacher and Elijah Muhammed. By changing his constructs throughout his lifetime, Malcolm went from being a highly promising student to a street criminal to an intolerant religious leader to a leader who wanted to unite all people through religion.

because he thought that Fenichel's review represented psychoanalytic politics at their worst. He also defended Fromm and was expelled from the International Psychoanalytic Association. Analysts were asked to choose between Freud and Sullivan; those who backed Sullivan were subsequently harassed in various ways, and this argument between interpersonal and traditional Freudian approaches continues in some psychoanalytic circles today. Sullivan was a brilliant lecturer but a terrible writer, and he published only one book, Conceptions of Modern Psychiatry (1940). After his death, his friends collected his best lectures and published them in four books: *The Interpersonal Theory of Psychiatry* (1953a), *Conceptions of Modern Psychiatry* (1953b), *The Psychiatric Interview* (1954), and *Clinical Studies in Psychiatry* (1956).

Sullivan was witty and charming, but he could also be moody and sarcastic. He had a reputation for being a heavy drinker and not always honest, and he was clearly a troubled soul. Despite his international fame, he became increasingly morose during the last ten years of his life. In 1940, he moved to a small house in rural Maryland where he lived alone. He was also alone when he died in a hotel room in Paris in 1949—on the anniversary of his mother's death—while attending a meeting of the World Federation of Mental Health. He seems deliberately to have stopped taking the medication that had been prescribed for his heart condition.

Core Problem: The Origins and Consequences of Anxiety

A key point of our book is that the important theories of personality all contain an autobiographical component, and this is particularly true in Sullivan's case. Sullivan's mother was unstable in the best of circumstances, and, as noted, she disappeared for a year when he was nearly three. Thus Sullivan was both physically and emotionally abandoned as a child. Modern psychological research clearly shows that this kind of separation is quite traumatic for most young children and has long-lasting effects.

It was rumored that Sullivan also had a psychotic episode after leaving college at seventeen. As a new psychiatrist, he was fascinated by schizophrenia—probably for "biographical" reasons—and he soon became famous for successfully treating schizophrenics. Sullivan believed that schizophrenia was an extension of normality—indeed, that everyone has the potential to become schizophrenic. As he put it, "Everyone and anyone is much more simply human than otherwise, more like everyone else than different" *(1962, frontispiece)*, and that includes every kind of psychological abnormality. Sullivan concluded that schizophrenia was caused by a person's efforts to control anxiety-provoking interpersonal situations, and that the symptoms could be interpreted as protecting the person from anxiety. This brings us to the key question underlying Sullivan's theory: Where does anxiety come from, and what are its psychological consequences?

Sullivan's View of Human Nature

Motivation

Sullivan's ideas about motivation are clear but not precise. He did not like the idea of instincts because he thought human behavior was too flexible to be explained in such terms. Rather, Sullivan *(1953b)* talked about tensions, which sound very much like instincts. Tensions take two forms. The first kind are the needs that humans share with other animals (e.g., hunger and thirst). For humans, the most important of these is the need for tenderness, the satisfaction of which requires another person. The second kind of tension is anxiety, a diffuse and painful emotion caused by social rejection and disrupted relationships. As there is no single or consistent way to relieve anxiety, Sullivan believed it is the most disruptive force in human relationships. According to Sullivan, the need to avoid anxiety is the primary force shaping personality. In short, to understand a person, we need to know how he or she avoids anxiety.

Where does anxiety come from? Infants "catch" it from their parents through the process of empathy, an innate sensitivity to the moods of others. Parents are always somewhat anxious when caring for their babies, and babies sense this, becoming anxious themselves. But there is nothing that babies can do to relieve their parents' anxiety, and there is often little that parents can do to relieve the anxiety of their babies.

Two implications of Sullivan's theory of motivation should be emphasized. First, he assumed that people have a deep need for secure relations with others—that people are biologically disposed to seek attention, acceptance, and approval from others. This need is particularly important in infancy and childhood, and anxiety occurs when it goes unfulfilled. Second, according to Sullivan, adult personality is largely formed out of the methods that people develop to avoid anxiety. Here Sullivan's theory resembles that of Freud, who likewise believed that adult personality is the crystallization of childhood defenses.

Personality Development

Sullivan analyzed the development of personality in childhood in considerable detail, but he wrote very little about personality in adulthood. There are two parts to his developmental theory: The first concerns how thought develops over time, the second concerns how relationships develop over time.

How Thinking Develops. Sullivan's ideas about cognitive development resemble those of the Swiss developmental psychologist Jean Piaget, whose work Sullivan had read. Both suggested that the way we think about the world changes over time and that such changes occur in a well-defined sequence, reflecting qualitative transformations in thought. Thus, although children at a higher stage of thought can regress to a lower level, children at a lower level cannot understand higher-level thought.

Sullivan called the first and most primitive form of thought **prototaxic thinking**. We know little about this stage, but we assume that, in very early childhood, feelings, sensations, and emotions are disconnected; for instance, an infant doesn't see the links between being hungry, crying, and being satisfied after food arrives. Concepts such as time, place, and causation have no meaning, and much of an infant's mental activity is taken up with discovering the difference between itself and the surrounding environment.

In the second year of life, prototaxic thinking gives way to **parataxic thinking**. During this stage, children are able to link feelings and events, but the links are often wrong. Parataxic thinking is essentially magical thinking in which two events become connected. For example, if a child cries and someone brings her food, she will notice the connection and conclude that the first event causes the second. In actuality, of course, such sequences are often coincidental; a child starts to cry, the family cat comes into the room, and the child concludes that crying made the cat appear. In addition to being magical, parataxic thinking is egocentric. Although children understand that there are other people in the world, these others are significant only insofar as they do things for the children.

Adults also engage in magical and egocentric thinking—more often than one might imagine. For example, if a young woman at college notices that a shy young man is isolated and invites him to join her group, the young man may conclude that she cares for him, not that she was simply being polite. Sullivan believed that schizophrenic thinking is primarily parataxic.
At some point between twelve and eighteen months, after the capacity for language has developed, children begin to use **syntaxic thinking**. Syntaxic thinking is characterized by a logical and realistic understanding of the world, and it depends on **consensual validation**, the

process of comparing one's understanding of the world with what others consider to be true. Thus, syntaxic thinking is not egocentric; a child at this age realizes that other people may understand the world better than he does and actively compares his understanding with that of other people.

The consensual validation that underlies syntaxic thinking is an important part of personality development. Consensual validation helps us understand ourselves by allowing us to compare our views of ourselves with how other people see us. Consensual validation also corrects parataxic distortions. During social interaction, we may discover that our views of ourselves differ from how other people see us. This discovery is particularly important for children who have developed negative self-images. Over time, they may realize that others see them as competent and attractive rather than unlikeable.

How Relationships Affect Personality Development. Sullivan believed that personality unfolds in a sequence of seven stages, each of which is defined by characteristic interpersonal events. This developmental sequence involves decreasing egocentrism and increasing skill at interpersonal relations. Jung and Erikson (Chapter 11) also argued that the stages in personality development are defined by the ability to solve certain developmental problems; but unlike interpersonal theorists, they focused on intrapsychic rather than interpersonal processes.

Sullivan's stages are as follows:

1. Infancy (0 to 2 years). Infancy begins at birth and ends with the development of true language. Infants are made human by the tenderness they receive from their caretakers. They cannot survive unless cared for by others, and nursing is the crucial first interpersonal experience. From their experience with nursing, babies, who think in the parataxic mode, develop a primitive theory of mothers, which Sullivan called a personification, or theory about ourselves or others. Mothers are identified with nipples, which are good if they arrive when desired but bad when they are late or missing or when the mother is anxious.

This experience of good and bad nipples *(Sullivan, 1953a)* generalizes into personifications of good and bad mothers. Sullivan believed that babies' relationship with their mother critically influences the development of their personality. Children of comforting mothers are confident in social interaction; children of anxious mothers fear interaction. Moreover, in contrast to Freud, Sullivan believed that children's relationship with their mother is more important than their relationship with their father.

On the basis of their early experience with their mother, children develop three kinds of personifications—or theories—of themselves called the good-me, the bad-me, and the not-me. The *good-me* results from tender treatment by the mothers. The *bad-me* results from feelings of anxiety and tension, which children pick up from their mothers. And the *not-me* is an unusual case whereby children feel dissociated from themselves. The not-me is a vision of oneself as evil, something that people rarely experience consciously; they know about it primarily through their dreams. According to Sullivan, schizophrenics experience the not-me personification almost continuously.

Although one of these self-personifications usually dominates in infancy, children normally fuse the three into one sometime after the age of three. Not surprisingly, children whose not-me personification dominates consciousness tend to have serious adjustment problems later in life.

2. Childhood (2 to 5 years). Childhood begins with the development of language and ends with the development of a need for playmates, or what Sullivan called the **need for intimacy**. Five changes occur during childhood. First, the good and bad mother personifications are fused into one that resembles the real mother, and children distinguish between their parents. Second, children integrate the three self-personifications into a single self-concept. Third, children develop imaginary playmates with whom they talk, a process that contributes to their self-understanding and ability to interact with others. Fourth, emotions become reciprocal during this period, such that children can give as well as receive tenderness, and their relationships become less one-sided.

It is also during this stage that children begin "as if" performances, or role playing. There are two forms of such role playing. In the first, children act as if they were their parents, presumably as a way of practicing adult roles in preparation for later life. In the second, they act as if they were preoccupied with something—a game, book, or toy—in order not to have to deal with others. This latter form of role playing is often used to avoid interactions that children think will make them feel anxious.

3. The Juvenile Era (5 to 8 years). The juvenile era begins when children want to spend more time with their peers than with their families—that is, when the need for intimacy first emerges—and it ends when a child finds a single friend with whom he or she can satisfy the need for intimacy. Sullivan *(1940)* suggested that the major interpersonal accomplishments of the juvenile era is development of the abilities to cooperate, compete, and compromise. The development of these abilities is critical for being able to get along with other people in later life. At this age, children no longer want to interact with authoritarian adults; they seek out, and need, interactions in which they will be treated as equals. The major opportunity for such interaction is, of course, with peers at school.

During this time, children are increasingly able to think on the syntaxic level. As a result, they begin to make discriminations among other people, both children and adults. For example, one teacher may be seen as kinder than the others, and one parent more indulgent than the other.

4. Preadolescence (8 to 13 years). The stage of preadolescence begins when the need for intimacy appears, and it ends with the onset of puberty. It is characterized by further social development and the formation of an important same-sex friendship based on real affection. According to Sullivan, this friendship becomes the most intense relationship in a child's life. For the first time, the well-being of another person becomes as important to children as their own well-being, and they begin to develop the capacity to love. In Sullivan's view, friendship in preadolescence is a way of practicing for the relationships with members of the opposite sex that begin in adolescence.

The need for intimacy grows out of the earlier need for tenderness. Tenderness and intimacy come before, but are related to, the concept of love. One can have a tender relationship with parents, friends, even pets; but intimacy involves a relationship with another person of similar status. Intimacy has nothing to do with sex; it develops well before puberty and usually involves a person of the same sex. Because it develops between equals, intimacy usually doesn't exist in parent-child relations.

An intimate relationship allows a child enough security to try new behaviors and to disclose personal feelings. This intense friendship also strengthens a child's sense of self-worth. In Sullivan's view, many children (and he would have included himself in this category) enter preadolescence with serious problems of self-esteem because of earlier rejections that made them doubt their value to anyone. And when such children develop a preadolescent friendship with someone who admires and respects them, this relationship may actually have therapeutic value. At about age eight, for example, Sullivan developed a close friendship with a neighbor that changed his life.

5. Early adolescence (14 to 18 years). Early adolescence begins when individuals reach puberty and ends when they fall in love with a member of the opposite sex. Again, in contrast with adherents of traditional psychoanalytic theory, Sullivan argued that sexual impulses in infancy and childhood are relatively unimportant when compared with adolescent sexuality. To dramatize the differences between the stages, Sullivan used the term lust to describe the sexual urges of adolescence.

As in preadolescence, relationships with others are the most important factor in an adolescent's life. In an ideal relationship, lust can be integrated with the need for intimacy. Sullivan also believed that intimate relationships can potentially correct earlier personality problems. In the shared intimacy of early adolescence, a young person can learn how to develop and maintain healthy interpersonal relationships—a skill that will be important throughout his or her life.

According to Sullivan, early adolescence is a turning point in personality development. At this time, young people either learn how to deal appropriately with intimacy and lust or they have serious problems with relationships in later life. Although sexual needs are important during this period, it is a mistake, he argued, for psychiatrists (inspired by Freud) to focus on their patients' sex lives, because sex is only one aspect of interpersonal relations.

6. Late adolescence (19 years to maturity). This stage of personality development begins when sexuality becomes a normal part of life and a young person becomes less egocentric and more socially responsible. It ends with the establishment of a lasting love relationship. The most important developmental challenge of this period is the acquisition of a vocational identity—the decision as to what one is going to do when one grows up. Here, for the first time, any psychological problems that developed earlier become important because they foreclose certain occupational choices or training opportunities. Prior to this stage, immaturity didn't matter. But as young persons enter the world of work, their shyness, insecurity, or delinquency will influence their career choices.

At this point, Sullivan argued, many young people begin *a life behind the mask*; they learn to play roles that are designed to disguise their feelings of inadequacy in various situations. But playing their disguised roles requires so much energy that personality development becomes impossible. Further development will depend on an integrated or coherent image of themselves that is not tied to any specific interaction—a topic that is discussed in the next section.

7. *Adulthood.* When individuals successfully complete the tasks of late adolescence—establishing a career and a lasting love relationship—they enter adulthood. With regard to this love relationship, Sullivan noted that "highly developed intimacy with another is not the principal business of life, but is, perhaps, the principal source of satisfaction in life" *(1953b, p. 34)*. Sullivan defined *love* as follows: "When the satisfaction or the security of another person becomes as significant to one as one's own satisfaction or security, then the state of love exists" *(1953b, pp. 42–43)*. This definition is purely interpersonal; it is also based on the complete absence of egocentrism.

Sullivan had little to say about adulthood, because everything that prevents it from occurring happens earlier. But the reason he analyzed overall development in such detail is that he thought personal growth and change occurred primarily at the transition points in development, which therefore needed to be specified as accurately as possible. Unlike Kelly, who believed that people can develop continuously simply by changing their thinking, Sullivan took the traditional view that development proceeds in a stage-like manner. In his view, development involves decreasing egocentrism and increasing skill at maintaining relationships.

Sullivan's stages of development are compared with those of Freud and Jung in Box 7.2.

Self-Knowledge

Sullivan used the term **self-system** to refer to the self-concept, which he believed is the central core of personality, because it regulates social interaction. Sullivan defined personality in terms of the emotional exchanges that occur between people. He was interested not in what people do in private but in what they do to one another. Personality, he said, is the "relatively enduring pattern of interpersonal situations that characterize a human life" *(1953a, pp. 110–111)*. In other words, personality is composed of habitual patterns of interpersonal behavior.

The two key terms in Sullivan's theory are **personifications** and **dynamisms**. Personifications correspond to Kelly's notion of a role construct—they are the theories that we have about ourselves and other people. And dynamisms are habits or traits. They are our characteristic ways of dealing with others, and they closely correspond to Kelly's notion of a role.

Sullivan defined the self-system in two very different ways. On the one hand, the self-system is a self-personification; it is our theory of ourselves regarding how we expect others to react to us. In this first sense, the self-system consists of the reflected appraisals of others; it is based on how others reacted to us in the past and how we evaluated those reactions. On the other

BOX 7.2 Stages of Development According to Freud, Jung, and Sullivan

Freud, Jung, and Sullivan were all interested in how the unconscious affects personality. Both Jung and Sullivan built on Freud's ideas, but their theories radically departed from traditional psycho-analytic theory and its definition of personality development as the result of symbolic expression of sexual and aggressive drives.

As you may recall from Chapter 3, Freud believed that personality develops as the libido of the child fixates on different parts of the body, advancing through the oral, anal, and phallic stages, then through a latency period, and culminating in a genital stage that begins at puberty. Signifi-cant personality changes do not occur after the end of the phallic period and the subsiding of the Oedipal conflict; thus, according to Freud, personality is more or less established by the age of five or six.

Jung rejected the importance of childhood sexuality in psychological development, arguing that the drive for individuation is the main force that creates personality. The first two stages of life—childhood and youth—are relatively unimportant if no significant trauma occurs during these periods. Personality does not really "blossom" until adulthood, which occurs around the age of forty. In old age, the last stage of life, people come more and more under the control of the uncon-scious, much as they were in childhood.

Neither Freud nor Jung put much emphasis on the role of other people in an individual's psycho-logical development (except for the father in psychoanalytic theory). But Sullivan took a completely different approach, arguing that relationships with others are the driving force that influence personality throughout our lives. At any stage of life, he said, a relationship with a friend or teacher can help us develop psychologically in either a positive or negative direction. In this way, Sullivan's theory resembles the ideas of Karen Horney, another theorist interested in how the unconscious affects personality. Horney did not identify a sequence of developmental stages, but she believed that the way we interact with others reflects the quality of our relationships early in life.

The different ideas of Freud, Jung, and Sullivan about the stages of psychological development are summarized in Table 7.2.

hand, the self-system describes the behaviors that we use to maintain the approval and avoid the criticism of others. In this second sense, the self-system consists of our typical ways of relating to others.

We develop a self-system to protect ourselves from criticism and rejection. The self-system is thus like a filter that focuses our attention on the interpersonal behaviors that parents, friends, teachers, spouses, or employers like or dislike. In short, the self-system is exclusively defensive, designed to prevent interpersonal mistakes. As a result, the self-system becomes the primary obstacle to growth, change, and development. The self-system—our theory about what others expect of us during social interaction—must be revised to reflect interpersonal reality more accurately—to reflect what others actually expect rather than what we think they expect.

TABLE 7.2 Stages of Development According to Freud, Jung, and Sullivan

Freud	Jung	Sullivan
Oral stage (First year of life)	Childhood (0 to adolescence)	Infancy (First two years of life)
Anal stage (Second year of life)	Youth (Puberty to 35)	Childhood (Ages 2 to 5)
Phallic stage (Ages 3 to 5)	Adulthood (About 35 to 70)	Juvenile era (Ages 5 to 8)
Latency (5 to puberty)	Old age (70 and older)	Preadolescence (Ages 8 to 13)
Genital stage (Puberty until death)		Early adolescence (Ages 14 to 18)
		Late adolescence (19 to maturity)
		Adulthood

In contrast to the standard view that personality is stable over time, Sullivan (like Murray and Kelly) argued that the self-system of a normal person constantly changes as people adapt to new interpersonal demands and try to guard against rejection and anxiety. Sullivan suggested that every interaction between two people can result in some small change in their self-systems. As more people join an interaction, the process becomes more and more complex. Participants act in accordance with their views of themselves and others, and these views change as an interaction proceeds. In Sullivan's view, it is surprising that social interaction proceeds as smoothly as it usually does, given the complexity of the multiple interacting self-systems.

Unconscious Processes

In Sullivan's view, people are primarily motivated to avoid the anxiety caused by interpersonal rejection and to seek acceptance, security, and approval. In the process, they use certain unconscious techniques that Sullivan called **security operations**. Security operations sometimes protect a person from feeling anxious; at other times they increase a person's emotional suffering. According to Sullivan, inappropriate security operations are the primary cause of interpersonal problems.

Although Sullivan criticized most of the Freudian defense mechanisms (i.e., repression, sublimation, projection, etc.), his concept of security operations serves the same purpose—to protect a person from anxiety. The most important of them, he said, is selective inattention, which refers to the process of unconsciously focusing our attention on a particular topic and ignoring everything else. If we are in an emergency, this focus allows us to concentrate on the problem at hand; but we more often use selective inattention to avoid recognizing unpleasant facts about ourselves. Selective inattention is also useful for lying. In a fascinating essay on compulsive liars, Sullivan noted that the distinguishing feature of such people is their ability to focus closely on present circumstances—that is, to focus on what they are saying at the moment in those circumstances—with no regard for what they may have said on other occasions. The focus is what allows them to lie effectively and without embarrassment— because they actually believe what they are saying at the moment.

The self-system uses selective inattention to filter experience and focus on the feedback that we receive from significant others. This process is much more common than we might realize; only a small part of our mental life is conscious and not influenced by selective inattention. The self-system may also keep people so closely focused on social feedback that they end up with a kind of interpersonal tunnel vision; in such cases, it restricts their ability to change by limiting the way they think about themselves. Because selective inattention is unconscious, self-systems can be extremely stable: "The self-system . . . is extraordinarily resistant to change by experience. This can be expressed in the theorem that the self-system from its nature . . . tends to escape influence by experience which is incongruous with its current organization and functional activity" *(Sullivan, 1953a, p. 190)*.

Children discover selective inattention when they first learn to put on an act for defensive purposes—for example, when they learn to behave as if they don't notice their parents' rejection. The results of selective inattention are identical to Freudian repression, but without the logical problems associated with the concept of repression. We avoid thoughts that might make us anxious—not by engaging the ego-repressing id instincts, but by acting as if we don't know that we have such thoughts.

Psychological Adjustment

Sullivan believed that psychological adjustment is primarily influenced by, and expressed in, interpersonal relations, particularly during the first years of life. In his view, adjustment problems are usually caused by disruptions in children's relationship with their mother—due to absence, illness, or rejection—but disruptions in the relationship between children and their father may also create problems. Such disruptions produce anxiety and negative self-personifications, problems that can be relieved by developing positive relationships later in life.

As noted, Sullivan was interested in normal personality development, and he believed that relatively few adults suffer from serious emotional problems. He also believed that a **tendency toward health** provides the ability to overcome early or childhood trauma. People are naturally disposed to avoid doing things that cause rejection and create anxiety. This is a constant tendency in life; thus, according to Sullivan, development moves inevitably toward a better capacity for relationships and an integrated self-personification, which is how he defined maturity.

Sullivan suggested that psychologists rarely see mature people in therapy and know little about them. Nevertheless, he suggested the following characteristics of maturity. Mature adults need, and have the capacity for, intimate interpersonal relations. They can perceive anxiety and insecurity in others, are sensitive to their needs, and understand their problems. In short, they have completely overcome the egocentrism of youth. They are not overtly anxious, they think primarily with syntaxic logic, they find life interesting and exciting, and they don't cause problems for themselves or others (Sullivan, 1953b).

The Individual and Society

Sullivan had a far more sophisticated understanding of the links between individuals and their societies than most theorists. As you may recall, his friends included some of the most important sociologists, anthropologists, and political scientists in the history of American social science (Mead, Sapir, Lasswell). He founded a journal—*Psychiatry*—dedicated to analyzing the social origins of psychiatric problems. And he subscribed to what he called a principle of communal existence that applies to all living forms: "The living cannot live when separated from what might be described as their necessary environment" (1953a, p. 31). In contrast with other animals, the necessary environment for humans is culture: "since culture is an abstraction pertaining to people . . . man requires interpersonal relationships or interchange with others" (1953a, p. 32). Sullivan believed that people need interaction in much the same way that they need food and oxygen. Unlike Freud, who saw culture as an external factor to which people must adapt, Sullivan believed that people are inherently social and that personality grows out of, and is sustained and modified by, social interaction—which always takes place in a cultural context. Thus people have a deep organic need for their cultures.

Sullivan's interest in the links between individuals and society was more than merely academic: He understood in a practical way the social origins of psychiatric problems. For example, as a psychiatrist in the Selective Service System during World War II, he warned that many men being drafted into the army would be stressed by the system and eventually become medical and financial burdens on the federal government. Sullivan's view contradicted official policy; General Lewis B. Hershey, the head of the Selective Service, wanted to build the army as quickly as possible, which meant inducting as many men as possible. Sullivan, however, was correct in his analysis, and he eventually resigned from the Selective Service as a result of this disagreement (Chapman, 1976).

In the last years of his life, Sullivan began to analyze social (as opposed to individual) problems. He took part in international conferences to promote communication between nations and ideologies, and worked for the World Health Organization and the United Nations. He died while attending an executive meeting of the World Federation of Mental Health in 1949.

Evaluating Sullivan

Four aspects of Sullivan's theory are problematical. The first is the writing; like that of Jung, Murray, and Kelly, Sullivan's writing is sometimes disorderly, abstruse, and idiosyncratic. This makes it hard to know precisely what his key terms mean.

BOX 7.3 Interpersonal Theory Since Sullivan

Freud has stimulated more "words" in response to his ideas than any other personality theorist, with the possible exception of the learning theorists (Chapter 8). But Sullivan's ideas have stimulated more empirical research in mainstream psychological journals than those of any theorist in this book.

The evolution of interpersonal theory since Sullivan's death can be described in terms of three phases. The first of these began in 1957 with the publication of Timothy Leary's *Interpersonal Diagnosis of Personality*. Leary's book sparked widespread interest in Sullivan's ideas among psychologists for two reasons. On the one hand, for Sullivan, personality was primarily seen during social interaction, and Leary developed a taxonomy of the structure of interpersonal behavior. Leary suggested that all social interactions are organized in terms of two themes: (a) love-hate and (b) dominance-submission. Every interpersonal act is a combination of some amount of love/hate and some amount of dominance/submission, such that, for example, the apparently open-hearted greeting of an aspiring politician would be a fusion of love and dominance: He likes you, and he wants to be your master.

On the other hand, Leary suggested that the underlying components of interpersonal behavior can be measured, using observer ratings, and that the scores from such ratings would form a circular structure that went clockwise from pure dominance with no elements of love or hate, to pure love with no elements of dominance or submission, to pure hate with no elements of dominance or submission, to pure submission with no elements of love or hate. Leary called this structure the interpersonal circle and suggested that it can be used to describe the typical interpersonal behavior of individuals, couples, or groups.

As we mentioned in Chapter 2, the development of research in personality—and any other field of scientific inquiry—depends on the availability of a taxonomy of the subject matter. Drawing on Sullivan's theory, Leary provided a particularly useful one for the study of interpersonal behavior. The second phase in the evolution of Sullivan's interpersonal theory involved the development of resource exchange theory *(see Foa & Foa, 1974; Foa & Foa, 1980; Foa et al., 1993)*. Following up on Sullivan's suggestion that interpersonal behavior is a kind of exchange, U.G. and E.B. Foa *(1974)* carefully analyzed the structure of the exchange process. Specifically, they described the kinds of resources exchanged during social interaction and the order in which these resources become important during development. They also provided a taxonomy of the relationships among the resource categories. According to the Foas, all resources can be organized in terms of two major dimensions—concrete-abstract and general-particular—which, in turn, can be arranged along the perimeter of a circle. In effect, then, there is a circular order to the relationship among the resources that are exchanged during social interaction.

The third phase has entailed the conceptual and psychometric synthesis of the ideas of Leary and Foa by a number of researchers including Lorna Benjamin *(1993)*, Robert Carson *(1991)*, Donald Kiesler *(1982)*, and especially Jerry Wiggins *(1996)*. Drawing on Sullivan, Leary, and Foa, Wiggins suggested that social life is organized in terms of two very broad dimensions that David Bakan

(1966) called agency and communion. Agency concerns actions designed to enhance oneself and one's position in life; communion concerns building relationships with others. According to Wiggins, people need status and love, which are fundamentally interpersonal needs because their satisfaction requires the presence of other people. They are also the primary resources that are exchanged during social interaction. That is, after dealing with another person, we always gain or lose a little bit of status and gain or lose a little bit of love.

Based on the degree to which an action involves giving to or taking away status from another person, as well as giving or taking away love, it is possible to specify the exact nature of every interpersonal exchange. In this connection, Wiggins and his associate P. D. Trapnell (1996) provided massive mounts of data showing that interpersonal behavior has a remarkably orderly structure—a circumplex—in terms of which all existing measures of personality can be interpreted. Others, too—including Benjamin and Kiesler—have drawn on Sullivan's ideas to generate a large volume of research as well as an impressive set of measurement procedures designed to measure personality and diagnose interpersonal problems.

Second, although anxiety is a key concept in Sullivan's theory, he uses the word to refer to "virtually all basic types of emotional suffering. . . . It perhaps would have been better if Sullivan had employed a different term to designate so broad a spectrum of painful feelings" *(Chapman, 1976, p. 79)*. For example, Freud distinguished among "neurotic anxiety," the unrealistic worrying of neurotics; "realistic anxiety," warning signals from the ego indicating that a person is in danger; and "moral anxiety," guilt caused by the knowledge that one has done wrong. More recently, Roy Baumeister distinguished among "social anxiety," fear that others will find one unattractive; "performance anxiety," fear that others will find one incompetent; and "guilt," fear that others will find one immoral. Baumeister thinks about anxiety in interpersonal terms, arguing that it is caused by the concern that one will be excluded, rejected, and driven out of one's social group. We believe that these kinds of distinctions are sensible and important, but that they are missing from Sullivan's model.

Third, Sullivan began his career studying schizophrenia. He believed that the overwhelming anxiety caused by being rejected by one's caretakers results in schizophrenia, and he claimed that it could be cured by developing a mature and enduring relationship with another person. This is an optimistic view of schizophrenia and probably true in some cases—today the term schizophrenia is often used to describe anyone who is profoundly disturbed and unable to get along in the world. But modern research strongly suggests that there is an important genetic component to schizophrenia. If so, then its cause is biological, and its cure requires using some form of biological or medical intervention rather than simply relying on interpersonal relations.

Finally, like Kelly, Sullivan had nothing to say about moral development—about where a person's sense of right and wrong comes from and how it affects his or her subsequent personality development. Whether or not one accepts the psychoanalytic analysis of this problem, Freud was correct in his view that superego development—acquiring a sense of right and wrong—is the most fundamental transformation in personality development.

Nevertheless, three features of Sullivan's theory are important and ensure his continuing relevance in the study of human nature. First, like Kelly, Sullivan identified the origins and nature of social skill. Although social skill critically determines a person's success at work and in life, the literature in vocational and industrial psychology yields virtually no definitions of social skill or methods to measure it. Yet Sullivan's theory provides some very clear hints. Social skill, he suggested, depends on overcoming egocentrism, so that one can think about what other people want, need, and expect of them. Social skill also depends on the ability to revise one's views of oneself and others in light of new feedback from others. In this respect, Sullivan's model of social skill closely resembles Kelly's.

Second, Sullivan's theory of motivation is important in light of what we know about the evolutionary origins of modern humans. Since we evolved as group-living animals, it is sensible to assume that we are innately oriented toward signs of acceptance and disapproval from other members of our group. There is obviously more to human motivation than a need to be accepted and liked—or, conversely, a need not to be rejected, spurned, and despised. But Sullivan, along with Karen Horney, defined what seems to be a quintessential human need that makes sense in terms of evolutionary theory.

Finally, Sullivan's importance is clearly demonstrated in the amount of research his theory has generated, in the quality of that research, and in the degree to which it has led to converging and replicable results. (For a review, see Wiggins & Trapnell, 1996.)

Box 7.3 considers some modern research in interpersonal theory.

Practical Application: The FIRO Awareness Scales

Although many American companies currently use a teamwork model, this was not always the case. Historically, the American workplace was organized around the concept of individual jobs and individual performance ratings. In one of the most famous studies done at the Hawthorne plant of the Western Electric Company *(Roethlisberger & Dickson, 1939)*, managers wanted to understand why new employees always started at a higher level of productivity than the existing workers, but soon reduced their productivity to the same level as the others. This was particularly puzzling given that people who produced more were paid more. Researchers were surprised to find out that employees were willing to sacrifice a higher level of compensation in order to have better relationships with their co-workers. Co-workers expressed their disapproval of anyone who produced at higher levels, so the new employees soon adjusted their own productivity levels downward.

Since the time of the Hawthorne studies, researchers have gathered an impressive body of evidence showing that interpersonal relationships in the workplace dramatically influence productivity, job satisfaction, accident rates, and other important variables. Today, employers are increasingly organizing their workplaces around the principle of teamwork. The basic idea behind teamwork is that workers will cooperate and share their skills in order to accomplish a task.

Not all teamwork approaches are successful, however, since being an effective team member requires some skill in interpersonal relations, a topic not taught in most schools. For this reason, many managers have instituted programs to help people identify and improve their own interpersonal styles. One measure of interpersonal skill widely used in industry is the Fundamental Interpersonal Relations Orientation (FIRO) Awareness Scales.

The FIRO Awareness Scales *(Shutz, 1958)* are designed to help people develop an awareness of themselves and the way they relate to other people. Although the FIRO scales address a number of interpersonal situations—including a child's behavior toward other children, a person's relationship with his or her parents, and a person's satisfaction with the feelings and behaviors of his or her partner—the most commonly used measure, the FIRO-B (B refers to behavior), assesses a person's relations to others at work.

The FIRO-B can help people understand how they communicate with others in terms of three interpersonal needs: Inclusion, Control, and Affection. Inclusion relates to the amount of contact with others that a person seeks, Control relates to a person's need for power or dominance, and Affection relates to the amount of closeness with others that a person desires. These three needs are further categorized along the dimensions of Expressed, which is the extent to which a person initiates a behavior, and Wanted, which is the extent to which a person wants or accepts a behavior from someone else.

Results from this measure can be used to identify the roles that people play within a teamwork situation. For example, people with low Wanted Inclusion scores tend to be individualists, those with high Wanted Affection scores tend to be listeners, and those with high Expressed Control and low Wanted Affection scores tend to be taskmasters.

Table 7.3 describes some FIRO-B results in terms of the impressions others may make.

TABLE 7.3 FIRO-B Results and the Impressions Others Make on You

If you have	Then you may perceive	If you have	Then you may perceive
High Wanted Inclusion	Most rejections as devastating Being away as "missing the action" Lack of acknowledgment as negative	Low Wanted Inclusion	Most invitations as obligatory Being singled out as threatening Group time as wasteful
High Wanted control	Any structuring as inadequate Standard procedures as important Sole responsibility as burdensome	Low Wanted Control	Any control as too much Plans and structures as pressure Competitive behavior as annoying
High Wanted affection	Lack of expressed concern as insensitive Infrequent feedback as frustrating Distance from others as a personal loss	Low Wanted Affection	Reassurances as superficial Personal questions as intrusive Emotions as distracting and trying

8

J. B. WATSON, E. L. THORNDIKE, B. F. SKINNER, AND ALBERT BANDURA

Learning Theory and Personality

- The Distinctive Features of Learning Theory
- A Brief History of Learning Theory
- Core Problem: Predicting and Controlling Behavior
- Learning Theory and Human Nature
- Evaluating Learning Theory
- Practical Application: The One Minute Manager

This chapter concerns what has historically been the most popular approach to personality in American psychology—learning theory, which encompasses classical conditioning, behaviorism, instrumental conditioning, operant conditioning, and cognitive social learning theory.

Despite the fact that behaviorism and learning theory have dominated American psychology, most personality psychologists are deeply critical of the behaviorist approach to personality. And most behaviorists are deeply critical of traditional personality theory. This antipathy is due to the assumptions that underlie learning theory. The four distinctive features of learning theory are discussed below.

The Distinctive Features of Learning Theory

Behaviorists and learning theorists have a particular and consistent view of how to make psychology scientific. They argue that the essence of science is public verification—that others must be able to replicate a researcher's findings before the findings can be accepted.

Because scientific psychology involves finding law-like relationships among observable phenomena, theoretical ideas that are not observable have no place in scientific psychology. According to this view, unobservable phenomena such as the ego, archetypes, the self, needs, and traits are probably not scientific. So the first distinctive feature of behaviorism is a self-conscious effort to be scientific by restricting research to relations among phenomena—such as behavior—that can be observed.

The second distinctive feature of behaviorism concerns the cause of behavior. Traditional personality psychology assumes that there are stable structures inside people that control and explain their behavior. Although traditional theorists disagree about the nature of these structures, they agree that the structures exist and determine behavior. Behaviorists reject this assumption on the grounds that internal structures cannot be observed. Indeed, they maintain that internal structures are irrelevant to our understanding, inasmuch as observable factors in the environment such as "cues" and "reward contingencies" cause behavior. This view, which amounts to a total repudiation of traditional personality psychology, has presented a formidable intellectual challenge to the field.

The third feature is closely related to the second. Every traditional theory of personality has some assumptions about human motivation at its core. But behaviorists regard such assumptions as futile; motivational concepts, they say, are not only unobservable but unnecessary, because what people do depends on factors in the external environment rather than on internal motives.

The fourth distinctive feature of behaviorism concerns the nature of personality development. In traditional personality psychology, development is stage-like and involves "qualitative transformations": In other words, adults are qualitatively different from children as a result of certain internal transformations associated with psychological development. Personality theorists may disagree as to the nature of these transformations, but they agree that the transformations occur. For the behaviorists, however, development involves acquiring new behaviors, or changing old ones, through learning. This is a steady process with no dramatic transformations, and adults differ from children only in that they are older and therefore have learned more behaviors.

We close this overview with two observations. First, behaviorism—and cognitive social learning in particular—dominates much of American psychology today. In fact, many people consider behaviorism literally the truth rather than one viewpoint among many.
Second, we agree with the behaviorists' view that, when studying people, what matters is what they do, not what they say or believe. We also agree that interventions such as psychotherapy and education are pointless unless they change how people behave. But behaviorists define the goal of psychology as the prediction and control of behavior, not the explanation of behavior. We typically wonder why people behave as they do, but behaviorists usually avoid the "why" question.

A Brief History of Learning Theory

Behaviorism, the dominant perspective in American psychology since World War I, is the foundation of modern experimental psychology. It evolved over time and several subschools have emerged, ranging from radical behaviorism to cognitive social learning theory. This section of the chapter traces the theoretical roots of the movement.

British Empiricism. Aristotle observed that events that are similar or opposite, or that occur close together in time or space, are perceived as being associated with each other. John Locke (1632–1704), the first British empiricist, developed Aristotle's ideas further in his *Essay Concerning Human Understanding (1690)*. Locke suggested that true knowledge comes from experience only, rather than from reasoning or logic. The mind of a newborn infant is a *tabula rasa,* or blank tablet, because the infant lacks experience but is ready to receive it. Knowledge comes from building mental links or associations between experiences. For example, when a child cries and a caregiver appears, the child then "knows" that crying and help are somehow linked.

Building on Locke's ideas, David Hume (1711–1776), the most important British philosopher of his age, criticized the concept of cause and effect. His view resembles Aristotle's proposal that, when events occur together, we often mistakenly assume the first caused the second. Hume argued that cause and effect cannot be demonstrated. For example, when one billiard ball hits a second, all we see is one event following another. The belief that the movement of one caused the movement of the other is a connection that we form in our minds, but it may not be true.

David Hartley (1705–1757), another British empiricist, explained the perception of cause and effect in terms of activity in the brain. Hartley proposed that intense vibrations within the central nervous system cause sensations and that less intense vibrations cause ideas. Finally, John Stuart Mill (1806–1873) suggested that simple ideas, based on simple associations formed out of experience, come together in the mind to form more complex ideas; he referred to this process as "mental chemistry." British empiricist philosophy, especially as applied to epistemology—the study of how we acquire knowledge—is the theoretical backbone of behaviorism.

Pavlov and Classical Conditioning. Ivan P. Pavlov (1849–1936), the son of a poor Russian village priest, won a government scholarship to the University of St. Petersburg, where he studied the new mechanistic physiology that had also intrigued young Sigmund Freud. Pavlov was particularly interested in the physiology of digestion. In 1890, after many years of poverty, he became a professor at St. Petersburg Military-Medical Academy. Equipped with a fine laboratory and a large staff, he began studying digestion in dogs, using surgical techniques that he invented. He was awarded the Nobel prize for physiology in 1904 for these studies, and his research on digestion is still cited in medical textbooks.

Among the digestive reactions that Pavlov studied was salivation. A splash of diluted acid on a dog's tongue produced a lot of saliva. Pavlov then noticed that dogs who became accustomed to the laboratory routine would salivate as they were being placed in the laboratory harness, before acid was placed on their tongues. Pavlov called this phenomenon "psychic secretions."

After receiving his Nobel prize, Pavlov spent the rest of his life studying psychic secretions. In his most famous experiment, Pavlov showed a dog some food, and the dog began to salivate. Next, Pavlov rang a bell just before showing the dog the food. After a few trials, the dog, upon hearing the bell, began to salivate; the dog had associated the bell with food. Pavlov called the food an **unconditioned stimulus**—because food normally caused the dog to salivate; he called the bell a conditioned stimulus; and when the bell caused the dog to salivate, Pavlov called the salivation in response to a bell a **conditioned response**. The link between the conditioned stimulus (the bell) and the conditioned response (salivation) constituted a **conditioned reflex**. Pavlov's study demonstrated that if one observable event—salivation—reliably follows another observable event—a bell ringing—then an association has been formed between the events. He argued that understanding associations of this sort is all one needs to develop a science of the mind. Knowing about the mental state of the dog is unnecessary to explain its salivation in these circumstances.

Pavlov's view of how two phenomena become associated in the central nervous system is called **classical conditioning**. Behaviorists use classical conditioning to explain how people acquire fears and aversions. Suppose, for example, that a person eats oysters and then becomes ill; he may later avoid eating oysters because of this unpleasant earlier experience. Through a process known as **stimulus generalization**, the person may associate oysters with scallops and refuse to eat scallops as well. In Pavlovian terms, the person's nervous system has been altered by an association between oysters and illness, but he will probably be unaware of the source of this attitude toward oysters.

While studying the process of stimulus generalization, Pavlov made a discovery that was even more important than the conditioned reflex. First he taught a dog to choose a circle over an ellipse by giving the dog treats for choosing the circle. Then he made the choice more difficult by making the ellipse more like a circle. At some point, as the ellipse neared a circular shape, the dog essentially experienced a "breakdown," becoming highly agitated, frantic, and unable to continue the experiment. Moreover, this agitation lasted for a long time. Pavlov suspected that the dog's reaction was much like a nervous breakdown in humans and referred to the dog's reactions as an "experimental neurosis."

Pavlov also noted individual differences in terms of how the dogs broke down. Dogs who were quite active prior to the experimental neurosis became even more so afterward—constantly chewing, howling, and scratching. In contrast, dogs who were more placid before the experiment seemed depressed afterward. Pavlov attributed these differences in behavior to differences in the activity level of the dogs' brains.

Many psychologists were excited to think that complex human behavior could be analyzed in terms of associations formed through conditioning. By the 1920s, Russian researchers were actively studying the effects of classical conditioning on human behavior, a tradition that continues in Russian psychology today.

John B. Watson and Behaviorism. Pavlov eventually became a Soviet national hero because his mechanistic psychology "proved" the materialistic basis of Marxist theory. Specifically, Pavlov had shown that learning could be produced using observable or material processes—as opposed to mental processes. By World War I, Pavlov's influence had spread to the United

States, where his ideas were instantly popular. Many younger psychologists, dissatisfied were the introspective psychology developed by Wilhelm Wundt, eagerly adopted Pavlov's research perspective.

Interest in behaviorism was further stimulated by an increasing concern with real-life problems. For example, Lightner Witmer, who in 1890 started the first psychological clinic in the United States at the University of Pennsylvania, did so after a teacher brought a student to him and remarked that, if psychology were worth anything, Witmer should be able to improve the boy's spelling (Witmer, 1908).

A growing interest in animal psychology also promoted behaviorism. Because animals cannot discuss their inner states, animal psychologists had to study their behavior. As knowledge about animal learning was accumulated, some psychologists began to apply it to human learning. In fact, it was in education and child psychology that behavioral psychology first became popular.

John B. Watson (1878–1958), the man who established behaviorism as a movement in American psychology, was born in South Carolina. His pious mother wanted him to be a clergyman, but he was a fiercely rebellious young man whose life was defined by taking contrary positions. He entered Furman University at sixteen, majored in philosophy and psychology, and then decided to do graduate work in psychology in order to disprove the ideas of his major professor at Furman. Watson studied at the University of Chicago with John Dewey, who, along with William James, developed the philosophy of pragmatism. Watson took a strong dislike to Dewey's pragmatic philosophy and his introspective research methods. He turned to the study of animal behavior and completed a Ph.D. dissertation on "The Psychical Development of the White Rat" in 1903. Watson was soon seen as a "star"—the youngest Ph.D. in the history of the psychology department at Chicago, a prolific writer, and a persuasive speaker.

Watson became a professor of psychology at the Johns Hopkins University in 1908 and chairman of the department the next year. His 1913 paper, "Psychology as the Behaviorist Views It," announced the birth of behaviorism:

> Psychology as the behaviorist views it is a purely objective experimental branch of natural science. Its theoretical goal is the prediction and control of behavior. Introspection forms no essential part of its methods, nor is the scientific value of its data dependent upon the readiness with which they lend themselves to interpretation in terms of consciousness. The behaviorist, in his efforts to get a unitary scheme of animal response, recognizes no dividing line between man and brute. (Watson, 1913, p. 158)

Watson argued that psychology concerns the study of *behavior*, not mental or psychological states. He also believed that the appropriate goal of psychology is to predict and control behavior, rather than to explain a person's psychological state. And finally, Watson argued that the laws of behavior are the same for animals and people, and that there is nothing distinctive about human behavior.

Having declared the traditional research methods of psychology bankrupt, Watson needed an alternative, which he found in Pavlov's classical conditioning. In 1919 Watson published *Psychology from the Standpoint of a Behaviorist*, which relied heavily on Pavlov's concept of conditioned reflexes. However, Watson had no real experimental data to support his behaviorist theory. He and his associate Rosalie Rayner gathered that data in his study of Little Albert—one of the most famous and controversial studies in the history of American psychology. The Little Albert study showed how fear could be conditioned in children.

Little Albert was a quiet and well-adjusted nine-month-old with no unusual fears. Like all children, however, he was afraid of loud noises. Watson wanted to determine if fear could be conditioned in an infant, if the conditioned fear would generalize to other objects, and if the fear would last beyond the experiment. Watson and Rayner put Little Albert on a table and then showed him a white rat. As Albert touched the rat, they hit a steel bar with a hammer, making a loud noise. After they had done this seven times, Albert began to cry as soon as he saw the rat.

Subsequently, Watson discovered that Albert was also afraid of a rabbit, a dog, a sealskin coat, a Santa Claus mask, and Watson's white hair. Albert was still afraid of these objects thirty-one days later. Albert's mother took him out of the experiment shortly thereafter. No one knows whether Little Albert's fear of rats and other furry objects ever went away *(Harris, 1979)*, but the experiment named after him certainly showed that emotion can be conditioned—that people can be trained to fear arbitrary objects.

Watson left his wealthy and politically influential wife and married Rosalie Rayner, causing a major scandal and forcing Watson to leave Johns Hopkins and academic life altogether. He moved to New York and began a very successful career in advertising. During his relatively short academic career, Watson changed the face of American psychology forever. In later years, he wrote an article on behaviorism for The Great Soviet Encyclopedia and lectured on the topic, but the Little Albert experiment was his last serious piece of psychological research.

Probably the most important point to remember about Watson's behaviorism is his emphasis on how the environment "shapes" adult behavior. Watson argued that all children are born with similar tendencies, that any differences in their adult behavior must be caused by environmental factors, and, therefore, that controlling a child's environment can determine adult behavior. In 1926, Watson issued his famous challenge:

> Give me a dozen healthy infants, well-formed, and my own specified world to bring them up in, and I'll guarantee to take any one at random and train him to become any type of specialist I might select—a doctor, lawyer, artist, merchant-chief and, yes, even into a beggar-man and thief, regardless of his talents, penchants, tendencies, abilities, vocations and race of his ancestors. *(1926, p. 10)*

Thorndike and Instrumental Conditioning. Edward Lee Thorndike (1874–1949) grew up in New England as the son of a Methodist minister. As an undergraduate at Wesleyan University, he edited the college newspaper, won his class tennis championship, excelled as a student, and read William James's *Principles of Psychology*. He went to Harvard to study literature, took some classes with James (who was an inspirational teacher), and decided to become a psychologist. Thorndike chose to build his academic reputation by studying learning in chickens.

Harvard had no tradition of animal research, so Thorndike kept his chickens in William James's cellar, much to the delight of James's children. He built a series of connected pens, separated one chicken from the rest of the flock, and observed how long it took the chicken to find its way back to the flock. He found that the chickens solved the puzzle more and more rapidly with practice.

In 1897 Thorndike won a graduate fellowship to Columbia University and moved to a New York apartment accompanied by "the most-educated hens in the world." With laboratory space at Columbia, Thorndike began to study cats, observing how they escaped from a set of "puzzle boxes." When placed in a puzzle box, the cat made a series of random actions—clawing, chewing, jumping—until it hit the switch that released it. When placed back in the box, the cat tended to repeat the last thing it did before escaping and, with practice, escaped the box increasingly sooner.

On the basis of his observations of animals in puzzle boxes and mazes, Thorndike *(1905)* proposed a theory of animal learning known as **connectionism** or **instrumental conditioning**. The theory encompasses two "laws." The first, the **Law of Exercise**, states that the tendency to repeat an action is related to the frequency with which it has occurred in the past. The second and more important **Law of Effect** states that actions that lead to positive outcomes are more likely to be repeated in similar situations in the future.

Thorndike *(1933)* also speculated somewhat about the physiological processes associated with reinforcement; but like Watson, he stressed that learning can be explained entirely in terms of environmental factors—particularly the connection between actions and rewards. His theory is known as instrumental conditioning because behaviors that lead to or are instrumental in bringing about rewards tend to be stamped in or retained *(Hilgard & Marquis, 1940)*. Thorndike had a long, active, and successful career: During his lifetime, he was the most famous psychologist in America after his teacher, William James. Out of all his many publications, however, he is primarily remembered for the Law of Effect.

B. F. Skinner and Operant Conditioning. B. F. Skinner is the most famous American psychologist in the history of the discipline. Burrhus Frederick Skinner—known as Fred—was born in 1904 in the little railroad town of Susquehanna, Pennsylvania. His father, a self-taught lawyer for a coal company, was passive and depressed; he often lamented during his crying spells that he and Fred were failures. Skinner's mother was dominant, vain, and manipulative, and frequently complained about the problems she had experienced while giving birth to Fred. Skinner's parents favored his younger brother, who died suddenly while Skinner was in high school. Skinner helped perform the autopsy on his brother, and the pathologist described his assistance as "helpful." Upset by their younger son's death, Skinner's parents tried to keep Fred close to them. Independence and emotional detachment thus became major issues in his life, and he saw behaviorism as a way to "protect" people from their emotions.

Fathers of learning theory (clockwise from upper left): Skinner, Watson, Pavlov, and Thorndike.
Sources: National Library of Medicine; Underwood & Underwood/ Corbis; San Faulk/New York Times Co./Archive Photos; National Library of Medicine.

Skinner described himself as an impossible child, but he was bright, did well in school, had considerable musical talent, and began writing for publication when he was ten. In 1926 he graduated Phi Beta Kappa from Hamilton College with a degree in English.

After college, Skinner returned home determined to be a novelist, but he encountered a writer's block, went into a depression, then discovered Pavlov and Watson. At that point he decided to become a behaviorist and, in 1927, entered the graduate program in psychology at Harvard. For two years, Skinner "would rise at six, study until breakfast, go to classes, laboratories, and libraries with no more than fifteen minutes unscheduled during the day, study until exactly nine o'clock at night and go to bed" *(Skinner, 1970, p. 9)*. In his eight years at Harvard he was a very successful student; it was there that he developed the essential features of his perspective, which he called "operant conditioning."

Skinner joined the psychology department at the University of Minnesota in 1936 and in 1938 he published *The Behavior of Organisms*. During World War II, he worked on a project in which he trained pigeons to serve as guidance systems for missiles. Although the project was successful, technological advances made the pigeon systems unnecessary, much to Skinner's regret. The war ended, and in 1945 Skinner became chair of the psychology department at Indiana University. This circumstance set off the second major crisis of his career: He was deeply ambivalent about leaving his practical army research for the tedium and triviality of academic life. On an impulse, and virtually overnight, he wrote his best-known work, *Walden Two*, a utopian novel that sold over two million copies and made Skinner an intellectual celebrity. *Walden Two*, published in 1948, describes an ideal society based on Skinner's ideas about behavioral engineering. In 1948, he returned to Harvard as professor of psychology. The energetic Skinner published *Science and Human Behavior* in 1953, *Verbal Behavior* in 1957, and *Schedules of Reinforcement* with Charles Ferster in 1957, and the American Psychological Association gave him a Distinguished Scientific Contributor Award in 1958. Thirteen years later, in 1971, he published *Beyond Freedom and Dignity*, where he argued that freedom is a myth and that the future of society depends on even greater control of human behavior. The book created a storm of controversy and made him even more famous. Skinner died in 1990, a few days after receiving a lifetime achievement award from the American Psychological Association.

Skinner's perspective is the endpoint of the tradition defined by Pavlov, Watson, and Thorndike. Skinner argued that Pavlov and Watson were incorrect in focusing on stimulus events that come before an action. Like Thorndike, Skinner argued that what matters is what happens *after* an action. That is, a stimulus may elicit a response, but what happens to a person after he or she responds determines what that person will do in the future. Skinner called the relationship between a response and the consequences of that response **operant conditioning**.

Assume, for example, that you step off a curb and into a street, you hear a horn, and you step back on the curb. The next time you step into a street and hear a horn, you step back on the curb even more quickly. Pavlov and Watson would have said that you became conditioned to the sound of the horn. Skinner, on the other hand, would have argued that what is important is that you weren't hit by the car. In Skinner's terms, behavior is a function of its consequences. You do something—that is, you perform what he called an operant response— and something happens. If what happens is positive or desirable, then you are more likely to repeat that action or operant response. (Table 8.1 illustrates the differences among the theories of Pavlov, Watson, Thorndike, and Skinner in the context of generous behavior.) Skinner's primary contribution to behaviorism is the concept of shaping. Shaping involves modifying someone's behavior in a desired direction by controlling the consequences of that person's behavior along the way, and behavior modification is the method used to shape human behavior. Behavior followed by reinforcement is more likely to be repeated than behavior that is not followed by reinforcement. Because behavior is a function of its consequences, behavior can be reinforced in order to increase the likelihood that it will reoccur. However, the behavior that one wants to change must be visible, observable, and measurable.

In summary, Skinner's operant conditioning differs from Pavlov's classical conditioning in that it ignores the physiological basis of behavior; it differs from Watson's behaviorism in its deemphasis on the role of a stimulus in learning. Above all, Skinner insisted that psychology should study only phenomena that can be observed. According to Skinner, the goal of psychological research is the prediction and control of behavior, a goal that makes a theory of human nature unnecessary.

TABLE 8.1 What Creates Generous Behavior? Explanations from Classical Conditioning, Behaviorism, Instrumental Conditioning, and Operant Conditioning

Learning Theory	Creator	Rationale
Classical conditioning	Ivan Pavlov (1849–1936)	Learning occurs when a person makes associations between stimuli. These associations become part of the neural structure.
Example: A parent hugs and praises his child whenever she shares her toys with her sister. On a neurological level, the child develops a reflex that associates sharing with pleasurable feelings. This reflex generalizes to other behaviors and the child grows into an adult whom others might describe as generous.		
Behaviorism	John B. Watson (1878–1958)	Learning occurs when a person is conditioned to respond in a certain way to a particular stimulus. Behaviorists believe that forces in the environment, rather than neural connections, cause behavior.
Example: A parent who hugs and praises his child for sharing creates an environment in which the child learns that pleasurable feelings will follow the act of sharing. As long as the child is in an environment that encourages sharing, she will continue to share with others.		
Instrumental conditioning	E.L. Thorndike (1874–1949)	The more times a specific response is linked with a specific stimulus, the more likely the response will occur in the future. Behavior is shaped by forces in the environment.
Example: If a parent only occasionally hugs and praises his child after sharing, the sharing behavior may not be learned. Consequently, the child may not grow into someone whom others would describe as a generous adult.		
Operant conditioning	B.F. Skinner (1904-1990)	Learning occurs on the basis of what happens after a person responds to a stimulus. What happens afterward is called a reinforcement.
Example: If a parent rewards sharing behavior with hugs and praise that are valued by the child (positive reinforcement) or does not require the child to go to bed at her usual time (negative reinforcement), the child is more likely to continue to share. Conversely, if the parent reacts to sharing behavior by scolding the child (punishment) or shows no reaction to sharing behavior (extinction), the child's sharing behavior will eventually disappear.		

Albert Bandura and Cognitive Social Learning Theory. In 1963, the same year that
Skinner published *"Behaviorism at 50,"* Albert Bandura and Richard Walters published *Social
Learning and Personality Development,* a book that changed learning theory forever. Their
book reported experiments showing that children can learn new behaviors simply by watching
others and without reinforcement, findings that challenged the foundation of traditional
behaviorist theory. Bandura and Walters called their approach cognitive social learning and
suggested that it could explain personality development better than traditional behaviorism
or any other theory. Cognitive social learning theory not only ignores reinforcement; it also
relies on cognitive factors—which are not observable—to explain learning. Because Bandura
emphasizes cognitive factors in the development of personality, he is known as a cognitive
social learning theorist. (Table 8.2 illustrates the differences between operant conditioning
and cognitive social learning—again, in the context of generous behavior.)

Albert Bandura was born in Mundara, Alberta (Canada), in 1925; his parents were Polish
immigrants. He graduated from the University of British Columbia and, in 1952, received
a Ph.D. in clinical psychology from the University of Iowa. A year later, Bandura moved to
Stanford University, where he spent the rest of his academic career.

In collaboration with Richard Walters (1918–1967), Bandura published Adolescent
Aggression in 1959, and their 1963 book *Social Learning and Personality Development*
elaborated the social learning model. In the years that followed, Bandura and his students
further refined the model, then extended it to analyze a variety of troubled or flawed
behaviors.

Bandura's basic argument is found in his first book, *Adolescent Aggression* (Bandura & Walters,
1959). In this excellent study, Bandura identified two samples of boys who were closely
matched on age, IQ, social class, family intactness, and geographical locale. The only
difference was that the boys in one group had been brought to the attention of the local
police for their overtly aggressive behavior. By studying closely the dynamics of the aggressive
boys' families, Bandura made an important observation. These families differed from the
families of the nonaggressive boys in two ways. First, the fathers of the aggressive boys were
themselves quite aggressive. And second, the fathers of the aggressive boys paid the most
attention to their sons when the conversation concerned the boy's aggressive (mis)behavior.
Bandura concluded that the boys' aggressiveness could be explained by two factors in their
environment: (1) an adult model for aggressive behavior, and (2) reinforcement—by adult
attention—for behaving like the adult model.

Here, Bandura believed, was the explanation for personality development. Individuals'
distinctive characteristics are a function of the models to which they have been exposed
and the behaviors for which they have been rewarded. Bandura's career has largely involved
analyzing the specific factors involved in modeling and showing how modeling can explain
everything from delinquency to prejudice.

Bandura has had an enormous influence on modern American psychology. Indeed, cognitive
social learning theory is probably the most popular theoretical perspective in social, clinical,
and personality psychology today. Bandura has written major papers on a variety of topics,

TABLE 8.2 What Creates Generous Behavior? Operant Conditioning versus Cognitive Social Learning

Operant Conditioning	In operant conditioning, what happens after the response will determine the likelihood of a response occurring in the future. For example, the parent's response to a child's sharing behavior (positive reinforcement, negative reinforcement, punishment, or extinction) determines the frequency with which the child engages in sharing behavior. The parent's reactions "shape" the child's behavior and generalize to behavior as an adult. In this way, the parent's reinforcement influences behavior so that the child grows up to be someone people would label as either generous or stingy.
Cognitive Social Learning	In social learning,—also known as observational learning—the child learns sharing behavior by observing the behaviors of others. The child sees what happens to others when they share and experiences vicarious reinforcement. But in order for the child to learn to share, four conditions must be fulfilled: the child must pay attention to the sharing behavior being performed by someone else; the child must remember the behavior; the child must have the skills to share (as well as something to share and someone to share with); and the child must be reinforced for sharing. This reinforcement can occur at a cognitive level and does not need to be observable. Although researchers who accept the operant conditioning model would not agree with this interpretation, cognitive social learning is currently the most popular model among learning theorists for how behavior is learned.

been active in professional psychology, and received many honors and awards for his research contributions. He was elected president of the American Psychological Association in 1974 and has served as David Starr Jordan Professor of Social Science in Psychology at Stanford. Bandura also received a Distinguished Scientific Achievement Award from the American Psychological Association and is currently a Fellow of the American Academy of Arts and Sciences.

Core Problem: Predicting and Controlling Behavior

At the turn of the twentieth century, American psychologists began trying to solve practical problems—curing mental illness, teaching children to read, eliminating prejudice, training good citizens. The laboratory psychology model, imported from Germany and based on introspection, seemed useless for solving such problems.

Psychoanalysis developed in Europe at about the same time that behaviorism developed in North America, and the two perspectives were competing alternatives to introspectionism. Although psychoanalysis seemed useful for treating certain kinds of emotional problems, it also had some obvious limitations as a science. For example, it attempted to explain a person's present behavior in terms of unverifiable events that happened in early childhood. In this sense, it took an approach known as retrospective explanation. Freud himself once commented that psychoanalysis could never be more than a retrospective science.

Pavlov and Thorndike showed that animals could be conditioned to behave in predictable ways. Watson and others demonstrated that human behavior could also be conditioned, and by the 1920s researchers in Pavlov's laboratories had conditioned humans to salivate just like the dogs they had conditioned earlier *(Smither, 1984)*. In short order, early behaviorists found that a wide variety of human behavior could be conditioned to respond to environmental cues such as lights, buzzers, or words from a hypnotist. Thus, in a real though limited sense, it can be said that behaviorists are able to predict and control a person's behavior. This achievement, they believe, is the proper scientific goal of psychology—which is why they see themselves as inherently more scientific than traditional personality psychologists.

Learning Theory and Human Nature

Motivation

Traditional personality psychology uses motivational concepts to explain people's behavior. In the early twentieth century, personality psychology was dominated by psychoanalysis and its emphasis on unconscious sexual and aggressive motives. Not surprisingly, behaviorists rejected the psychoanalytic theory of motivation because unconscious instincts are unobservable.

Like the British empiricists, most behaviorists assume that people are naturally motivated to seek pleasure and avoid pain, and that these tendencies can be demonstrated in the laboratory. Specifically, according to Skinner, the consequences of a response will be either pleasant or aversive. After a large meal, for example, a person may feel either satisfied or stuffed; how much that person eats at the next meal will be affected by the results of the prior meal. For that matter, when a person does anything, one of four consequences will affect the likelihood that the person will do it again. These four consequences are positive reinforcement, negative reinforcement, punishment, and extinction, and they are defined as follows.

Positive reinforcement is what takes place when an action is followed by pleasant outcome. Food, which fulfills a biological need, is a primary reinforcer; praise, which fulfills a nonbiological need, is a secondary reinforcer. Being praised, winning a competition, eating a great dessert, and making money in the stock market are all positively reinforcing. Behaviors that are followed by positive reinforcement are likely to reoccur in the future. In Skinner's view, positive reinforcement is the most powerful influence on behavior.

Negative reinforcement occurs when an action is followed by the cessation of an unpleasant condition. People take off heavy clothing when they become too hot, parents stop closely supervising their children when they begin acting responsibly, and criminals are granted parole when they appear to be reformed—and actions, such as these, that are followed by the termination of an unpleasant experience tend to be repeated. Students who take required courses "to get them over with" are responding to negative reinforcement.

Punishment occurs when an action is followed by unpleasant consequences. Flunking courses, getting fired, and being humiliated in public are punishments. Even the mere prospect of punishment can control behavior. For example, people pay taxes to avoid going to jail, practice religion to avoid going to hell, and diet and exercise to avoid becoming unattractive. In such cases, other behaviors are avoided because of their possible unpleasant consequences.

Extinction is the gradual disappearance of a behavior that is not reinforced. For example, when Skinner first tried to write a novel, his efforts were neither rewarded nor punished. As a consequence, his interest in writing fiction began to decline. Because his behavior—novel writing—was not followed by any consequence, and thus was not reinforced, the behavior eventually ceased.

Paradoxically, the behaviorist contribution to the theory of motivation is the argument that the concept itself is unnecessary—on the grounds that behavior can be more simply and scientifically understood in terms of schedules of reinforcement than in terms of motivation. Note, however, that Bandura departs from the strict behaviorist view inasmuch as he believes that people can think about the consequences of their actions. And if they think about these consequences, he argues, they can be self-motivating. For example, once a boy learns to be aggressive, he may also learn that aggression can lead to positive outcomes. The anticipation of a positive outcome can then motivate him to commit future aggressive behavior. Bandura's view of motivation closely resembles that of George Kelly, who also argued that the concept of motivation is useless.

Personality Development

Traditional models of development, such as psychoanalysis, believe that development unfolds from the inside, and that it unfolds in the same way for each child. In behaviorist terms, by contrast, "personality"—defined as the way people behave in public—reflects each child's unique learning history: Development is directed from the outside, and it unfolds differently for each child. From infancy, people retain behaviors that were followed by desirable outcomes, and personality is essentially the sum of these experiences. Moreover, development never ends, because experiences constantly change and people adjust their behavior to the demands of changing life circumstances. In 1945, Skinner proposed creating special environments for infants that would stimulate their development in desirable ways. Box 8.1 describes one such environment: Skinner's baby-in-a-box.

Bandura also defines personality development in terms of learning more sophisticated responses to problems; he believes that learning results from observing others rather than from being punished or rewarded. Vicarious reinforcement, he points out, occurs when consequences experienced by someone else change the behavior of the person who observed these consequences. For example, a young girl may see a movie about a doctor who becomes famous for his research, then decide to become a doctor herself. Similarly, vicarious punishment can occur if a child sees a movie in which a criminal is punished.

Not all behavior that is observed is also learned. Watching a professional tennis player will not automatically improve one's tennis serve. For observational learning to take place, Bandura (1986) believes that four conditions must occur. First, the viewer must pay attention to the behavior that is being modeled. Second, the viewer must remember the behavior. Third, the

viewer must have the skills necessary to reproduce the behavior that has been observed. And finally, the model's behavior must lead to positive outcomes. Only when these four conditions are met will people learn by observing and be able to perform the observed behavior.
In summary, the social learning view of personality development closely resembles the general behaviorist view that development consists of learning new behaviors, and that adults differ from children only in that they have learned more behaviors.

Self-Knowledge

According to Skinner, we know about ourselves in exactly the same way that we know about other people—by observing our own behavior and looking for trends. Self-knowledge is the same as knowledge of others, and we don't know anything about ourselves that other people couldn't know if they watched us.

Behaviorists are often accused of ignoring consciousness. Skinner *(1974)* suggested that this is not true; behaviorists, he said, regard consciousness as necessary in order for people to report their feelings to others, but consciousness is not very useful as an explanatory concept. For example, a person who believes that he is happy will base that belief on some kind of evidence. To the behaviorist, it is the evidence—and not the reported feeling—that is important. In the behaviorist paradigm, a person can say that he is happy because he smiles, whistles, and sings—but not vice versa. In other words, the inner state of conscious happiness does not cause the behavior.

People often describe themselves as "friendly," "honest," or "intelligent," but behaviorists believe that these words tell us very little. Not only do they mean different things to different people, but there is no way to determine whether individuals have described themselves correctly without some additional behavioral evidence. As a result, conscious self-reflection is not a reliable source of self-knowledge.

In contrast to mainstream behaviorists, Bandura *(1986)* developed a view of the self that explains how people can reflect on and change their behavior. According to Bandura, there are three steps in the self-regulation of our behavior. First, we must observe it; in a tennis game, for example, we must observe how we serve (tossing the ball, bending the knees, turning the upper body, etc.). Second, we must evaluate our behavior by comparing it to our expectations or the behavior of others; —for example, we must compare our serve to that of an expert player. Third, we must experience self-reactions—feelings of competence or incompetence that result from the comparison process.

Bandura *(1989)* describes peoples' beliefs about their competence in terms of self-efficacy. People who are high in self-efficacy believe they can take charge of problems and resolve them successfully; self-efficacy is thus the behaviorist version of self-confidence. And, indeed, confidence affects performance in many ways. For example, people with a strong sense of self-efficacy do better in school, practice birth control, make more money in life, and are less likely to smoke cigarettes *(Myers, 1990)*. In addition, they are more persistent at tasks and tend to be less anxious and depressed *(Maddux & Stanley, 1986; Scheier & Carver, 1988)*.

BOX 8.1 Baby in a Box

In 1945, Skinner wrote an article for Ladies' Home Journal describing the manner in which he and his wife had raised their newborn daughter. Skinner's attempt to make the care of infants more scientific and efficient spurred a brief interest in the application of technology to childcare. Skinner's environment for his daughter was a closed compartment about the size of a crib, but with a window on one side so the child could see out. Temperature inside the box was controlled so that the baby needed only to wear a diaper. Skinner discovered that her crying and fussing could be stopped if he slightly lowered the temperature from its usual 78 degrees. Because the child wore no clothing, she was able to exercise freely and to develop strong back, leg, and stomach muscles.

The mattress for the compartment was a tightly stretched canvas on a roller. When the baby soiled the mattress, Skinner simply unrolled the canvas further. The canvas was ten yards long and lasted about a week before it needed washing, greatly reducing the baby's laundry. Moreover, because the baby wore only diapers, her personal laundry was minimal. Skinner wrote that the baby needed bathing only once a week.

A current of warm air flowed above the canvas to keep it dry, and even the air the baby breathed was filtered. Skinner believed that the sanitary conditions of the compartment contributed greatly to his daughter's health. At the time of writing, she had never experienced a stomachache or missed a daily bowel movement. The total time necessary for infant care was about one and a half hours per day.

Despite the positive aspects of Skinner's baby compartment, some persons objected to its use. Usually, such complaints focused on its "artificiality":

> One of the commonest objections was that we were going to raise a "softie" who would be unprepared for the real world. But instead of becoming hypersensitive, our baby has acquired a surprisingly serene tolerance for annoyances. She is not bothered by the clothes she wears at playtime, she is not frightened by loud or sudden noises, she is not frustrated by toys out of reach, and she takes a lot of pommeling from her older sister like a good sport. . . . It is not, of course, the favorable conditions to which people object, but the fact that in our compartment, they are "artificial." All of them occur naturally in one favorable environment or another, where the same objection should apply but is never raised. It is quite in the spirit of the "world of the future" to make favorable conditions available everywhere through simple mechanical means. (1982, p. 122)

Skinner arranged to have compartments manufactured by the Aircrib Corporation, but the company's founder died and no further cribs were built. According to Skinner, the negative predictions about the consequences of being raised in an Aircrib environment were not borne out: His daughter did not commit suicide, descend into psychosis, or sue her father. Rather, she married and became a successful artist.

Given the advantages of the Aircrib, why didn't it become popular with the general public? According to Skinner, the infant care industry is so large and profitable that manufacturers have no incentive to make childrearing easier for mothers.

Self-efficacy is related to self-esteem, but the two concepts are not identical. Self-efficacy refers to one's sense of competence, but not to how one feels about the competence. For example, a criminal lawyer might believe she has the skills needed to defend guilty people successfully, but she may not feel good about what she does. Nonetheless, a person's self-efficacy and self-esteem are usually aligned with one another.

Unconscious Processes

Behaviorists are generally uninterested in questions about the unconscious because they believe that environmental factors are sufficient to explain behavior. In addition, they believe that all behavior is basically unconscious in the sense that it is shaped and maintained by contingencies that are not usually observed or analyzed. In Skinner's view, for example, we do what we do because the same actions in the same circumstances in the past were reinforced. But we are not always aware of the links between our actions and the rewards. The unconscious consists of nothing more than unrecognized links between behavior and subsequent outcomes; thus, it is built up through experience. In every case where a behavior seems unconsciously motivated, Skinner argued, the environmental factors that created the behavior can be identified.

Psychological Adjustment

In 1948, Neal Miller published a famous study demonstrating that neurotic behavior not only can be created by environmental factors but also can continue without being reinforced. In this study he put rats in a box with two compartments—one white and one black—with a door between them. The floor of the white compartment was electrified and shocked the rats' feet. Miller trained the rats to escape the electric shock by running into the black compartment. Later, when the floor of the white compartment was no longer electrified, the rats continued to run quickly into the black compartment. Miller then shut the door, trapping the rats in the white side of the box. Although the floor was not electrified, the rats were obviously afraid of the white side—they were tense, and they crouched and urinated. Miller concluded that the rats had developed a neurotic fear of the white compartment.

From a behaviorist perspective, neuroses are patterns of maladaptive or self-defeating behavior that have been learned *(Wolpe, 1964)*. The goal of behavior therapy, then, is to help a person "unlearn" dysfunctional behaviors and replace them with more productive alternatives. One of the most common forms of dysfunctional behavior is learned helplessness *(Seligman, 1975)*. Learned helplessness can be manifested in one of two ways: (1) as a failure to take action to help oneself or (2) as an inability to learn how to help oneself *(Miller, Rosellini, & Seligman, 1977)*. To demonstrate how helplessness is learned, J. Bruce Overmier and Martin Seligman *(1967)* placed dogs in slings so that they were unable to avoid a series of painful electric shocks; this situation taught the dogs helplessness. Later, the dogs were placed in boxes with two compartments and an open door between them. The dogs were shocked in one compartment, but rather than move into the shock-free compartment, they stayed where they were and endured the shocks. According to Seligman, people often experience the same thing: Helplessness learned in one situation is carried over to another. Box 8.2 describes a procedure for changing the way a person thinks about depression.

BOX 8.2 Learning New Thinking Skills

One of the most valuable aspects of the learning theory approach to human nature is its practical focus. As described in this chapter, learning theory grew out of an attempt to improve educational methods and to ease the suffering of people with psychological problems.

Indeed, learning theory has been widely used to manage depression—a particularly interesting problem in that twice as many women as men suffer from it. In his book What You Can Change and What You Can't, psychologist Martin Seligman (1993) proposes a behavioral approach to dealing with this problem. According to Seligman, women are more prone to depression not because they are more willing to talk about their problems, have worse jobs than men, or have a different body chemistry that causes depression. Rather, Seligman believes the incidence of depression is higher among women for three reasons.

The first is learned helplessness. Because our society often praises or criticizes boys' behavior while ignoring that of girls, boys learn self-reliance and activity whereas girls learn passivity and dependence. No matter what a woman achieves, she may still feel passive and dependent. Learned helplessness is a recognized cause of depression.

The second reason is rumination, or the tendency to think about one's problems. Women ruminate; men are more likely to act. A woman who loses her job, for example, may brood about the events leading up to getting fired; a man, on the other hand, is more likely to get drunk, to get into a fight with someone, or even to look for a new job immediately without thinking about why he lost his job in the first place. In this way, the man avoids the negative thinking that characterizes depression.

The third reason is women's pursuit of thinness, a possible cause of depression because (1) our society idealizes thinness, (2) lost weight almost always comes back, and (3) women worry more about their weight than men do. Seligman points out that in cultures that do not have a thinness ideal, the rates of depression between men and women are equal.
One approach to treating depression is cognitive therapy, which is designed to change the way a person thinks. Cognitive therapy has five components:

1. The client learns to recognize the automatic thoughts (e.g., "I am not attractive") that come at those times when she feels worst.
2. The client learns to dispute the automatic thoughts by focusing on contrary evidence. For example, she might think of friends who don't seem to care about their weight, of particular times in the past when she felt attractive, or even of people who are thin but unattractive.
3. The client learns to make reattributions, which are different explanations for the automatic thoughts. For example, instead of thinking "I'm not attractive," she might recognize that she feels most unattractive when something negative happens—such as when she receives a low grade on a test or when plans with friends fall through.
4. The client learns to control her ruminations by monitoring both the contents and the timing of her thoughts.
5. Finally, the client learns to question the assumptions underlying our thin-is-ideal society, such as the likelihood that anyone will achieve the thinness of a magazine model or that being thin automatically results in a happy, glamorous, and exciting life.

Seligman claims that this cognitive approach to dealing with depression is effective for about 70 percent of the people who use it. Changing the way a person thinks takes a few months, starting about one month after the person begins therapy. But perhaps the best aspect of cognitive behavior therapy is that it teaches new thinking skills that can be used to address other problems as well.

Learned helplessness has been used to explain depression and even susceptibility to disease *(Visinteiner, Volpicelli, & Seligman, 1982)*. According to Seligman, people become helpless when they believe their problems are caused by conditions that are (1) permanent rather than temporary, (2) located inside themselves rather than in the environment, and (3) generalized rather than specific to a single problem area *(Abramson, Seligman, & Teasdale, 1978)*. When behavior therapists deal with learned helplessness, they do not try to strengthen the ego, help the patient achieve insight, or improve object relations; rather, they focus on controlling very specific behaviors.

In summary, behaviorists regard psychological adjustment as a function of the fit between a person's behavior and his or her environment. Healthy people respond to stimuli in ways that do not make them anxious. Changing peoples' behavior is a more effective way to help them than providing them with insight into their problems.

The Individual and Society

Skinner was deeply concerned about the relationship between the individual and society, and he actively promoted behavioral methods as a way to improve society. *Walden Two (1948)* and *Beyond Freedom and Dignity (1971)* describe a society based on Skinner's principles. In *Walden Two*, a world-weary psychology professor visits a community organized according to the principles of operant conditioning. The community, which bears the same name as the book title, is run by an idealist named Frazier, and it provides its members the maximum opportunity for personal satisfaction with a minimum of waste and inefficiency. Unlike Thoreau's Walden, *Walden Two* does not urge people to seek a simpler way of life; rather, it suggests that people should use technology to promote happiness and a higher standard of living. Using behaviorist technology, the community leads a carefully planned and structured life in which the optimal development and satisfaction of each person are promoted.

Walden Two operates on a system of work credits, in which the people who have the least desirable jobs—such as collecting garbage or washing dishes—earn the most free time. No one works more than four hours per day, however, and in their free time people do the things they have always dreamed about. They perform in plays, exhibit artwork, and pursue their special interests—activities for which they would have neither the time nor opportunity in the real world. Because the community members are satisfied with their lives, there are virtually no problems with alcoholism, personal relationships, labor relations, or crime. Environmental planning and management in Walden Two have eliminated most of the difficulties that plague society.

The psychology professor is accompanied by a philosopher who is suspicious of Frazier's community. The philosopher constantly looks for faults and eventually concludes that Walden Two is a fascist and totalitarian society controlled by Frazier. Frazier shrugs off this accusation, noting that members can leave Walden Two any time, but they stay because they cannot find the same quality of life and level of personal satisfaction anywhere else.

In 1971, Skinner published his most controversial and best-known book, *Beyond Freedom and Dignity*. This book attacks two of society's most cherished beliefs: (1) that people have free will and (2) that people have a natural capacity for morality. These cherished beliefs, Skinner argues, have produced a world of waste, corruption, and unhappiness. Future social progress depends on giving up these unrealistic notions.

Behaviorists believe that people's actions reflect their earlier experiences. If criminal behavior leads to a higher standard of living, then criminal behavior will persist; if people feel better after using drugs, then they will continue to use drugs. In reality, people are not free to choose how to behave—factors in the environment cause them to "choose" specific behaviors. Consider the case of an alcoholic who stops drinking. Although society may praise the ex-alcoholic for his courage and self-control, he may not deserve any credit. He probably stopped drinking because of the marital, financial, and health problems that drinking caused. Because he would not have stopped except for these problems, environmental factors—and not courage—made him quit.

Similarly, according to Skinner, a teenager who uses drugs is not inherently immoral; rather, the feelings associated with drug use are more powerful and dependable than the feelings of social disapproval that may accompany drug use. Just as we shouldn't praise someone for doing what society values, we shouldn't blame someone for antisocial behavior. Behavior is caused by environmental factors, not individual choice. There are no bad people, only poorly designed social environments.

Skinner argued that controlling the environment would produce better social behavior, but critics have countered that people dislike social control because it seems to rob them of their human dignity. In Skinner's view, however, the concept of dignity is meaningless. We do what we do because we have been reinforced for doing it in the past; freedom and dignity have nothing to do with our behavior. According to Skinner, the concepts of freedom and dignity have prevented scientists from designing environments that optimize human abilities. People prefer to live in an inefficient world that gives them the illusion of choice rather than allow behavioral specialists to create a world in which everyone could be happy. In contrast with those who work to increase the amount of human freedom and dignity in the world, Skinner argued that the world needs less of that and more control.

Not surprisingly, *Beyond Freedom and Dignity* stimulated widespread—and often hostile— debate about behaviorism. Many readers objected that centralized control of individual behavior to make society more efficient sounded like totalitarianism. An elite corps of behavioral scientists constructing contingencies of reinforcement for the rest of society, they said, could quickly become a way to train people to follow blindly their masters' orders—with no one supervising the masters.

In retrospect, however, the hostile response to Skinner's ideal society seems to have been an overreaction. Although it is possible to use conditioning for undemocratic purposes, it is equally possible to use it to enhance the quality of life. Whether or not we believe it, many of our behaviors reflect conditioning rather than conscious choice. Obvious examples of things we do without thinking include saying "Fine" when someone asks us how we are, taking notes when a professor begins to speak, and looking in every mirror that we pass. More complex but equally habitual behaviors include taking turns in a conversation, being reverent in places of worship, and seeking attractive friends.

Bandura's cognitive social learning theory likewise suggests that society can be restructured to bring about positive change. The aspect of this theory that has the greatest implications for the welfare of society is Bandura's research on aggression *(Bandura, 1965; Bandura, Ross, & Ross, 1961, 1963)*. In this research, children who observed an adult acting aggressively, and who then experienced frustration, were significantly more likely to be aggressive themselves. The original studies used live models, but Bandura later demonstrated that children who viewed aggressive behavior on television became more aggressive. In short, there are links between televised aggression and children's behavior.

Bandura's studies have since prompted further research indicating the dangers of unrestricted television watching. One longitudinal study of television and violence *(Eron et al., 1972)*, for example, suggested that boys who viewed a great deal of televised violence in the third grade were more violent than their peers ten years later. Many researchers are now convinced that children learn violent behavior through modeling—that is, watching television.

Evaluating Learning Theory

Learning theory—especially behaviorism—changed the history of psychology. In a sense, the behaviorists were the first people to divorce psychology from both philosophy and physiology. By relying exclusively on observable behavior for their data, the early behaviorists helped to establish psychology as an empirical and scientific discipline. Not surprisingly, behaviorism is America's best-known contribution to psychology. It has influenced virtually every area of psychology, and concepts such as reinforcement are part of our everyday language.

One reason behaviorism is so popular is that it can be applied to numerous problems. For example, reinforcement is used to teach severely retarded people and schizophrenics to care for themselves, to eliminate undesirable behaviors in children, to minimize absenteeism and tardiness in the workplace, and to bring about a wide variety of behaviors that facilitate the smooth operation of society. Behaviorism is practical, it works, and it relies upon methods that almost anyone can learn.

Another important behaviorist claim—and one that sharply distinguishes it from psychoanalysis—is that learning goes on throughout one's lifetime. Psychoanalysts maintain that personality is more or less set somewhere between the first year of life and the end of the phallic period—around the age of five or six. In contrast, behaviorists argue that what we do reflects our prior conditioning—and that conditioning goes on throughout life. Thus, behaviorists can point to examples of adults who have dramatically changed their behavior in response to changes in reinforcement.

The behaviorists have undoubtedly made important contributions to understanding the origins of dysfunctional behavior. Classical conditioning, for example, shows how fears and avoidances can be conditioned. And Pavlov's research on the experimental induction of neurosis seems to explain the origins of what today is called post-traumatic stress disorder. Pavlov suggested that animals and people break down when they are placed in situations where they must perform but have no idea what constitutes successful performance. Imagine a child with an erratic parent who, at the end of each schoolday, either hugs or slaps the child. And imagine an erratic boss whose employees never know whether their performance will be greeted with a smile or a curse. Both cases would be extraordinarily stressful if they persisted—a phenomenon that Pavlov was the first to illuminate.

It is important to recognize that behaviorism is about behavior, not personality. Skinner, Bandura, and the other behaviorists almost certainly did not intend to develop a theory of personality. Nonetheless, their ideas about how people learn—especially how they learn positive and negative social behavior—have greatly influenced personality psychology. Bandura, in particular, has almost inadvertently created a theory of personality with more empirical support and scientific credibility than many of the standard views of human nature. His most important contribution has been to integrate cognitive processes into a behaviorist framework. Indeed, his concepts of self-reinforcement and self-efficacy, which are concerned with individual differences, have moved behaviorism into the mainstream of psychological thinking. For these reasons, cognitive social learning theory is the most active area of behaviorist research today.

Bandura's analysis of the observational process in learning is another important contribution. Bandura and Walters took psychologist E. C. Tolman's *(1933, 1935)* earlier distinction between learning and performance—that reinforcement is not necessary for learning although it may encourage performance—and applied it to human learning. This distinction clarified many issues that traditional behaviorist learning theory cannot explain. For example, the cognitive social learning explanation of how children learn to speak grammatically—that they learn by imitating adults—is far more logical than an explanation based on trial-and-error learning accompanied by reinforcement. In Bandura's view, society offers so many possibilities for learning though observation (e.g., movies, television, and reading) that conditioning must be only a special case of learning.

Social learning has several practical applications. For example, behavior modeling is used to improve skills in everything from interpersonal relations to golf or tennis by having students observe the performance of professionals. Along the same lines, Bandura's conclusion that children learn aggression by watching television has caused a revolution in public attention to televised violence. Although a few researchers dispute the claim that television causes aggressive behavior, the major networks now present most violent programs later in the evening, when young people are more likely to be asleep.

Despite these contributions, behaviorism has some significant shortcomings as a theory of personality. First, most early behaviorist research was based on rats and pigeons, and critics argue that it is impossible to generalize from rats and pigeons to humans. Second, as noted, behaviorism could lead to the authoritarian control of society if the principles of reinforcement were used to channel people's emotions and behavior in the service of a totalitarian political ideology. After all, books and movies describe worlds in which people no longer have control of their lives because they are conditioned to respond to the wishes of their political masters. And, theoretically, behaviorism could be put to such uses; but it could just as well be employed to structure a world in which everyone's needs are met and all people are able to achieve their potential.

Interestingly, many of the complaints about behaviorism testify to its power. It is indisputable that the principles of reinforcement can be used to influence behavior. But why, then, is reinforcement used so ineffectively? One problem has to do with the difficulty of providing consistent reinforcement over time. In a review of reinforcement theory in management settings, for example, Bernard Bass (1985) concluded that behavioral techniques are an extremely powerful method for shaping employee behavior, but almost no one can apply a consistent reinforcement schedule over a long period of time. Therefore, it would seem that the threat of using behaviorism for political purposes is highly exaggerated.

Other critics complain that behaviorism ignores characteristics inside people. Indeed, Skinner consistently denied that thinking affects behavior; in his final speech to the American Psychological Association (1990), he referred to the study of cognition as the "creationism" of American psychology—meaning that he thought the study of cognition was unscientific. Nonetheless, behaviorists such as Bandura believe that, to understand behavior, we need to understand how people think. The cognitive social learning approach has become so popular that most behaviorists now ignore Skinner's warning about the folly of studying mental processes.

Another problem with behaviorism—especially Skinner's version—is its atheoretical nature. It is more a method (i.e., for training animals, children, and certain adults) than a theory. And in some respects, it is rather slippery intellectually. For example, Skinner did not specify in advance what would count as a reinforcement: In effect, anything that changed behavior was a reinforcement and if it didn't change behavior, it wasn't. Consequently, Skinner's definition of reinforcement—the core idea in his system—is circular.

There is also a problem with Bandura's concept of self-efficacy and its relationship to self-esteem. As you may recall, self-esteem refers to feelings of self-worth, whereas self-efficacy concerns feelings of competence. Theoretically at least, self-esteem without self-efficacy is not a problem for most people, but self-efficacy without self-esteem may well be. This issue merits further research, as it has not been carefully studied.

The question of how self-esteem is related to self-efficacy raises a more general problem with social learning theory. Although adding cognitive concepts to the behavioral model was an important step forward, cognitive social learning, like Skinnerian behaviorism, works best as an explanation for the development of relatively simple skills. What it cannot do is explain the development of more complex behaviors such as patterns of irrational or self-destructive behavior. Moreover, despite their many achievements, cognitive social learning theorists have yet to specify clearly how cognitive factors influence learning and behavior; they have only argued that such factors do so. In addition, these theorists have not explained the mechanisms of reinforcement and modeling. People differ greatly in terms of what they find reinforcing; they also differ greatly in terms of how easily they are influenced by models and in terms of the kinds of models to whom they will respond. But why these differences exist is not well understood.

Finally, it is important to note that behaviorism represents a profound and radical challenge to the very existence of personality psychology. Personality psychology is ultimately concerned with the nature of human nature—with answering the question of what people are like at the deepest level. In this respect, personality psychology is a continuation of the Socratic quest for self-knowledge. But for the behaviorists such a quest is, in principle, a futile endeavor. In their view, the reasons for our actions are located not within us but outside in the environment of reinforcers that shape our behaviors. For the behaviorists, the search for self-knowledge is pointless as long as it is directed inward. The only kind of self-knowledge worth having is knowledge of the reinforcers to which we respond.

Similarly, behaviorists dismiss the core concepts of personality psychology as useless baggage: Motivation, the unconscious, the self-concept, dreams, and aspirations are empty notions because they refer to phenomena that cannot be observed—and, in any case, the behavior they are supposed to explain can be explained more parsimoniously by the principles of reinforcement. If the behavioral approach to personality is correct, then traditional personality theory is seriously wrong. Conversely, if traditional personality psychology is correct—if concepts such as the self and the unconscious are important—then behaviorism is seriously wrong. Students should not be dismayed by this stark contrast, however, because such disputes are the essence of science. Whatever the shortcomings of the behaviorist approach, it is a powerful force—perhaps even the dominant force—both in American academic psychology and in the practice of psychotherapy.

Box 8.3 describes the life of Benjamin Franklin from a behaviorist perspective.

Practical Application: The One Minute Manager

In 1982, management professor Kenneth Blanchard and physician Spencer Johnson created an extremely popular program called *The One Minute Manager: The Quickest Way to Increase Your Own Prosperity*. The "one minute" approach was initially geared toward getting results in the workplace, but the authors soon extended their discussion to improving performance in other areas in life such as parenting and sports.

Told in the form of a story of a young manager who questions an older manager about how to become more effective, *The One Minute Manager* offers three simple rules for getting the best performance from other people.

First, successful managers are completely clear about what they expect from others. Using a practice called **One Minute Goal Setting**, managers and subordinates specify certain

BOX 8.3 Biography: Benjamin Franklin

Benjamin Franklin, the fifteenth child of a Boston candlemaker, was born on January 17, 1706. From 1718 to 1723, Franklin served as an apprentice to his brother as a printer; then he moved to Philadelphia and established himself as a printer and journalist. The publication of *Poor Richard's Almanack* (1733–1758), a book of advice and sayings such as "Time is money," made him famous in the American colonies.

In Philadelphia, Franklin started a discussion club that eventually became the American Philosophical Society. During the same period, he established such institutions as the public library, fire department, city hospital, and post office, and invented the Franklin stove and lightning rod. His book *Experiments and Observations on Electricity* (1751) was published in several languages, making him internationally famous.

From 1757 to 1775, Franklin represented American interests in England; but he eventually despaired of preserving American liberty within the confines of the British empire. In 1775, he returned to Philadelphia, was elected to the Continental Congress, and helped draft the Declaration of Independence. From 1778 to 1785, Franklin served as ambassador to France; he also helped negotiate with Great Britain at the end of the Revolutionary War. In one of his last papers, he argued for the abolition of slavery. Franklin died in 1790.

One of the most remarkable men of his age, Franklin began writing an autobiography in 1771 that detailed a self-management system that several researchers *(Knapp & Shodahl, 1974; Mountjoy & Sundberg, 1981; Snortum, 1976)* have compared to a modern behavior modification program. Franklin apparently recognized the importance of predicting and controlling his behavior, and he developed a systematic program for doing so. Two hundred years before Watson and Skinner, Franklin reported using sophisticated behavioral techniques such as recording behavior prior to shaping, stimulus control, and negative reinforcement.

When Franklin was twenty-two years old he conceived the idea of achieving moral perfection, which he intended to accomplish by breaking bad habits and developing good ones. Toward this end he identified thirteen virtues and the behaviors necessary to achieve them. These virtues and behaviors are listed below.

1. Temperance   Eat not to dullness; drink not to elevation.
2. Silence   Speak not but what may benefit others or yourself: avoid trifling conversations.
3. Order   Let all your things have their places; let each part of your business have its time.
4. Resolution   Resolve to perform what you ought; perform without fail what you resolve.
5. Frugality   Make no expense but to do good to others or yourself; i.e., waste nothing.
6. Industry   Lose no time; be always employ'd in something useful; cut off all unnecessary actions.
7. Sincerity   Use no hurtful deceit; think innocently and justly; and, if you speak, speak accordingly.
8. Justice   Wrong none by doing injuries; or omitting the benefits that are your duty.
9. Moderation   Avoid extreames; forbear resenting injuries so much as you think they deserve
10. Cleanliness Tolerate no uncleanliness in body, cloaths, or habitation.

11. Tranquility   Be not disturbed at trifles, or at accidents common or unavoidable.
12. Chastity   Rarely use venery but for health or offspring; never to dulness, weakness, or the injury of your own or another's peace or reputation.
13. Humility   Imitate Jesus and Socrates *(Franklin, 1899, pp. 88–89)*.

Having set his behavioral goals, Franklin next embarked on a program of successive approximation to achieve those goals:

> *My intention being to acquire the habitude of all these virtues, I judg'd it would be well not to distract my attention by attempting the whole at once, but to fix it on one of them at a time; and, when I should be master of that, then to proceed to another, and so on, till I should have gone thro' the thirteen: and, as the previous acquisition of some might facilitate the acquisition of others, I arrang'd them with the view, as they stand above. (1899, p. 89)*

Franklin developed a chart in which he noted the number of times he fell short in achieving perfection in each of the virtues. From this chart, he could quickly determine how close he had come to his goals. During the period he worked on this project, Franklin rose at 5 a.m., washed, planned his day, and ate breakfast. From 8 until noon he worked, ate, and read; from noon until 2 p.m. he did his bookkeeping; from 2 until 6 p.m. he worked; and from 6 until 10 p.m. he ate dinner, socialized, or engaged in his hobbies. Like Freud, he reserved a portion of each day for self-analysis; but unlike Freud he focused on actual rather than symbolic behavior.

Interestingly, Franklin regarded his greatest failure to be in the virtue of Order, and one reason he gave for this failure was a lack of training early in life. Nevertheless, he believed that his program of behavioral self-management had greatly improved both his behavior and the quality of his life:

> *In truth, I found myself incorrigible with respect to order; and now I am grown old, and my memory bad, I feel very sensibly the want of it. But, on the whole, tho' I never arrived at the perfection I had been so ambitious of obtaining, but fell far short of it, yet I was, by the endeavor, a better and happier man than I otherwise would have been if I had not attempted it. (1899, pp. 93–95)*

goals and agree on what the goals mean. Then the subordinates write out each goal on a single piece of paper using fewer than 250 words, occasionally reread the goal, and think about their performance several times a day to determine whether their behavior matches the goal.

Second, successful managers use a practice called **One Minute Praising**. Specifically, they tell subordinates that they are going to give them feedback on their performance and then praise them immediately, identifying exactly what they did right and how what they did benefits the company. Next, the managers stop for a moment of silence so the subordinates can "feel" how good the managers feel, thus encouraging them to do more of the same. Finally, the managers shake hands in a way that shows they support their subordinates' efforts.

Third, successful managers use the **One Minute Reprimand**. When things aren't going right, they reprimand subordinates immediately by telling them very specifically what they did wrong. The managers then stop for a moment of silence—again, so they can "feel" how the managers feel. Subsequently, the managers shake hands in a way that communicates the subordinates still have the managers' support. The managers remind the subordinates that each of them is valued personally—that their performance in this particular situation is not what matters most.

Finally, the managers realize that when the reprimand is over, it's over.

Although *The One Minute Manager* created a sensation and stayed on bestseller lists for months, its three core ideas are based on techniques that were developed by Skinner and Bandura some time earlier. In the book, successful managers attribute their effectiveness to One Minute Goal Setting, which, in behavioral terms, identifies the behaviors the managers want to see performed. The managers then shape behavior by using positive reinforcement (praise) and punishment (reprimand) to motivate people to accomplish their goals. In addition, the managers use the cognitive social learning technique of allowing subordinates to reflect on their own behavior.

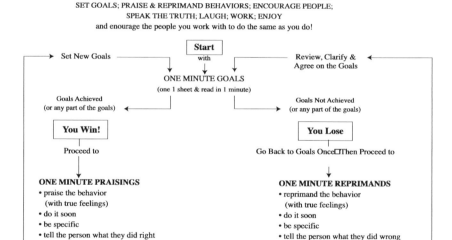

A very brief summary of
THE ONE MINUTE MANAGER'S "GAME PLAN"

How to give yourself & others "the gift" of getting greater results in less time
SET GOALS; PRAISE & REPRIMAND BEHAVIORS; ENCOURAGE PEOPLE;
SPEAK THE TRUTH; LAUGH; WORK; ENJOY
and enourage the people you work with to do the same as you do!

The One Minute approach to successful management, though deceptively simple, reflects the powerful impact that conditioning can have on all kinds of behavior.

Figure 8.1 summarizes this approach.

PART FOUR

Social Psychological Theory

9

GEORGE HERBERT MEAD, ERVING GOFFMAN, AND THEODORE R. SARBIN

Role Theory and the Sociological Approach to Personality

- Historical Context
- Core Problem: The Social Origins of Personality
- The Sociological View of Human Nature
- Evaluating the Sociological Approach to Personality
- Practical Application: The Employment Interview

Although Gordon Allport is best known for his analysis of traits and the self-concept, he often remarked that everything important in personality is related to a person's social class. Allport's comment reflects the key insight of this chapter, which concerns models of personality based on social psychology and especially sociology. Most personality theories explain human behavior in terms of factors inside people. In contrast, sociology explains behavior in terms of concepts or structures, such as social class, that exist outside people in society.

Like the behaviorists, sociologists regard concepts such as traits, needs, and unconscious motivations as irrelevant for understanding personality. Because sociological models emphasize social factors as the cause of behavior, they challenge the relevance and significance of virtually every other theory presented in this book.

Sociological approaches to personality enter psychology in the form of role theory; George Herbert Mead, the great University of Chicago sociologist, provided the first detailed statement of role theory in the 1920s. Later, role theory was elaborated in important ways by Erving Goffman and Theodore Sarbin in the 1950s and 1960s. Today, the role theory explanation of human nature is overlooked by most personality texts, but the perspective is too interesting intellectually, and too well substantiated empirically, to be ignored.

In our earlier discussion of George Kelly (see Chapter 7), we noted that his key concepts are role constructs—our theories about what others expect of us during social interaction—and roles—how we behave during social interaction based on our role constructs. We also noted that Kelly considered calling his point of view "role theory." The present chapter concerns role theory as well, so how do the two approaches differ? The difference is in the way roles are defined. For Kelly, once again, roles are what we do based on our theories about others, and every person's roles are unique. But for adherents of sociological role theory, roles are units of the social structure (e.g., father, mother, professor, student); generally speaking, our behavior is directed or controlled by the social roles that we occupy and the roles are given to us by the society or culture in which we live. Kelly's roles are unique and idiosyncratic; sociological roles are common to a culture.

Historical Context

Sociological Perspectives on Human Nature

Philosophers have always speculated about the nature of society, but Auguste Comte (1798–1857) was the first philosopher to suggest that we study social processes in the same way that we study any other natural process. In his six-volume publication, *Cours de Philosophie Positive (1842)*, Comte proposed using the methods of natural science to analyze the relationship between people and their social systems. Toward this end he distinguished between social statics—the forces that keep societies stable—and social dynamics—the forces that cause change. He also invented the term sociology.

In the same work, Comte developed a three-stage model to describe the history of human thought. The first stage, he said, is a "theological" phase that ends when religion can no longer explain the puzzles of life. Next comes a "metaphysical" phase during which the world is analyzed in philosophical terms, but without leading to progress. Last is the "scientific" phase, which Comte considered the high-water mark of human thought.

Karl Marx (1818–1883) was also a major figure in the development of modern sociology. According to Marx, the people who control the economic resources of a society (e.g., the farms and factories) will always conflict with those who have no resources. Marx believed that people are naturally cooperative, but differences in economic resources force them to compete for survival. As a result, history is an unending struggle between the haves and the have-nots, and in this sense, economics—not biology—ultimately determines human behavior. In *The German Ideology (1848)*, Marx further argued that individual personalities are primarily shaped by the conditions under which people work, a view that became a major theme in modern sociology.

Emile Durkheim (1858–1917), the father of academic sociology, was influenced by Comte, as well as by Wilhelm Wundt—the first experimental psychologist. Durkheim, too, wanted to transform the study of society into a rigorous empirical science. He believed that social facts such as the religion, culture, and economy of a particular group should be explained by other social facts rather than by the actions and desires of individuals. Durkheim also argued that societies are held together by the shared beliefs of their members, and that individual personality is shaped by the culture into which a person is born.

In his best-known book, *Suicide* (1897), Durkheim proposed that suicide is caused by poverty and urban decay rather than by individual psychological problems such as depression. The development of modern industry, he said, forced people to move from farming communities into large urban centers. In these large, anonymous industrial slums, the power of traditional social institutions such as the church, neighborhood, and family began to decline. When people no longer feel rooted in their communities, they experience anomie—a sense that life lacks meaning and purpose. According to Durkheim, **anomie**, caused by a lack of ties to one's community and traditional social institutions, is the cause of crime, alcoholism, suicide, and other social ills.

Max Weber (1864–1920), a German historian and sociologist, also studied the effects of the industrial revolution on individuals. In his best-known book, *The Protestant Ethic and the Spirit of Capitalism* (1904–1905), he discussed how religious values influence personality and behavior. Weber noticed that Protestants were usually more successful in business than Catholics. According to Protestant theology, God chooses who will go to heaven and people on earth can never know whether they have been chosen; becoming wealthy, however, is a possible sign of being chosen. Accordingly, Protestant religions encourage people to work hard, accumulate wealth, and shun worldly pleasure to improve their chances of a heavenly afterlife. As a result, the personalities of Protestant children are primarily shaped by the religious beliefs of their culture; in the ideal case, they become hardworking, tenacious, serious, thrifty, and pious.

We like to summarize the classic sociological approach in terms of the metaphor of "the river of history." Think of life as a giant river with people floating on its surface. They swim this way and that, thinking they are the cause of their motion, when in fact it is the river that sweeps them along. Events such as World War II and the Great Depression of the 1930s change forever the lives of millions of people, and there is very little that a single individual can do to avoid their effects. These and other world historical events are the river of history.

There are two points to be remembered about this metaphor. First, our lives are controlled by huge forces outside of us, forces of which we are often unaware and about which there is little we can do. Second, the river of history has a beginning and an end. It begins in a state called "community," an ideal form of human relationships that people feel are sanctioned by history—relationships in which people trust one another and depend on one another. Unfortunately, however, the river of history ends in what Durkheim referred to as anomie, the feeling that we are living in the company of strangers, most of whom we cannot trust, and that our lives have no historically sanctioned meaning.

Sociologists have accumulated considerable data to support the first point—that our lives are controlled by vast impersonal social forces. For example, Allport's remark that everything important in personality is correlated with social class appears to be true. Social class is defined by parents' income, occupation, and education, each of which can be quantified. Social-class background can predict not only one's income, occupation, and level of educational attainment but also one's choice of mates, religious preference, reading tastes, consumer behavior, dietary practices, clothing choices, sexual behavior, medical care, life expectancy, and cause of death. For this reason, sociologists are fond of saying that personality exists in the cracks and chinks of the social structure, meaning that what matters in life is the social structure and that the personalities of individuals are unimportant.

Although sociologists have collected a great deal of data showing that important aspects of our lives can be predicted by social-class background, the sociological approach confuses prediction with explanation. Much of our behavior can be predicted by our social-class background, but background doesn't explain it. To explain *why* we behave as we do, we must turn to microsociology and role theory.

Sociologists distinguish between macrosociology and microsociology. *Macrosociology* deals with large-scale issues such as the structure of society and the links between the economy and mental health. Marx, Durkheim, and Weber were macrosociologists. Microsociology, on the other hand, deals with relations between people; by definition, personality theory deals primarily with microsociological issues.

Role theory is the version of microsociology most important for personality psychology; sociologists who developed this perspective include Charles Horton Cooley, George Herbert Mead, and Erving Goffman. According to role theory, interactions between individuals become standardized and ritualized with the passage of time. These standardized interactions (e.g., the rules of etiquette) become the structures that form society—structures that, once formed, begin to control the interactions from which they originated.

Charles Horton Cooley (1864–1929) is best known today for his theory of the *looking glass self*: "Each to each a looking glass, reflects the other as he doth pass." Cooley's thesis is that we come to know ourselves based on how others react to us. William James based his famous analysis of the self-concept on Cooley's theory of the looking glass self, and Gordon Allport (Chapter 7) cited it in his discussion of traits. Cooley argued that people are inherently social and attuned to feedback from others; people internalize this social feedback, and it turns into their self-concepts. For our purposes, Cooley is important because he provided the founding insight for role theory—that personality (the self-concept) arises out of, and then feeds back into, social interaction.

George Herbert Mead and Symbolic Interactionism

George Herbert Mead (1863–1931) was a philosopher at the University of Chicago whose analysis of social interaction had a powerful influence on subsequent sociological theory and research. He studied philosophy at Harvard with William James and was also influenced by C. H. Cooley, Wilhelm Wundt, and John Dewey; it was with Dewey that he founded the Chicago school of pragmatism. Mead's ideas are an interesting blend of utilitarianism, behaviorism, and Darwinian evolutionary theory. He published little during his life but was a very influential teacher. His only book, *Mind, Self, and Society* (1934), is a collection of his lectures published by his students after he died. This book provides the conceptual basis for most modern theories of social interaction in the social sciences, and Mead himself is considered the father of role theory.

Mead's role theory can be summarized in terms of two themes—cognitive development and the development of our sense of self or identity. Starting with cognitive development, Mead believed that small children are egocentric, asocial, and dissociated. That is, they never think about how their actions affect others, they are unable to participate in society, and their personalities depend on the person to whom they are talking. In contrast, most adults think about how their actions affect others, they are able to take part in society, and their personalities are the same regardless of the person to whom they are talking. The key to these changes is development of what Mead called **role-taking ability**.

Role-taking ability, which concerns putting oneself in another person's place and thinking about oneself from the other person's perspective, develops in the process of playing games in childhood. For example, in order to play a game, even one as simple as jumprope, a child must think about what the other children in the game are doing and coordinate her actions with theirs; she can't simply twirl the rope as she pleases. If she is unwilling or unable to engage in this elementary role taking, the other children won't allow her to play jumprope.

Role taking reduces egocentrism and makes social interaction possible in the following way. From their experience in games, children generalize their various role-taking experiences. They gradually realize that playing in any game, and taking part in any social interaction, requires thinking about what others expect and then acting accordingly. Mead referred to this process as "adopting the role of the generalized other"—by which he meant thinking about what one does from the perspective of other people in general, rather than from the perspective of the specific people with whom one is presently dealing. According to Mead, cognitive development is complete when a person can adopt the perspective of the generalized other.

The second theme in Mead's role theory concerns the origins of our sense of self. According to Mead, we learn about ourselves by watching how others react to us. When we think about ourselves in terms of how others see us, we become self-aware, and the "self" that we are aware of develops out of feedback from others. In this respect, a person's sense of self or identity—which is the most private part of personality—actually begins in public. It is shaped by the manner in which other people react to us.

Mead's theory is called **symbolic interactionism**, which refers to the idea that, during interaction, we guide our behavior by what we think others expect of us. Other people rarely tell us directly what they expect; rather, their behavior expresses their expectations symbolically. Social interaction resembles play in games, in which there are various parts to play. In order to interact, one must have a part to play and one must play by the rules. And in social interaction, as in games, there are winners and losers. From a sociological perspective, we move from one interaction to another in which we play our roles, and outside these roles we don't have a personality—or at least one that matters.

Society itself is the sum of the interaction rituals that go on constantly—weddings, baseball games, drinks after work, public lectures, financial transactions, sexual encounters. In Mead's view, each interaction that we participate in gives us more information about how others see us and we revise our self-images or identities accordingly.

Mead's ideas were not very influential during his lifetime; it was his student, Herbert Blumer *(1969)*, who turned symbolic interactionism into one of the most important schools of modern sociology. In personality theory, the influence of symbolic interaction is particularly obvious in the writings of Kelly and Sullivan (Chapter 6), Sarbin (this chapter), Erikson (Chapter 11), and Hogan (Chapter 12).

Erving Goffman and Impression Management

Erving Goffman (1922–1982) received his undergraduate degree from the University of Toronto and his Ph.D. from the University of Chicago. He later taught at the University of Edinburgh, the University of California at Berkeley, and the University of Pennsylvania. In contrast with Mead, who thought about social interaction as a kind of game, Goffman likened social interaction to dramatic performance. Goffman based his analysis of interpersonal behavior on these well-known lines from Shakespeare: "All the world's a stage, And all the men and women merely players: They have their exits and entrances; And one man in his time plays many parts" (*As You Like It*, act II, scene 7).

Goffman became famous with the publication of his Ph.D. dissertation, *The Presentation of Self in Everyday Life* (1959). His six books systematically explore the links between staged theatrical performances and everyday social interactions. Although Goffman's ideas are rarely discussed in psychology textbooks, he was an influential and popular writer whose use of the dramaturgical metaphor "cemented his reputation as one of the most illuminating—and disturbing—cartographers of that shadowy terrain where man plays at being a social animal without fully understanding exactly what he is doing" *(Time, January 10, 1969, p. 50)*.

In the theater there are actors and an audience; in everyday social interaction there are actors—those who are talking and putting on a performance—and there are observers—those who are watching and waiting to perform. This actor-observer distinction is important, given the rules that govern the behavior of both parties in an interaction.

According to Goffman, when others meet us, they want to know what we are like and what we are up to. Because they watch us carefully for cues regarding our personalities, it is in our best interest to control the impressions we make. In a play the performers enact their assigned parts and carefully stay in their roles, but in social interaction we engage in what Goffman calls **impression management**, whereby we try to control the impressions that others form of us by maintaining a consistent performance.

Box 9.1 describes Goffman's ideas about the effectiveness of a restaurant metaphor for describing the way we attempt to manage impressions.

In social interaction we try to teach others how to think about us, and they try to decide if we are the persons we claim to be. Others compare what we say about ourselves with cues—such as our accent, dress, body language, vocabulary, and personal grooming—in order to form their impressions of us. So, for example, not only should we say that we are glad to see someone, we must also *act as if* we are glad to see that person.

In the process of managing the impressions we make on others, we use many tricks of stagecraft. For example, we use scenery (in the sense that we meet with the others in the location that we choose); we use props, such as cell phones, briefcases, and athletic equipment; we plan the clothes (costumes) that we wear for the occasion and may use makeup or other accouterments such as wigs, hair dye, padded bras, elevator shoes, and contact lenses; and, finally, we assume a manner, whether determined, aggressive, casual, bored, attentive, or concerned. The scenery, props, costumes, makeup, and manner that we choose for an interaction all convey a message to observers about how we want them to regard us.

There are clear but implicit rules governing both theatrical performance and social interaction. Two of these, concerning the behavior of the actor and the behavior of the audience, are especially important. First, actors on stage should stay in character (i.e., follow the script), and actors in life should be who they claim to be. For example, if a person suggests that he is a great tennis player, he should actually have some talent for tennis. Second, the audience should be respectful of an actor's efforts and applaud politely, even if the performance isn't very good; similarly, during social interaction, we should avoid challenging or criticizing another person's performance. Rather, we should be polite and pretend that we believe the other person is, for example, a good tennis player. If actors and observers obey these rules, the play can go on—and social interaction can continue. If they violate the rules, then the play—or the interaction—comes to an end.

Four implications of Goffman's dramaturgical perspective should be highlighted. First, his theory is really an elaborated and extended metaphor: "Let's pretend that social interaction is a stage performance in a play." Obviously real life is not a stage performance; nonetheless, the metaphor is useful for helping us think about aspects of social interaction that we might otherwise not notice.

Second, during social interaction, according to Goffman, we try to control the impression that others receive of us. Assume, for example, that we want to be seen as cheerful and optimistic. But when we get discouraged, we must pretend to be more upbeat than we actually feel. This raises the problem of sincerity: How do people know when we are being sincere as opposed to merely acting? The problem turns out to be an interesting and rather tricky one, because convincing others that we are sincere is, in itself, a role performance.

Third, some people believe that in dealing with others, they should "be themselves," pure and simple, and they refuse to put on a performance. From Goffman's perspective, however, this view is superficial and somewhat naïve. Whenever you observe the most elementary rules of politeness—covering your mouth when you cough, for example, or using toilet facilities rather than relieving yourself in public—you are putting on an act in Goffman's sense. But more important, no matter what you do in the company of others, they will assume that you are doing it deliberately in an effort to manage their impression of you—and they will evaluate you accordingly. Worrying excessively about how you might be evaluated by others and, conversely, refusing to consider how others might evaluate you are thus equally self-defeating and maladaptive.

Finally, we need to point out specifically how Goffman thought about personality. During social interaction, people try to tell others how they want to be regarded. They do this by putting on performances for the benefit of others—or by pretending not to put on a performance, which is the same thing. Other people watch these performances and make inferences about who we really are. However, they are mistaken because, according to Goffman, the only thing we can know for sure about another person is his or her performance. Personality is a dramatic effect, something that others attribute to us, based on our manner and appearance, the setting, and the response of the audience to our performance. To sustain a consistent performance, we as actors must constantly modify and fine-tune our actions in response to the problems that inevitably occur—buttons come off, people interrupt us, the audience is hostile. But to say that we are all actors is not to say that we are all deceitful. Rather, Goffman's point is that part of what it means to be human is to communicate with others using words, actions, and props, and to control these words and actions so as to convey our intentions and desires and acquire our desired ends.

Core Problem: The Social Origins of Personality

Beginning with Durkheim, sociologists have argued that personality is explained by social structure, not biology. Sociologists provide extensive evidence that personality is linked to social-class background; the work of Mead, Goffman, and Sarbin extends this line of analysis in an important way. Specifically, the problem with traditional sociological theory is that although we know that personality is correlated with social class, we don't know why. The contributions of Mead, Goffman, and Sarbin are their detailed analyses of the processes by which social structures create individual personality. Sarbin's ideas are especially relevant to this line of inquiry.

Theodore Sarbin and Role Theory

In the 1880s Theodore Sarbin's parents immigrated to Pennsylvania from Eastern Europe. They settled in Cleveland where Ted, the fourth of six children, was born in 1911. Samuel Sarbin was a cigar maker whose income, relative to the needs of his large family, was only marginal, and Ted grew up in working-class neighborhoods where no one went to college. Though a passionate reader, he was an indifferent student who dropped out of high school in 1928 and went to work. Later, however, he enrolled at an adult evening school and soon became a top student, graduating in 1931 at the height of the Great Depression.

Sarbin wandered the country for a while, living hand to mouth. In 1934 he entered the Ohio State University, subsisting on federal work-study money and part-time jobs in fraternity houses. He took introductory psychology with Frank Stanton, who later became president of the Columbia Broadcasting System. Sarbin decided to major in psychology; two years later, he graduated *cum laude* and Phi Beta Kappa. Sarbin completed a Master's degree at Case Western Reserve in Cleveland, then returned to Ohio State in 1938 to begin a Ph.D. program in psychology. He began studying hypnosis—a life-long interest—and published a paper on hypnotizability in 1938. Then, in the spring of 1939, he took a job in the counseling center at the University of Minnesota, where he specialized in the treatment of students with serious problems, and began work on his dissertation. Norman Cameron *(e.g., 1943)*, who pioneered role theory as a way to analyze psychiatric problems, persuaded Sarbin to think about psychiatric patients as actors putting on a particular kind of performance—playing a role—rather than as victims of disordered internal mental structures. At that point Sarbin began to analyze his "problem students" in terms of role theory.

Sarbin finished his Ph.D. in 1941. He received a two-year postdoctoral fellowship at the University of Chicago to work in the psychiatric unit at University Hospital, as well as in the sociology department. Here he discovered the ideas of George Herbert Mead: "[T]he ghost of G. H. Mead had a profound effect on me . . . [and] I began to formulate some ideas about role as a possible link between social structure and personality" *(Sarbin, 1994, p. 4)*. During this time he also attended seminars at the Chicago Institute for Psychoanalysis.

In 1943 Sarbin went into private practice, first in Chicago, then in Los Angeles, where he became very successful. In Los Angeles he interviewed a number of successful actors about their trade secrets. Despite the money and glamorous lifestyle, however, he missed "the life of the mind" and in 1949 joined the faculty at the University of California, Berkeley. During the next few years Sarbin was highly prolific, publishing a number of experimental studies of role theory. This research culminated in a major theoretical statement in 1954, after which his name became virtually synonymous with role theory in American psychology.

In 1957 Sarbin started the Center for Social Science Theory at Berkeley. Erving Goffman was a member of the group, and Sarbin described their conversations as a "turning point" during which he realized that people use their roles for purposes of impression management. Five years later, in 1962, Sarbin went to Oxford University as a Fulbright Fellow; during his time there, he began to identify himself as a "symbolic interactionist" in the tradition of Mead and Goffman. In 1969 he moved to the new campus of the University of California at Santa Cruz. And during the 1970s, influenced by the philosopher Stephen Pepper, he began to use the narrative as a metaphor for psychology. Narrative psychology maintains that people should be understood in terms of the stories they tell about themselves rather than in terms of in-dwelling psychic entities such as traits or superegos.

Sarbin retired in 1976; since then he has continued to develop his ideas about role theory, identity, social deviancy, hypnosis, and narrative psychology. A charming, magnetic, and intensely intellectual man, he inspired generations of graduate students at Berkeley. Although he is best known for role theory, his 1948 doctoral dissertation was an important paper in the history of clinical psychology—especially with respect to the clinical versus actuarial prediction problem (Sarbin, 1943). This problem concerns how best to predict a person's behavior—through tests or through the judgment of trained psychologists. Moreover, his 1960 book, co-written with Ronald Taft and Daniel Bailey, strongly influenced the development of cognitive theory models of clinical psychology. Sarbin's many contributions make him one of the most important writers of his generation.

Overview of Role Theory

Sarbin argues that psychology has historically made a mistake by basing its theories on natural-science metaphors. As an alternative, he proposes the use of metaphors from history and drama. He suggests that social behavior is governed by roles, some of which exist in society (e.g., student and teacher) and some of which we make up for ourselves (e.g., rock fan, fitness buff, tropical fish fancier). Social behavior, then, consists of playing these roles, behaving as if they were real. Roles are always played in relation to other people in other roles. Consequently, role playing depends on paying attention to the expectations of others, guiding our actions by what we think they expect us to do. A major goal of social interaction is to create an impression, to persuade others that we have certain desirable characteristics and don't have certain undesirable ones. In essence, our roles define our personality, and outside our roles it is hard for us to interact with other people.

Sarbin argues that our behavior should be understood in terms of the roles we are playing and, indeed, that roles are part of the social system; even the roles that we make up for ourselves are taken from our culture. In short, our behavior is caused not by hypothetical intrapsychic structures such as traits, ego defenses, and feelings of inferiority but, rather, by the roles that we are playing at the moment—motorist, customer, student, football fan, and so forth. Social life thus consists of moving from one role to another, as we move from one interaction to the next.

Since the emergence of their discipline, sociologists have been trying to predict peoples' behavior using patterns of events in society. For example, when they correlate rates of mental illness with the state of the economy, they find that admissions to mental hospitals increase as the economy gets worse. However, as we pointed out earlier, prediction is not explanation. Sociologists can predict a boy's delinquency on the basis of his parents' education, occupation, and income, but these factors do not explain why the boy is delinquent. The problem is that social facts and individual personalities do not exist at the same level of analysis: People don't interact with social facts, they interact with other people. Why, then, is personality correlated with social class—and how are individuals linked to the social structure? The role-theoretical answer is deceptively simple. Roles are units of the social structure—for example, every business or governmental agency has an organizational chart that specifies the roles that exist within it. And associated with each role are certain standards of performance. For example, an important role in a university organization is that of faculty member. There are specific requirements regarding how people should behave while in that role—show up for class, be prepared, answer questions—and others expect them to do just that. Moreover, they know what is expected of them and will either respond to these expectations or risk being fired. In short, roles and role expectations form the link between the individual and the social structure.

Box 9.2 illustrates role theory's usefulness in the context of biography.

The Sociological View of Human Nature

Motivation

Although Sarbin doesn't talk about motivation, his two major motivational assumptions are easy to identify: first, that life consists primarily of social interactions, and, second, that it is during those interactions that one's personality emerges. In fact, Sarbin notes emphatically that "[i]n order to survive as a member of society, the individual must be able accurately to locate himself in the social structure" *(1968, p. 506)*. The initial step in any interaction is to decide who we are (what role we will play), who the other players are (what roles will they play), and what norms or expectations apply to the roles (how the roles are supposed to be played). This is a cognitive process that takes place very quickly. The process is driven by a need for predictability: We need to know who we are, who the others are, and what the rules are in order to have a competent if not satisfactory interaction.

After determining our own roles, the roles of others, and the norms governing our interaction, we actually play the role. In Sarbin's terms, we enact it. Moreover, we do so according to a large number of rules, maintaining a certain posture, gaze, tone of voice, level of attentiveness, vocabulary style, and so forth in order to retain the approval or avoid the disapproval of others. If our role performance doesn't meet the expectations of others, they may reject us: "[I]n role enactment we always remain alert to other persons, real or imagined, and to their actual and their likely reactions to our behavior" *(Sarbin and Allen, 1968, p. 529)*. Thus,

BOX 9.2 Biography: Ronald Reagan

The biography of Ronald Reagan, the fortieth president of the United States, is ideally suited to reveal the shortcomings of traditional personality theories as models for interpreting individual biographies, while at the same time revealing the strengths of role theory for the same purpose. Reagan was not introspective and rarely if ever engaged in self-analysis. His lack of introspection probably reflects the fact that he was a profoundly optimistic person who "had a genius for happiness" *(Bosch, 1998, p. 27).*

In any case, it seems difficult to interpret Reagan's life in terms of underlying conflicts, traumas, or dark preoccupations. He was sunny, contented, and supremely self-confident, and nothing made him defensive. His lack of introspective tendencies appears to have thoroughly confounded his observers. Reagan chose Edmund Morris, the Pulitzer Prize–winning biographer of Teddy Roosevelt, to be his official biographer; but Morris interviewed Reagan repeatedly over fourteen years and finally gave up trying to understand him. Morris's controversial *(1999)* biography of Reagan is essentially a novel or fabrication. Others, too, found Reagan to be enigmatic. As his son Ron reported, "You are not going to figure him out. That's the first thing you need to know. I haven't figured him out. I don't know anybody who has figured him out" *(Bosch, 1998, p. 13).* We believe role theory provides a sensible clue to Reagan's biography. But first we need to ask, What about Reagan needs to be explained?

In our view, the most interesting aspect of Reagan's life is his success. He was successful at everything he tried to do. He was born in 1911 in Tampico, Illinois, the second son of an Irish father who was charming and affable but also a drunk and ne'er-do-well, and a devout Scottish mother who was intensely ambitious. Reagan's father moved the family constantly until 1922, when they settled in Dixon, Illinois. Reagan describes as a turning point in his life the occasion when, at age eleven, he found his father passed out on the front porch. He dragged him inside—it was winter—and never forgave him for his public display of drunkenness. Reagan described his mother as "a lovely Christian lady who devoted her life to helping other people." She enjoyed staging morality plays in which good triumphs over evil. Reagan frequently performed in his mother's morality plays and learned to love acting.

At the time of his baptism, Reagan's mother gave him a book that, he told his biographer, was the most important book he ever read. "It is the story of a young Christian man born in a rather ugly industrial midwestern town, who discovers through a series of bitter experiences with an alcoholic father that he has the gift of oratory. He is able to inspire young people in the town toward good works. . . . And through his good looks and his voice and his convictions he manages to create a whole social movement in this town. And at the end of the book, the young man . . . goes off to Washington to take his message to the world" *(Bosch, 1998, pp. 30–31).* The message concerned independence, self-reliance, and decency, and Reagan told his mother that he wanted to be just like the hero of the novel.

According to role theory, people should be understood in terms of the stories they tell about themselves and their lives, rather than in terms of psychic entities such as traits or superegos. The story Reagan told about his life was precisely the story of the novel's hero. The interesting point here is that very few of Reagan's observers believed his simple story; they all thought that there must be more to Reagan than his commitment to his simple Christian script of saving others through good work and persuasive oratory.

Reagan had a very successful high school career; a handsome, athletic young man, he played varsity football, captained the swim team, had the lead role in all the school plays, was class president and school president, and wrote short stories and poetry. For seven summers, the last three of high school and the four during his college years, Reagan was a lifeguard at Lowell Park on the Rock River. During that time he pulled seventy-seven people from the river and further elaborated the role he loved best—the hero. After leaving the White House in 1988, and though suffering from Alzheimer's disease, he still enjoyed talking about his days as a lifeguard on the Rock River.

In 1928 Reagan entered Eureka College, a religious school founded by his mother's sect, the Disciples of Christ. He had a marvelously successful college career. He was a reporter for the school paper and president of the Booster Club, played varsity football for three years, and became head cheerleader for the basketball team, the school's number-one swimmer, editor of the yearbook, member of the student senate for two years, and president for one. Again, he had the lead role in most of the school plays.

Reagan graduated in 1932, at the height of the Great Depression, and set off in search of a job in radio, the dominant entertainment medium of the day. He went from station to station, starting in Chicago and slowly moving west; eight months later, he landed a job as a sportscaster and staff announcer in Davenport, Iowa, at a very attractive salary. He was an immediate success and by spring he was promoted to NBC's main radio station in Des Moines, Iowa. He worked there for five years and became a midwestern celebrity: "Handsome and well dressed, he had his pick of the most eligible women and was welcome at Des Moines' most fashionable establishments" *(Bosch, 1998, 38)*.

In 1937, Reagan followed the Chicago Cubs to Southern California for spring training; he then went to Hollywood and took a screen test with Warner Brothers. Based on his poise, grooming, and good looks, he was immediately signed to a contract. When he stepped onto a movie set for his first film, he felt immediately at home. He also felt at home working for a large corporation—he was a born "company man." Although he never achieved the status of an Errol Flynn or a James Cagney, Reagan's movie career was quite successful prior to World War II; he was regarded as a highly promising young man and one of Hollywood's most eligible bachelors. He moved from success to success, signing a million-dollar contract with Warner Brothers at the time he was inducted into the Army Air Force. Because he had terrible eyesight, Reagan spent the war making propaganda and training films in Culver City. He said he developed a profound respect for those who actually went into combat, and he made this point repeatedly during the rest of his career.

When Reagan was released from the army in 1945, he decided to dedicate his life to trying to save the world through politics. He joined the Screen Actors Guild and rapidly rose in the organization, first becoming a board member, then being elected president six times. In the Screen Actors Guild, Reagan learned about communism and concluded that the communists who were active in the unions were more interested in promoting communism than in improving working conditions for union members. Reagan witnessed violence at the studio gates—buses overturned, windows smashed, bloodshed—and became a passionate anticommunist as a result. He also became an FBI informant and testified at the House Un-American Activities Committee hearings.

In 1948 Reagan's first wife, the actress Jane Wyman, sued him for divorce. This outcome was due in part to politics—she was more radical than he—and in part to the fact that her career was rising rapidly and his was beginning to fade. After his divorce, Reagan went through the only "down" period of his life. He quickly revived after meeting Nancy Davis in 1951; they were married the next year and entered into the closest partnership in political history. Nancy was as ambitious as his mother, very protective of Reagan and his reputation, and thereafter their lives were continuously interwoven. Their relationship was so close that even their children felt excluded.

Reagan's movie career continued to flounder. He was out of work during most of 1953 and in debt when General Electric hired him in 1954 to host General Electric Theater on weekly television. Reagan's weekly TV appearances made him a national celebrity. More important, his contract required that he visit GE facilities ten weeks a year, giving speeches and boosting morale. Between 1954 and 1962, Reagan visited all 135 GE plants and met 250,000 employees. No politician had ever met so many ordinary Americans on the campaign trail. During this period, he came to despise government interference in business. By 1959 his political beliefs were in place: He would save America from communism, on the one hand, and from government intrusion in business, on the other.

By the late 1950s, Reagan was the second most sought after speaker in the United States (after Dwight Eisenhower). His hostility toward communism and big government made him the favorite of conservatives everywhere. He also attacked socialized medicine, income tax, and Social Security. In 1962, after criticizing the Tennessee Valley Authority—a major client of GE—he was fired. Reagan strongly disliked Lyndon Johnson's Great Society, and he became co-chair of the Goldwater for President Committee. In 1964, his speech on national television nominating Barry Goldwater raised $8,000,000 in campaign contributions and made Reagan a national political celebrity. Two years later, in 1966, he ran for governor of California and used his simple but effective conservative vision to win by a landslide. After he was reelected in 1970, people began urging him to run for president. As his aide Lynn Nofziger noted, "What got me when I began working for Reagan . . . was the fact that people out there were excited about him. . . . He was just an instinctually nice man who attracted people to him and he was articulate and he was a man of conviction. No, there was never anything phony about Ronald Reagan, and maybe that's what it was" *(Bosch, 1998, p. 114)*.

Reagan thought he was the heir apparent to the presidency after Richard Nixon, and he ran in 1976 as an outsider (a person not part of the Washington establishment). He lost the primary to Gerald Ford in a close contest. At the Republican convention, after announcing his acceptance, Ford invited Reagan to the platform. Reagan gave a short, impassioned speech rallying the faithful and mending fences, and the speech was judged "magical." Many people believed the Republicans had chosen the wrong nominee—and then, four years later, it was Reagan's turn. During the 1980 presidential campaign, Reagan presented himself as the person who could save America from a period of poisonous self-doubt and loss of direction. In 1981, at age seventy, Ronald Reagan became president of the United States.

Our argument here is that the distinctive feature of Reagan's biography is success. There is some debate about how successful his presidency was, and there were major problems during his second term. But Reagan is generally credited with winning the Cold War and bringing about the demise of the Soviet Union, restoring public confidence in America, and precipitating the longest economic recovery in financial history. After winning reelection in 1984, Tip O'Neill, the

Democratic Speaker of the House and Reagan's primary political antagonist, told Reagan: "In my fifty years of public life, I've never seen a man more popular than you with the American people" (Bosch, 1998, p. 250).

How can Reagan's success be explained? Four factors are important, though they've been overlooked by biographers and psychologists. First, he was very bright: As an actor he learned his lines effortlessly, his staff suggested that he had a photographic memory, and he repeatedly detected the political mood of the country before his staff. Second, he was extremely competitive and ambitious, though outwardly so smooth, charming, and genial that few people appreciated how intense and focused he actually was. Third, he was very well organized; Tip O'Neill said that Reagan's transition into the White House in 1980 was the smoothest and most efficient in history. But most important, from the perspective of this chapter, Reagan had superb role-playing skills.

Reagan was poised, graceful, witty, relaxed, and charming—a master of self-presentation. He could "read" an audience, sense what they wanted to hear, and deliver a message more effectively than any politician in recent memory. Reagan loved to go on television and get his message out.

All you wanted to do is fix the camera on his head and let him talk. . . . He was able to speak in ways that the American people believed and in a language that they understood and agreed with. . . . [H]e vocalized their frustrations and hopes and fears and gave them a vision. He said, you know, there really is a shining city on a hill. And they wanted to believe it. . . . His communication was . . . empathetic, and that's really what established that special link between Ronald Reagan and the American public. (Bosch, 1998, p. 155)

As noted, Reagan's biographers and observers found him mysterious and enigmatic. They were unable to determine what he was really like, way down deep. The legacy of psychoanalysis is that people are best understood in terms of their dark side. However, from a role-theoretical perspective, Reagan is more readily comprehended in terms of his public role than in terms of his private thoughts, feelings, insecurities, and repressed memories. Reagan wanted to be a hero, to save America from communism, from government interference, and from the mood of pessimism and self-doubt that prevailed in 1980. That was the role he chose to play—and, indeed, role theory offers a better model for understanding him than traditional depth psychology.

the assumption behind role enactment is that normal people are sensitive to the reactions of others, and that they need positive feedback from others during social interaction.

In fact, all microsociologists—including Cooley, Mead, and Goffman—implicitly assume that people need predictability and positive social feedback, and that these needs govern social interaction. But why, one might wonder, are sociologists so reluctant to analyze human motivation? The reason, we believe, is that they want to put as much distance as possible between themselves and psychoanalysis. This is an interesting aspect of Freud's legacy.

Personality Development

Sarbin describes development in terms of three themes: the development of the self, social identity, and role learning. These developmental changes are directly tied to the pattern of interactions in which a person is involved. As observers, what we see when we interact with other people are their role enactments. As actors, our role enactments are controlled and explained by (1) our self-concept, (2) our social identity, and (3) the repertoire of social roles that we know how to play.

The Self. The self is the sum total of all the inferences that we make about ourselves, based on past interaction: "The term 'self' refers to the inferences the person makes about the referent for 'I.'" *(Sarbin and Allen, 1968, p. 522).* Sarbin *(1952)* describes the development of the self in terms of five stages.

1. *Somatic Self:* During the period from birth to about one month, children learn that their body is different from the rest of the world, and that there are limits to their being.

2. *Physiological Self:* During the period from two to six months, children learn that they have internal states (i.e., that they can be hungry, wet, cold, or in pain). They also learn that, because these states are internal, they belong to themselves and not to the external world.

3. *Primitive Construed Self:* During the period from six to nine months, children learn that people are different from, for example, bottles and blankets. They also begin to recognize particular people on the basis of their typical gestures and ways of handling the children.
4. Introjecting Self: During the period from nine to twelve months, children learn to play and to take part in "pretend" activities such as peekaboo. They also begin to discern and imitate a few words.

5. *Social Self:* After the first year, children are increasingly able to distinguish others on the basis of their social roles, to see themselves from an external perspective, and to assign labels to themselves such as "bad boy," "good girl," "brave," and "stupid." By the end of this fifth stage, they have a small but real sense of self and are ready to take part in social interaction.

Social Identity. Social identity is the view we have of ourselves during social interaction; it answers the questions "Who is he?" "Who are you?" "Who am I?" If someone asks you who you are, you will answer in terms of your social identity. In many cases, this amounts to telling the other person about your occupation—for example, teacher, bull fighter, actor, student.

Social identity varies along three dimensions: status, value, and involvement. Status concerns the power and social esteem associated with an identity. Value concerns the social acceptance associated with an identity. And involvement concerns the amount of time a person spends in an identity each day. The status and value associated with a social identity depend on how a person performs in that role. That is, one can't simply claim to be, for example, a college professor and then expect respect and acceptance from others on that basis. A person who claims to be a professor must also act the part—which means being well read, well spoken, intellectually motivated, and concerned about trying to pass along one's intellectual enthusiasm to younger people.

Social identity is at the heart of Sarbin's theory. Life in society, he said, consists of a continuous series of interactions, and interaction depends on having an identity. But our identity also puts constraints on our behavior: We must make sure that our behavior supports, and doesn't undermine, our social identity. Thus, for Sarbin, social behavior is a function of a public concept—social identity—and not a private desire.

Role Repertoire. In order to interact with others, we must have a social identity; we must also know how to act so as to support that identity. Maintaining a social identity depends on fulfilling the requirements of certain roles. Sarbin defines a role as "an organized set of behaviors that belongs to an identifiable position" *(Sarbin and Allen, 1968, p. 545)*. Moreover, role enactments always occur vis-à-vis complementary roles, which he defines as counterplayers—mother-son, teacher-student, lawyer-client. Thus, according to Sarbin, learning a role requires learning what others expect of us when we are in that role and what we can expect of people in complementary roles: "[I]n role enactment we always remain alert to other persons, real or imagined, and to their actual and their likely reactions to our behavior" *(Sarbin and Allen, 1968, p. 529)*.

Role learning in childhood essentially consists of learning to do what one is told. The roles that adults play are less explicit and less well defined; and in many cases, adults invent the roles they play. Sarbin *(Sarbin and Allen, 1968)* suggests that people probably learn roles in adulthood through the process of imitation and modeling, as described by Albert Bandura *(1986; see also Chapter 8)*.

Unconscious Processes

As a clinical psychologist, Sarbin knows that people sometimes do things without being able to report the reasons for their actions. He explains this phenomenon in terms of organismic involvement, by which he means that people play their roles with varying degrees of intensity or absorption.

Sarbin identifies eight levels of role involvement. At Levels I and II, people play their roles with considerable detachment. Level III refers to the degree of involvement that the reader is currently experiencing. At Level IV, people are absorbed in a role to the point that they temporarily forget who they are and, for a short period of time, identify themselves with the role. For example, they might briefly lose their temper while driving in traffic.

At Level V, people are so thoroughly engrossed in a role that they act as if they *are* the role. Sarbin's example is a person who has been hypnotized—and whose physiology has changed in response to hypnotic suggestion. While playing the role of a hypnotic subject, the person is substantially engrossed by it.

Level VI characterizes hysterics, people who take their social roles so seriously that they act

BOX 9.3 Two Views of the Self: Jung Versus the Sociologists

Of all the personality theorists, none was more interested in the self than Carl Jung. In fact, Jung believed that our most basic drive is to achieve individuation by discovering the self.

As you may recall, Jung defined the persona archetype as the mask we wear in social situations. All societies have rules about social interaction, and it is the job of the persona to organize our behavior so that we can successfully interact with others. But to achieve individuation, Jung argued, we must move beyond the persona and explore deeper, more complex aspects of our personality such as the shadow and hero archetypes. In Jung's view, people who live solely at the level of the persona are, at best, superficial and uninteresting. At worst, they can be overwhelmed by other archetypes in the collective unconscious and become seriously ill.

No sociologist would concur with Jung's view of the self. From a sociological perspective, what lies in the unconscious (a concept that not all sociologists accept in the first place) is knowledge about social rules that helps us conduct social interaction. In short, personality consists of the performances that we provide for other people. Even when we are alone, according to sociologist George Herbert Mead, we still perform for what he called the "generalized other."

This difference between the Jungian and sociological approaches to personality highlights a point from the first chapter regarding the definition of personality: Whereas sociologists see personality as the role performances that create reputation, Jungians see personality as an inner core. Sociologists would argue, for example, that we know a person is polite because other people say so. But Jungian psychologists would wonder if politeness is merely part of that individual's persona, rather than a genuine aspect of his or her personality. This issue of whether our inner core or our reputation reflects our personality more accurately is one of the most intriguing questions in personality psychology.

as if they have no personality other than their roles. Unlike hypnotic subjects, hysterics stay in their roles for long periods of time.

Level VII is called "ecstasy"; it refers to a level of role involvement not frequently seen in everyday life. Ecstasy occurs, for example, during religious conversion experiences in which people are "possessed," they speak in tongues, walk on burning coals, or enter trance states. People remain in ecstatic states for only short periods of time.

Level VIII, or "bewitchment," is the most extreme form of role involvement. At this level, people enter a state of possession and remain there, often with fatal consequences. Examples include victims of black magic or voodoo death:

> The man who discovers that he is being boned by an enemy . . . stands aghast. . . . His cheeks blanch and his eyes become glassy. . . . His body begins to tremble and the muscles twitch involuntarily. He sways backward and falls to the ground, and after a short time appears to be in a swoon. . . . From this time onwards he sickens and frets. . . . Unless help is forthcoming in the shape of a countercharm administered by . . . the medicine man, his death is only a matter of a comparatively short time. *(Basedow, 1925)*

This discussion of role involvement suggests that Sarbin defines the unconscious in terms of the degree to which people are engrossed in their roles. When deeply absorbed, he suggests, they are controlled by factors outside their awareness. Sarbin's analysis thus closely resembles Jung's discussion of the persona; as Jung noted, to the degree that people are consumed by their social roles, their actions are under the control of unconscious processes. Box 9.3 contrasts the Jungian and sociological views of the unconscious and the self.

More recently, Sarbin (1995) has analyzed the development of identity using what he calls the **Quixotic principle**. Don Quixote, the protagonist of Miguel de Cervantes' novel, read extensively about medieval Spanish chivalry, overidentified with the figure of a knight-errant, and set out in search of adventures such as slaying dragons and saving damsels in distress. Sarbin notes that at various points in history, entire generations of young people have similarly been caught up in identities that were vividly portrayed in the entertainment media; consider, for example, the 1960s teenagers who imitated the appearance and lifestyle of British rock musicians. Their behavior, like that of Don Quixote, seemed unconsciously motivated. Indeed, one of the most useful contributions of the sociological tradition is the finding that peoples' behavior is often controlled by themes from their culture—roles, values, and other social expectations—of which they seem completely unaware.

Self-Knowledge

Like Sullivan and Mead, Sarbin defines **self-knowledge** in terms of reflected appraisals: What we know about ourselves depends on how others react to us; by observing others' reactions to our role performances, we come to understand ourselves.

Self-knowledge is not factual; we don't know ourselves in the same way that we know how tall we are, how much we weigh, and what color our eyes are. Rather, self-knowledge is like a story we tell about ourselves, based on our memory of the reactions of the other people with whom we have dealt over the years. Because we base our self-narrative on the reactions of many different people, and because we creatively compose our self-narrative, self-knowledge is also like a theory that can be only partially verified. For Sarbin, then, it is misleading to ask about the accuracy of a person's self-knowledge. The story that we tell about ourselves is our story; it is the only one we have, and its accuracy is purely relative. Thus self-knowledge is subjective.

At the same time, however, self-knowledge has consequences. Every social interaction, according to Sarbin, begins with a series of questions: What role will we play in that situation? What role is the other person playing? And what rules or expectations will govern the interaction? Those people who answer these questions in idiosyncratic ways, or who cannot accurately locate themselves and others prior to an interaction, will fail, be rejected, or suffer some sort of punishment. Thus, although self-knowledge is subjective, it has important practical consequences.

Psychological Adjustment

For Sarbin, psychological adjustment has nothing to do with inner psychological states such as unconscious trauma and repressed emotions. Rather, he argues, adjustment involves three cognitive variables that underlie the process of role playing. The first concerns the fit between our self-concept/social identity and the roles that other persons expect us to play. For example, women who see themselves as intelligent, competent, and worthy of high-status roles in business, government, or the military must often deal with the fact that men expect them to play more subservient roles. This scenario inevitably results in tension, which continues until either the women change their views of themselves or the men change their expectations.

The second cognitive variable influencing psychological adjustment is the number of roles we are able to play. As Norman Cameron put it, "[T]he person whose repertory includes a variety of well-practiced, realistic social roles is better equipped to meet new and critical situations than the person whose repertory is meager, relatively unpracticed and socially unrealistic" *(1947, p. 465)*. Thus psychological adjustment depends on our being able to play enough different roles, in a sufficiently competent fashion, to meet the expectations of the other people with whom we must deal.

The third cognitive variable is role-taking ability—the ability to understand the expectations of others during social interaction. In this context Cameron *(1943)* argued that the essence of paranoia is an inability to understand others' expectations, leading people to develop a theory about others' expectations that is disconnected from reality—and to act accordingly. Similarly, Harrison Gough *(1948)* argued that psychopathy, or serious delinquency, is caused by a failure of role taking and a loss of self-control. To the degree that people understand what others expect in a social situation, they will regulate their behavior accordingly. Conversely, if they do not understand what others expect, there will be no social constraints on their behavior, leading them to be both impulsive and insensitive to the consequences of their actions.

There is considerable evidence to support Sarbin's claim that people classified as maladjusted are deficient in role-taking and role-playing skills. Sarbin would explain the origins of this deficiency in terms of early social experience. Modern research, however, increasingly suggests that neurological deficits may account for a person's inability to understand the expectations of others during social interaction *(Lykken, 1995)*. In fact, a potential problem with sociological models is that they minimize the importance of biological variables and, in doing so, risk cutting themselves off from the mainstream of scientific thinking.

The Individual and Society

We have noted several times in this chapter that sociologists have found consistent links between social structural variables such as social class and personality variables. Because these concepts exist at two different levels of analysis, there is the problem of explaining how they are linked.

This is the core problem in Sarbin's theory, and, as we noted earlier, he solves it in a deceptively simple but logically persuasive manner. Roles, he argues, are elements of the social structure, and they are defined by social rules, regulations, and historical custom. The role of president, for example, is defined by the U.S. Constitution. When a person is playing a particular role, we know that there are certain standards that apply to the performance of that role, and we expect the person to live up to those standards. To continue with our example, we expect a person in the role of president to be honorable, to represent us well when dealing with foreign powers, and to be the president of all the people rather than just a small group of friends.

People playing roles are usually sensitive to the expectations of others; they know that if they ignore these expectations, they won't be allowed to stay in the roles for long. Thus, expectations link individuals—who occupy roles—to the social structure—which is made up of rules. In our view, this is the major contribution of role theory: It provides the best possible answer to the question of why personality variables correlate with social class.

Evaluating the Sociological Approach to Personality

The sociological approach to personality began with Durkheim, but George Herbert Mead was its most important proponent. Mead strongly influenced an earlier generation of psychologists and is still frequently cited today. As suggested above, his ideas are a major force in current personality research as psychologists attempt to identify the cognitive processes underlying interpersonal interaction.

Sarbin developed what is thus far the most systematic account of a sociological model of personality by extending Mead's and Goffman's ideas into all aspects of social life. In addition, between 1948 and 1972 he and his students published scores of studies evaluating aspects of role theory. In terms of sheer empirical data, Sarbin's model of personality probably has more support than any other theory considered in this book except for cognitive social learning. Nonetheless, our sense is that Sarbin's writing isn't as well known today as it should be. There are three probable reasons for this.

First, Sarbin's theory is, in a sense, a victim of its own uniqueness. Specifically, because his model is creative and original, it falls outside the modern mainstream. Recall that Sarbin rejects the conventional models of explanation from traditional personality psychology. He explains peoples' actions in terms of the role they are playing and the social identity they are trying to support rather than in terms of psychological structures and processes inside people. This approach puts Sarbin beyond the limits of traditional measurement-based personality research.

At the same time, Sarbin and his students (e.g., Coe & Sarbin, 1966; Orne & Scheibe, 1964) have substantially undermined the claims of experimental social psychology. Consider what goes on, from a role-theoretical perspective, in the typical social psychological experiment. The experimental subjects have a social identity, and the experiment involves a form of social interaction like any other—except that it is more artificial and the subjects don't know how they will be evaluated. Nevertheless, the subjects carefully monitor the experimental situation in order to determine how to behave so as to maintain the best possible identity. The implication of this analysis is that many experiments show only that subjects will do what they think the experimenter expects and, hence, that experiments say little about the hypotheses the experimenters think they are testing. Such a radical critique of experimental social psychology effectively leaves Sarbin with few mainstream professional allies.

A second problem with Sarbin's theory is that his writing is quite abstract and often expressed in terms of jawbreaking neologisms—words like *emplotments* and *mythoclastic rhetoric*. This style presents a formidable barrier to understanding what he is saying, especially for nonspecialists.

Finally, like Durkheim, Mead, Sullivan, and Goffman, Sarbin minimizes the importance of biology, thus relegating his theory to the outer realm of mainstream science. It should be noted, however, that Sarbin is in good company there, including most sociologists and social psychologists.

Practical Application: The Employment Interview

At some time or another, almost everyone will experience an employment interview. From the perspective of personality theory, this setting is interesting because it so clearly illustrates a typical role enactment as described by Sarbin. During the employment interview, each person is trying to guess what the other person is expecting. The applicant tries to appear to be exactly the person the interviewer is looking for, whereas the interviewer tries to figure out if the applicant's performance is sincere. The interview also entails scenery (a business office), props (a notepad for the interviewer, a résumé and perhaps a briefcase for the applicant), and costumes (business attire appropriate to the job under discussion). To prepare for this encounter, both interviewer and applicant often consult the many books available about successful interviewing.

Although the employment interview is supposed to be about qualifications, the applicant's performance, during which certain personality factors are exhibited, usually influences the interviewer's decision to a greater degree. Indeed, research indicates that interviewers hold stereotypes of what they consider the ideal employee and measure applicants' performance against that standard *(Rowe, 1989; Webster, 1982)*. Moreover, most applicants know this and adjust their performance to fit what they believe the interviewer's stereotype to be. After the applicant has convinced the interviewer that he or she has the general qualifications necessary to do the job, the interviewer begins to assess whether the applicant will fit in with other employees *(Adkins, Russell, & Werbel, 1994; Finney, 1996)*. During this part of the interview process, the interviewer pays more attention to personality factors inferred from the applicant's performance and less attention to objective qualifications.

For example, we know that interviewers respond favorably to qualities such as likeability, initiative, and intelligence *(Hitt & Barr, 1989; Liden, Martin, & Parson, 1993; Raza & Carpenter, 1987)*. We also know that interviewers prefer attractive candidates of either sex *(Marlowe, Schneider, & Nelson, 1996)*; that they like applicants who dress like people already working for the company *(Rafaeli & Pratt, 1993)*; and that they respond favorably when female applicants dress in a masculine rather than feminine manner *(Forsythe, Drake, & Cox, 1985)*.

Interviews have three distinct phases: (1) the initial period, when the interviewer forms an impression of the candidate from his or her résumé, test scores, or references; (2) the interview process itself; and (3) the period during which the interviewer makes a judgment about the suitability of the candidate. Some interviewers are so convinced of their skills at assessing people that they claim not to need the interview performance to make a decision—basing it instead on the first phase, when they can form an impression of the applicant from the written material provided *(Macan & Dipboye, 1990)*. Although many researchers consider this approach to be more objective than making a decision on the basis of an applicant's interview performance, most applicants prefer to have the opportunity to perform for the interviewer. As Goffman *(1959)* has pointed out, interviewers will usually be polite and pretend that most performances are good, even when they are not.

PART FIVE

Responses to Social Psychological Theory

10

ABRAHAM MASLOW AND CARL ROGERS

Humanistic Psychology

- The Influence of Existentialism on Humanistic Psychology
- The Lives of Abraham Maslow and Carl Rogers
- Core Problem: The Question of Values
- The Humanistic View of Human Nature
- Evaluating Humanistic Psychology
- Practical Application: Humanistic Psychology and Education

In the 1940s Abraham Maslow, a well-trained behaviorist, began a study of his two most respected and famous teachers, the anthropologist Ruth Benedict and the Gestalt psychologist Max Wertheimer. Maslow concluded that Benedict and Wertheimer were exceptional individuals who could not be understood in terms of behaviorist psychology *(Maslow, 1971)*. What made them exceptional were their high levels of maturity, productivity, and openness to experience. Maslow then surmised that there must be other people capable of such high-level -functioning and that superior functioning must be a natural human -capacity.

Humanistic psychologists would call Benedict and Wertheimer *self-actualized*, a term (discussed below) that refers to performance at the highest level of which a person is capable. Although self-actualized people are rare, humanistic psychologists believe that everyone is motivated by a need to develop his or her capabilities and that the major goal in life is to achieve self-actualization. By emphasizing the development of human potential, humanistic psychologists are essentially advocating that the entire focus of psychological research be redirected. As stated in the Articles of Association of the American Association of Humanistic Psychology:

> Humanistic psychology is primarily an orientation toward the whole of psychology rather than a distinct area or school. It stands for the respect for the worth of persons, respect for differences of approach, open-mindedness as to acceptable methods, and interest in exploration of new aspects of human behavior. As a "third force" in contemporary psychology, it is concerned with topics having little place in existing theories and systems: e.g., love, creativity, self, growth, organism, basic need-gratification, self-actualization,

higher values, being, becoming, spontaneity, play, humor, affection, naturalness, warmth, ego-transcendence, objectivity, autonomy, responsibility, meaning, fair play, transcendental experience, peak experience, courage, and related concepts. *(1962, p. 2)*

Although humanistic psychology includes a variety of perspectives today, the core of the movement is the self-actualization theories of Abraham Maslow and Carl Rogers. To put their ideas in context, however, we need to briefly review existentialism, a school of philosophy that was the precursor to humanistic psychology in the 1950s.

The Influence of Existentialism on Humanistic Psychology

Existentialism, a distinctive European perspective on human nature, has no single author. We have chosen five people—Soren Kierkegaard, Friedrich Nietzsche, Ludwig Binswanger, Viktor Frankl, and Rollo May—to illustrate the major themes of this viewpoint.

Existentialists argue that, although most of us believe that our everyday activities are meaningful, from a longer perspective most of our concerns are not crucial. Indeed, most personal triumphs and achievements are trivial, if not meaningless. Existentialists also believe that if we acknowledge the folly of most human ambition, we will see the world more clearly.

1. Many people consider *Søren Kierkegaard* (1813–1855) to be the first existentialist. Although Kierkegaard was raised in a strict Lutheran home, he came to believe that conventional religion is a fraud because it assumes that people know what God expects of them. Kierkegaard argued, to the contrary, that God's wishes are inscrutable and that no one—including theologians and church officials—can know what God wants them to do. Kierkegaard further suggested that when people think they are talking to God, they may actually be listening to the voice of their own pride—this voice being a typical trick of the Devil. Consequently, we can never know for certain what our religious duties are. Kierkegaard concluded that we should passionately embrace our religious views, but that we should do so "in fear and trembling" because God's will is beyond our understanding. What he meant by this, from an existential perspective, is that we are responsible for our own actions and must choose how to live our lives rather than follow the dictates of the church, which also does not know what God really expects of us.

2. Like Kierkegaard, *Frederich Nietzsche* (1844–1900) was raised in a strict Lutheran family and eventually came to criticize conventional Christianity. But whereas Kierkegaard thought God was unknowable, Nietzsche believed that religion was a myth designed to persuade people not to think for themselves. Nietzsche argued that all philosophy from Plato to the late nineteenth century was a mistake because it was based on the idea that people can rationally analyze the world. But, Nietzsche argued, our philosophical theories are only rationalizations of unconscious biological impulses—an argument that Freud later adopted. Nietzsche also believed that psychology should replace philosophy as the "Queen of the Sciences," because people need to understand themselves before they can understand the world. Without self-understanding, people's theories of the world reflect only their unconscious biases.

Nietzsche was not a systematic thinker, but his views can be summarized in terms of three themes. First, he argued that science and the principle of intellectual honesty have led many modern people to doubt the claims of orthodox religion. As a result, many religious people are hypocrites because they know, at some level, that their religious beliefs are unjustified.

The second part of Nietzsche's argument concerns what he called the *Will to Power*. He suggested that human biology pushes people to develop their talents to the utmost—in effect, "wills them to power"—and that the highest form of the Will to Power is the search for self-knowledge or self-understanding. He further suggested that self-knowledge is the true goal of life, but that organized religion diverts us from the search by making the goal of this life the preparation for another life.

Finally, Nietzsche argued that if there is no God, or if what God requires is unknowable, then there is no ultimate justification for anything we do. Whatever we do we must do because we want to do it, and not because we think God wants us to. In other words, we must accept responsibility for our own actions.

3. *Ludwig Binswanger* (1881–1966) was a leader of the *Daseinanalyse* (existential analysis) movement in European psychology and psychiatry after World War I. Among his many accomplishments is the fact that he was a lifelong friend of Freud and yet seriously disagreed with Freud's ideas about human nature. Binswanger's book, *Foundations and Knowledge of Human Existence* (1942), applied the philosophical method known as **phenomenology** to the study of how we live in the world. Phenomenology was first developed by Edmund Husserl (1859–1938), who argued that the best way to understand the world is to forget our preconceptions, look at the world through the eyes of a naive child, then report what we see.

Binswanger reported three major findings based on phenomenology. First, he noted that two kinds of things exist in the world. On the one hand, there are things that exist *in themselves*, such as pencils, spark plugs, and bowling balls—things that are not self-reflective. On the other hand, there are things that exist *for themselves*; these things—primarily people—are self-reflective. Both existentialists and humanistic psychologists use the distinction between things and people as a guide for how to treat others.

Second, Binswanger noted that there are three ways to live in the world. When we live in the *Umwelt*, the first mode of existence, we focus on our personal satisfaction and treat others as objects rather than as people. In the *Mitwelt*, we try to find ways to live with other people. The Mitwelt takes two forms: the **anonymous mode** and **the mutual mode**. In the former we react to others in terms of our roles, but in the latter we encounter others in an open and accepting way. An encounter in the mutual mode, where we appreciate and accept the existential reality of others and expect them to accept us in the same way, is the ideal form of human relationship. The philosophical concept of an encounter is the basis for the *encounter groups* that are an important part of humanistic psychology. In the third mode of living—the *Eigenwelt*—we assimilate other people and the world for the purpose of self-affirmation. This mode involves the process of self-actualization that we associate with humanistic psychology.

Binswanger's third point is that people exist in the world without knowing why. This is a problem because people need to feel that their lives have significance. The tension between the human need for purpose and the absence of any obvious purpose creates stress, which people resolve by becoming neurotic, by adopting a religion, or by developing a personally chosen lifestyle. This final path is what Binswanger, other existentialist writers, and the humanistic psychologists recommend.

4. *Viktor Frankl* (1905–1997) was a Viennese psychoanalyst who survived a Nazi concentration camp during World War II. The Nazis' pointless persecution and murder of so many innocent people caused Frankl to question the meaning of life and led him to three conclusions. First, from a phenomenological perspective, people have free will and can rise above or transcend their biological needs, their environment, and their own past. This conclusion came from Frankl's observation that some people in the concentration camp transcended the horrible conditions and found meaning in their lives even as prisoners. The capacity for transcendence, however, carries a burden of responsibility; if we become victims of our biological or personal history, it is because we have chosen to do so. We cannot explain or excuse our actions by saying that we had no choice—we are free and, therefore, responsible for the attitude that we take toward our lives.

Second, Frankl concluded that people want to believe their lives are meaningful and that the need for meaning is the most important human motive, more important even than self-actualization: "Self-actualization is a good thing; however, I maintain that man can only actualize himself to the extent to which he fulfills meaning. Then self-actualization occurs spontaneously" *(Frankl, 1968, p. 8)*.

Finally, Frankl concluded that we achieve meaning by actively committing ourselves to a cause. Commitments vary, and the fact of being committed is more important than the merits of one's project: "Man must risk committing himself to a cause not worthy of his commitment" *(Frankl, 1967, p. 13)*. Meaning can also be found in the way one deals with "the tragic triad of human existence": pain, death, and guilt. Sometimes people are defeated by circumstances beyond their control, but they can make their lives meaningful through the stance they take toward their defeat.

5. *Rollo May* (1909–1994) is the major proponent of existential psychology in the United States. According to May *(1967)*, people today often feel powerless and empty, and these feelings cause anxiety, which is a generalized discomfort that has no specific object *(May, 1977)*. People then turn to alcohol, drugs, religion, careerism, and other distractions to avoid feeling anxious.

May *(1953)* further argues that people are primarily motivated by a need for self-development, a need that evolves through four stages. In the stage of innocence, infants are unaware that they are separate from the world around them. In the stage of rebellion, young people struggle to gain self-consciousness and independence. In the stage of ordinary consciousness, individuals are able to function successfully in the world. Finally, in the stage of creative consciousness, they transcend the problems of everyday life and see the world as it really is. According to May, few people reach this fourth stage. Personal growth depends on going beyond what we think we are and discovering what we really are—which is also the goal of humanistic psychology.

The Fathers of Existentialism (clockwise from upper left): Kierkegaard, Frankl (with Joerg Haidov), May and Nietzsche.

Sources: Bettmann/Corbis; AP Photo/Ronald Zak; Archive Photos; Lulten-Deutsch Collection/Corbis.

The interconnection between existentialism and humanistic psychology can be summarized as follows. First, humanistic psychology uses the existential method of phenomenology, the view that by looking at the world naively and openly, we can discover important truths about life. Second, existentialists criticize behaviorism and psychoanalysis for assuming that people's actions are always determined by forces outside their awareness. Existentialists believe, on phenomenological grounds, in the reality of free will: The laws of science explain the movement of inanimate objects, but humans can and should control their own lives. To the degree that our actions can be explained by factors other than free choice—including unconscious motivations or conditioning—we have become objects and lost our humanity. Third, existentialism and humanistic psychology emphasize self-actualization as the primary human motive. They assume that our self-actualizing tendencies are frustrated by modern life, making us unhappy and unable to develop our true natures.

Box 10.1 illustrates another interconnection—that between humanistic psychology and medieval philosophy.

Abraham Maslow.
Source: Bettman/Corbis.

The Lives of Abraham Maslow and Carl Rogers

Both Abraham Maslow and Carl Rogers were trained in scientific psychology, but each eventually concluded that the normal research methods of academic psychology do not allow us to understand what it is to be human. In their view, mainstream psychology ignores the basic problem of life—namely, how to maintain one's natural drive toward wholeness and psychological growth, and how to avoid a lifestyle that prevents this growth.

Abraham Maslow. Abraham Maslow was born in 1908 in Brooklyn, New York, the son of working-class immigrants from Russia. As a child, Maslow felt isolated as a Jew in a non-Jewish neighborhood and he preferred to read rather than play. Maslow attended the University of Wisconsin, studied animal behavior, and became a committed behaviorist. He stated that his life "truly began" when, at the age of twenty, he became acquainted with the works of John B. Watson and married Bertha Goodman *(Hall, 1968)*. As a graduate student, Maslow also read Freud. He received his Ph.D. in 1934.

In 1937, Maslow took a position at Brooklyn College. During the next fifteen years, he went through psychoanalysis, studied with Benedict and Wertheimer, and took courses with Horney, Adler, and Fromm. Maslow eventually rejected behaviorism because, using behavioristic principles, he couldn't control his baby or explain her striving for growth and competency, and he couldn't understand great people like Benedict and Wertheimer.

Shortly after the Japanese attack on Pearl Harbor in 1941, Maslow dedicated his life to studying human potential:

> I was too old to go into the army. It was at that moment that I realized that the rest of my life must be devoted to discovering a psychology for the peace table. . . . Since that moment in 1941 I have devoted myself to developing a theory of human nature that could be tested by experiment and research. I wanted to prove that human beings are capable of something grander than war and prejudice and hatred. (Hall, 1968, p. 54)

In 1951, Maslow moved to Brandeis University, where he chaired the psychology department for ten years, and in 1967, he was elected president of the American Psychological Association. He helped found the American Association of Humanistic Psychologists in 1962 and the Division of Humanistic Psychology (Division 32) within the American Psychological Association in 1970. Maslow died of a heart attack in 1970 while writing an analysis of the implications of humanistic psychology for economics, political science, and ethics.

Maslow argued that people have a powerful need to develop their potential to the highest degree possible; he referred to this as a need for *self-actualization*. Unfortunately, for most people, the process of self-actualization is blocked by other factors in their lives. Maslow (1959) estimated that perhaps only one person in two hundred is self-actualized, because outside influences such as parents, peers, teachers, and religion direct the need for psychological growth into socially acceptable channels. Instead of growing naturally, we "adjust" to our circumstances. Consequently, most of us strive for goals that do not promote self-actualization.

Freud is famous, but Maslow has been even more influential. Indeed, because of his theory of needs, he is probably the most influential personality theorist in the history of organizational psychology. According to Maslow (1954), human motivation can be characterized in terms of a hierarchy whereby needs at the lower levels must be met before higher-order needs become important. This hierarchy of needs has become a key tool for evaluating management practices. It is discussed in greater detail below.

Carl Rogers. Carl Ransom Rogers (1902–1987) was born into a large, religiously-oriented family in Oak Park, Illinois. He described his childhood as characterized by hard work and strict Protestantism; the family, though close, did not dance, play cards, attend movies, smoke, drink, or mention sex (Rogers, 1967). Rogers was a solitary child who spent his time reading and dreaming about the future.

Rogers majored in agriculture at the University of Wisconsin; during his junior year he visited China with the World Student Christian Federation and then gave up his parents' fundamentalism for a more liberal religious view. He attended Union Theological Seminary in New York City, then Teachers College of Columbia University, where he earned a degree in clinical and educational psychology in 1931. Rogers worked with delinquent and

Carl Rogers.
Source: Roger Ressmeyer/Corbis.

underprivileged children in Rochester, New York, for several years before moving to Ohio State University. In 1945 he became director of the Counseling Center at the University of Chicago, where he began pioneering research on the effectiveness of psychotherapy. In 1946, he was elected president of the American Psychological Association.

Rogers moved back to the University of Wisconsin in 1957, and in 1964 he joined the Western Behavioral Sciences Institute in La Jolla, California, where he helped to found the Center for Studies of the Person. In his later years, Rogers studied marriage, interpersonal conflict, and international relations. Like Maslow, Rogers wanted to use psychology to promote world peace. He died in La Jolla at the age of 85.

Rogers developed his ideas before Maslow, but their approaches are unusually compatible, particularly with regard to motivation. In Rogers' view, a person's ability to self-actualize depends on how he or she was treated in childhood.

According to Rogers, children are oriented at birth toward personal growth and self-enhancement, but their capacity for growth is often subverted by their parents and society. Rogers believed that childhood socialization is almost always a negative experience—children are taught to suppress their natural feelings and to behave according to socially acceptable rules. Later in life, too, people ignore what they really want and try to live up to ideals that have little to do with happiness or fulfillment. Consequently, the self—the core of personality—is buried under layers of rules about "appropriate" behavior. People become neurotic when they live their lives in terms of others' standards; so the basic problem in life, said Rogers, is to outgrow their need to please others and learn to pursue their own real needs.

Core Problem: The Question of Values

In modern society, most people value power, prestige, and worldly possessions more than the development of their personalities. Humanistic psychology became popular in the 1960s when many Americans began to question these societal values. Even earlier, however, sociologists complained about such values in books like William Foote Whyte's *The Organization Man* (1954); filmmakers expressed their concern about the effects of oversocialization in movies like "The Man in the Grey Flannel Suit" (1956); and psychoanalysts such as Erich Fromm (1941) criticized society's preference for "automaton conformity."

In many respects, humanistic psychology was a reaction to the prevailing values of the 1950s, including the traditional family and its division of sex roles, the belief that all persons in authority must be respected, and the view that mainstream American life is superior to all other ways of life. These values are not inherently wrong, but humanistic psychologists object to their being imposed on everyone. From a humanistic standpoint, people who do not belong to a traditional family, do not pursue promotions, and do not respect authority or support Wall Street should not automatically be seen as maladjusted.

The humanistic psychologists found that, ironically, many people who embrace the mainstream values of our society—God, family, money, and country—feel empty and isolated, whereas many people who reject these values feel psychologically healthy. This is because the values of society can be illogical and contrary to human nature. As one humanistic psychologist observed:

> [W]ho is more dangerous, the seventeen-year-old girl who claims that an atom bomb sits within her, or the nuclear strategist who helps the Pentagon find efficient means of destroying, within minutes, one hundred million people? The girl is diagnosed as schizophrenic and is institutionalized, whereas the Pentagon consultant is wined, dined, fawned over, and paid extremely handsome fees. We grow accustomed to these absurdities, to a point where we can read about the My Lai atrocities [in which American troops slaughtered innocent Vietnamese civilians] in the morning, suffer brief pangs of shock and guilt, and then return our attention to the day's activities. And we do all this while managing to sustain the conviction that we really care about the plight of our fellow man. *(Shaffer, 1978, p. 55)*

The values taught by our culture are, for the most part, superficial and incapable of helping people reach their fullest potential. Thus, humanistic psychologists believe that the basic problem in life is to choose values that are right for the individual. People need to resist the tendency to accept society's values automatically, and they need to establish their own identities. According to Maslow, "the average 'normal,' 'well-adjusted' person often hasn't even the slightest idea of what he is, of what he wants, of what his own opinions are" (1956, p. 172).

Humanistic psychologists urge people to choose their own values. Consistent with Jung's concept of individuation, they believe that psychological growth involves outgrowing the demands of conventional society and developing the person latent within each of us—much as the existentialists originally suggested.

FIGURE 10.1 Maslow's Hierarchy of Needs

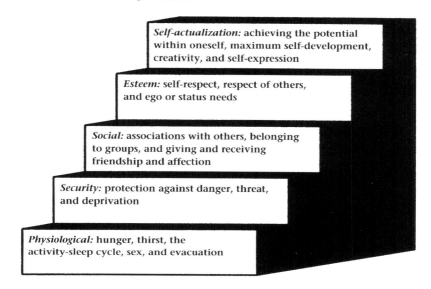

Self-actualization: achieving the potential within oneself, maximum self-development, creativity, and self-expression

Esteem: self-respect, respect of others, and ego or status needs

Social: associations with others, belonging to groups, and giving and receiving friendship and affection

Security: protection against danger, threat, and deprivation

Physiological: hunger, thirst, the activity-sleep cycle, sex, and evacuation

The Humanistic View of Human Nature

Although Maslow and Rogers were concerned with different aspects of personality, their theories are so similar that they can be considered together. Details of each are discussed below.

Motivation

In *Motivation and Personality,* Maslow *(1954)* introduced his hierarchy of needs, which has been widely influential for decades and continues to be popular in organizational psychology today. As noted earlier, Maslow proposed that humans are motivated by five distinct patterns of needs that form a hierarchy. The first four levels of needs concern what Maslow *(1955)* referred to as **d needs**—"d" for deficiency. It is only after these deficiency needs are fulfilled that the higher-order need for self-actualization becomes important.

Maslow's hierarchy is illustrated in Figure 10.1.

The first level of the hierarchy encompasses **physiological needs** related to survival, including the needs for oxygen, food, sex, sleep, and warmth. **Safety needs**, which include desires for stability, order, predictability, and economic security, make up the second level. The third level of the hierarchy concerns the interpersonal **need for love and belongingness**—that is, for affection and meaningful social interaction. The fourth level of the hierarchy involves the **need for self-esteem**, which comes from a sense of accomplishment, autonomy, competence, and recognition from others. Finally, at the highest level of the hierarchy is the **need for self-**

actualization, which concerns what Maslow *(1955)* called the **b needs**—"b" for being. Maslow defined self-actualization as

> the full use and exploitation of talents, capacities, potentialities, etc. Such people seem to be fulfilling themselves and to be doing the best that they are capable of doing, reminding us of Nietzsche's exhortation, "Become what thou art!" They are people who have developed or are developing to the full stature of which they are capable. *(Maslow, 1970, p. 150)*

Maslow believed that self-actualized people are different from the rest of us, and that they respond to a different set of motives. He suggested, in fact, that the entire concept of motivation may be relevant only for those who are not self-actualized, because those who are do not "strive"; rather, they seek to "develop" *(Maslow, 1954, p. 173)*.
Nevertheless, he proposed that self-actualized people are motivated by the following **metaneeds:**

wholeness	perfection	completion
justice	aliveness	richness
simplicity	beauty	goodness
uniqueness	effortlessness	playfulness
truth	self-sufficiency	

The metaneeds associated with self-actualization are very different from the deficiency motives of the first four stages of the hierarchy: Whereas deficiency needs concern a person's survival, being needs concern the development of his or her true potential.

Although Maslow first thought about self-actualization while studying his two favorite teachers (Ruth Benedict and Max Wertheimer), he later studied the nature of self-actualization in general. Starting with a broad sample of people, Maslow observed, interviewed, and tested potentially self-actualized adults. As he collected data and refined his original criteria, he eventually identified a group of about sixty people whom he considered self-actualized. Most of these people were well-known public figures such as Albert Einstein, Eleanor Roosevelt, Albert Schweitzer, Sigmund Freud, Adlai Stevenson, and Abraham Lincoln.

Based on his studies, Maslow concluded that self-actualization depends on three conditions. First, the lower-level needs—the d needs—must be satisfied. Second, self-actualized persons can't be motivated solely by personal gain; they must also pursue universal values such as freedom and justice. Finally, although Maslow studied people of all ages, he eventually concluded that most self-actualized people are sixty or more years old. In a group of 3,000 college students, for example, he found only one person whom he considered to be on the road to self-actualization.

Although not all humanistic psychologists believe that Maslow's hierarchy of needs is the essence of human motivation, humanistic psychology overall is defined by the view that people are fundamentally motivated by a need for growth. As Rogers *(1954)* stated in *Client-Centered Therapy*, "The organism has one basic tendency and striving—to actualize, maintain, and enhance the experiencing organism" *(p. 487)*. Indeed, humanistic psychologists describe as harmful anything that limits the development of human potential. For this reason, they criticize many of the institutions of our society, including scientific psychology, behaviorism, psychoanalysis, personality assessment, IQ testing, experimental psychological research, the educational and judicial systems, organized religion, the traditional family, psychiatry, advertising, the defense industry, and modern art. In their view, these institutions subvert healthy human values and cause people to ignore self-actualization.

Box 10.2 presents a discussion of the tension between humanistic and scientific psychology.

Personality Development

Whereas Maslow's major contribution to personality psychology is his theory of motivation, Rogers' major contribution is his analysis of personality development. Rogers' ideas were based on years of clinical experience, and he began to spell them out in the 1940s. In Counseling and Psychotherapy, Rogers *(1942)* introduced the **client-centered** approach to counseling—a term that in later years he changed to **person-centered**—and in Client-Centered Therapy *(1954)*, he outlined his theory of personality and behavior. The most thorough statement of Rogers' theory of personality change actually appears as a chapter in Psychology: A Study of a Science *(Koch, 1959–1963)*—a chapter that Rogers described as "the most thoroughly ignored of anything I have written" *(1980, p. 60)*.

According to Rogers, children are born predisposed toward psychological growth, but they lack an organized sense of self; in time, however, they begin to discover how they are different from the rest of the world. Rogers believed that one of the first tasks of life is to separate oneself psychologically from one's family. With experience, children develop a self-concept, which Rogers defined as "an organized, fluid, but consistent conceptual pattern of perceptions of characteristics and relationships of the 'I' or the 'me,' together with values attached to these concepts" *(1951, p. 498)*. The self is, of course, the center of personality.

As children gather experience, they assign values to different experiences—for example, "I like being held," "I don't like a wet diaper," "I like to chase the cat." Rogers referred to this process, which starts in infancy and continues throughout life, as the **organismic valuing process**.

Very early in life, however, the valuing process undergoes an important change. Babies begin to realize that they are being evaluated by others, and that these evaluations are not always positive. And small children learn, for example, that crying in public or chasing the cat are no longer "good" things to do. Although these activities reflect children's true feelings, parents consider them bad. In this way, the children experience what Rogers called **conditional positive regard**, in which parental love and affection depend on children's acceptance of parental values.

Over time, children learn that in order to receive positive regard—to be liked and accepted—they must live up to the expectations of others. Consequently, children develop an ideal self that reflects the values of others but denies their own natural values, which are based on their real self. Feeling insecure, the children then develop an unhealthy need to be accepted by others on their terms. According to Rogers, the end result of this process is that children believe that their parents' values are their own.

Rogers believed that suppressing the organismic valuing process—that is, ignoring one's own values and adopting the values of others—blocks the growth instinct and limits the development of one's potential. First babies learn to devalue their own experiences and to introject the values of their parents; then they grow up with relatives, friends, teachers, clergy, and other members of society who impose other values on them. According to Rogers, this process is usually so effective that most adults no longer know what they truly value. Having lost their original sense of self, they look to others to tell them what is good, beautiful, or true. From a humanistic viewpoint, few children have the opportunity to develop normally; more typically, their own natural sense of values becomes suppressed as they learn to deny their own experiences and adopt the values of other people. In this way children become "socialized" or "adjusted" to a world that may be very different from what they would have chosen on their own. In Rogers' view, the basic problem of life is to become able to choose one's own values. Maslow, like Rogers, believed that for most people the growth process is stultified in childhood.

Self-Knowledge

If, as Rogers argues, the self begins to be distorted shortly after birth, how can people ever know—let alone act according to—what they truly value? Rogers *(1951)* suggested that most people really don't know what they value, and that they live in **incongruence**—a state in which their daily behavior is inconsistent with their self structures or emotions.

It is easy to find examples of incongruence: the wealthy and respected surgeon who wishes he were a jazz musician, the career woman who wishes she could stay home with her children, the college student who majors in business rather than theater. In Rogerian terms, these people may be successful at what they do, but their daily lives do not reflect who they really are. Despite their apparent success, they are privately dissatisfied or anxious, and they may eventually experience other more serious psychological symptoms. In essence, people who reject their own values and adopt the values of their parents and society—who live in incongruence—are doomed to be unhappy.

Incongruence and its opposite, congruence, are illustrated in Figure 10.2.

Rogers believed that if the organismic valuing process—the ability to live by one's own standards—can be rediscovered, then people can become happy, content, and grow psychologically. Unfortunately, the values that society endorses and that most people accept usually lack real significance for human development or personal satisfaction. Some of these are even absurd:

> Let me give another instance from a class of mine, a group of prospective teachers. I asked them at the beginning of the course, "Please list for me the two or three values which you would most wish to pass on to the children with whom you will work." They turned in many value goals, but I was surprised by some of the items. Several listed such things as "to speak correctly," "to use good English, not to use words like ain't." Others mentioned neatness—"to do things according to instructions"; one explained her hope that "When I tell them to write their names in the upper right-hand corner with the date under it, I want them to do it that way, not in some other form." *(Rogers, 1964, p. 163)*

FIGURE 10.2 Congruence Versus Incongruence

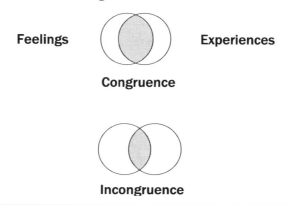

Feelings   Experiences

Congruence

Incongruence

For Rogers, people can discover their true selves only if they don't have to conform to the values of others in order to be accepted. By offering a person warmth, acceptance, and empathic understanding, close friends—or a psychotherapist—can create the kind of environment that a person's parents should have provided: one in which the person is able to make his or her own choices and, at the same time, be regarded positively by others. If people's choices reflect their innermost values, they will not be harmful to others. Humanistic therapists never reinforce, punish, or interpret a client's statements; nor do they recommend what actions to take. Rather, they attempt to understand the client and to demonstrate respect for all of the client's feelings—an attitude known as unconditional positive regard. Humanistic therapists believe that, at the deepest level, only you know what is best for yourself—and you can discover what is best only in an environment that is psychologically safe.

In summary, humanistic psychology suggests that it is hard to know our true selves. Because we are always being evaluated by others and trying to live up to their expectations, most of us are out of touch with our own values. Consequently, we have become what we were told to be.

Unconscious Processes

The concept of the unconscious has a real but limited role in humanistic psychology. Specifically, the manner in which children assigns values to their experiences is almost certainly unconscious, and children adopt their parents' values through the unconscious mechanism of introjection. Nevertheless, humanistic psychologists devote little attention to analyzing the unconscious. In their view, it is difficult enough to understand the contents of a person's conscious mind, let alone the alleged contents of that person's unconscious. Humanistic psychologists also believe that unconscious processes such as introjection undermine individual responsibility.

In contrast with their views about the unconscious, humanistic psychologists are very interested in one aspect of consciousness—the **peak experience**. As examples of this phenomenon, Maslow *(1964)* pointed to the experiences of ecstasy or transcendence that religious people have reported throughout history. In addition, he asked the self-actualized people whom he studied to describe "their most wonderful experiences: happiest moments, ecstatic moments, moments of rapture, perhaps from being in love, or from listening to music, or suddenly 'being hit' by a book or a painting, or from some great creative moment" *(1968, p. 71)*. From their responses, he hypothesized that peak experiences occur at a higher level of consciousness—one that we can all potentially attain. Although the insights produced by peak experiences can be painful, they are never harmful or undesirable.

During a peak experience, people may feel at one with the universe. They may feel detached and able to see reality clearly. They may feel wonder, awe, love, compassion, and a lack of inhibition or anxiety. Or they may feel disoriented with regard to time and space:

> *[There is the] frequent report, especially by lovers, of the complete loss of extension in time. Not only does time pass in their ecstasies with a frightening rapidity so that*

a day may pass if it were a minute but also a minute so intensely lived may feel like a day or a year. It is as if they had, in a way, some place in another world in which time simultaneously stood still and moved with great rapidity. (Maslow, 1968, p. 81)

Maslow also suggested that a peak experience lasting only moments can profoundly affect a person's life. It can change an individual's view of himself or the world; in cases of neurosis, it may even relieve the symptoms. Maslow believed that most normal people have peak experiences, but that self-actualized people have them more frequently. Those who have never had a peak experience, according to Maslow, tend to be "organization men" or bureaucrats. In the case of religious people, Maslow believed that "peakers" develop the faiths and that "nonpeakers" codify and enforce the rules. In recent years, psychologist Mikhail Csikszenmihalyi (1991) has sharpened and extended Maslow's study of peak experience with his analysis of the concept of flow.

Psychological Adjustment

The nature of psychological adjustment is something of a puzzle for humanistic psychologists. For most personality theorists, being well-adjusted means being comfortable with the prevailing social system and culture. But humanistic psychologists suggest that people who fit in are forced to operate on a level far below their actual capabilities. Thus being normal is somewhat pathological. Fortunately, in relationships characterized by unconditional positive regard, people can learn to listen to their "selves" and decide what values are appropriate for them. According to Rogers *(1964)*, people moving toward personal growth and maturity tend to avoid facades, pretense, and defensiveness. Less concerned about the expectations of others, they begin to positively value self-direction—and "this openness becomes the client's most valued resource."

In *Motivation and Personality*, Maslow *(1954)* outlined the characteristics of self-actualized people. Over the years, his list of characteristics has been expanded and modified to some degree, but it still represents the views of most humanistic psychologists. These characteristics are as follows:

1. *More efficient perception of reality and more comfortable relations with it.* Self-actualized people have an unusual ability to detect the spurious, the fake, and the dishonest in human affairs. In addition, they are able to see "concealed or confused realities" more clearly in art, music, science, politics, and public affairs.

2. *Acceptance of self, others, and nature.* Self-actualized people lack strong feelings of guilt, shame, or anxiety. They accept their own shortcomings, and they are intolerant of the artificial behavior of others.

3. *Spontaneity.* Self-actualized people are more spontaneous than others, and they are rarely concerned about doing things in a conventional way when they consider a task to be important.

4. *Problem-centering.* Self-actualized people feel they have some mission in life that is outside themselves. This mission is generally not personal, and it often concerns philosophical and ethical issues.

5. *Detachment and the need for privacy.* People who are self-actualized have a greater-than-average need for solitude and privacy. In fact, others sometimes see them as aloof and overly reserved.

6. *Autonomy, independence of culture and environment.* Maslow suggested that self-actualized people do not depend on their physical and social environments for support. Rather, their major satisfaction comes from reaching their potential. This contrasts with deficiency-motivated people, who need the support of others.

7. *Continued freshness of appreciation.* Self-actualized people have the ability "to appreciate again and again, freshly and naively, the basic goods of life—with awe, pleasure, wonder, and even ecstasy, however stale these experiences may have become to others" *(p. 214).* Maslow made special note of the sexual experiences of some of his self-actualized subjects: For them, orgasm was not a passing pleasure but, rather, something that provided them with a mystical kind of strengthening.

8. *The "mystic experience," the "oceanic feeling."* Mystical experiences were fairly common among Maslow's subjects. These were sometimes tied to sexual experiences.

9. *Gemeinschaftsgefühl.* This term, coined by Alfred Adler, refers to a desire to aid humanity. Despite the imperfections of others, self-actualized people feel a basic underlying kinship with them and want to help.

10. *Interpersonal relations.* Maslow's subjects seemed to have deeper and more enduring interpersonal relations than many other adults. Yet they also tended to have only a few close friends, perhaps because being friends with self-actualized people takes a great deal of time and energy.

11. *A democratic character structure.* Without exception, Maslow found his self-actualized subjects to be democratic in the most basic sense. Regardless of social class, education, political beliefs, race, or religion, they treated everyone the same.

12. *Discrimination between means and ends.* Self-actualized people are certain about right and wrong in matters of daily living. They act ethically, have definite moral standards, and always attempt to do the right thing. Interestingly, none of Maslow's self-actualized subjects had traditional religious views. Only one of the subjects labeled himself an atheist; many others stated that they believed in God as a metaphysical concept but not as a personal figure.

13. *Philosophical and nonhostile sense of humor.* Self-actualized people tend to have a sense of humor different from that of the average person. They are interested in "rather thoughtful, philosophical humor which elicits a smile more usually than a laugh" *(p. 222).*

14. *Creativity.* Without exception, self-actualized people are creative. This creativity is not of "genius" caliber but, instead, resembles the creativity of innocent children. Maslow suggested that everyone is born with this capacity, but only self-actualized people retain it through life.

The foregoing list may suggest that self-actualized people are secular saints whose personal qualities are far beyond those of most people. But Maslow did not believe that self-actualized people are perfect; if anything, he made a special effort to describe their shortcomings. Far from being always kindly, noble, and warm, self-actualized people, he said, can be boring, vain, irritating, ruthless, and absent-minded. In particular, he noted that self-actualized people recovered so quickly from the deaths of people close to them that they appeared to be heartless, and their socially inappropriate or rude behavior often shocked or hurt others. In fact, because such people do not automatically obey normal social conventions and are not afraid to offend others, they often feel lonely and alienated.

Humanistic psychologists propose high standards for adjustment but argue that these standards refer to normal behavior. Indeed, what most of us regard as well-adjusted behavior is a compromise between our true selves and the realities of our lives—a compromise known as incongruence. In humanistic psychology, incongruence is not natural to humans; what's natural is striving for self-actualization.

The Individual and Society

Consistent with mainstream psychology—and in contrast with sociology—humanistic psychologists believe that life in society changes individuals in unhealthy ways. Socialization, where natural motives and values are overwhelmed by the demands of culture, is almost always seen as damaging. Creativity is stifled, and people are taught to ask others to define for them what is good, just, or beautiful. In essence, the individual's true self is sacrificed to the dictates of the prevailing culture. Society, as represented by our parents, teachers, and other authority figures, tries to make us "fit in" with the mediocrity that characterizes modern life rather than fostering the truly remarkable potential that exists within us.

Barry Stevens, a high school dropout who wrote several books about her experiences *(e.g., Stevens, 1984, 1985)* and co-authored a book with Carl Rogers *(Rogers & Stevens, 1967)*, blended examples from her life with her reactions to the ideas of Rogers. Although her experiences were not particularly unusual, they exemplify the humanistic approach to solving life's problems:

> *When I was forty years old, I was baffled and confused because I couldn't seem to know what I wanted. In my own terms, I had gone crazy. In trying to find my way out of this, I went two ways at once: a search inside myself for what had gone wrong, and a search outside myself for something to believe that would set me right. The outside search was a flop. I never did find anything that I could entirely go along with. The inside search was rewarding, and it was there that I found that I didn't need to believe anything at all. Everything that I needed was already inside me. . . . But when I did get in touch with my*

inner valuing again, it was terribly hard to trust it, because in important ways it went against what everyone says. The more I use it, the more I trust it. (Rogers & Stevens, 1967, p. 29)

Despite their hostility toward conventional society, humanistic psychologists believe that social change is possible. Societies that encourage human potential, they say, are an ideal against which other societies can be compared. That is, the societies in which we live are quite different from the kinds of societies in which humans should naturally live. For example, a society of self-actualized persons would never tolerate war, starvation, and the denial of human freedom and dignity. Despite the sorry state of the modern world, Rogers *(1980)* was optimistic about the changes in society that he saw taking place.

Humanistic psychologists also strongly believe in the need to respect the uniqueness of each person. The purpose of society, they argue, is to provide a framework within which individuals can meet their needs and become self-actualized. Because people naturally value justice, beauty, and freedom, society can only benefit by treating people in a more flexible, tolerant, and individualized way.

Evaluating Humanistic Psychology

Five points about humanistic psychology are distinctive and worth remembering.

1. *Its optimistic view of life.* Probably the most striking feature of humanistic psychology is its optimistic view of human nature. Based upon their research and experience, Maslow and Rogers believed in the basic "goodness" and worth of every human being. This is not to say that they approved of the actions of all people, but they believed that every individual has intrinsic worth and that this worth deserves respect.

   The optimistic tone of humanistic psychology had wide appeal in the 1960s, and it was adopted by various social change movements that were active at the time. As world attention increasingly focused on civil rights in the United States, human rights in Indochina, and the effects of automation and bureaucratization in industrial society, the vision of human nature offered by humanistic psychologists struck a resonant chord in many people. According to Maslow and Rogers, personality can unfold only when the world is person-centered, not technology-centered.

2. *Its relation to existentialism.* Like existentialism, and in sharp contrast with behaviorism and sociology, humanistic psychology distrusts the prevailing values of society. Existentialists as well as humanistic psychologists argue that the values American society represents and enforces prevent people from deciding how to live their own lives. To live by the values of mainstream society and not realize one has other choices is to live inauthentically, according to the existentialists—and to fail to develop one's potential, according to the humanistic psychologists.

   For the existentialists, the freedom to choose one's values brings with it the responsibility to choose. In fact, Rogers *(1980)* provided many examples of people who decided to choose their own values, to reject what they considered wrong for themselves, and to develop their unique potentialities. In the humanistic view, and in person-centered therapy especially, no one can help another person make the decision to choose self-actualization. That decision must come from within.

3. *Its personal style.* Another distinctive feature of humanistic psychology is the candid and disarming writing style of its proponents—particularly Rogers himself. In his later years, Rogers stopped doing empirical research, and most of his later writing concerns the universal problems of everyday life: doing an unsatisfactory job and feeling bad about it, working with people we don't like or trust, feeling overwhelmed by situations, and so forth. Rogers' candor contrasts sharply with other theorists we have discussed, most of whom were careful not to disclose anything personal to their readers. As you may recall from Chapter 3, Freud broke his own golden rule ("During free association, always say whatever comes into your mind") when he refused to give Jung some personal information while Jung was interpreting one of Freud's dreams—and this hypocrisy ruined their relationship. Rogers (1972, 1980), on the other hand, wrote about his having wept when he received the APA award for scientific contribution to psychology and about his problems with sexual performance in middle age. For Rogers, humanistic psychology was more than a theory of personality—it was his way of life.

4. *Its emphasis on interpersonal communication.* Humanistic psychologists in general, and Rogers in particular, have made a valuable contribution by discussing the nature of mature interpersonal relations. Their emphasis on the importance of being nonevaluative suggests an alternative to traditional forms of communication. Over and over, they describe how people start to "develop" at those times when the normal evaluative pattern of communication is altered. In many cases, people have gained significant personal insights through their exposure to person-centered communication. The influence of this nonjudgmental approach on the practice of psychotherapy has been enormous.

5. *Its link to cognitive psychology.* A fifth distinction concerns the fact that humanistic psychology paved the way for the shift in academic psychology from the study of behavior to the study of cognition. Virtually all humanistic psychologists have made frequent, acid comments about behaviorism, which dominated American psychology after World War I. For that matter, humanistic psychologists are largely responsible for traditional behaviorism's loss of influence over the years. In essence, humanistic psychology argues that there is more to people than their behavior, and that individual phenomenology has to be studied if human nature is to be understood. As a theoretical perspective, behaviorism is simply too limited to give an adequate account of why people are as they are.

There are also, however, some distinctively troubling aspects of humanistic psychology, and we will mention four.

1. *Its failure to develop beyond their original insights.* The cornerstone concepts of humanistic psychology—self-actualization, the hierarchy of needs, unconditional positive regard—appeared in Rogers' *Client–Centered Therapy* in 1954 and Maslow's *Motivation and Personality* in the same year. These books contain virtually all the theoretical

BOX 10.3 Biography: Wassily Kandinsky

The Russian-born painter Wassily Kandinsky (1966–1944) is considered the founder of abstract art. His emphasis on form, line, and color in the early part of the twentieth century greatly influenced the later abstract expressionists such as Mark Rothko and Jackson Pollock. Kandinsky was descended from Mongolian princes, and he grew up in a household that encompassed a mixture of European and Asian cultures. The family was wealthy and enjoyed traveling; as a child, Kandinsky visited Venice, Rome, and Florence. In 1871, he finished high school in Odessa and became an amateur performer on the piano and cello. At the same time, he began to paint as a hobby.

In 1836, Kandinsky enrolled at the University of Moscow, where he studied law and economics. During his college years, he did well in his studies, but he never lost his interest in art. In 1889, he visited the Hermitage Museum in St. Petersburg to see the Rembrandts there and, in the same year, made a trip to the museums in Paris.

Kandinsky received his doctorate in jurisprudence from the University of Moscow in 1893. Although he had lost some of his enthusiasm for the law, he felt that a career in art was a luxury he could not afford. After graduation, he taught at the university but eventually accepted a job as director of the photography department of a printing company.

When Kandinsky was thirty, he was offered a professorship in jurisprudence at the University of Dorpat in Estonia. Confronted with this opportunity, he was forced to examine his values. To the surprise of those around him, he turned down the offer, resigned from the printing company, and moved to Munich and enrolled in a private art school. Kandinsky was of royal descent and held a doctorate in law from a prestigious university, but at the art school he was just an ordinary student.

Kandinsky graduated in 1900 and, during the next few years, gained a reputation as a competent modern artist. Around 1910 he developed a style that eliminated subject matter altogether, concentrating instead on form, space, and color. Kandinsky's goal was to create a visual abstract language in the same way that composers had created an aural abstract language. His initial painting in this mode—"First Abstract Watercolor"—is generally recognized as the first abstract work in the history of art (see Figure 10.3).

At the outbreak of World War I, Kandinsky returned to Russia; during the war and ensuing revolution, he continued to paint. The new Bolshevik government was initially supportive of his work, and in 1921 Kandinsky founded the Russian Academy of Artistic Sciences. Over time, however, the Bolsheviks became more interested in works that glorified socialism and less enthusiastic about abstract art. Finding the atmosphere in Moscow less favorably disposed toward his work, Kandinsky immigrated to Berlin, where he joined the famous Bauhaus school of architecture and applied art. When the Gestapo closed the Bauhaus in 1933, however, Kandinsky moved to Paris, where he lived and painted until his death in 1944.

Kandinsky's life is a good model of the humanistic approach to life. Descended from royalty and the holder of a prestigious degree, Kandinsky abandoned a prosperous and secure future as a lawyer and professor to become an entry-level student in a German art school. However promising his future, Kandinsky obviously could not live in incongruence. He valued art above law, and his decision to pursue art was an expression of what motivated him at the deepest level. Although we cannot know what contributions Kandinsky would have made as a lawyer, the world has been greatly enriched by his choice of art as a career.

contributions made by the two authors in their lifetimes. Although humanistic psychology became widely popular in the following decades, the original theoretical structure remained unchanged—in contrast to Freud's ideas, which have continued to develop and change. Looking through back issues of the *Journal of Humanistic Psychology*, one gets the impression that there is little difference between articles published last year and those published twenty years ago. It seems reasonable to expect that, more than forty years after humanistic theory's original formulations, either a greater body of evidence supporting it would have been developed or that the theory would have been modified to account for discrepancies. Unfortunately, neither seems to be the case.

2. *Its link to individualism.* Humanistic psychology is frequently criticized for promoting the individual at the expense of society. Humanistic psychologists seem truly to believe that if personal needs are appropriately satisfied, the world will automatically be a better place in which to live. This view also contradicts existentialism, which maintains that, as individuals, we are responsible for opposing tyranny and alleviating unnecessary human suffering, regardless of the price we pay in terms of our own gratification. Accordingly, the existentialists would not agree that behaving responsibly depends on being self-actualized.

There is also a problem with the way humanistic psychology conceptualizes individualism and interpersonal relations. According to Maslow and Rogers, people become unhappy when they feel estranged from the prevailing values of society, thus becoming likely to feel estranged from other people as well. Yet humanistic psychology recommends that people deal with feelings of alienation and loneliness by becoming even more individualized and alienated from society in the interest of personal mental health.

As Maslow suggested, self-actualization can be lonely. And in a related vein, Rogers (1980) described his wife's illness and death in a moving passage concerning the relationship between individualism and personal obligations. In their last years together, he felt he should care for his wife through her illness, but he was no longer certain that he loved her. At the same time, he wanted to be free to do the things that he enjoyed. When Rogers eventually left his dying wife in order to pursue his own self-actualization, she felt betrayed, and their relationship during her last years was not happy. Whatever we may think of Rogers' actions, he was true to his belief that responsibility to oneself comes before responsibility to others.

3. *Its emphasis on self-actualization.* By now, the term self-actualization has become a part of ordinary language. It is common for people in various programs and institutions to say that they are committed to helping others become self-actualized. Despite years of research, however, there is little evidence that such a state of being actually exists. Although Maslow described a personality type (the self-actualized person) that virtually

everyone seems to recognize, it has been impossible to develop a measure of self-actualizing tendencies.

Moreover, the qualities that Maslow said typified self-actualized people, such as "aliveness," "goodness," and "wholeness," are so ill-defined as to be neither interpretable nor amenable to empirical analysis. Indeed, "aliveness" probably means entirely different things to an athlete, a religious ascetic, a drug user, and a motivational speaker. Furthermore, the concept of self-actualization becomes quite confusing when it is transported across cultures. For example, the extreme individualism of humanistic psychology makes it improbable that anyone from a traditional, family-centered culture such as Japan could become self-actualized.

4. *Its elitist approach.* A final problem with humanistic psychology concerns its elitism. Humanistic psychologists repeatedly stress that the optimal level of psychological functioning should be considered the *norm*. In their view, those of us who are not self-actualized live on an inferior plane of being: "Could these self-actualizing people be more human, more revealing of the 'original nature' of the species, closer to the 'species type' in the taxonomical sense? Ought a biological species be judged by its crippled, warped, only partially developed specimens, or by examples that have been overdomesticated, caged, and trained?" *(Maslow, 1954, p. 211).* The assumption that people who adapt to the demands and values of their society are psychologically immature is illogical and, in some respects, even condescending.

Box 10.3 applies a humanistic interpretation to the life of the Russian painter Wassily Kandinsky.

Practical Application: Humanistic Psychology and Education

Rogers wrote extensively about education, but he had few good words to say about our current methods of instruction. In his view, as expressed in "Learning to Be Free" *(1963),* modern education emphasizes conformity, docility, and rigidity; regards personal values as irrelevant; and stifles students' creativity or channels it into forms that the teachers consider socially acceptable. Two years earlier, Rogers *(1961)* had suggested that the educational process should become less teacher-centered and more student-centered, thus leading students to recognize that they are responsible for their own learning. Students, he said, should not expect their instructors to provide them with information; rather, an instructor should assist students as they teach themselves. In this way, the teacher becomes both an academic resource and a model of behavior. However, Rogers observed that when teachers acted this way, students often became anxious and even angry.

According to Rogers *(1961),* students in a teacher-centered classroom demand that instructors "do something" during class. By contrast, an instructor in a student-centered classroom listens carefully and responds openly and honestly to all comments—leaving it up to the students to "do something." In the latter situation, said Rogers, students eventually recognize that they are free to learn—for example, they can design a program in any way that they feel is appropriate. In fact, according to Rogers, student-centered education often engenders in students a voracious appetite for learning and doing far more work than they would have if the teacher had defined the subject matter and the grading requirements.

Rogers believed that the classroom should promote both academic learning and personal growth. Because the humanistic classroom discards the strictly defined roles of student and teacher, people can get to know one another on a personal level. When people are not constrained by traditional roles, he argued, they learn to value others for who they are rather than for the titles that they hold.

"Open" approaches to education have also been proposed by Maria Montessori *(1988)*, John Dewey *(1999)*, and A. S. Neill *(1995)*, but Rogers went beyond these theorists by insisting on the importance of interpersonal factors in the classroom. In his view, if we are satisfied with the world as it is, then education should stick to the facts. If, however, we are not satisfied with the world, then education should be designed to develop interpersonal skills and personal creativity.

In summary, Rogers believed that the approach he developed for therapy could be applied equally well in educational settings. In order for learning to be effective, students must decide what they want to learn, and they must take responsibility for learning it. Neither teachers nor parents should dictate the "proper" values or goals for young people.

11

ERIK ERIKSON
and Psychosocial Theory

- The Development of Ego Psychology
- The Life of Erik Erikson
- Core Problem: The Concept of Identity
- Psychosocial Theory and Human Nature
- Evaluating Erikson
- Practical Application: Choosing a Career

Freud dominated the development of psychoanalytic theory until his death in 1939. His primary theoretical concern was analyzing the id—how it operates, how it is controlled, and what happens after it is controlled. Moreover, as a psychiatrist, he was interested in the origins and treatment of psychopathology, and he seemed almost obsessed with demonstrating how the id is the source of psychological problems. As a result of his obsession, he ignored the ego and the question of how we deal with the normal demands of ordinary life.

Freud would tolerate no deviation from his theories, and anyone who challenged his views regarding the importance of the id was expelled from the psychoanalytic movement. After his death, however, some psychoanalysts turned their attention to the ego and the processes by which people adapt to everyday life. Freud's daughter Anna was a leader in this movement, which is known as **ego psychology**.

The ego psychologists altered Freud's gloomy view of our struggle to control the id, and they did so in three ways. First, they suggested that there is a natural fit between the individual and society—that the process of adjusting to society's demands is not traumatic. Second, they proposed that a mother's care is crucial for normal personality development. And third, they focused more on how the ego adapts to the demands of everyday life than on how the id disrupts it. Erik Erikson became the best known of the ego psychologists, and his ideas spread to many fields outside personality theory—including anthropology, history, and sociology. Erikson also created the discipline of psychohistory and wrote compelling biographical analyses of Gandhi, Martin Luther, Hitler, George Bernard Shaw, William James, and Thomas Jefferson.

Erikson was primarily influenced by Anna Freud and Heinz Hartmann, the founders of ego psychology. This chapter begins with a brief overview of ego psychology, then examines Erikson's ideas in detail.

The Development of Ego Psychology

Anna Freud

Anna Freud (1895–1982) was Sigmund Freud's youngest child and his intellectual heir. She grew up around Viennese psychoanalysts, was analyzed by her father (a practice now considered taboo), and eventually became an analyst herself. She specialized in the problems of children, and after the Freud family fled the Nazis and moved to England in 1938, she worked in a London nursery. In collaboration with Dorothy Burlingame, Anna Freud wrote several books based on her experiences with troubled children during World War II. In 1947, she founded and began directing the Hampstead Child Therapy Course and Clinic. She remained there until her death in 1982.

According to traditional psychoanalytic theory, when id impulses become conscious they create anxiety that the ego controls through repression; in other words, the ego simply drives unacceptable thoughts out of consciousness. In her book *The Ego and the Mechanisms of Defense*, however, Anna Freud *(1936)* described several additional mechanisms that the ego uses to avoid anxiety. These defense mechanisms, as you may recall, are discussed in Chapter 3.

Rather than studying how the id disrupts everyday life—as her father did—Anna Freud focused on how the ego handles anxiety-provoking impulses. She believed that the best way to understand another person is in terms of that person's typical defense mechanisms, and that studying defense mechanisms allows us to understand ego functioning in general.

Anna Freud believed that normal childhood development is less traumatic than her father suggested—indeed, that most children are born into environments to which they adapt in a natural, rather than traumatic, way. Children's development is not promoted by psychological struggles with their parents; rather, parents help their children develop. Anna Freud's emphasis on the importance of the ego in psychological development was further spelled out by another Viennese psychoanalyst, Heinz Hartmann.

Heinz Hartmann

Heinz Hartmann's lectures to the Vienna Psychoanalytic Society in 1937 were important events in the development of ego psychology. These lectures, published in English in 1958, were collectively entitled *Ego Psychology and the Problem of Adaptation*. Whereas Freud believed the ego develops by drawing energy from, and serving, the id, Hartmann (1894–1970) argued that the ego develops by organizing and interpreting a person's experience. The ego grows not by controlling the id but by helping one adapt to the social environment—a critical idea in Erikson's psychosocial theory as well. According to Hartmann *(1958, p. 12),*

Anna Freud
*Source: National
Library of Medicine.*

children are born with an "undifferentiated matrix" of psychic energy so that the ego develops separately from the id.

As suggested earlier, Freud believed that parents and children conflict over the need for children to control their instincts, and that these struggles are often traumatic, causing adult neurosis. In contrast, Hartmann believed that the ego develops in a "conflict-free sphere" *(1958, p. 8)*, so that most children adapt to their parents' demands with little psychological trauma. Hartmann further suggested that children are born pre-adapted to an "average expectable environment" *(p. 35)*; in other words, parent-child conflict is not inevitable, and children's needs are usually not a problem for their parents. In further contrast with Freud, Hartmann argued that the key to normal development is the quality of the mother-child relationship.

The ego's job, Hartmann said, is to help infants adapt to their parents rather than to control infantile sexual instincts. In this way the ego organizes personality, and neurosis usually reflects failures in ego development *(Rapaport, 1951)*. In summary, then, Hartmann argued that (I) neurosis is not the normal result of childhood development; (2) children are born pre-adapted to an average expectable social environment, so struggles with their parents are not a necessary part of normal development; and (3) the ego, not the id, is the center of personality.

Though seemingly slight, the differences between Sigmund Freud, on the one hand, and Anna Freud and Heinz Hartmann, on the other, are actually quite substantial. In fact, ego psychology changed psychoanalysis in significant ways. Whereas Freud argued that civilization imposes a burden on children, ego psychologists maintain that children are born ready to adapt to the demands of society—and that society is actually necessary for normal psychological development. Erik Erikson further developed and expanded these ideas about the relationship between a child and its parents, and therefore between the individual and society.

The Life of Erik Erikson

Erik Homburger Erikson was born June 15, 1902; his parents were Danish but living in Germany. Erikson's father was a Protestant who abandoned the family just before Erik's birth without marrying his mother. In 1905 Erikson's mother, who was Jewish, married Theodor Homburger, who was also Jewish. As a child, Erikson was confused about his background because his mother refused to tell him anything about his real father *(Bloland, 1999)*. Erikson called himself Erik Homburger until he was almost forty years old, which suggests that he had a personal interest in the problem of identity.

Erikson attended a technical school in Denmark where he studied art. After graduating, he was not sure that he wanted a career as an artist and began wandering about Europe. He twice arranged for galleries to show his work and each time left town before the exhibit opened—perhaps because he was ambivalent about his early occupational choice. Then, in 1927, Erikson began teaching art at a small school in Vienna attended by the children of Freud's patients. He became interested in education and enrolled in a Montessori training school. The Viennese psychoanalysts liked young Erikson; he eventually began psychoanalytic training and was analyzed by Anna Freud.

In 1933, Erikson immigrated to Boston, where he worked with Henry Murray (Chapter 6) at the Harvard Psychological Clinic, becoming the first child analyst in the city. Like Jung, Erikson was keenly interested in the psychology of native peoples. In 1938, he visited a Sioux Indian reservation in South Dakota, and his observations during that experience became the basis for *Childhood and Society (Eriksond, 1950, 1963)*, which many people regard as his most important book.

In 1939, Erikson joined the Institute of Child Welfare at the University of California at Berkeley; but he resigned in the 1950s—during the McCarthy period—when asked to sign a loyalty oath. This action required great courage and dedication to the principles of intellectual freedom. Erikson returned to Massachusetts and eventually became a professor at Harvard. His book *Gandhi's Truth (1969)* won both a National Book Award and a Pulitzer Prize. In 1970 he moved back to California, where he was affiliated with Mount Zion Hospital and the San Francisco Psychoanalytic Institute. In 1987, Erikson retired to Cambridge, Massachusetts, where he died in 1997.

Core Problem: The Concept of Identity

Erikson agreed with Freud that the core of personality is a set of unconscious biological needs or instincts. He also agreed with Freud that events in childhood strongly influence adult personality. And finally, he agreed with Freud that childhood experiences cause adult unhappiness. But Erikson differed from Freud in four important ways. First, his research with native peoples taught him what sociologists and anthropologists have always known—that

Erik Erikson and his wife in
their home, 1988.
*Source: New York Times Co./
Sarah Putnam/Archive Photos.*

personality is influenced by culture as well as biology. Second, he believed that certain important problems in development occur *after* the Oedipal conflict. Third, he argued that problems in development do not reflect conflicts between a child's id and the demands of his or her parents but, rather, that most such problems reflect a child's efforts to deal with the changing demands of reality. And finally, Erikson thought the major cause of modern unhappiness is not repressed sexuality but peoples' inability to understand how they fit into their society.

The question of how people fit into their society—a question of identity—is the central issue in Erikson's theory of personality. According to Erikson, the manner in which children develop in a social environment gives structure and meaning to their life. Although the problems of psychological development are the same in all societies, each culture is unique, which means that people in different cultures solve their problems in different ways.

As noted, identity was a major issue in Erikson's own life, and it is a theme to which he repeatedly returned in his writing. In *Childhood and Society (1950, 1963)*, he argued that the problems of the Sioux—alcoholism, alienation, and unemployment—were caused by their adoption of the identity of a buffalo hunter, a choice that deviates from the mainstream of American society. In *Young Man Luther (1958)*, he argued that Martin Luther's life was primarily shaped by his efforts to find a place for himself, first in his father's business, then in the Catholic Church. And in *Gandhi's Truth*, he argued that Gandhi's militant nonviolence reflected the manner in which Gandhi resolved his own identity conflict. In each case, the key themes in the person's life had to do with identity, not sexual adjustment.

It was also in terms of identity that Erikson conceptualized the links between the individual and society, and explained the problem that Durkheim *(Chapter 9)* described as **anomie**.

Anomie is caused by the development of the modern industrial state, where people live in overcrowded and anonymous large urban centers while working at alienating and unfulfilling jobs. One natural consequence of this circumstance, Erikson believed, is that parents raise children to fill roles in a society that no longer exists, which then leads to the problem of identity.

Throughout history, Erikson noted, human groups existed in different environments. To survive, each group developed a culture—a set of methods for dealing with their specific environment. And one aspect of each culture was its childrearing practices: Children were raised to share the values and attitudes necessary to survive in that environment. But when childrearing practices no longer fit the environment—because the environment has changed—children grow up with identities that fit the new environment badly. Anomie reflects the fact that many parents raise children to participate in cultures that no longer exist. And this situation, in turn, creates the problem of identity on a widespread cultural basis.

Psychosocial Theory and Human Nature

Motivation

According to Erikson, the most basic human motive is not sex but a desire to fit into one's social environment. Sexuality is a problem only if it prevents a person from developing normally, which involves completing the tasks associated with each stage of development. Although people want to fit into their society, the way they do so takes different forms at different periods in life. Erikson describes development in terms of eight stages, each of which assumes a particular motive: a need for nurturance and care (Stage 1); a need to explore the environment (Stage 2); a need to do things for oneself (Stage 3); a need to feel competent (Stage 4); a need to know where one fits in one's society (Stage 5); a need for a sexual and romantic partner (Stage 6); a need to guide the next generation (Stage 7); and a need for meaning in one's life (Stage 8). (The stages themselves are discussed more fully in the section on personality development.)

This complex list of motives can be reduced to a smaller number. The need to be cared for, the need for intimacy, and the need to care for and guide the younger generation all involve social interaction. The need to do things for oneself, to explore, and to feel competent are versions of the mastery motive that is so important in ego psychology. And finally, Erikson's identity and integrity stages imply the need for meaning that Jung analyzed.

Nonetheless, Erikson was somewhat careless in his discussion of motivation. He believed, on the one hand, that personality is rooted in biology but, on the other, that history and culture have profoundly altered human nature. Consequently, according to Erikson, aside from sex and aggression—the traditional motivational basis for psychoanalysis—there is little about the biological nature of motivation on which psychologists can agree. In short, as Erikson never clearly spelled out his motivational assumptions, the foregoing discussion represents our best guess about what he would have said.

In summary, Erikson argued that human motivation varies with the major task associated with each stage of life. The guiding principle underlying human development is the ego's effort to adapt to the social conditions in which a person lives. Sexuality, mastery, and the Jungian search for meaning are major motives only at certain times and in certain cultures.

Personality Development

Erikson's view of development is widely recognized as a major contribution to personality theory. As noted, he proposed that personality develops across the life cycle through a series of eight stages. Although Erikson initially adopted Freud's five psychosexual stages (oral, anal, phallic, latency, and genital), he modified Freud's theory in three ways. First, he borrowed Hartmann's view that the ego develops in a "conflict-free sphere," such that psychological development is far less traumatic than Freud described. Second, he argued that the manner in which young persons solve the problem of identity is as important as the manner in which they deal with the Oedipus complex. And third, he suggested that each stage of development has a counterpart in a broader institution within society:

> Each successive stage and crisis has a special relation to one of the basic elements of society, and this for the simple reason that the human life cycle and man's institutions have evolved together. . . . This relation is twofold: man brings to these institutions the remnants of his infantile mentality and his youthful fervor, and he receives from them—as long as they manage to maintain their actuality—a reinforcement of his infantile gains. (1963, p. 250)

Erikson referred to this process as the "cogwheeling of the lifecycle," whereby each individual's development links into the development of persons younger and older than the individual (1964, p. 152). Societies are organized to provide both reassurance to their older members as well as methods for meeting the needs of the younger generation. Psychological development, then, is not necessarily as difficult and unhappy as Freud described; rather, society normally promotes each person's development—as the role theorists (Chapter 9) suggested.

Psychological and biological development are connected with society during Erikson's "Eight Ages of Man," as described in *Childhood and Society* (1950, 1963). These eight stages are summarized below.

1. *Basic Trust vs. Basic Mistrust (birth to one year).* According to Erikson, when babies are born, they expect to be fed, held, and cared for. A baby's caretakers also have expectations—"based on some intrinsic wisdom, some intrinsic planning, and much superstition" (1980, p. 60)—about how their child should behave and develop. Because of these expectations, parents begin almost immediately to mold their children. Babies form impressions of the world based on their early experiences. Some may sense that it is a warm, caring place; others, that it is an uncaring place where no one responds to their cries. During this first stage of life, infants learn to trust or mistrust other people. Erikson's stage of basic trust parallels Freud's oral stage, during which time an infant explores the world through tasting and biting.

In Erikson's view, the stage of basic trust versus mistrust is the most critical stage in life. A failure to develop a sense of trust has profound psychological implications and can lead to schizophrenia, depression, or criminal behavior in adulthood. The development of trust depends more on the quality of the interaction between a mother and her infant than on the quantity of love or food that she provides. Erikson believed a sense of trust develops only when a mother has a particular bond with her child. Considerable research suggests that Erikson's views about the developmental importance of this first stage are essentially correct.

The social institution corresponding to the stage of basic trust is *religion*. Religion provides people with comfort and reassurance in the same way that parents comfort and reassure their children. Erikson noted that all religions ask their believers to depend on them for both earthly and spiritual well-being, and that they emphasize how small and powerless humans are in comparison with the universe. In contrast with Freud, Erikson *(1968)* regarded religious faith as normal rather than pathological.

Erikson also believed that successfully dealing with the issue of trust in this first stage of development produces the virtue of hope. Hope is the enduring belief that one's wishes can be fulfilled and obstacles overcome. Essential to development throughout the lifespan, it depends on "the new being's first encounter with trustworthy maternal persons, who respond to his need for intake and contact with warm and calming envelopment and provide food both pleasurable to ingest and easy to digest, and who prevent experience of the kind which may regularly bring too little too late" *(1964, p. 116)*.

According to Erikson, mothers who provide adequate nurturance must themselves have been adequately mothered, must think of motherhood in a way that is congruent with society's conceptions, and must have a world image that explains the links between their lives and the past, present, and future. Such mothers provide a perfect psychological environment in which hope can be developed.

2. *Autonomy vs. Shame and Doubt (one to three years)*. During the first stage of life, children learn that the external world is predictable and orderly. In the second stage, however, children must learn to control their impulses. This primarily concerns delaying gratification, acting in socially appropriate ways, and controlling their bowels. Accordingly, Erikson's autonomy stage resembles Freud's anal stage. Children with internal control have a sense of autonomy and a feeling that, in many cases, they can control the environment and the reactions of other people. Conversely, those who lack internal control tend to feel shame and doubt. Competent mothers help their children develop a sense of autonomy by not shaming them unnecessarily when accidents occur or when they fail at some undertaking.

In Erikson's *(1980)* view, Western values have influenced toilet training in a negative way. He noted that many parents believe toilet training is the most difficult problem in all child training; they try too hard, and their children suffer accordingly. Specifically, many modern parents believe that bowel movements should be mechanical, orderly, and produced on demand like any other product in an industrial society. This attitude—which reflects a "time is money" worldview—can make children neurotic.

During the autonomy stage, children learn that they and others have rights that must be respected. Accordingly, the autonomy stage corresponds to the social institution of *law and order*. The principle of law and order requires that the rights of individuals be respected within the context of the larger society; failure to develop self-control during the autonomy stage usually leads to problems with authority later in life. Erikson believed that this period leads to the virtue of *will*, which concerns children's exercise of both free choice and self-restraint despite having experienced shame and doubt in infancy *(1964, p. 119)*. Will enables children to behave in a socially acceptable behavior, which, in turn, relates to self-control. According to Erikson, nothing in life requires as much self-control as when a child in the autonomy stage must give in to the demands of a younger sibling.

3. *Initiative vs. Guilt (three to five years)*. In Erikson's view, a child's abilities begin to come together in the third stage of development:

> *There is in every child at every stage a new miracle of vigorous unfolding, which constitutes a new hope and a new responsibility for all. Such is the sense and pervading quality of initiative. . . . He appears more himself, more loving, relaxed and brighter in his judgment, more activated and activating. He is in free possession of a surplus of energy which permits him to forget failure quickly and to approach what seems desirable (even if it also seems uncertain and even dangerous) with undiminished and more accurate direction. (1963, p. 255)*

The initiative stage resembles Freud's phallic period, and it includes the feelings associated with castration anxiety and the incest taboo. During this stage, children begin to rely less on their parents and more on themselves to solve problems. They deal with the world using what Erikson called the intrusive and inclusive modes. In the *intrusive mode*, children attack others, make noise, and intrude into adult space—such as their parents' bed—and other unexplored spaces simply because they are curious. In the *inclusive mode*, they respond to the desires and feelings of others.

According to Erikson, this is the time when boys and girls first experience culture-driven distinctions between the sexes. Although girls can be as intrusive as boys, most societies demand that they be inclusive, while allowing boys to be intrusive. For example, girls at this age are encouraged to "play house" or "take care of baby" whereas boys are encouraged to play in groups, build structures out of blocks, and play aggressive games such as space invaders or cowboys.

Box 11.1 discusses differences between boys' and girls' patterns of play.

It is also during the initiative stage that children practice the roles that society will require later. Erikson recognized that some girls find this period to be especially difficult. Children of both sexes who fail to develop a sense of initiative often become fearful and withdrawn, and feel guilty about their fearfulness. Unwillingness to take initiative and the corresponding guilt are usually caused by parents who overcontrol, criticize, or punish children's attempts to explore during this stage. These children learn to feel guilty even about their own natural curiosity and, rather than openly exploring the world, become restricted and overcontrolled.

Erikson suggested that resolving the Oedipus complex, which occurs during this period, gives children a moral sense and a vision of future possibilities. During this stage, children develop fantasies and games from which they develop images of adult roles that reflect the economic roles available within society as a whole. Accordingly, the institution associated with this stage is the economic system into which the children are born. The virtue that develops in this stage is a sense of purpose, the courage to pursue one's goals. This sense of purpose is developed in play:

> *Play is to the child what thinking, planning, and blueprinting are to the adult, a trial universe in which conditions are simplified and methods exploratory, so that past failures can be thought through, expectations tested. . . . Thus infantile play (like mature man's inspired toys: dance, drama, ritual) affords an intermediate reality in which purposefulness can disengage itself from fixations on the past.* (1964, pp. 120–121)

4. *Industry vs. Inferiority (six to sixteen years)*. The first three stages of life strongly affect adult personality. By the end of these three stages, at age six, children are ready to move outside the home and begin participating in the world, usually by beginning their education. Education does not have to take place in a formal institution; according to Erikson, it can be in a "jungle or classroom" *(1963, p. 258)*. Reflecting his Montessori training, Erikson recommended that classroom training should strike a balance between traditional and progressive education.

Erikson's fourth stage coincides with Freud's latency period. During this time, children stop simply playing and begin seeking social recognition by doing what adults value. They develop a sense of industry—a willingness to work—and they learn to use the technology of their culture. In Erikson's view, this stage prepares children for adult careers. Children whose parents build or make things often have an advantage over children whose parents have service or intellectual careers, because they learn technical skills. Children who are unable to master the technology of their culture often develop a sense of inferiority; those who perform poorly in school, for example, may begin to feel inadequate. As a result, they may regress to an earlier stage such as the Oedipal period. On the other hand, a child who has been rejected at home may be encouraged by a warm teacher to develop a sense of industry.

The industry stage has important social implications. Earlier stages concern relationships between child and their parents, but in order to learn the technology of their culture, children must interact with nonfamily members. These people, in turn, usually reward the children for their accomplishments rather than for simply existing. A possible consequence is that some children may become overly conforming and too concerned with pleasing others.

BOX 11.1 Sex Differences in Patterns of Play

Throughout his career, Erikson was particularly interested in children, and when he immigrated to the United States in 1933, he was the only child psychoanalyst in America. Erikson developed many of his ideas about children by observing how they played with the various toys that he kept in his consulting room.

One striking difference between boys and girls, Erikson pointed out, is their pattern of play, particularly during the initiative stage, which corresponds to Freud's phallic period. Erikson observed that girls liked to play with toy houses and dolls, pretending that the latter were members of a family. Erikson called this style of play the inclusive mode, and he argued that the girls' activities were preparing them for their roles later in life.

By contrast, the boys Erikson observed operated in the intrusive mode. Whereas the girls preferred to play quietly in a small area, the boys were loud and disruptive. They were also more likely to build towers and other phallic-like structures. As with the girls, Erikson believed that the boys' mode of play helped prepare them for the kinds of behavior that society would expect of them in the future.

Although Erikson believed that these patterns of play had a genetic basis, he also recognized that society often stereotypes the types of play expected from boys or girls. For this reason, he noted, girls who enjoy being assertive and intrusive, and boys who prefer being inclusive, may earn the disapproval not only of the adults around them but also of their peers.

Because the industry stage emphasizes learning to use tools and becoming productive, Erikson believed that *technology* is the social institution, and *competence* the virtue, associated with this stage. Hope, will, and purpose—the virtues of the first three stages—only anticipate a child's future life, but competence provides a child with concrete skills with which to build an identity. By developing competencies in response to the demands of people outside their family, children link themselves to the surrounding culture.

5. *Identity vs. Identity Confusion (sixteen to twenty years).* Erikson's fifth stage of life concerns the topic that he made famous: developing a sense of identity. The identity concept was so important for Erikson that we discuss it further in the section on self-knowledge.

Childhood comes to an end when young people learn to work and to use the tools of their culture. At the onset of puberty, and with the tasks of adult life looming before them, adolescents begin to wonder who they are relative to the larger world and what they will become in the future. During earlier stages of development, young persons' identities are defined by others; at this point, however, they need to define their own identities.

The key to establishing identity is for young people to align their self-concepts with the way in which they are seen by other people, such that when they like themselves, the people who are significant in their lives also like them. Teenagers who are uncertain about their identities often experience "role confusion" and may behave in strange ways, adopting unusual clothing, food preferences, religious activities, and so forth. Although their behavior can be disruptive, it is positive if it leads to a sense of identity.

Interestingly, while trying to discover who they are by rejecting adult norms, teenagers typically conform rigidly to the standards of their own peer group. They try out various extreme behaviors in order to see what happens, or they fall in love as a way of defining their own identity. Similarly, finding a best friend who agrees with them on everything helps young people develop an identity.

Erikson (1963) pointed out that young people who lack a sense of identity are easy targets for politicians selling totalitarian doctrines—such as Hitler's youth movement in Germany, Mao's Red Guards in China, and militias in the United States. He noted that, throughout history, politicians have always taken advantage of the adolescent need to belong to a group or movement, exploiting that need to recruit young people to their cause.

The institution of *ideology* is the key to developing a sense of identity. When young people adopt an ideology—a political, historical, or religious theory regarding the purpose and meaning of their social group—they develop an early form of identity. Erikson also noted that the rise of science, the decline in religious belief, and the impersonal nature of life in large cities (the forces that create Durkheim's sense of *anomie*) make identity development much harder for adolescent city dwellers than for youths who live in simpler societies.

Young people in this stage move between impulsiveness and caution as they search for values. Erikson refers to the virtue associated with this search as *fidelity*, which is the ability to stay loyal to a value system that has inevitable contradictions (1964). Historically, fidelity has been attached to religion, but today it is more often directed toward nonreligious ideas—such as civil rights or capitalism—that give meaning to social life. According to Erikson, young people have a sense of identity when they are acting in a way that is consistent with liking themselves and, at the same time, are valuable to the significant people in their lives.

When the identity stage is completed, a person is ready for the tasks of adulthood. Erikson's three final stages concern the psychological problems of later life.

6. *Intimacy vs. Isolation (twenty to thirty years)*. In the sixth stage of psychological development, people must deal with intimacy. Once they have established a sense of identity, they will want to fuse that identity with another person. Knowing who they are allows them to develop mature relationships such as sexual unions, close friendships, and alignments with important mentors. Conversely, individuals who lack a sense of identity have problems with intimacy. As Erikson pointed out, many people expect their partners to provide them with an identity. These relationships will be under stress from the beginning.

Erikson further suggested that mature sexuality develops only during this sixth stage of

---

BOX 11.2 Characteristics of Mature Sexuality

In traditional psychoanalysis, love occurs when we transfer our unconscious feelings about our parents onto someone else. Accordingly, many psychoanalysts believe that men marry women who remind them of their mothers, and that women marry men who resemble their fathers. In this view, then, marriage is a vehicle for symbolically enacting fantasies from the Oedipal period—sex with the desired parent.

Erikson's perspective on sexuality is considerably broader than this traditional view. What he called the "utopia of genitality" *(1963, p. 266)* is a sharing process that has significance for society as well as for individuals. Erikson criticized psychoanalysts who believe that more and better sexual relations are the key to greater happiness. Happiness, he insisted, can occur only when sexuality is related to the needs of society.

Erikson's six conditions for mutual sexuality are as follows:

1. mutuality of orgasm
2. with a loved partner
3. of the other sex
4. with whom one is able and willing to share a mutual trust
5. and with whom one is able and willing to regulate the cycles of (a) work, (b procreation, and (c) recreation
6. so as to secure to the offspring, too, all the stages of a satisfactory development.
   (Erikson, 1963, p. 266)

---

life. Sexual activity in earlier periods is usually motivated by identity needs or unresolved conflicts from the initiative or Oedipal stage of life.

Mature sexuality, which depends on meeting the demands of the six preceding stages, is described in Box 11.2.

People who are unable to resolve their intimacy issues experience a sense of isolation. They not only want to be alone but sometimes also want to destroy others who seem foreign or different—a state of mind that reflects prejudice and intolerance. Erikson suggested that, in addition to prejudice, "character-problems" often emerge at this stage. He also noted, however, that it is possible for two persons, neither of whom is capable of intimacy, to live together in "isolation *à deux.*"

The virtue associated with the intimacy stage is *love*. Erikson believed that, although love is important during every stage, the mutuality of mates or partners in a shared identity makes it especially important during this one. Love means more than an intimate partnership: Erikson commented that love can even be "in the service of some territoriality, be it bed or home, village or country" *(1964, p. 130).*

7. *Generativity vs. Stagnation (thirty to sixty years).* Generativity is a matter of being productive in an occupation and guiding the next generation of young people. As people

lose a part of themselves in intimacy, they gain the ability to be involved in matters outside themselves. Consequently, in the seventh stage of life, people become interested in making a contribution to their society. Having found intimacy, they can develop a career and begin to help the next generation prepare for its future. In Erikson's view, generativity does not require becoming a biological parent, since having children is not proof of maturity. Rather, his point is that people who have successfully dealt with the demands of generativity naturally want to help and encourage younger people.

Erikson believed that adults who are unproductive have experienced a failure in development. Unproductive adults become self-indulgent and indifferent to the needs of others; in a sense, they treat themselves as their own children. A common way to escape the demands of this stage of generativity is to become preoccupied with ones' own physical and emotional health. Generative people are altruistic, but stagnated people are narcissistic and self-absorbed.

The goal of the seventh stage is to pass along the wisdom of one's society. Accordingly, *every social institution* that protects and reinforces society's teachings promotes development in this stage. Similarly, care is the virtue associated with generativity. Mature people care about the younger generation and the institutions of society, thus overriding their normal ambivalence toward young people and existing social institutions. In fact, said Erikson, the concept of an all-caring God is a projection of the human need to care for others.

8. *Integrity vs. Despair and Disgust (sixty-five years and beyond).* In the last stage of life, people who are mature will have met their social responsibilities and accepted their triumphs and failures. Although they understand that other lifestyles are valid, they believe their own lives were the most appropriate for them. Overall, they can reconcile what has happened in their lives with what might have happened. Successful completion of this stage gives a person integrity:

> *It is the acceptance of one's one and only life cycle and of the people who have become significant to it as something that had to be and that, by necessity, permitted of no substitutions. It thus means a new and different love of one's parents, free of the wish that they should have been different, and an acceptance of the fact that one's life is one's own responsibility. It is a sense of comradeship with men and women of distant times and of different pursuits who have created orders and objects and sayings conveying human dignity and love.* (Erikson, 1968, p. 139)

The opposite of integrity is despair, along with the feeling that time is too short to make up for past shortcomings. Despair often appears as a kind of misanthropy, or rejection of humanity. Moreover, individuals who lack integrity frequently experience an unrealistic fear of death. The virtue associated with this final stage of life is *wisdom*—a detached concern with life itself. Wisdom conveys the integrity of experience despite one's declining physical abilities.

Table 11.1 summarizes Erikson's eight stages of life.

Psychosocial Crises

		1	2	3	4	5	6	7	8
Old Age	VIII								Integrity vs. Despair, WISDOM
Adulthood	VII							Generativity vs. Stagnation. CARE	
Young Adulthood	VI						Intimacy vs. Isolation. LOVE		
Adolescence	V					Identity vs. Role Confusion. FIDELITY			
School Age	IV				Industry vs. Inferiority. COMPETENCE				
Play Age	III			Initiative vs. Guilt. PURPOSE					
Early Childhood	II		Autonomy vs. Shame, Doubt. WILL						
Infancy	I	Basic Trust vs. Basic Mistrust. HOPE							

TABLE 11.1 Erikson's Eight Stages of Life

Self-Knowledge

Despite the fact that Erikson always aligned himself with traditional psychoanalysis, his theory actually departs from Freud in a number of ways. For example, Freud believed we acquire self-knowledge by consulting a therapist, whereas Erikson believed it comes from social feedback during development. In addition, Erikson regarded self-knowledge as changing and evolving during each stage of development rather than being fixed by age five. Finally, according to Erikson, the core of self-knowledge is a sense of identity, and his concept of identity is similar to the self-concept as described by Harry Stack Sullivan (Chapter 7) and George Herbert Mead (Chapter 9).

People normally solve the problem of identity during the fifth stage of the life cycle, but identity development actually begins at birth. Children are born into cultures that have clear—though often unwritten—rules about the values and beliefs that children should develop. Parents are products of the same culture, and they raise their children using these rules. Psychologists tend to ignore the fact that socially shared values affect personality development, leaving the study of these issues to anthropologists and sociologists.

Margaret Mead *(1965)*, F.L.K. Hsu *(1961)*, and George and Louise Spindler *(1983)*, for example, studied the influence of culture on child-rearing in American culture. According to these anthropologists, American culture teaches values such as success, self-reliance, sociability, honesty, competence, the need to work, and a distrust of authority. Americans whose values do not exactly fit the dominant culture—and this often includes persons from minority groups—find themselves outside the mainstream, possibly with identity conflicts.

In Erikson's view, being raised in a subculture that is outside the mainstream of American life is likely to cause problems with identity and, therefore, with psychological adjustment. One of Erikson's best-known essays, "Hunters Across the Prairie" *(1963)*, concerns the problems that develop when children learn values at home that are inconsistent with those of the dominant culture. In 1938, Erikson visited a Sioux Indian reservation in South Dakota "to find out whence came the tragic apathy with which Sioux Indian children quietly accepted and then quietly discarded many of the values taught them in the immensely thoughtful and costly experiment of federal Indian education" *(p. 115)*.

Erikson reported that these Sioux, once known for their fierceness and pride, had become apathetic and depressed. Their teachers and social workers were particularly concerned about the truancy, stealing, and sexual activity they observed among the children, and they blamed the children's behavior on their parents' permissiveness regarding toilet training and masturbation. One teacher even believed that the Sioux were unable to love their own children. According to Erikson, the teachers and social workers evaluated the manner in which the Sioux raised their children in terms of their own Anglo culture and values; consequently, they misunderstood the source of the apathy and depression of the Sioux.

In contrast with the Anglo teachers, Erikson was amazed at how healthy the children were despite growing up in circumstances that, according to Freud, would likely have caused serious neuroticism. Erikson believed that the Sioux parents were trying to raise their children in such a way as to perpetuate the buffalo-hunting culture of their ancestors. The Anglo teachers and social workers, on the other hand, were attempting to force the Sioux to adopt the values of a new capitalist culture—and this was the cause of their widespread apathy and depression.

> [T]here could be only passive resistance to the senseless present and dreams of restoration: when the future would lead back to the past, time would again become ahistoric, space unlimited, activity boundlessly centrifugal, and the buffalo inexhaustible.
>
> Their federal educators, on the other hand, continued to preach a life plan with centripetal and localized goals: homestead, fireplace, bank account—all of which receive their meaning from a space-time in which the past is overcome and in which the full measure of fulfillment in the present is sacrificed to an ever higher standard of living in the ever distant future. The road to this future is not outer restoration but inner reform and economic "betterment." (1963, p. 132)

The case of the Sioux clearly shows that identity crises are created when young people learn, then try to live by, values inconsistent with those of the larger the culture.

A person's sense of identity forms for the first time in the fifth stage of life, although it continues to change thereafter. Those people who have not established a sense of identity by the end of adolescence are unable to develop intimacy, generativity, or integrity. Accordingly, the ability of a person to move into adulthood depends on identity formation, which Erikson (1968) regarded as the final stage of ego development.

In his later writing, Erikson (1980) distinguished between two kinds of identity that differ in subtle but important ways. The first, *personal identity*, resembles the Jungian persona; it is defined by our perception that we are the same person over time and that others perceive us to be the same person. The second, *ego identity*, concerns the fit between the person we know ourselves to be and the person whom others think we are. According to Erikson, this dual identity depends on several factors, including the following: (1) one's inherited constitution, (2) strong needs that develop in early childhood, (3) special abilities such as artistic or athletic skills, (4) significant identifications or role models, (5) preferred defenses for dealing with anxiety, (6) successful sublimations, and (7) consistent ways of interacting with others (1980, p. 125). In essence, these seven factors combine to provide people with a sense of who they are as well as how they fit into the historical context in which they live. Erikson believed that some people in the United States find adolescence difficult because, at roughly the same time that they must deal with the problem of identity, they must also learn to deal with peer competition, physical intimacy, and career development. Not surprisingly, many young people begin their adult lives with a confused sense of identity, making it difficult for them to decide on their future careers.

For those people who are not ready to choose an identity, society provides a **psychosocial moratorium**—a socially sanctioned "time out" from the process of choosing an identity. In our culture, a psychosocial moratorium might involve joining the military, going to college and graduate school, entering psychotherapy, using drugs, or devoting oneself to a political cause or spiritual leader. All of these activities allow one to avoid choosing a mate or a vocation—and thus to avoid the issues of marriage and career. As suggested earlier, some young people turn to sexual relationships for the same reason.

In response to the problem of choosing an identity, other young people may choose a **negative identity**, thereby becoming something that society doesn't want. Like many adolescent identity choices, this negative identity is an experiment. In Erikson's view, identity confusion in late adolescence is not a problem; in fact, our culture encourages it to some degree. Problems do occur, however, when society's authority figures—as represented by judges, teachers, and so on—react to the negative identity that a young person has adopted in such a way as to lock it in. When that happens, the negative identity becomes a "real" identity. This phenomenon is discussed further in the section on psychological adjustment.

In summary, Erikson introduced the self-concept to psychoanalytic theory. The self doesn't simply reflect sexual drives and early childhood experiences; rather, it is shaped by feedback from the culture into which a person is born. In Erikson's view, psychological problems are rarely caused by sexual frustration; more often they result from not fitting into the culture within which one is born. This view is a radical departure from traditional psychoanalytic thinking and, as such, accords well with the role-theoretical model discussed in Chapter 9.

Unconscious Processes

"What a good dreamer can do for himself, psychoanalysis must restore to the patient," Erikson wrote in *Insight and Responsibility* (1968, p. 201). This statement reflects Erikson's argument that, for most of us, unconscious processes are a normal—even helpful—part of our lives. Drawing on ego psychology, Erikson believed that the primary task of the ego is to help people adapt to their social environments, which it does in an unconscious way. Erikson suggested that much of our everyday behavior expresses unconscious processes in a symbolic way, and that these symbolic expressions are often meaningless outside the cultural contexts in which they occur. His position is thus somewhere between Freud's and Jung's, in the sense that he did not believe the unconscious must be kept under strict control or that coming to terms with the unconscious is the goal of life; rather, his argument was that the unconscious helps a person meet the developmental tasks that come up in each stage of the life cycle.

In Erikson's view, understanding another person requires understanding how universal unconscious processes—such as the need for a sense of identity—are worked out for that person in specific social contexts. For example, in Somalia an adolescent boy might become a gunman in a warlord's army, but in the United States he might become a football player. Both are identity choices and, at an unconscious level, they fulfill the same psychological need.

Psychological Adjustment

During World War II, Erikson worked at the Mt. Zion Veterans' Rehabilitation Clinic treating veterans with combat neuroses. He concluded that most combat neuroses were caused not by "shellshock" but by a loss of "historical sameness and continuity" (1968, p. 17). Many soldiers with combat neuroses had lost their sense of inner control; they suffered from a kind of disorientation that Erikson described as an identity crisis. Over time, Erikson came to believe that many disorders of adolescence and early adulthood reflected a similar kind of identity crisis. Although identity crises are a normal part of development, serious problems occur when a young person who is poor or otherwise disadvantaged is unable to resolve them because of the conditions of his or her life.

In Erikson's view, adjustment problems occur when a person is unable or unwilling to resolve a normal developmental problem. And as we just noted, the adjustment problem that he primarily focused on was the identity crisis. Typically, during a crisis, young people experience **identity diffusion** or develop a negative identity. Persons who suffer from identity diffusion seem disorganized, changeable, and unable to finish their projects; they drift through life in a planless and purposeless manner.

Persons with a negative identity have chosen an identity that is the opposite of what they were expected to be. Negative identities are formed from roles that, at various stages of development, were dangerous or undesirable. For example, a boy who was taught to be sober and thrifty might adopt the negative identity of a drinker and gambler; a girl who was taught to be successful in everything she tried might become incompetent and helpless. Young people often use alcoholism, political radicalism, promiscuity, and other deviant behaviors to reject the conventional identities preferred by their parents or community.

Erikson suggested that the parents of adolescents who choose negative identities have some characteristics in common. Typically, the mother is concerned about status and meddles in her children's lives. She worries about social approval and recognition, and often complains to her children about their father. The father, on the other hand, tends to be successful in his work, but is excessively dependent on his wife and jealous of his own children. Erikson suggested that children with severe identity crises are quite hostile toward their parents.

Erikson believed that the way to treat identity diffusion and negative identity is with a psychosocial moratorium. During the moratorium, a person can explore alternative identities. In severe cases, the person must be physically sheltered from the expectations of his or her family. Generally speaking, Erikson was skeptical of psychiatric diagnosis, and he believed that psychiatric labels are often applied to people who are going through a psychosocial crisis that will pass with time.

In summary, Erikson believed that psychological health results from normal childrearing experiences and people's willingness to accept the roles available in their society and culture. As the case of the Sioux Indians shows, severe psychological problems occur when the identity that children have been raised to fulfill doesn't fit the society in which they must live—when the roles that are available to young people are unacceptable because they are foreign or degrading.

The Individual and Society

Freud thought the rules of society are designed to control human nature; they must be imposed on each developing person for the benefit of society, but at great personal cost to the individual in question. In contrast, Erikson believed that society supports and promotes individual development. Personal development and the mechanisms of society intertwine: Society contains the rules of mothering and childcare and other structures—school, work, marriage—that are designed to foster and promote individual welfare. For most people most of the time, Erikson said, society encourages individual growth. In fact, he criticized psychoanalysts who ignore society's role in personality development.

Erikson also criticized social scientists who ignore the fact that early childhood experience shapes individuals, who then transform their societies:

> *Academic minds, whose long-range perspectives can ignore the everyday urgencies of the curative and educative arts, blithely go on writing whole world histories without a trace of women and children, whole anthropological accounts without any reference to the varying styles of childhood. As they record what causal chain can be discerned in political and economic realities, they seem to shrug off as historical accidents due to "human nature" such fears and rages in leaders and masses as are clearly the residue of childish emotions.* (Erikson, 1964, p. 44)

Erikson gave the name **psychohistory** to the study of the links between psychological development and a person's historical circumstances. Psychohistory explains people's behavior not merely in terms of unconscious motives—as Freud did in his essay on Leonardo da Vinci *(1910)*—nor merely in terms of social forces—as Durkheim did in Suicide *(1897)*—but also in terms of how individuals adapt their childhood experiences to the environments in which they live.

Although historians have been interested in psychology for some time *(see Barnes, 1925)*, Erikson's 1958 book, *Young Man Luther*, is generally regarded as the first major work in psychohistory *(Runyon, 1988)*. Erikson's approach to psychohistory assumes that great leaders spell out the problems faced by many people in their societies and become leaders because they find a solution for these problems. Erikson *(1974)* referred to the conditions faced by everyone in a particular society at a given time—and, more specifically, the life history of an individual considered within his or her historical context—as the **historical actuality**.

From his studies of Martin Luther, Gandhi, Thomas Jefferson, and other leaders, Erikson identified several common themes in their development. These include an infantile "curse"— such as guilt over sexual experimentation or brutal treatment by parents—that had to be overcome; a feeling that their greatness was inevitable despite physical weakness or shyness; and a strong moral conscience even in early childhood. In addition, these people had great energy, an unusual ability to concentrate, and the capacity to "bide their time, until they find their public even as their public finds and drafts them" *(1968, p. 203)*.

Erikson also focused on dictators such as Hitler (see Box 11.3). He was particularly interested in the question of how famous leaders influence cultural identities in the eras in which they live. Their unique historical circumstances give these people an opportunity to define their own identities, and in doing so they provide new identities for subsequent generations of young people. The psychological study of historically significant people is important, not only for understanding history but also for understanding the psychological development of the persons who follow them.

Some historians *(e.g., Stannard, 1980)* criticize psychohistory on the grounds that psychoanalysts have not found significant links between experiences in early childhood and later adult behavior, or that great leadership is more the product of social forces than of individual characteristics. Nevertheless, psychohistory continues to be an influential discipline. All biographers must at some point deal with the psychological development of their subjects and try to determine how they dealt with the problem of identity.

Evaluating Erikson

Like all theories, especially the important ones, Erikson's has some distinctive strengths and some notable shortcomings. Let us begin with the latter.

First, Erikson always took pains to demonstrate his loyalty to traditional Freudian psychoanalysis. Consequently, his theory can be criticized for sharing many of the problems with psychoanalysis in general: lack of evidence for the existence of intrapsychic structures such as the id, ego, and superego as well as the oral, anal, and phallic stages of psychosexual development; retrospective explanations rather than predictions of behavior; and disproportionate attention paid to male sexuality.

Second, according to some writers, the view that people are born preadapted to an average expectable environment is politically conservative. Harry Guntrip *(1973)*, for example, criticizes what he regards as the "anti-person" stance of ego psychology, suggesting that Erikson's argument that people need to fit into the society in which they were born encourages conformity and, hence, a loss of individual uniqueness. Indeed, many people are born into environments that are bad for them, yet Erikson claimed that their major developmental task is to adapt to their unhealthy environments. How, if people are biologically predisposed toward adaptation to their social environments, can social change come about? Some writers (e.g., Erich Fromm) answer that human potential can be maximized and human suffering can be minimized only by restructuring society—something that ego psychology and Erikson's theory cannot envision.

Third, Erikson argued, on the basis of his own experience, that his eight stages of psychosocial development are universal—that every person in every culture must undergo the same eight stages. And if so, then other researchers should be able to observe these eight stages in the psychological development of people in other cultures. Unfortunately, however, there has been no independent verification of these stages. This is not to say that Erikson's stages cannot be found in other cultures—only that their existence has thus far not been independently verified.

A related issue concerns the mechanisms of stage transition: What causes a person to move from one developmental stage to the next? Erikson suggested that the transitions are biologically programmed; at a certain point in biological time, he said, a person automatically

BOX 11.3 Biography: Adolf Hitler

During World War II, the Office of Strategic Services commissioned a psychobiographical study of Adolf Hitler—a first of its kind. In later years, many historians and psychologists have analyzed the psychological factors that affected Hitler's behavior. One of the best known of these is Erikson's "The Legend of Adolf Hitler's Childhood," which appeared in Childhood and Society *(1950, 1963)*.

Hitler was born in Branau, Austria, on April 20, 1889. His father, the illegitimate son of a poor peasant woman, had run away from home at the age of thirteen. Failing to make a better life, Hitler's father returned at the age of forty-six and began a career as a minor customs official. Hitler always despised his father for accepting such a lowly position, and he was determined never to take such a job himself, even though this was his parents' wish.

Erikson pointed out that Hitler's family situation probably made resolution of the Oedipal conflict difficult. Hitler's mother was twenty-three years younger than his father. In addition, his father drank excessively and physically abused his mother. However, although childhood experience undoubtedly affected Hitler's psychological development, Erikson suggests that Oedipal rivalry alone is insufficient to explain the excesses of Hitler's adult life.

Hitler was a poor student in school, and his low grades prevented him from graduating. After his father died in 1907, he left home to seek his fortune in Vienna. He applied to art school and was rejected twice, but he continued to dream of becoming an artist. During this period, he fell into total poverty, moved into a hotel for transients, and supported himself by painting postcards. Erikson believed that Hitler developed his identity as a German nationalist and patriot during World War I. In 1913, Hitler enlisted in the Bavarian infantry. During the war, he experienced extensive combat, received a wound to the leg, and was exposed to poison gas; he was also cited for his conspicuous bravery. After the war, he gave up his dream of becoming an artist and taught political indoctrination for the army. At this job Hitler discovered he had great ability as a public speaker, and in 1919 he left the army to join the German Workers' Party, which later became the Nazi Party.

In Erikson's view, Hitler's success was based on the fact that his personal identity problems were the same as those faced by a generation of German working-class youth. Erikson pointed out that, judging from Mein Kampf *(1941)*, Hitler was seriously confused about who he was: He was born in Austria but considered himself a German; his parents wanted him to be a customs official but he wanted to be a painter; he could not become a painter because he was rejected by the art school; his dreams of greatness were contradicted by his squalid and impoverished lifestyle. Totally disregarding these facts, Hitler ultimately described his childhood as a kind of romantic fairytale.

Erikson also believed that, at least in his early years, Hitler's story was prototypical for most working-class German youth of that period. Before the war, German culture emphasized order and obedience—and this was the culture on which Hitler's childrearing was based. But German culture after the war was radically different: Now the country faced a great financial depression, combined with a racy public life in which all the old conventions were flaunted. Obedience to traditional authority was an inadequate basis for adolescent identity, especially compared to the newly emerging German nationalism. Like the Sioux elders we discussed earlier in the chapter,

German parents at that time were raising their children for a culture that no longer existed:

> When the father comes home from work, even the walls seem to pull themselves together (nehmen sich zusammen). The mother—although often the unofficial master of the house— behaves differently enough to make a baby aware of it. She hurries to fulfill the father's whims and to avoid angering him. The children hold their breath, for the father does not approve of "nonsense"—that is, neither of the mother's feminine moods nor of the children's playfulness. . . . Sons are bad, and punishment is always justified. Later, when the boy comes to observe the father in company, when he notices his father's subservience to superiors, and when he observes his excessive sentimentality when he drinks and sings with his equals, the boy acquires the first ingredient of Weltschmerz, a deep doubt of the dignity of man—or at any rate of the "old man." *(Erikson, 1963, pp. 331–332)*

Indeed, the working-class youth of Hitler's time saw traditional German society as hypocritical and dysfunctional; thus the establishment of a new order that would provide a new German identity was badly needed. In the social and economic disarray that characterized Germany after World War I, Hitler's struggle for identity, his nationalist politics, and his extreme views of the inferiority of non-Germans appealed to an entire working-class generation.

In Erikson's view, Germany's defeat in World War II did little to solve the identity problem of German youth. The division of Germany into two countries with antagonistic ideologies merely delayed the formation of a uniquely German political identity. Erikson further argued that, until German youth acquired a means for establishing identity, they would experience problems. From an Eriksonian perspective, the reunification of East and West Germany undoubtedly affected German character, but the emergence of skinheads and neo-Nazis in what used to be East Germany is just the sort of ominous development that Erikson predicted.

moves to the next stage. But there is no evidence for this claim, either. On the other hand, it is easy to imagine the expectations that people have about the behavior of children at each point in their development. In the United States, for example, three-year-olds are expected to be toilet trained, six-year-olds are expected to know how to read, eighteen-year-olds are expected to have career goals, and so on. And, indeed, if cultural expectations are the mechanisms that explain stage transitions, then the number and timing of the stages are not universal, as Erikson claimed. Rather, the number and timing of the stages would depend on the expectations that exist in a given culture.

Despite these shortcomings, Erikson's theory has a number of features that make it arguably the most important modern theory of personality. One attractive quality is its overall positive tone. Erikson saw life as a series of obstacles that must be faced—but once faced, they provide people with a sense of satisfaction and rightness about their lives. He also believed that human development is, in most cases, untraumatic and relatively free of psychopathology. Erikson was neither as pessimistic as Freud nor as optimistic as the humanistic psychologists. He regarded life as an interaction in which society creates the people it needs, and individuals create societies in which they can grow and develop.

Erikson's notion that people are biologically disposed to live in society contrasts strongly with traditional psychoanalytic theory. According to Freud, the instincts of sex and aggression guarantee conflict; accordingly, Freud predicted that life in society will be painful for most people. But Erikson and the ego psychologists replaced the most basic element of psychoanalysis—the antisocial instincts of sex and aggression—with a drive to fit in with one's culture. Although Erikson's ideas are inconsistent with Freud's, they are quite consistent with modern thinking about our evolution.

Erikson is probably best known for his theory of development across the life cycle. His notion that different tasks must be completed at different points during development has influenced writers both inside and outside psychology. This idea also appeals to people who do not believe that personality is fixed after the age of five.

Erikson's theory of the life cycle promotes analysis of the problems of adult development, a topic largely ignored by every theorist except Jung. Certainly the difficulties involved in choosing an occupation, finding a mate, and guiding the next generation have profound implications for the health of both individuals and society, and Erikson is one of the few personality psychologists who recognized these implications.

In addition, Erikson's term *identity crisis* has become part of everyday language; the concept is widely used in social work, clinical psychology, anthropology, and other fields. With the concept of identity, Erikson brought the self-concept into psychoanalysis. Freud believed that the instincts controlled human behavior, and he regarded conscious mental phenomena, such as a socially bestowed self-image, as trivial. By contrast, Erikson's identity concept placed a social—that is, nonbiological—element at the center of personality.

As we noted in the first chapter of this book, one of the most crucial questions in social theory is how to understand the relationship between the individual and society. America's founding fathers adopted the answer provided by eighteenth-century English philosophers, and it survives largely intact in modern psychology—namely, that people create their societies for reasons of self-interest, and if the societies stop serving their self-interest, the people will change them. The direction of influence is one-way; people create societies. But like Hegel and Marx, most sociologists take exactly the opposite perspective: They argue that large social forces such as history and economics control the lives of individuals. Again, the direction of influence is one-way; but this time, people are the creatures of large social forces.

Erikson's most important contribution, in our view, is his analysis of the relationship between individuals and societies—an analysis that is among the most sophisticated in the social sciences. In a nutshell, he argues that people need their cultures in order to survive in their physical environments. One element of culture is the manner in which its members raise their children. People create culture, but culture in the form of childrearing practices creates individuals. Thus, according to Erikson, people are inextricably embedded in culture, and the direction of influence goes both ways: People create, then are created by, their cultures.

Another attractive feature of Erikson's theory concerns its integrative nature. Although Erikson always thought of himself as a psychoanalyst, his work brings together ideas from anthropology, literature, sociology, political science, and, of course, history. Probably more so than any other theorist discussed in this book, Erikson carried the lessons of psychology into other disciplines. The concept of human nature contained in his work is much more balanced and complete—as well as believable—than those developed by many other theorists. Indeed, Erikson's understanding of how the social sciences fit together makes him one of the most influential and honored psychologists outside his own discipline.

Practical Application: Choosing a Career

In psychosocial theory, each developmental stage has a crisis that must be resolved before individuals can move to the next stage. During the identity stage, people face two particularly challenging decisions: They must decide the kind of person they wish to spend their life with, and they must decide the kind of vocation they will pursue. These choices are the cornerstone of Erikson's concept of identity.

The latter—career choice—has long been an area of interest for psychologists. Today, most psychologists believe that our career interests reflect many of our personal characteristics. In other words, all occupations have certain personality characteristics associated with them, and career success and satisfaction usually require that we match our personal qualities with the qualities demanded by specific jobs.

Most modern vocational interest inventories use a classification system developed by psychologist John Holland (1985), who has proposed that all careers can be classified into six broad categories:

1. Realistic careers (e.g., airline pilot, mechanical engineer, geologist, carpenter) appeal to people who like to see the concrete outcome of their efforts. These careers tend to be "hands-on," practical, and applied.

2. Investigative careers (e.g., surgeon, veterinarian, anthropologist, economist, psychiatrist) attract individuals who enjoy analyzing information and coming up with solutions to problems. In contrast with realistic careers, investigative careers tend to be more scientific and deductive.

3. Artistic careers (e.g., architect, composer, dancer, reporter) appeal to people who need a creative outlet for their abilities. Artistic careers often attract individuals who like flexible work schedules and changing job duties.

4. Social occupations (e.g., professional athlete, clinical psychologist, industrial/ organizational psychologist, political scientist) attract people who are interested in teaching or helping others. These individuals prefer jobs in which they interact with others and probably would not be happy working alone.

5. Enterprising occupations (e.g., real estate agent, supervisor or manager, teacher, lawyer, sales representative) appeal to individuals who like a changing work environment that offers opportunities for growth and reward.

6. Conventional careers (e.g., programmer, accountant, financial analyst, restroom attendant) appeal to people who enjoy analyzing and managing data. These individuals like work environments that are orderly, predictable, and structured.

Holland's career theory further states that people will be most successful in occupations that fit their personality characteristics. Although people make vocational decisions on the basis of factors other than personality (income potential, availability of jobs, years of training, and so forth), Holland argues that we will be most satisfied with our choice if our career allows us to express our personality. This view accords well with Erikson's theory, which maintains that we cannot make a successful career choice until we are clear about our identity.

MODELS OF PERSONALITY BASED ON SOCIOANALYTIC THEORY AND EVOLUTIONARY PSYCHOLOGY

- Historical Context
- Core Problem: What Do People Really Want?
- The Socioanalytic View of Human Nature
- Evaluating Socioanalytic Theory and Evolutionary Psychology
- The Life of Sigmund Freud

Socioanalytic theory describes a model of human nature that synthesizes the best modern thinking about human evolution, which includes evolutionary psychology *(e.g., Buss, 1991)*, psychometrics *(e.g., Wiggins, 1996)*, and human behavior genetics *(e.g., Lykken, 1996; Tellegen et al., 1988)*. Because people evolved as group-living and culture-using animals, we have a deep, organic need for social interaction and the comforts provided by the universal elements of human culture—religion, family, authority structures, and morality.

Specifically, socioanalytic theory suggests that the *inner core* of personality—motivation—is composed of needs that promoted survival in our ancestral past; these primarily concern the desire to be liked and accepted, to have status, power, or control over others, and to make sense out of the world. And the *surface* of personality—our conscious and nonconscious intentions—consists of the strategies we have developed to gain acceptance, to gain power, and to make the world predictable, all in the context of modern life. In short, the core of personality reflects our ancestral past, whereas the surface of personality reflects the demands of what the philosophers call the "specious present."

The major themes of everyday life—as seen in the development of history, politics, and economics—therefore involve the pursuit of acceptance and approval, status and power, and predictability and control. Given that motivation concerns the universal features of human nature, but also that personality is about how people differ from one another, socioanalytic theory further suggests that *the most important differences among people concern how well we get along with others, how much status we have, and how we make sense out of their lives*. Thus, we are ultimately concerned here with individual differences in people's ability to get along, get ahead, and find meaning.

Historical Context

Evolutionary theory began with Darwin's book, *Origin of Species (1859)*. Darwin noted that species live in particular environments—frogs live in ponds, parrots live in treetops, and so on. If the members of one species use the resources of their environment more effectively than others, then they have an advantage, and their numbers will increase. Darwin further noted that species change over time—they get smaller, larger, faster, and so forth. Changes that increase a species' ability to exploit its environment are retained; changes that reduce its ability to exploit an environment disappear—as do the species that exhibit those changes. Likewise, the demands of environments gradually change over time, which usually means that species must also change, if they are to survive.

The bottom line in evolutionary theory is "fitness." The fitness of any member of a species can be defined in terms of the number of its offspring that survive to maturity. The more offspring who survive, the greater the fitness and vice versa. The final element of traditional evolutionary theory is the concept of "adaptation." Adaptation affects behaviors as well as physical and mental abilities: Those behaviors and abilities that enhance fitness (i.e., that promote the survival of offspring) are "adapted" and will appear in the next generation. Most of the behaviors and abilities of existing creatures are adapted; for example, cats are adapted to hunt for small animals at night, dogs are adapted to hunt in packs, and parrots are adapted to eat nuts and seeds in trees. But the crucial question for our present purposes—and one to which we will return shortly—is "For what are people adapted?"

Some modern writers (e.g., Dawkins, 1986) also emphasize the role of sexual selection in human evolution. They argue that within a group, individuals competed for mates—who were obviously needed for reproduction. Characteristics that made individuals more attractive to members of the opposite sex were retained, sometimes to the point of jeopardizing adaptation to the larger environment. An obvious example of sexual selection in the animal world is the huge tail on male peacocks.

In short, human evolution was driven by pressures from the external environment in which groups lived, as well as by pressures within the groups. Among the external pressures were other human groups, one of the most potent forces shaping human evolution. Warfare was a universal feature of early human existence; characteristics that allowed one group to survive at the expense of its neighbors were also adaptive and retained. These characteristics were usually cultural (e.g., weapons and child-training strategies), but adapting to culture must have exerted some evolutionary pressure, too. That is, individuals who could use the elements of culture (e.g., language and finance) must have had an advantage relative to other members of the group.

All living creatures—including humans—are products of millions of years of evolutionary development. But Darwin tried to avoid talking about how his ideas apply to people because he feared the criticism that would inevitably follow. Thus, although he invented the theory, others brought it into psychology. Four people were especially important in introducing evolutionary theory to personality psychology.

1. Francis Galton, who was Darwin's half-cousin, immediately realized that Darwin's ideas applied to people as well as to other animals (an idea that is still controversial in nonscientific circles). Galton argued in *Hereditary Genius* (1869) that if mental, emotional, and physical characteristics are inherited, then they will run in families—and he provided data to support this point. He thus pioneered the scientific study of individual differences and human behavior genetics, both of which are active areas of research in modern psychology *(see Rowe, 1997)*.

2. William James, the first true giant of American psychology, was also a committed Darwinian. In 1889 he published Principles of Psychology, the greatest textbook of its era; and a few years later he wrote *Psychology: Briefer Course*, which Gardner Murphy *(1962, p. 6)* described as "the first really full-fledged evolutionary psychology." The latter book is primarily devoted to the origins and structure of consciousness, but Chapter 25 is about instincts. James defined an instinct as "the faculty of acting in such a way as to produce certain ends, without foresight of the ends, and without previous education in the performance" *(1962, p. 592)*. According to James, the influence of instincts on behavior can be seen only in babies; in adults, instincts are buried under a layer of habits.

3. William McDougall is largely forgotten today, but many of his ideas are quite modern. His *Social Psychology* (1908) was a founding text in social psychology, although it actually concerns personality. Revised and updated over a period of thirty years, it analyzes human nature from an evolutionary perspective. In both this book and *Outline of Psychology* (1923), McDougall argued that social behavior is initially triggered by a small number of instincts, but because these are quickly modified by experience, social behavior primarily reflects social influence. He also proposed a list of instincts that he modified several times, but that always ended up resembling James's original list.

4. Evolutionary theory initially addressed the question of how natural selection shapes the physical features of a species—how giraffes developed long necks, for example. But E. O. Wilson's *(1975)* book, *Sociobiology*, showed that the same principles apply to social behavior. Specifically, Wilson demonstrated that there are important advantages to group living (e.g., social species often out-compete solitary species) and that there are adaptive advantages to cooperating with and caring for others.

Galton, James, McDougall, and Wilson all suggested that human nature must be understood in the context of human evolution. Although future personality theories must be consistent with evolutionary theory, evolutionary theory *per se* tells us nothing specific about personality:

"Evolutionary theory is a theory about the origins of human nature, but it is not itself a theory of that human nature" *(Buss, 1997, p. 328).* Box 12.1 presents a discussion of evolutionary psychology from an interdisciplinary perspective.

Core Problem: What Do People Really Want?

The traditional personality theorists—Freud, Jung, Erikson, Rogers, Sullivan—assumed that the most important generalization we can make about people is that everyone is somewhat neurotic. They also assumed that the most important problem in life is to overcome our neurosis. There are two problems with these standard assumptions. First, they are empirically false: Not everyone is neurotic. Second, it is easy to show that such theories about neurosis reflect the biographies of their authors—Freud had problems with authority, Erikson had problems with his identity, and so on. We, on the other hand, believe that it is important to analyze human nature using generalizations that are both true and independent of one's own biography.

Sociology, anthropology, and primate research are helpful in this regard, and they lead to three generalizations that are both true and "impersonal." The first generalization is that primates and people always live in groups. This suggests that they are inherently social, that in a deep and important sense they need companionship and are adapted for group living *(see Baumeister & Leary, 1995).* Moreover, group living has clear survival implications; solitary primates and humans don't live very long.

The second generalization is that every primate and human group has a status hierarchy. This suggests that, in a deep and important sense, primates and people need status. Moreover, because status permits better choices in mates, food, and other commodities that promote fitness, people must be adapted to pursue it. Finally, anthropology tells us that religion is both an ancient human practice and a cultural universal. This suggests a need for predictability, a need to understand how the world works and what our place in the world might be. The need for predictability led to religion, but also to culture and technology; and it is culture that sets us apart from the rest of the primates. Obviously, then, the need for predictability has evolutionary significance.

People also have physiological needs—food, air, water, sleep. But these needs are not unique to people. The three motivational themes just described provide a general answer to the question "What do *people* really want?" What people want reflects what early humans needed to survive. However, to say that people are motivated by biologically based impulses is not to say that consciousness is irrelevant. Biology sets up life's problems, but consciousness allows us to solve those problems. As William James noted, consciousness evolved to solve the problems posed by biology—by human motivation. And a model of motivation based on evolutionary theory answers the question of how people are alike. But we must also account for the individual differences among people. People differ most importantly in terms of the strategies they have developed for dealing with the problems of getting along, getting ahead, and making sense out of the world—and, indeed, some strategies are more effective than others.

The Socioanalytic View of Human Nature

Motivation

As noted, at a deep and perhaps unconscious level, people are motivated by three broad needs: (1) attention, approval, and acceptance; (2) status and control of resources; and (3) predictability and order in their everyday lives. We refer to these needs as "getting along," getting ahead," and "finding meaning." These are powerful motives: People will kill to gain acceptance and status, they will kill to avoid losing them, and they will sometimes kill themselves when they think they have lost a sense of meaning and purpose *(Chapter 10)*. These needs explain the universal themes in human affairs (e.g., "It's still the same old story, the fight for love and glory . . . as time goes by.")

The first two motives are familiar themes. David Bakan *(1966)*, in a spirited *tour de force*, demonstrated that participation in larger social units (Communion/getting along) and efforts at self-promotion (Agency/getting ahead) are universal themes in human affairs. In evolutionary psychology, David Buss *(1991)* observed that successful reproduction depends on forming alliances (getting along) and negotiating status hierarchies (getting ahead). In anthropology, Robert Redfield *(1960)* observed that the survival of any social group depends on its members *living together* and *getting a living*. And in sociology, Talcott Parsons and Richard Bales *(1955)* demonstrated that every human group depends on successful completion of two activities: socio-emotional tasks (getting along) and tasks related to group survival (getting ahead).

Getting along and getting ahead are also major motive patterns in personality psychology. Dan McAdams *(1993)*, in the tradition of Erikson (Chapter 11) and Sarbin (Chapter 9), shows that the stories that people tell about themselves to support their identities can be organized around these two themes, which he calls intimacy and power. The same two motives are also important in social exchange theory *(Foa & Foa, 1980)*, which proposes that social interaction is organized around the exchange of love and status. Similarly, Jerry Wiggins *(Wiggins & Trapnell, 1996)*, in a brilliant quantitative elaboration of Sullivan's interpersonal theory (Chapter 7), argues that the exchange of love and status is the principal dynamic in social life.

The demands of getting along and getting ahead have two consequences. First, social interaction is a major human preoccupation because attention and status are the results of interaction. Second, when we gain status, others begin to resent us even as they congratulate us; conversely, we usually gain acceptance by conforming to the expectations of others—which makes high achievement difficult. Thus, there is an inherent tension beneath the surface of social life as people try to advance themselves without alienating others.

The need for predictability and order also has a long history in psychology. Pavlov's studies (Chapter 8) showed that when dogs are required to perform in unpredictable circumstances, they become neurotic. Donald Hebb and Richard Thompson *(1954)* pointed out that chimpanzees have a strong need for predictability, are highly sensitive even to small changes in the behavior of others, and become quite upset when others deviate even slightly from their normal behavior. In the context of personality psychology, Kelly's theory (Chapter 7) depends on the assumption that people need to be able to predict how others will respond to them. And, finally, Durkheim's (Chapter 9) key concept, anomie, refers to the condition that people experience when their lives no longer make sense in traditional terms. In short, anomie assumes a need for predictability and meaning, which established culture and tradition provide.

Over the course of human history, people with more status, more acceptance, and more predictability in their lives were at an advantage in the process of reproduction—they had a better choice of marital partners, food supplies, shelter, and other resources *(Daly & Wilson, 1983)*. With some qualifications, this is still true today. To summarize this discussion: People are fundamentally motivated by a need for structure and predictability, a need for attention and approval, and a need for status and control of resources. We meet these needs during social interaction: By virtue of the unique features of human evolution, we are compelled to interact. But because human nature is rooted in biology, individual differences are inevitable. Thus, some people need social acceptance more than others (e.g., actors versus anchorites), some people need status more than others (e.g., politicians versus social workers), and some people need predictability and meaning more than others (e.g., observers of orthodox religion versus agnostics). Finally, some people are more successful than others in attaining these goals, and these individual differences are what socioanalytic theory tries to explain.

Personality Development

From an evolutionary perspective, personality development can be thought of in terms of both the development of the species and individual development.

Phylogenesis: The Development of the Human Species. Two adaptations gave our ancient ancestors an advantage over chimpanzees, baboons, and other competitors: the development of an upright stance and the development of tool use. Upright stance freed the hands to grasp tools. And better tools—including clubs, spears, and sharp stones—allowed early humans to hunt and fight more effectively than other primates. (Today, better tools still give human groups an advantage when competing with other groups.) Tool use—and culture in general— also encouraged the development of larger brains, which then permitted the development of more sophisticated tools.

The mechanics of birth requires that human babies have small heads, but human intelligence—fostered by tools and culture—has promoted larger heads. The result is that human infants need a long period of development while their brains grow and they learn the lessons of their culture—language, tool use, and so on. Moreover, during that long period of development, infants must be cared for. The ability of adults to provide care depends on "pair bonding" and a division of labor between males and females. Consequently, all human groups are organized around partnerships *(Eibl-Eibesfeldt, 1989, p. 186)*.

Iraneus Eibl-Eibesfeldt notes that "the basic principles of human society are fully developed in hunter-gatherer peoples" *(1989, p. 615)*. Hunter-gatherers live in groups of twenty to fifty people, each of which is composed of a family unit containing grandparents, parents, and offspring. The groups stay together, live in a fixed region, and defend it against other groups. They maintain group solidarity through gift giving and other forms of exchange, as well as through ritualized social interaction—including festivals and religious ceremonies. Some groups are egalitarian, others are authoritarian; but all have status hierarchies. In addition, all believe that they are a special people and distrust foreigners. Haggling and disputes are constant; warfare is universal. The groups with superior technology and social organization overwhelm, enslave, or destroy groups with inferior technology and social organization. Technology and social organization are the keys to group survival, which explains why the younger generation needs to learn the culture of its group.

The foregoing themes, reflecting perhaps 1,000,000 years of human experience, are the unconscious background in terms of which individual personality develops. People lived in hunter-gatherer groups until agriculture was invented about 10,000 years ago; agriculture, in turn, allowed much larger human communities (cities) to develop. Modern industrial society is perhaps 150 years old and has led to huge urban centers. Life in these large cities is easier in some ways than life in a hunter-gatherer group (e.g., food, water, electricity are generally available) but more difficult in other ways (e.g., we no longer know our neighbors, or even trust them). We are adapted to living in conditions that no longer exist, which explains much of the malaise of modern urban living—a malaise that Durkheim referred to as anomie.

Ontogenesis: The Development of Individuals. A study of the natural history of humans *(e.g., Eibl-Eibesfeldt, 1989)* suggests that individual development takes place in four broad stages, and that these stages occur in every culture.

1. *Infancy.* Infancy extends from birth until the child enters a children's play group somewhere between three and five years of age. Parent-infant relations are usually

characterized by tenderness and affection; even such notoriously ferocious people as the Yanomamis of Northern Brazil treat their babies and small children with great kindness. Just as parents want to care for their babies, the babies want to be cared for by, and interact with, their parents. In normal circumstances this two-way motivation leads to the development of an "attachment bond" *(Ainsworth et al., 1978)*, a strong emotional link between an infant and its caretakers. The development of a mother-child bond is preprogrammed, forming the basis not only for an infant's sense of security and well-being but also for a child's subsequent social relationships. Accordingly, the development of an attachment bond is the key event during this first period of life. If the mother becomes psychologically impaired (through mental illness or substance abuse) or absent (through death, illness, or some other misfortune), and if there are no other adults to take her place, then the consequences for the child's later development are usually unfavorable. The data on this contingency are quite clear *(see Bowlby, 1969, 1971)*.

2. *Childhood.* Childhood extends from the time children enter their play group until the onset of adolescence. Children expect their parents to coddle and support them, a pattern that encourages childish egocentrism. To interact with their peers, they must outgrow this egocentrism. The opposite of egocentrism is social sensitivity, and this, as George Herbert Mead *(1934)* pointed out, develops through playing games in childhood. Eibl-Eibesfeldt concurs: "By playing together in the children's group the members learn what aggravates others and which rules they must obey" *(1989, p. 601)*. Children learn how to interact with adults by following the adults' rules; and they learn how to interact with other children by anticipating their expectations—which, in turn, they learn to do by playing games. In short, the crucial lessons of childhood involve overcoming infantile egocentrism and learning to interact successfully within the peer group.

3. *Adolescence.* All cultures describe adolescents in somewhat negative terms, probably because their behavior is neither childlike nor mature. For example, the Bushmen of the Kalahari Desert in southern Africa refer to adolescents as "lazy, lounging lords of the shade." Moreover, adults generally want adolescents to give up their childish interests and begin contributing to their group, tribe, or family as soon as possible. To dramatize adolescents' transition to adulthood and to encourage them to follow the rules of adult behavior, many societies use puberty rites to mark the point at which adolescents are supposed to change.

Puberty rites can be quite dramatic—even cruel. Depending on the culture, they may include beatings and ritual mutilation (tattoos, circumcisions, etc.), seclusion in special huts or compounds, or pressure to wear peculiar clothes, eat nasty foods, and shave bodily hair. In contemporary American society, the Marine Corps uses ritualized harassment to encourage new recruits to leave adolescence for adulthood. But whereas adults want adolescents to become productive citizens, adolescents want status among their peers. Indeed, they care primarily about feedback and approval from their peer group, not from adults.

We agree with Erikson that the primary task of adolescence is to develop an identity. Our identity is an idealized view of ourselves—as scholar, dancer, athlete—that we use to organize our lives and our social interactions. Identity answers the question of who we are, what we do, what we stand for, and how we should be treated. During adolescence, young people try out a variety of identities—musician, cheerleader, mystic. Feedback from the peer group (e.g., "Who do you think you are?") is often what gradually determines the final choice.

4. *Adulthood.* Adult social life consists of an extended series of interactions, usually with the same people, and it can be described in terms of four characteristics. The first concerns the goal of adulthood—namely, the pursuit of status and social acceptance. Second, there are two major strategies for interaction: competing and trying to outperform others, and affiliating and trying to build coalitions. High status depends on the support of others, which involves building relationships. But high status also depends on aggression, if for no other reason than high-ranking individuals must be able to defend their position against the subordinates who will challenge them. As Freud *(1913)* noted, these challenges usually come from younger people, they are inevitable, and, over the long run, they will be successful.

A third point is that status leads to the sense of being the center of attention—a feeling that is directly related to self-esteem. When a low-ranking chimpanzee becomes the alpha male, he seems to get bigger, and his physiological signs of stress diminish *(DeWaal, 1980)*. The same appears to be true for people who suddenly achieve high status. This observation is somewhat obvious, but it is also irresistible: "[E]ven relatively intelligent people cannot escape the force of status seeking" *(Eibl-Eibesfeldt, 1989, p. 308)*. Box 12.2 describes the universality of status seeking.

Finally, as Wiggins *(1996)* notes, social interaction is an exchange process—and what gets exchanged are status and respect. After every interaction each person gains or loses a little bit of status and a little bit of respect. Interacting with others is a kind of social performance: Athletes, actors, and politicians are only as good as their last performance, so the saying goes—but the same is true for most of us. Every interaction is followed by a short accounting process, after which we either gain or lose points.

Self-Knowledge

Along with William James, William McDougall, and George Herbert Mead, we believe that the self is the core of personality, and that it is created during social interaction based on feedback from others. Once the self is formed, it guides our actions vis-à-vis others, and feedback from others then further shapes the self. Ultimately, this sense of self is the same as our identity. Because interaction is so central to adult social life, it is important to ask, What do we need in order to have an interaction? The answer is that we need two things: a pretext for the interaction (e.g., "Let's get together and watch football") and a role for each participant to play (e.g., "You be the host and I will bring some beer").

The Games Children Play. Think for a moment about the kinds of interactions you can have with a child. Some examples follow.

1. *"Ah Boo" Games (birth to nine months).* Children as early as six months can "interact" in very simple games. For example, hold a child on your lap and slowly bring your hand down to cover the child's face, then quickly take your hand away and say "Boo"; by the second or third repetition the child will show signs of enjoyment. The reason is that the baby is receiving attention and interaction in a structured and predictable way, and this is inherently pleasant.

2. *"What's That" Games (nine to eighteen months).* By nine to twelve months of age, more complicated interactions are possible. Place a child on your lap, open a magazine, point to a picture, and say "What's that?" Then turn the page and repeat the sequence. Children love this game because, once again, it gives them attention in a structured and predictable fashion. Note also that this game contains the elements of adult interaction: a pretext or reason for interaction (looking at the book) and mutual parts to play (page turner and page ripper).

3. *"Mother-Baby" Games (twenty months).* By twenty months, many children can play "mother-baby" games in which a mother changes her tone of voice and talks to her child as if he were a baby and the child responds by "acting like a baby." This is the child's first experience at assuming a role in order to interact with another person.

4. *"Pretend" Games (thirty-six months).* By thirty-six months, most children are able to initiate

versions of adult interaction. One child will say to another, "Pretend the couch is a monster" or "Pretend the dolly is sick and we are doctors." The children will then use the pretend statement to organize their play until they have exhausted its possibilities. Moreover, at this age some children are so sophisticated about constructing interactions that they can manipulate the process. For example, the authors of this book have a videotape of a little girl saying to a little boy, "Pretend you were the mommy and I was the daddy." The little boy, looking puzzled, protests weakly. The girl repeats the request. The boy mumbles that she can't be the "daddy." The girl begins laughing and repeats the request. The boy, now near tears, threatens to tell the teacher if he can't be the "daddy." Laughing, the girl skips off, saying she doesn't want to play anyway. This sequence suggests the girl has mastered the interaction process sufficiently well that she can invent a pretext and assign bogus roles.

As noted, children at play receive attention in a structured and predictable manner. But realize also that adults don't simply get together and bask in one another's company; they get together and "do something"—have a cup of coffee, drink a beer, talk something over—and their interactions are essentially identical to the play among three-year olds. To interact with another person, we need a pretext and a role to play. Our identity guides social interaction because we use it to decide what roles we will play and how we will play them. Some roles, in fact, we won't play because they are inconsistent with our identity. Recall that in the example given above, the little boy's identity forbade him to play the role of "mommy."
Where do identities come from? Mead said that other people teach you who you are. This is true, but you also choose your identity from a "menu" that is available in your culture. The menu is usually found in the entertainment world—in movies, books, TV shows, and so on. However, the real you comes from a menu provided by society. You may choose to reject the identities that are available in your culture, but you will have to find another one in order to join in the game of life and interact with others.

People's identities include their values, and their values are tied to their social class; in fact, social class is defined by values. For example, wealthy people with working-class values seem working class, whereas working-class people with good taste and civil manners seem "well bred." In short, personality—identity—is linked to social class through our values, which explains Allport's generalization that everything of importance in personality is correlated with social class.

Identity and Reputation.   There are two components of personality: identity and reputation. Our identity guides our behavior during social interaction; it controls the roles we are willing to play and how we play them. For example, all of the participants in a college classroom are playing the role of student, but *how* they do so varies widely, depending on their identities.

Other people evaluate our behavior during social interactions and create our reputation. Identities are personality from the perspective of the actor; they concern the person that *we* think we are. Reputations, on the other hand, are personality from the perspective of the observer; they concern the person that *others* think we are. Most people can describe their identities, but few people can accurately describe their reputations, even though they usually care deeply about them (see Figure 12.1).

BOX 12.3 The Importance of Reputation

In the past, personality psychologists ignored reputation, claiming that it had nothing to do with personality. From a "real world" perspective, however, they were clearly wrong. People actually care deeply about their reputations and will work hard to preserve them. Consider the case of professional football player Mark Chmura. Rich, handsome, and famous, he served as star tight end of the Green Bay Packers, was selected to the Pro Bowl three times, and earned a Super Bowl Championship ring. Chmura is also a devout Catholic, a former altar boy who famously refused to meet with President Bill Clinton at a White House reception because he disapproved of Clinton's morals.

On April 9, 1999, after an evening of heavy drinking with a friend, he went to the friend's house for a nightcap. The friend's teen-aged daughter was having a post-prom party with some high school friends. A seventeen-year-old girl at the party, who was a member of a gang called "The Sexy Bitches," remarked, as Chmura arrived, that she hated him, and called him an unprintable name. More drinking followed, at which point observers described Chmura as drunk, red-faced, and giggling. In his underwear, Chmura got into a hot tub with some girls. Later he went into a bedroom, and the aforementioned seventeen-year-old, after being told not to, followed him.

At 2:00 a.m. on April 10, the police came to Chmura's house and arrested him on charges of sexual assault with a minor—a charge tantamount to pedophilia. During the next few months, Chmura was quite depressed, had frequent crying spells, and started losing his hair. He was afraid to go out—especially to restaurants, because he thought cooks might defile his food. Life as he knew it was over; his fame, his money, his championship rings and trophies no longer mattered. Life had become a nightmare—because his reputation was ruined.

A jury, after deliberating for two hours, found Chmura not guilty. He then began trying to put his life back together, exercising, working out, and exploring job offers. But as a reporter at Sports Illustrated (February 12, 2001) asked, Would he ever be able to rebuild his reputation? People have been known to kill themselves over damaged reputations—an option Mark Chmura considered seriously—and this fact speaks poignantly to the emotional power of such events. Reputation is indeed at the core of personality, and any serious theory of personality must take this into account.

Gordon Allport (1961) argued that reputation was not part of personality. His viewpoint has been widely influential, but we think he was wrong. In fact, we believe that there are five reasons why reputations are important for the study of personality. First, they develop quickly and are stable over time: Different observers tend to agree quite substantially about a person's reputation—which means that reputations can be studied objectively. In contrast, identities are fluid and much harder to evaluate or study. Second, most people spend a great deal of time and energy trying to establish and maintain their reputations. Even criminals, for example, care deeply about their reputations, which usually reflect the kind of crimes in which they have specialized and how notorious they have become. Some people pretend not to care how others evaluate them, but they are playing the part of being indifferent; indeed, their indifference is a carefully cultivated part of their reputation (cf. Schlenker & Weigold, 1990). Third, because the best predictor of future behavior is past behavior, and because reputations reflect a person's past behavior, reputations are quite useful for predicting many, if not most, aspects of social performance (e.g., academic achievement, occupational success, delinquency, and career choice). Fourth, psychologists have a well-defined taxonomy of reputations—namely, the Five-Factor Model (Chapter 6). People tend to think about and describe others in terms of five categories or dimensions—self-confidence, social presence, likeability, conscientiousness, and curiosity/creativity. Fifth, and last, our reputations reflect the amount of social acceptance and status we have within our community (see Box 12.3).

We have said many times in this chapter, and in various ways, that a primary goal of socioanalytic theory is to explain individual differences in peoples' ability to achieve love, power, and purpose or meaning. Two sets of reasons account for these individual differences. The first are obviously biological: Height, body build, temperament, appearance, and intelligence are inherited and have implications for success in adulthood. Tall, smart, well-built extraverts have an immediate, though not necessarily overwhelming, advantage in the game of life compared to people with the opposite characteristics.

The second set of reasons for individual differences in life's success concern how people analyze the world, which is the subject matter of George Kelly's theory and that of the cognitive social psychologists who followed him (including Albert Bandura and Walter Mischel). After all, what we do depends on what is on our minds, and some people are more insightful about how to conduct themselves than others. The mental models most responsible for individual differences are (a) our identities and (b) the interpersonal behaviors we have developed to express and defend our identities. The latter are known as *self-presentational behaviors*.

We must all have an identity in order to take part in social interactions. And identities vary enormously, a fact that largely explains the differences between people. College professors are different from stockbrokers; but people with the same identity—college professors—express the identity differently.

There is little research explaining why people choose the identities they do, or why they express them as they do. So we are left to assume that individual differences are largely a function of identity choice and identity expression.

Successful people know how to manage their reputations, and they manage them one interaction at a time. This observation is what prompted Goffman (1959) to remark that, during every interaction, we run a major risk of minor embarrassment and a slight risk of utter humiliation—because our reputation is evaluated after each interaction in the same way that a musician's reputation is evaluated after each performance.

But what is it that we know when we know ourselves? There are two perspectives on self-knowledge—the actor's and the observer's. There is the person that we know, and there is the person that others know. On the one hand, self-knowledge from the actor's perspective involves becoming aware of our identity and the self-presentational strategies that we use to support it (i.e., being mindful of what we are doing when we interact with others). On the other hand, self-knowledge from the observer's perspective involves becoming aware of how others perceive and describe us. Identity and reputation are indeed the major components of self-knowledge, and they are related in interesting ways. For example, the person we think we are may not be the person that others think we are—and to the degree that this is true, we will have trouble achieving our goals in life.

To summarize this discussion: Our evolutionary history as group-living animals suggests that, at a deep and often unconscious level, we need social acceptance, status, and predictability. We get these through social interaction. All social interaction follows the model of a game. For an interaction, we need a pretext or agenda, and we need roles or parts to play. Identities, agendas, and roles all come from the culture in which we live—which explains the links between personality and culture, or social class. We use our identity to guide our social behavior; there are roles we won't play because they just aren't us. We spend our days in various roles assigned to us by others—student, employee, son, daughter—and we all play the roles differently because of our identities.

Our identities guide our social interactions, in conjunction with the agendas for the interactions and the roles that are available. Thus, what we do at any point in time (e.g., our behavior) is a function of our identity, and of the roles and agendas that structure the particular interaction in which we are involved. Finally, self-knowledge involves becoming aware of our identities, the way in which we present our identities to others, and the way in which others evaluate our self-presentations. In short, it concerns becoming aware of our identities and our reputations—and people who are successful in the game of life are mindful of these issues.

Unconscious Processes

Freud's view that we are often unaware of the reasons for our actions is correct. However, we believe that people can become aware of these reasons if they pay attention. We believe that there are at least three sets of unconscious causes underlying social behavior.

The first set of unconscious causes is biological in nature. As noted above, we need attention and approval, status and control of resources, and order and predictability. Although much of our everyday behavior concerns these needs, we are rarely conscious of this fact. Loneliness usually indicates a need for interaction; depression indicates lost status and control; and anxiety is caused by chaos and unpredictability. We become conscious of these needs, therefore, primarily when they are unfulfilled. We also include temperament (Buss & Plomin, 1984) and mood (Tellegen, 1985) in this category of unconscious biological processes. People are born predisposed toward certain characteristic moods and emotions: Some people are naturally cheerful, others are naturally gloomy; some are naturally energetic, others are naturally lethargic; some are naturally sociable, others are naturally shy; some are naturally calm and relaxed, others are naturally tense and edgy. Because we live inside our own mood states, they color our perceptions like tinted glasses and we tend to think they are universal, that others see the world the same way we do. In any case, our mood states focus our attention and shape our perceptions in ways that are simultaneously profound, idiosyncratic, and unconscious. Being unaware of our characteristic moods can cause problems, as, for example, when shy people decide they want to be politicians or work in sales and then discover that constant interaction with strangers is stressful.

The second set of unconscious causes is a function of our natural egocentrism. That is, we tend to be unaware of, or even ignore, what others expect or believe during interactions. For example, when managers are asked to describe how they are seen and evaluated by their staff, they are surprisingly inaccurate. Even couples in close relationships can't accurately describe how they are perceived by their partners. Although we constantly interact, the data suggest that our interactions are based on very superficial mutual understanding. This raises a serious question about how social interaction is possible.

One answer is that the rules governing interaction are "prewired" in our nervous systems, so that our responses to others don't depend on understanding others or knowing what they expect. In this respect, human social interaction may resemble the mating dance of dragonflies, wherein gestures, colors, smells, and postures trigger corresponding gestures, postures, and behavior. Eibl-Eibesfeldt *(1989)* argues that the rules of social interaction are inherited, that there is "a universal grammar of social behavior according to which verbal and nonverbal interactions are similarly structured" *(p. 499)*. The result is that "[m]any of the basic strategies of social interaction . . . follow their course automatically according to phylogenetically evolved programs" *(p. 516)*. Indeed, people all over the world respond to the same nonverbal gestures (e.g., sticking one's tongue out is a universal sign of impertinence) and recognize the same emotions in others. Eibl-Eibesfeldt further suggests that "we can speak of a universal grammar of human social behavior. . . . With the discovery of the universal interactional strategies . . . [w]e have recognized the existence of a universal . . . regulating system governing all interactions" *(1989, p. 517)*.
Consequently, it seems that much of our behavior during social interaction—posture, facial expressions, gaze, pace, and so on—occurs automatically and is therefore unconscious. Politicians, actors, and other entertainers understand this and often undergo elaborate coaching in order to master and control these very subtle and otherwise unconscious interpersonal behaviors.

The third set of unconscious causes comprises the values, attitudes, and norms of our culture that we assume are true and therefore do not question or evaluate. These include rules about what we should eat, how we should dress, and how we should treat people above or below us on the corporate ladder. This third category includes a much wider range of beliefs, attitudes, and behaviors than we may realize; it corresponds to the sociological model of the unconscious that we described in Chapter 9. As we noted in that chapter, the first goal of every social reform movement is to make people aware of as-yet-unexamined unconscious ideas and practices that need to be changed. As the great Oklahoma humorist Will Rogers said, "It isn't what you don't know that will hurt you, it is what you do know that isn't true."

We can summarize this discussion as follows. Although social behavior is largely guided by forces or processes outside people's awareness, many of these nonconscious determinants can be made conscious through social feedback, education, and self-reflection. To the degree that they remain unconscious, people are liable to act in ways that are foolish, self-defeating, or even immoral (as when they engage in racist or sexist behavior).

Psychological Adjustment

As we have noted several times, at a deep and perhaps unconscious level people need attention and approval, status and success, and structure and predictability. This observation provides a framework for understanding psychological stress and poor adjustment. William James suggested that stress is caused by having expectations about our own performance that exceed our actual capacities. That is, if we expect to perform at a certain level, or if others expect us to, stress is created when we don't perform at that level. If the stress persists long enough, we will break down physically or psychologically. Consider three examples.

First, children vitally need the attention and approval of their parents and caretakers. Imagine what life is like for children with unpredictable parents. When they return from school, or otherwise seek support and affection from their parents, they never know if they will be hugged or abused. Although they need their parents' attention and acceptance, they won't be able to perform in a way that ensures parental availability. Because such children's expectations exceed their capacity to perform, the result will be extreme stress, lowered self-esteem, and various psychological symptoms that may last a lifetime. Second, imagine a conscientious working man with a family to support, who loses his job because the corporation for which he works must shut down. He expects to be able to provide for his family but loses his capacity to do so because of forces beyond his control; here, too, the result can be extreme stress. Third, imagine a nervous and sensitive young soldier thrust into combat. He expects to be brave but finds himself terrified. The contrast between his expectations and his capacity to perform will cause great stress, perhaps resulting in a nervous breakdown. In all three cases, the solution lies in controlling expectations, which is often very hard to do.

The absence of stress does not automatically mean the presence of happiness. Happiness depends on solving the three great problems in life: gaining acceptance and social approval, gaining status and the control of material resources, and finding a way to make life predictable and interpretable.

Social Approval. Some people are more likeable than others, and the reasons are generally well understood. From the observer's perspective, a likeable person is one who is rewarding to deal with. Rewarding people are predictable and fun. Predictable people live up to their obligations—they are on time, keep their word, honor their commitments, and follow the ordinary rules of social interaction. Predictable people also express their emotions in a mature manner; they don't yell, rant, get angry, hurt, depressed, accusatory, or defensive but, instead, maintain an even emotional keel. People who are fun generally seem to care about us. They express concern, pay attention to our expectations, respect our feelings, and never offend us. In the best case, they are also entertaining, funny, colorful, and engaging.

From the actor's perspective, being rewarding is a function of caring about that aspect of one's reputation and having sufficient social skills to be an interesting interactional partner. The popular appeal of former President Bill Clinton was due in large part to his unusual ability to project concern and empathy. But there are many people who genuinely don't care whether others like them; others sense their lack of concern, and find them unlikeable. Moreover, some occupations actually require indifference to being liked. Examples include law enforcement, quality control engineering, safety enforcement—in short, any job where one is required to give others negative feedback on a routine basis.

Generally speaking, people who are liked and have many friends seem content, stress-free, and happy. Conversely, people who are friendless and isolated are usually stressed, have a poor quality of life, and are likely to experience health problems *(Diener et al., 1999)*. Consider the particular problem faced by shy people. On the one hand, they want to be liked; on the other, their shyness makes them socially awkward, which, in turn, often makes them unrewarding to deal with. This is another clear case of expectations exceeding capability: They want to be liked but lack the skill to make it happen on a regular basis.

Status. Most personality psychologists disapprove of people who are ambitious and want to get ahead. Freud characterized ambitious people as having unresolved Oedipal problems (they are potential father murderers, he said), Jung believed that ambitious people were overly involved in their personas, Erikson thought ambitious people had identity problems, and so on. In contrast, the field of organizational psychology recognizes ambition as the key to high status, as seen most obviously in the attainment of leadership roles.

Four status-related generalizations have been proposed *(Hogan & Hogan, 1991)*. First, most high-status people are ambitious: They want status, it is an explicit value for them, and they evaluate themselves in terms of their progress toward status attainment. Second, most high-status people are persistent: They work hard, and they are willing to endure setbacks, reversals, discouragement, disappointments, and failures to reach their goals. Third, most high-status people are strategic in the pursuit of their career goals, often choosing these goals when they are quite young and then spending their early years in conscious preparation. They deliberately develop the skills and personal contacts necessary for success, and they think carefully about what they do well and about the strengths and shortcomings of their competition. Fourth, most high-status people have something to prove: They have doubts about their personal worth and use their accomplishments to demonstrate their worthiness to themselves and others. Some may thus work hard and seek success in order to compensate for feelings of inadequacy. Beyond these generalizations, however, the keys to success depend on a person's chosen field. Successful artists and scientists are often quite disagreeable; for them, intelligence and creativity seem more important than likeability. Conversely, high status in public life—especially politics and business—depends on social skill as well as intelligence and creativity.

Ultimately, happiness appears to depend on having friends and a social network. Many low-status people who are popular seem happy; high-status people with few friends seem unhappy. Thus, status doesn't necessarily lead to happiness. Rather, much of life concerns getting along and getting ahead (see Box 12.4).

Finding Meaning. There is substantial agreement that mature people have "unifying philosophies of life," which involve a commitment to something outside themselves. Academic psychology has traditionally been hostile toward religion, and few researchers have studied the psychology of commitment. Carol Ryff (1989) is an exception. She provides clear evidence that having a "purpose in life" is empirically related to health and happiness. What remains to be analyzed is how people go about constructing such a purpose for themselves.

The Individual and Society

Most theories of personality define maturity in individual terms—mature people have high self-esteem, are self-actualized, are at peace with themselves, and so on. However, these individualistic definitions ignore a person's impact on, or responsibility to, others. A person can have high self-esteem, be self-actualized, and still be immature. Having high self-esteem is no guarantee that one will not exploit, manipulate, and betray others. Being self-actualized is no guarantee that one will act responsibly with regard to one's obligations to society at large.

We believe that maturity must be defined simultaneously from the perspectives of both the person and his or her social group. Maturity depends on balancing one's egoistic and altruistic impulses as well as one's self-critical and self-accepting tendencies. Mature people are both comfortable with themselves and open to critical feedback; they are both actively engaged in helping others and reasonable about advancing their own self-interest. A sign of maturity, therefore, is the degree to which individuals are integrated into their society without, at the same time, losing a sense of who they are vis-à-vis others. A commitment to social causes and to the welfare of others is necessary to overcome egocentrism; a critical distance from those causes is necessary in order to avoid becoming a true believer. Similarly, a measure of maturity is the degree to which one is self-accepting while at the same time realizing that one is not perfect. Within the context of overall self-approval, mature people listen carefully to negative feedback from others, including spouses, children, students, and employees—

especially others with less status than themselves.

Our view of maturity calls to mind the ideal citizens of Greek city-states during the time of Plato and Aristotle. Such persons were expected to develop their skills and seek excellence, but always within the context of what was good for their community as a whole. They were expected to balance personal pride against their duties as citizens. In contrast to those who adhere to the prevailing individualism of modern psychology, which defines maturity in a social vacuum, we believe that the concept of maturity must take into account the relationship between the individual and his or her society.

Evaluating Socioanalytic Theory and Evolutionary Psychology

At least three problems with the foregoing model of personality should be mentioned. First, as Marilyn Brewer and Linnda Caporael (1991) note, human evolutionary theory has at times been put to political rather than scientific purposes. Specifically, evolutionary arguments have been used to support racism, sexism, and even genocide. The argument is easy to construct. One need merely note that there are consistent differences between two groups—for example, men and women—and then argue that the characteristics that typify the group to which one belongs—usually the group that is in power—are innately and biologically superior to the characteristics of the other group, precisely because it is one's own group that is in power. One is then "justified" in stigmatizing the other group on the grounds of one's natural superiority. We, of course, deplore arguments of this sort because they are circular, pseudoscientific, and hateful.

A second problem with thinking about human nature in terms of evolutionary theory is that it requires an interdisciplinary perspective. One must learn, for example, about ethology, paleoanthropology, primatology, behavior genetics, and sociobiology, and this difficult assignment takes a long time to complete. Moreover, when academic psychologists become interdisciplinary, they sometimes put their careers at risk.

A third problem has to do with the fact that, from a research perspective, the two key elements of socioanalytic theory are identity and reputation. Reputation (personality from the observer's perspective) is easy to study and has a well-defined structure—the Five-Factor Model. The discovery of this model generated a substantial amount of interesting and useful research. On the other hand, personality from the actor's perspective—identity—is hard to study. Dan P. McAdams (1993) pioneered this very difficult and labor-intensive line of research, and has many interesting findings to report. Nonetheless, the research base on the topic of identity—the core of socioanalytic theory—is substantially underdeveloped.

As for the strong points of the evolutionary model, we point to two in particular. First, most of the ideas presented in this chapter are consistent with research results in the empirical literature. But more important, this model answers an old question—namely, How is it that people can both create and be created by society? The answer, we believe, lies in the fact that people evolved as group-living animals. The requirements of keeping a group together—internal organization and coordination—were key factors shaping human evolution. Consequently, society exists not only "out there" in the form of social structures, as the sociologists suggest, but also inside us, as McDougall and others suggest, in the form of inherited tendencies toward cooperating, helping others, complying with social norms, craving acceptance and status, and fearing social rejection. In short, evolutionary theory provides the best answer so far to the question about the relationship between the individual and society.

The Life of Sigmund Freud

As noted in Chapter 3, Sigmund Freud was one of the most creative and influential writers of the twentieth century, and not just in psychology. It is interesting to compare what psychoanalysis and socioanalytic theory have to say about his life story, because, one could argue, psychoanalysis should provide the better account. From the perspective of socioanalytic theory, three features of Freud's biography stand out. First, he was intensely ambitious; his family expected him to be famous, he wanted to be famous, and his surviving letters show how much he craved the respect and recognition of his peers. Second, he worked very hard—and for a very long time. He published more, and better, material after the age of sixty-five than most people do in a lifetime. And he did this by working all day and part of every night each day of the week. Third, according to his first biographer, Ernest Jones, between the ages of thirty-four and forty-four(1890–1900), Freud was quite neurotic. He suffered from depression, severe self-doubts, anxiety attacks, extreme mood changes, cocaine addiction, and a vast array of hysterical symptoms including migraines and palpitations of the heart—in addition to exhibiting a pathological dependence on his strange friend, Wilhelm Fliess.

How can we understand these major features of Freud's biography—the hard work, the ambition, and the neurosis? In fact, Freud himself offered a tidy account of how these features hang together, because they are the very features that his theory is designed to explain. For Freud, they all stemmed from his relationship to authority (i.e., to his father) and, therefore, from his Oedipus complex. Freud's argument can be quickly summarized as follows: His unresolved Oedipus complex explains his neurosis, his ambition, *and* his hard work. Freud developed his theory of the Oedipus complex based on ten years of self-analysis, which focused especially on his relationship with his father. In Freud's view, his superego prevented him from expressing his sexual desires, and the unexpressed sexual energy was turned into work through a process he called sublimation. His unanalyzed Oedipus complex prevented him from acknowledging his resentment of his father—whose voice was still heard in Freud's superego—and his hard work was a symbolic attempt to defeat his not very successful father by outperforming him. And his neurosis was caused by repressed sex and aggression trying to break into consciousness. In a nutshell, then, Freud believed his neurosis, as well as the ambition and hard work that led to his fame, resulted from his overly strict (but unanalyzed) conscience that developed around age five. Through self-analysis, Freud came to understand all of this and his neurosis went away.

The only problem with Freud's account is that, after his neurosis went away, he was still as ambitious and hardworking as ever. Freud thought his neurosis caused his ambition and hard work. But we believe it was just the other way around—that his ambition caused his hard work and his neurosis. We know that he was ambitious, and we think we know why. He experienced enormous family pressure to be successful. His ambition was further intensified by a comment that his angry father made after young Freud urinated in his parents' bedroom—

that he (young Freud) would never amount to anything. Freud's family expected him to be successful, and alternately pampered him—creating unusual self-confidence—and goaded him with doubts about his potential—creating a desire to prove himself. On the one hand, his self-doubt was an antidote to the complacency that pampering might have created. On the other, his self-confidence led to his persistence. In short, Freud seemed to have the precise balance of confidence and self-doubt needed to generate intense striving for success.

The biographies of highly successful men frequently reflect such themes as a critical and disapproving father *(see MacKinnon, 1965)* and constant efforts to win the acceptance and approval of the father. This, we suggest, was the source of Freud's ambition and his neurosis. Imagine Freud at the age of thirty-four. At that time he was an almost desperately ambitious man who was also deeply in debt to people whom he despised, living hand to mouth with a growing family to support and no professional or academic prospects in sight. Recall our claim that stress is caused by aspirations that exceed one's capacities. Freud's frustrated ambition was indeed the source of his neurosis. But even more important, his neurosis disappeared as soon as his career and fortunes improved, around 1900, with the publication of his masterpiece, *The Interpretation of Dreams*. The neurosis went away, but the ambition, drive, and desire for status remained intact until his death.

REFERENCES

Abramson, L. Y., Seligman, M.E.P., & Teasdale, J. D. (1978). Learned helplessness in humans: Critique and reformulation. *Journal of Abnormal Psychology, 87*, 49–74.

Adkins, Russell, & Werbel, (1994)*

Adler, A. (1927). *The practice and theory of individual psychology*. New York: Harcourt, Brace and World.

Ainsworth, M. S. (1979). Infant-mother attachment. *American Psychologist, 34*, 932–937.

Ainsworth, M.D.S., Blehar, M. C., Waters, E., & Wall, S. (1978). *Patterns of attachment: a psychological study of the strange situation*. Hillsdale, N.J.: Lawrence Erlbaum Associates.

Allport, G. W. (1937). *Personality: A psychological interpretation*. New York: Holt.

_____ (1942). *The use of personal documents in psychological science*. New York: Social Science Research Council.

_____ (1961). *Pattern and growth in personality*. New York: Holt, Rhinehart & Winston.

_____ (1963). Behavioral science, religion, and mental health. *Journal of Religion and Mental Health, 2*, 187–197.

_____ (1965). *Letters from Jenny*. New York: Harcourt, Brace & World. Boston: Beacon Press.

_____ (1968). An autobiography. In G. W. Allport (Ed.), *The person in psychology: selected essays*. Boston: Beacon Press.

Allport, G. W., & Odbert, H. S. (1936). Trait-names: A psycho-lexical study. *Psychological Monographs, 47* (Whole No. 211).

Allport, G. W., & Vernon, P. E. (1933). *Studies in expressive movement*. New York: The Macmillan Company.

American Association of Humanistic Psychology. (1962). *Articles of association.*

Atwood, G. E., & Tomkins, S. (1976). On the subjectivity of personality theory. *Journal of the History of the Behavioral Sciences, 12*, 166–177.

Bain, D. (1990). *Simone de Beauvior: A biograpy. New York*: Summit Books.

Bakan, D. (1966). *The duality of human existence*. Boston: Beacon Press.

Bandura, A. (1977). *Social learning theory, 2nd ed*. Englewood Cliffs, N.J.: Prentice-Hall.

_____. (1986). *Social foundations of thought and action*. Englewood Cliffs, N.J.: Prentice-Hall

_____. (1989). Human agency in social cognitive theory. *American Psychologist, 44*, 1175–1184.

Bandura, A., & Walters, R. (1959). *Adolescent Aggression: a study of the influence of child-training practices and family interrelationships*. New York: Ronald Press Co.

_____. (1963). *Social learning and personality development*. New York: Free Press.

_____. (1963). Imitation of film-mediated aggressive models. *Journal of Abnormal and Social Psychology, 66*, 3–11.

Barnes, H. E. (1925). *Psychology and history*. New York: Century.

Basedow, H. (1925). *The Australian aboriginal*. Adelaide: Preece.

Bass, B. M. (1985). *Leadership and performance beyond expectations*. New York: William Morrow.

Baumeister, R. F., & Leary, M. R. (1995). The need to belong: Desire for interpersonal attachments as a fundamental human motivation. *Psychological Bulletin, 117*, 497–529.

Beauvoir, de, S. (1949). *The second sex*. New York: Knopf. (Translated into English in 1953.)

Belenky, M. F., Clinchy, B. M., Goldberger, N. R., & Tarule, J. M. (1986). *Women's ways of knowing: The development of self, voice, and mind.* New York: Basic Books.

Belknap, T. (1996, October 28). Is the grumble gap shrinking? *Business Week*, p. 8.

Bem, S. (1974). The measurement of psychological androgyny. *Journal of Consulting and Clinical Psychology, 42,* 152–155.

Benjamin, L. S. (1993). *Interpersonal diagnosis and treatment of personality disorders.* New York: Guilford Press.

Binswanger, L. (1942). *Grundformen und Erkenntnis menschlichen Daseins.* Zürich: M. Niehans.

Blanchard, K., & Johnson, S. (1982). *The one minute manager: The quickest way to increase your own prosperity.* New York: William Morrow.

Block, J. (1995). A contrarian view of the five-factor approach to personality description. *Psychological Bulletin, 117,* 187–215.

Bloland, S. E. (1999, November). Fame: The power and cost of a fantasy. *Atlantic Monthly,* 51–62.

Bluen, S. D., Barling, J., & Burns, W. (1990). Predicting sales performance, job satisfaction, and depression by using the achievement strivings and impatience-irritability dimensions of Type A behavior. *Journal of Applied Psychology, 75,* 212–216.

Blumer, H. (1969). *Symbolic interactionism: perspective and method.* Englewood Cliffs, N.J.: Prentice-Hall.

Booth-Kewley, S., & Friedman, H. S. (1987). Psychological predictors of heart disease: A quantitative review. *Psychological Bulletin, 101,* 343–362.

Bosch, A. (1998). *Reagan: An American story.* New York: TV Books.

Bowlby, J. (1969). *Attachment and loss, Vol. I.* New York: Basic Books.

_____. (1971). *Attachment and loss, Vol. II.* New York: Basic Books.

Brewer, M. B., & Caporeal, L. R. (1990). Selfish genes versus selfish people: Sociobioology as origin myth. *Motivation and Emotion, 14,* 237–243.

Brown, L. M., & Gilligan, C. (1992). *Meeting at the crossroads: Women's psychology and girls' development.* Cambridge, Mass.: Harvard.

Burtt, E. A. (1954). *The metaphysical foundations of modern science.* Garden City, N.Y.: Doubleday.

Buss, A. H., & Plomin, R. (1975). *A temperament theory of personality.* New York: Wiley.

_____ (1984). *Temperament.* Hillsdale, N.J.: Earlbaum.

_____ (1999). *Evolutionary psychology.* Boston: Allyn & Bacon.

Caldwell, D. F., & O'Reilly, C. A., III. (1990). Measuring person-job fit with a profile-comparison process. *Journal of Applied Psychology, 75,* 648–657.

Cameron, N. A. (1943). The development of paranoic thinking. *Psychological Review, 50,* 219–233.

_____. (1947). *The psychology of behavior disorders.* Boston: Houghton Mifflin.

Campbell, D. C. (1965). Egoism, altruism, and other egocentric motives. *Nebraska Symposium on Motivation.* Lincoln: University of Nebraska Press.

Carson, R. C. (1991). The social-interactional viewpoint. In M. Hersen, A. Kazdin, & A. Bellack (Eds.), *The clinical psychology handbook*, 2nd ed. (pp. 185–199). Elmsford, N.Y.: Pergamon Press.

Cattell, R. B., & Stice, G. F. (1957). *Handbook for the sixteen personality factor questionnaire.* Champaign, Ill.: IPAT.

Chanin, M. N., & Schneer, J. A. (1984). A study of the relationship between Jungian personality dimensions and conflict-handling behavior. *Human Relations, 37*, 863–879.

Chapman, A. H. (1976). *Harry Stack Sullivan: His life and work*. New York: Putnam.

Chodorow, N. (1978). The reproduction of mothering. Berkeley: University of California Press.

_____. (1989). *Feminism and psychoanalytic theory*. New Haven: Yale University Press.

Coe, W. C., & Sarbin, T. R. (1966). An experimental demonstration of hypnosis as role enactment. *Journal of Abnormal and Social Psychology, 71*, 400–406.

Conway, F., & Siegelman, J. (1979). *Snapping*. New York: Delta.

Cooley, C. H. (1902). *Human nature and the social order*. New York: Scribner's. (Reprinted in 1962.)

Costa, P. T., Jr., & McRae, R. R. (1985). *The NEO personality inventory manual*. Odessa, Fla.: PAR.

Csikszenmihalyi, M. (1991). *Flow: The psychology of optimal experience.* New York: HarperCollins.

Daly, M., & Wilson, M. (1988). *Homicide*. New York: Aldine de Gruyter.

Darwin, C. (1858). *Origin of species*. London: Murray

Dawkins, R. (1986). *The blind watchmaker*. New York: Norton.

DeWaal, F. (1980). *Chimpanzee politics*. New York: Harper.

Dewey, J. (1999). *Liberalism and social action*. New York: Prometheus.

Diener, E., Suh, E. M., Lucas, R.F.W., & Smith, H. L. (1999). Subjective well-being: Three decades of progress. *Psychological Bulletin, 125*, 276–302.

Digman, J. M. (1990). Personality structure: The emergence of the Five-Factor Model. In M. R. Rosenzweig and L. W. Porter (Eds.), *Annual review of psychology* (Vol. 41, pp. 417–440). Palo Alto, Calif.: Annual Reviews.

Dunn, J., Bretherton, I., & Munn, P. (1987). Conversation about feeling states between mothers and their young children. *Developmental Psychology, 23*, 132–139.

Durkheim, E. (1897). *Le Suicide*. Paris: F. Alcan.

Eibl-Eibesfeldt, I. (1989). *Human ethology*. Chicago: Aldine.

Ekman, P., Friesen, W. V., O'Sullivan, M., Chan, A., Diacoyanni-Tarlatzis, I., Heider, K., Krause, R., LeCompte, W. A., Pitcairn, T., Ricci-Bitti, P., Scherer, K., Tomita, M., & Tzavaras, A. (1987). Universals and cultural differences in the judgment of facial expressions of emotion. *Journal of Personality and Social Psychology, 53*, 712–717.

Ellenberger, H. (1970). *The discovery of the unconscious*. New York: Basic Books.

Erikson, E. H. (1958). *Young man Luther*. New York: Norton.

_____. (1963). *Childhood and society*, 2nd ed. New York: Norton.

_____. (1964). *Insight and responsibility*. New York: Norton.

_____. (1968). *Identity, youth, and crisis*. New York: Norton.

_____. (1969). *Gandhi's truth*. New York: Norton.

_____. (1974). *Dimensions of a new identity*. New York: Norton.

_____. (1980). *Identity and the life cycle*. New York: Norton.

_____. (1982). *The life cycle completed*. New York: Norton.

Eron, L. D., Huesmann, L. R., Leftkowitz, M. M., & Walder, L. O. (1972). Does television violence cause aggression? *American Psychologist, 27*, 253–263.

Eysenck, H. J. (1967). *The biological basis of personality*. Springfield, Ill.: Charles C. Thomas.

Fairbairn, W.R.D. (1952). *Psychoanalytic studies of the personality*. London: Tavistock with Routledge and Kegan Paul.

Ferster, C., & Skinner, B. F. (1957). *Schedules of reinforcement.* New York: Appleton–Century-

Crofts.

Feuerbach, L. (1841). *Essence of Christianity*, 2nd Ed. New York: C. Blanchard.

Fitzgerald, H. E. (1977). Infants and caregivers: Sex differences as determinants of socialization. In E. Donelson & J. Gullahorn (Eds.), *Women: A psychological perspective*. New York: Wiley.

Flanagan, O. (2000). *Dreaming souls: Sleep, dreams, and the evolution of the conscious mind*. New York: Oxford University Press.

Foa, U.G., Converse J., Jr., Tornblum, K.Y., & Foa, E.B. (1993). *Resource theory: Explorations and applications*. San Diego: Academic Press.

Foa, U.G., & Foa, E.B. (1974). *Societal Structures of the Mind*. Springfield, IL: Charles C. Thomas.

_____. (1980). Resource theory of social exchange. In J. W. Thibaut, J. T. Spence, & R. C. Carson (Eds.), *Resource theory of social exchange. Contemporary topics in social psychology*. Morristown, N.J.: General Learning Press.

Forsythe, S., Drake, M. F., & Cox, C. E. (1985). Influence of applicant's dress on interviewer's selection decisions. *Journal of Applied Psychology, 72*, 387–392.

Fox, R. (1975). *Encounter with anthropology*. London: Peregrine.

Frankl, V. (1967). *Psychotherapy and existentialism: Selected papers in logotherapy*. New York: Simon & Schuster.

_____. (1968). *Man's search for meaning*. New York: Washington Square Press.

Franklin, B. (1899). Autobiography. *Poor Richard Letters*. New York: D. Appleton.

Frazer, J. G. (1911). *The golden bough*, 3rd ed. London.

Freud, A. (1938). *The ego and the mechanisms of defense*, rev. ed. New York: International Universities Press.

_____. (1900). The interpretation of dreams. In J. Strachey (Ed. and Trans.), *The standard edition of the complete works of Sigmund Freud*, Vols. 4–5. London: Hogarth Press.

_____ (1910). *Leonardo da Vinci and a memory of his childhood*. New York: Norton. (Reprinted in 1965.)

_____. (1913). Totem and taboo. In J. Strachey (Ed. and Trans.). *The standard edition of the complete works of Sigmund Freud*, Vol. 13. London: Hogarth Press.

_____. (1921). Group psychology and the analysis of the ego. In J. Strachey (Ed. and Trans.). *The standard edition of the complete works of Sigmund Freud*, Vol. *?. London: Hogarth Press.

_____. (1923). The ego and the id. In J. Strachey (Ed. and Trans.). *The standard edition of the complete works of Sigmund Freud*, Vol. 19. London: Hogarth Press.

_____. (1925). Some psychical consequences of differences between the sexes. In J. Strachey (Ed.), *The complete psychological works*. New York: Norton. (Reprinted in 1976.)

_____. (1927). The future of an illusion. In J. Strachey (Ed. and Trans.). *The standard edition of the complete works of Sigmund Freud*. London: Hogarth Press.

_____. (1930). Civilization and its discontents. In J. Straachey (Ed. and Trans.), *The standard edition of the complete works of Sigmund Freud*, Vol. 21. London: Hogarth Press.

_____. (1931). Female sexuality. In Strachey, J. (Ed.), *The complete psychological works*. New York: Norton. (Reprinted in 1976.)

_____. (1933). Femininity. In J. Strachey (Ed.), *New introductory lectures on psychoanalysis*. New York: Norton.

_____. (1938). Moses and monotheism. In J. Strachey (Ed. and Trans.). *The standard edition* *of the complete works of Sigmund Freud,* Vol. *?. London: Hogarth Press.

———. (1939). The psychopathology of everyday life. In J. Strachey (Ed. and Trans.), *The standard edition of the complete works of Sigmund Freud,* Vol. 6. London: Hogarth Press.

Friedlander, J. W., & Sarbin, T. R. (1938). The depth of hypnosis. *Journal of Abnormal and Social Psychology, 33,* 453–475.

Friedman, M., & Rosenman, R. (1974). *Type A behavior and your heart.* New York: Knopf.

Fromm, E. (1941). *Escape from freedom.* New York: Holt, Rinehart & Winston.

Fukuyama, F. (1992). *The end of history and the last man.* * New York: Wm. Morrow.

Funder, D. C. (1991). Global traits: A neo-Allportian approach to personality. *Psychological Science, 2,* 31–39.

Galotti, K. (1999). *Cognitive psychology in and out of the laboratory,* 2nd ed. Belmont, Calif.: Brooks-Cole.

Galton, F. (1869). *Hereditary genius.* Gloucester, Mass.: Peter Smith.

———. (1874). *English men of science: Their nature and nurture.* London: Macmillan.

Gay, P. (1988). *Freud: A life for our time.* New York: Norton.

Gergen, K. J. (1982). T*oward transformation in social knowledge.* New York: Basic Books.

Gilligan, C. (1982). *In a different voice.* Cambridge, Mass.: Harvard University Press.

———. (1987). Adolescent development reconsidered. C. E. Irwin, Jr. (Ed.), Adolescent social behavior and health. *New Directions for Child Development, No. 37.* San Francisco: Jossey-Bass.

Goffman, E. (1959). *The presentation of self in everyday life.* New York: Anchor.

Goldberg, L. R. (1971). A historical survey of personality scales and inventories. In P. McReynolds (Ed.), *Advances in psychological assessment* (Vol. 2, pp. 293–336). Paolo Alto, Calif.: Science and Behavior Books.

———. (1993). The structure of phenotypic personality traits. *American Psychologist, 48,* 26–34.

Goldstein, K. (1939). *The organism.* New York: American Book Co.

———. (1947). *Human nature in the light of psychopathology.* Cambridge: Harvard University Press.

Goodstein, J. D. (1994). Institutional pressures and strategic responsiveness: Employer involvement in work-family issues. *Academy of Management Journal, 37,* 350–382.

Gough, H. G. (1948). A sociological theory of psychopathology. *American Journal of Sociology, 53,* 359–366.

———. (1987). *Manual for the California Psychological Inventory.* Palo Alto, CA: Consulting Psychologists Press.

Greenwald, A. G. (1992). Unconscious cognition reclaimed. *American Psychologist, 47*(6), 766–779.

Grover, S. L., & Crooker, K. J. (1995). Who appreciates family-responsive human resource policies: The impact of family-friendly policies on the organizational attachment of parents and non-parents. *Personnel Psychology, 48,* 271–288.

Guilford, J. S.. Zimmerman, W., & Guilford, J. P. (1976). *The Guilford-Zimmerman Temperament Survey handbook.* Palo Alto, CA: Consulting

Guntrip, H. (1973). *Psychoanalytic theory, therapy and the self.* New York: Basic Books.

Guthrie, J. P, & Olian, J. D. (1991). Does context affect staffing decisions? *Personnel Psychology, 44,* 263–292.

Hall, G. S. (1904). *Adolescence.* New York: Appleton.

Hall, M. H. (1968). Conversation with Abraham H. Maslow. *Psychology Today, 2*, 35–37; 54–57.

Hardesty, C., Wenk, D., & Morgan, C. C. (1995). Paternal involvement and the development of gender expectations in sons and daughters. *Youth and Society, 26*, 283–22297.

Harris, B. (1979). Whatever happened to Little Albert? *American Psychologist, 34*, 151–160.

Hartmann, H. (1958) . *The ego and the problem of adaptation*. New York: International Universities Press.

Hathaway, S. R., & McKinley, J. C. (1943). *Manual for the Minnesota Multiphasic Personality Inventory*. New York: Psychological Corporation.

Haviland, J. (1977). Sex-related pragmatics in infants. *Journal of Communication, 27*, 80–84.

Hawley, P. H., & Little , T. D. (1999). On winning some and losing some: A social relations approach to social dominance in toddlers. *Merrill-Palmer Quarterly, 45*, 185–214.

Heilman, M. E., Block, C. J., Martell, R. F., & Simon, M. C. (1989). Has anything changed? Current characterizations of men, women, and managers. *Journal of Applied Psychology, 74*, 935–942.

Heymans, G. & Wiersma, E. (1906). Beitrage sur speziellen psychologie auf grund einer wassenunrerschung. *Zeitschrift für Psychologie, 43*, 81–127, 258–301.

Hilgard, E. R., & Marquis, D. G. (1940). *Learning and conditioning*. New York: Appleton–Century.

Hirsch, S. (1984). *Using the Myers–Briggs Type Indicator in organizations: A resource book*. Palo Alto, CA: Consulting Psychologists Press.

Hitler, A. (1941). *Mein kampf*. New York: Reynal & Hitchcock.

Hogan, R., & Hogan, J. (1991). Personality and status. In D. G. Gilbert & J. J. Connolly (Eds.), *Personality, social skill, and psychopathology*. New York: Plenum.

_____. (1996). *Hogan Personality Inventory Manual*. Tulsa, OK: Hogan Assessment Systems

Holland, J. L. (1985). *Making vocational choices: A theory of personalities and work environments*. Englewood Cliffs, New Jersey: Prentice–Hall.

Hollenbeck, J. R., Ilgen, D. R., Ostroff, C., & Vancourver, J B. (1987). Sex differences in occupational choicel pay, and worth: A supply–side approach to understanding the male–female wage gap. *Personnel Psychology, 40*, 715–743.

Horney, K. (1926). The flight from womanhood. *International Journal of Psychoanalysis, 7*, 324–339.

_____. (1937). *The neurotic personality of our time*. New York: Norton.

_____. (1939). *New ways in psychoanalysis*. New York: Norton.

_____. (1942). *Self–analysis*. New York: Norton.

_____. (1945). *Our inner conflicts*. New York: Norton.

_____. (1950). *Neurosis and human growth*. New York: Norton.

_____. (1967). *Feminine psychology*. New York: Norton.

Hughes, R. L., Ginnett, R. C., & Curphy, G. J. (1999). *Leadership*. Boston: Irwin McGraw–Hill.

Izard, C. E. (1971). The face of emotion. New York: Appleton, Century Crofts.

Jackson, L. A., Gardner, P. D., & Sullivan, L. A. (1992). Explaining gender differences in self–pay expectations: Social comparison standards and perceptions of fair pay. *Journal of Applied Psychology, 77*, 651–663.

James, W. (1892). *The principles of psychology*. Cambridge, MA: Harvard University Press.

_____. (1902). *The varieties of religious experience*. New York: Modern.

_____. (1962). *Psychology (Briefer Course)*. London: Collier Books.

Johnson, P. R., & Indivik, J. (1994). Workplace violence: An issue of the nineties. Public *Personnel Management, 23*, 515–523.

Jones, E. (1953). *The life and work of Sigmund Freud*. New York: Doubleday.

Jones, E. E. (1979). The rocky road from acts to dispositions. *American Psychologist, 34*, 107–117.

Jourard, S. M., & Landsman, T. (1980). *Healthy personality: An approach from the viewpoint of humanistic psychology*, 4th ed. New York: Macmillan.

Jung, C. G. (1906). Studies in word association. In Experimental researches. *Collected works*, Vol. 2. Princeton, N.J.: Princeton University Press. (Reprinted in 1974.)

_____. (1910). Experimental researchers. *Collected Works*, vol. 2. Princeton, N.J.: Princeton University Press. (reprinted 1953.)

_____. (1912). Symbols of transformation. *Collected works*, Vol. 5. Princeton, N.J.: Princeton University Press. (Revised in 1952; reprinted in 1956.)

_____. (1921). Psychological types. *Collected works*, Vol. 6. Princeton, N.J.: Princeton University Press. (Reprinted in 1971.)

_____. (1953a). The psychology of alchemy. *Collected works*, Vol. 7. Princeton, N.J.: Princeton University Press.

_____. (1953b). Two essays on analytical psychology. *Collected works*, Vol. 12. Princeton, N.J.: Princeton University Press.

_____. (1959). The archetypes and the collective unconscious. *Collected works*, Vol. 9. Princeton, N.J.: Princeton University Press.

_____. (1960). The structure of the psyche. *Collected works*, Vol. 8. Princeton, N.J.: Princeton University Press.

Jung, C. G. (Ed.). (1964). *Man and his symbols*. London: Aldus Books.

Jung, C. G., & Jaffe, A. (1964). *Memories, dreams, reflections*. New York: Vintage Books.

Kant, I. (1798). *Anthropology from a pragmatic point of view*. The Hague: Nijhoff. (Reprinted in 1974.)

_____. (1990). *Critique of Pure Reason* (1781), ed. Norman Smith. New York: St. Martin's Press.

Karraker, K. H., Vogel, D. A., & Lake, M. A.. (1995). Parents' gender-typed perceptions of newborns. *Sex Roles, 33*, 687–701.

Kelly, G. A. (1955). *The psychology of personal constructs*. New York: Norton.

Kiesler, D. J. (1982). Interpersonal theory for personality and psychotherapy. In J. C. Anchin & D. J. Kiesler (Eds.), *Handbook of interpersonal psychotherapy*. New York: Pergamon Press. (pp. 3–24).

Kilman, R. H., & Thomas, K. W. (1975). Interpersonal conflict-handling behavior as reflections of Jungian personality dimensions. *Psychological Reports, 37*, 971–980.

Knapp, T. J., & Shodall, S. A. (1974). Ben Franklin as a behavior modifier: A note. *Behavior Therapy, 5*, 656–660.

Koch, S. (Ed.). (1959–1963). *Psychology: A study of a science* (6 vols.). New York: McGraw-Hill.

Kohler, W. (1929). *Gestaltpsychologie*. New York: Liveright.

Kretschmer, E. (1925). *Physique and character*. New York: Harper. (Translated into English in 1938.)

Kuhn, T. (1965). *The structure of scientific revolutions*. Chicago: University of Chicago Press.

Latham, G. P. and Saari, L. M. (1979). Application of social learning theory to training through behavioral modeling. *Journal of applied psychology, 64*, 239–246.

Leary, T. (1957). *Interpersonal diagnosis of personality*. New York: Ronald Press.

Lewin, K. (1935). *A dynamic theory of personality*. New York: McGraw-Hill.

Liden, R. C., Martin, C. L., & Parson, C. K. (1993). Interviewer and applicant behaviors in employment interviews. *Academy of Management Journal, 36*, 372–386.

Little, B. R. (1972). Psychological man as scientist, humanist and specialist. *Journal of Experimental Research in Personality, 6*, 95–118.

Lykken, D. T. (1995). *The antisocial personalities*. Hillsdale, N.J.: Earlbaum.

Lynn, K. S. (1987). *Hemingway*. New York: Simon & Schuster.

Maccoby, E. E. (1992). The role of the parents in the socialization of children: A historical review. *Developmental Psychology, 28*(6), 1006–1017.

MacKinnon, D. W. (1965). Personality and the realization of creative potential. *American Psychologist, 20*, 273–281.

Maddi, S. R., & Costa, P. T. Jr. (1972) *Humanism in psychology: Allport, Maslow, and Murray*. Chicago: Aldine.

Mahler, M. S., Pine, F., & Bergman, A. (1975). *The psychological birth of the human infant*. New York: Basic Books.

Marcuse, H. (1955). *Eros and civilization*. New York: Beacon Press.

Marlowe, C. M., Schneider, S. L., & Nelson, C. E. (1996). Gender and attractiveness biases in hiring decisions: Are more experienced managers less biased? *Journal of Applied Psychology, 81*, 11–21.

Marx, K., & Engels, F. *The German ideology* (1848). (Translation published by International Publisher in 1937.)

Maslow, A. H. (1954). *Motivation and personality*. New York: Harper & Row.

_____. (1955). Deficiency motivation and growth motivation. *Nebraska Symposium on Motivation*. Lincoln: University of Nebraska Press.

_____. (1959). Psychological data and value theory. In Abraham H. Maslow (Ed.), *New knowledge in human values*. New York: Harper & Brothers.

_____. (1961). Are our publications and conventions suitable for the personal sciences? *American Psychologist, 16*, 318–319.

_____. (1964). *Religions, values, and peak-experiences*. New York: Viking.

_____. (1968). *Toward a psychology of being*, 2nd ed. New York: Van Nostrand Reinhold.

_____. (1970). *Motivation and personality*, rev. ed. New York: Harper & Row.

_____. (1971). *The farther reaches of human nature*. New York: Viking.

May, R. (1953). *Man's search for himself*. New York: Norton.

_____. (1977). *The meaning of anxiety*. New York: Norton.

McAdams, D. (1993). *The stories we live by: Personal myths and the making of the self*. New York: William Morrow.

McClelland, D. C. (1961). *The achieving society*. New York: Van Nostrand Reinhold.

McClelland, D. C., & Boyatzis, R. E. (1982). The leadership motive pattern and long-term success in management. *Journal of Applied Psychology, 67*, 737–743.

McClelland, D. C., & Burnham, D. (1976). Power is the great motivator. *Harvard Business Review, 25*, 159–166.

McCrae, R. R. (Ed.). (1992). The Five-Factor Model. [Special issue.]. *Journal of Personality, 60*(2).

McCrae, R. R., & Costa, P. T., Jr. (1987). Validation of the five-factor model of personality across instruments and observers. *Journal of Personality and Social Psychology, 52*, 81–90.

McCully, R. S. (1987). *Jung and Rorschach*. Dallas: Spring.

McDougall, W. (1908). *Social psychology*. London: Methuen.

McDougall, W. (1923). *Outline of psychology*. New York: Scribner's.

Mead, G. H. (1934). *Mind, self, and society*. Chicago: University of Chicago Press.

Mead, M. (1965). *And keep your powder dry*. New York: William Morrow.

Meichenbaum, D. (1977). *Cognitive behavior modification: An integrative approach*. New York: Plenum.

Merton, R. M. (1957). *Social theory and social structure*. Glencoe, Ill.: Free Press.

Milgram, S. (1974). *Obedience to authority*. New York: Harper & Row.

Miller, G. (2000). *The Mating Mind*. New York: Doubleday.

Miller, W. R., Rosellini, R. A., & Seligman, M.E.P. (1977). In J. D. Maser, & M.E.P. Seligman (Eds.), *Psychoathology: Experimental Models*. New York: W. H. Freeman

Mills, J., Robey, D., & Smith, L. (1985). Conflict-handling and personality dimensions of project-management personnel. *Psychological Reports, 57*, 1135–1143.

Mischel, W. (1973). Toward a cognitive social learning reconceptualization of personality. *Psychological Review, 80*, 252–283.

Mischel, W. (1968). *Personality and assessment*. New York: Wiley.

Montessori, M. (1988). *The Montessori method*. New York: Random House.

Moreau, C. (1991). The many-sided animus. Paper presented at the Annual Jungian Winter Seminar, C. G. Jung Institute, Zurich.

Morris, E. (1999). *Dutch: A memoir of Ronald Reagan*. New York: Random House.

Mountjoy, P. T., & Sundberg, M. L. (1981). Ben Franklin the protobehaviorist, Vol. 1: Self-management of behavior. *Psychological Record, 31*, 13–24.

Murdock, G. P. (1945). The common denominator of culture. In R. Linton (Ed.), *The science of man in the world crisis*. New York: Columbia University Press.

Murray, H. A. (1938). *Explorations in personality*. New York: Oxford University

_____. (1959). Preparations for a scaffold of a comprehensive system. In S. Koch (Ed.), *Psychology: The study of a science*. New York: McGraw-Hill.

_____. (1967). The case of Murr. In E. G. Boring & G. Lindzey (Eds.), *A history of**

Murray, H. A., & Kluckhohn, C. (1981). Outline of a conception of personality. In E. Schneidman (Ed.), *Endeavors in Psychology*. New York: Harper & Row. Pp. 204–234.

Murray, H. A., with staff (1948). *Assessment of men*. New York: Rinehart & Co.

Murray, H. A., & Kluckhohn, C. (1981). Outline of a conception of personality. In E. Schneidman (Ed.), *Endeavors in psychology*. New York: Harper & Row. Pp. 204–234.

Myers, I. (1962). *The Myers-Briggs Type Indicator manual and test*. Palo Alto, Calif.: Consulting Psychologists Press.

Myers, I., & McCaulley, M. H. (1985). *Manual: A guide to the development and use of the Myers-Briggs Type Indicator*. Palo Alto, Calif.: Consulting Psychologists Press.

Myers. (1990).*

National Center for Health Statistics. (1992). As reported in *The 1994 information please almanac*. Boston: Houghton Mifflin.

Neill, A. S. (1995). *Summerhill School*. New York: St. Martin's Press.

Norman, W. T. (1963). Toward an adequate taxonomy of personality attributes: Replicated factor structure in peer nomination personality ratings. *Journal of Abnormal and Social*

Psychology, 66, 574–583.

O'Leary-Kelly, A. M., Griffin, R. W., & Glew, D. J. (1996). Organization-motivated aggression: A research framework. *Academy of Management Review, 21*, 225–253.

Ohlott, P. J., Ruderman, M. N., & McCauley, C. D. (1994). Gender differences in managers' developmental job experiences. *Academy of Management Journal, 37*, 46–67.

Ones, D., Visweswaran, C., & Schmidt, F. (1993). Comprehensive meta-analysis of integrity test validities: Findings and implications for personnel selection and theories of job performance (monograph). *Journal of Applied Psychology, 78*, 679–703.

Orne, M. T., & Scheibe, K. E. (1964). The contribution of nondeprivation factors in the production of sensory deprivation. *Journal of Abnormal and Social Psychology, 68*, 3–12.

Overmeier, J. B., & Seligman, M.E.P. (1967). Effects of inescapable shock upon subsequent escape and avoidance learning. *Journal of Comparative and Physiological Psychology, 63*, 28–33.

Oyserman, D. & Markus, H. (1993). *The sociocultural self*. Hillsdale, N.J.: Lawrence Erlbaum Associates.

Parsons, T., & Bales, R. F. (1955). *Family, socialization and interaction process*. Glencoe, Ill.: Free Press.

Perry, H. S. (1982). *Psychiatrist of America: the life of Harry Stack Sullivan*. Cambridge: Harvard University Press.

Peterson, D. R. (1968). *The clinical study of social behavior*. New York: Appleton.

Piaget, J. (1964). *The moral judgment of the child*. New York: Free Press.

Pinker, S. (1997). *How the Mind Works*. New York: Norton.

Popper, K. (1959). *The logic of scientific discovery*. New York: Basic Books.

Prince, M. (1924). *The unconscious*, 2nd ed. New York: Wiley.

Provost, J. A. (1985). *A casebook: Applications of the Myers-Briggs Type Indicator in counseling*. Gainesville, Fla.: Center for Applications of Psychological Type.

Quinn, S. (1987). *A mind of her own: The life of Karen Horney*. New York: Summit Books.

Rafaeli, A., & Pratt, M. G. (1993). Tailored meanings: On the meaning and impact of organizational dress. *Academy of Management Review, 18*, 32–55.

Rajagopalan, N., & Datta, D. K. (1996). CEO characteristics: Does industry matter? *Academy of Management Journal, 39*, 197–215.

Ramul, K. (1963). Some early measurements and ratings in psychology. *American Psychologist, 18*, 653–559.

Rapaport, D. (1951). *Organization and pathology of thought: selected sources*. New York: Columbia University Press.

Raza, S., & Carpenter, B. (1987). A model of hiring decisions in real employment interviews. *Journal of Applied Psychology, 72*, 596–603.

Redfield, R. (1960). How society operates. In H. L. Shapiro (Ed.), *Man, culture, and society* (pp. 345–368). New York: Oxford University Press.

Rieff, P. (1959). *Freud: The mind of a moralist*. New York: Doubleday.

Roazen, P. (1968). *Freud: Political and social thought*. New York: Vintage.

Roethlisberger, F. J., & Dickson, W. J. (1939). *Management and the worker*. Cambridge, Mass.: Harvard University Press.

Rogers, C. R. (1951, 1954). *Client–centered therapy, its current practice, implications, and theory*. Boston: Houghton Mifflin.

Rogers, C. R., & Stevens, B. (1967). *Person to person: The problem of being human*. Boulder,

Colo.: Westview Press.

Rogers, C. R. (1942). *Counseling and psychotherapy*. Boston: Houghton Mifflin.

Rogers, C. R. (1961). *On becoming a person*. Boston: Houghton Mifflin.

Rogers, C. R. (1963). Learning to be free. In Farber & Wilson (Eds.), *Conflict and creativity*. New York: McGraw-Hill.

Rogers, C. R. (1964). Toward a modern approach to values: The valuing process in the mature person. *Journal of Abnormal and Social Psychology, 68*, 160–167.

Rogers, C. R. (1967). Autobiography. In E. G. Boring & G. Lindzey (Eds.), *History of psychology in autobiography*, Vol. 5. New York: Appleton-Century-Crofts.

Rogers, C. R. (1972). *Becoming partners*. New York: Dell.

Rorschach, H. (1921). *Psychodiagnostik*. New York: Grune & Stratton. (Reprinted in 1949.)

Ross, L., & Nisbett, R. E. (1991). *The person and the situation*. New York: McGraw-Hill.

Rostan, L. (1824). *Cours elementaire d'hygiene*. Paris: Bechef jeune.

Rowe, D. (1997). Genetics, temperament, and personality. In R. Hogan, J. Johnson, & S. R. Briggs (Eds.), *Handbook of personality psychology*. San Diego: Academic Press.

Rubin, J. Z., Provenzano, F. J., & Luria, Z. (1974). The eye of the beholder: Parents' views on sex of newborns. *American Journal of Orthopsychiatry, 44*, 512–519.

Runyon, W. M. (1988). A historical and conceptual background to psychohistory. In *Psychology and historical interpretation*. New York: Oxford University Press.

———. (1994). Coming to terms with the life, loves and work of Henry A. Murray. *Contemporary Psychology, 39*, 701–704.

Samples, K. R., de Castro, E. M., Abanes, R., & Lyle, R. (1994). *Prophets of the Apocalypes: Kavid Koresh and other American messiahs.* ∗

Sampson, E. E. (1985). The decentralization of identity: Toward a revised concept of personal and social order. *American Psychologist, 40*, 1203–1211.

Samuels, A. (1985). *Jung and the post-Jungians*. London: Routledge & Kegan Paul.

Samuels, A., Shorter, B., & Plaut, F. (1987). *A critical dictionary of Jungian analysis*. London: Routledge and Kegan Paul.

Sarbin, T. R. (1943). A contribution to the study of actuarial and individual methods of prediction. *American Journal of Sociology*, 593–602.

———. (1952). Contributions to role–taking theory, Vol. 3: A preface to a psychological analysis of the self. *Psychological Review, 59*, 11–22.

———. (1954). Role theory. In G. Lindzey (Ed.), *Handbook of social psychology* (pp. 223–258). Reading, Mass.: Addison–Wesley.

———. (1994). Steps to the narratory principle: An autobiographical essay. In D. J. Lee (Ed.), *Life and story: Autobiographies for a narrative psychology*. Westport, CT: Praeger.

Sarbin, T. R., & Allen, V. (1968). *Role theory*. In G. Lindzey and E. Aronson (Eds). Handbook of social psychology (pp. 488–567). Reading, Mass.: Addison-Wesley.

Sarbin, T. R., Taft, R., & Bailey, D. E. (1960). *Clinical inference and cognitive theory*. New York: Holt, Rinehart & Winston.

Schlenker, B. R., & Weigold, M. F. (1990). Self-consciousness and self-presentation: Being autonomous versus appearing autonomous. *Journal of Personality and Social Psychology, 59*, 820–828.

Schnell, E. R., & Hammer, A. (1993). *Introduction to the FIRO-B in organizations*. Palo Alto, Calif.: Consulting Psychologists Press.

Schur, M. (1972). *Freud: Living and dying*. New York: International University Press.

Schutz, W. (1958). *FIRO: A three-dimensional theory of interpersonal behavior*. New York: Holt, Rinehart, & Winston.

Sears, R. R., Maccoby, E. E., & Lewin, H. (1958). *Patterns of childrearing*. New York: Harper & Row.

Seligman, M.E.P. (1975). *Helplessness*. San Francisco: W. H. Freeman.

Senge, P. M. (1994). *Fifth-discipline fieldbook*. New York: Doubleday.

Shaffer, J.B.P. (1978). *Humanistic psychology*. Englewood Cliffs, N.J.: Prentice-Hall.

Shapiro, D. (1965). *Neurotic styles*. New York: Basic Books. (Reprinted in 1999.)

Sheldon, W. H., Dupertuis, C. W., & McDermott, E. (1954). *Atlas of men*. New York: Harper.

Siever, L. J. (1992). Schizophrenic spectrum of personality disorders. In A. Tasman & M. B. Riba (Eds.), *Review of Psychiatry*, Vol. 11. Washington, D.C.: American Psychiatric Press.

Simmel, G. (1984). *Georg Simmel: On women, sexuality, and love*. Guy Oakes, Trans. New Haven: Yale University Press.

Simpson, J. A., & Kenrick, D. T. (1997). *Evolutionary social psychology*. Mahwah, N.J.: Earlbaum.

Skinner, B. F. (1938). *The behavior of organisms*. New York: Appleton-Century-Crofts.

_____. (1948). *Walden two*. New York: Macmillan.

_____. (1953). *Science and human behavior*. New York: Macmillan.

_____. (1957). *Verbal behavior*. New York: Appleton–Century–Crofts.

_____. (1971). *Beyond freedom and dignity*. New York: Knopf.

_____. (1982). *Baby in a box*. In J. K. Gardner (Ed.), Readings in developmental psychology. Boston: Little, Brown.

_____. (1990). Can psychology be a science of the mind? *American Psychologist, 45*, 1206–1210.

Smither, R. D. (1984). *Competitors and comrades: Personality, economics, and culture*. New York: Praeger.

_____. (1998). *The psychology of work and human performance*, 3rd ed. New York: Longman.

Snortum, J. R. (1976, April). Ben Franklin's pursuit of perfection. *Psychology Today*, pp. 80–83.

Spence, L., & R. C. Carson (Eds.), *Contemporary topics in social psychology*. Morristown, N.J.: General Learning Press.

Spindler, G., & Spindler, L. (1983). Anthropologists view American culture. In B. J. Siegel, A. R. Beals, & S. A. Tyler (Eds.), *Annual review of anthropology*. Palo Alto, Calif.: Annual Reviews.

Spranger, E. (1928). *Types of men*. Halle: Niemeyer.

Stagner, R. (1937). *Psychology of personality*. New York: McGraw-Hill.

Stannard, D. E. (1980). *Shrinking history: Freud and the failure of psychohistory*. New York: Oxford University Press.

Stern, W. (1921). *Die menschliche Personlichkeit*. Leipzig, Germany: J. A. Barth.

Stevens, A. (1983). *Archetypes: A natural history of the self*. New York: Quill.

Stevens, B. (1984). *Burst out laughing*. Berkeley: Celestial Arts.

_____. (1985). *Don't push the river*. Berkeley: Celestial Arts.

Sullivan, H. S. (1953a). The interpersonal theory of psychiatry. New York: Norton.

_____. (1953b). *Conceptions of modern psychiatry*. New York: Norton.

_____. (1954). *The psychiatric interview.*, ed. H.S. Perry & M.L. Gawel. New York: Norton.

_____. (1956). *Clinical studies in psychiatry.*, ed. H.S. Perry & M.L. Gawel. New York: Norton.

_____. (1962). *Schizophrenia as a human process*. New York: Norton.

Symonds, P. M. (1931). *Diagnosing personality and conduct*. New York: Appleton-Century-Crofts.

Tanner, J. M. (1978). *Educational and physical growth*. New York: International Universities Press.

Tellegen, A. (1985). Structures of mood and personality and their relevance to assessing anxiety, with an emphasis on self-reports. In A. H. Tuma & J. D. Masser (Eds.), *Anxiety and the anxiety disorders* (pp. 681–716). Hillsdale, N.J.: Erlbaum.

Tellegen, A., Lykken, D. J., Bouchard, T. J. Jr., Wilcox, K. J., Segal, N. L., & Rich, S. (1988). *Personality similarity in twins reared apart and together. Journal of Personality and Social Psychology, 54*, 1031–1039.

Thorndike, E. L. (1905). The elements of psychology. New York: A. G. Seiler.

_____. (1933). A theory of the action of the after-effects of a connection upon it. *Psychological Review, 40*, 434–439.

Tolman, E. C. (1933). The determiners of behavior at a choice point. *Psychological Review, 45*, 1–41.

_____. (1935). Psychology versus immediate experience. *Philosophy of Science, 2*, 356–380.

Tomkins, S. (1980). Affect as amplification. In R. Plutchik & H. Kellerman (Eds.), *Emotion: Theory, research, and experience*. New York: Academic.

Tupes, E. C., & Crystal, R. E. (1961). Recurrent personality factors based on trait ratings (USAF ASD Tech. Rep. Nos. 61–97). Lackland Air Force Base, Tex.: U.S. Air Force.

Unger, R. K. (1989). *Representations: Social constructions of gender*. Amityville, N.Y.: Baywood.

Viola, G. (1909). *Le legge de correlazione morfologia del tipi individuali*. Padua: Prosperini.

Walraven, M. (1974). Mother and infant cardiac responses during breast and bottle feeding. Unpublished doctoral dissertation, Michigan State University, East Lansing.

Watson, J. B. (1913). Psychology as the behaviorist views it. *Psychological Review, 20*, 158–177.

Watson, J. B. (1926). Experimental studies on the growth of the emotions. In C. Murchison (Ed.), *Psychologies of 1925*. Worcester, Mass.: Clark University Press.

Waxman, H. S. (1995, September). Putting workplace violence in perspective. *Security Management*, pp. 123–126.

Weber, M. (1904–1905, 1930). *The Protestant ethic and the spirit of capitalism*, trans. T. Parsons. New York: Scribner.

Whyte, (1954). *The organization man*.*

Wiggins, J. S. (1973). *Personality and prediction: Principles of personality assessment*. Reading, Mass.: Addison–Wesley.

_____. (1996). *The Five-Factor Model of personality*. New York: Guilford.

Wiggins, J. S., & Trapnell, P. D. (1996). A dyadic-interactional perspective on the Five-Factor Model. In J. S. Wiggins (Ed.), *The Five-Factor Model of personality*. New York: Guilford.

Wilson, E. O. (1975). *Sociobiology*. Cambridge, Mass.: Harvard University Press.

_____. (1980). *Sociobiology*. Cambridge, Mass.: Belknap.

Winnicott, D. W. (1965). *The maturational processes and the facilitating environment.: studies in the theory of emotional development*. New York: International Universities Press.

Witmer, L. (1908). *The psychological clinic*. Old Penn, 9, 10.

Wolff, T. (1956). *Structural forms of the feminine psyche*. Zurich (privately printed).

Wolpe, J. (1964). *Psychotherapy by reciprocal inhibition*. Palo Alto, Calif.: Stanford University Press.

Wright, R. (1994). *The Moral Animal*. New York: Little, Brown.

Wundt, W. (1903). *Grundzuge der physiologischen psychologie*, 5th ed. Leipzig: Engelmaner.

Zimbardo, P. G. (1972). The Stanford prison experiment. A slide/tape presentation produced by Philip G. Zimbardo, Inc., P. O. Box 4395, Stanford, CA, 94305.

INDEX

Behavior
  expressive, 142
  predicting, 17
  self-presentational, 305–306
  unconscious, 307
  violent, 40–41
Behavioral modeling, 165
Behavior genetics, 295, 296
Behaviorism
  biographical example of, 209
  core problem of, 196–197
  distinctive features of, 185–186
  evaluation of, 205–208
  historical overview of, 188–190
  See also Learning theory
Behavior modification, 193
Behavior of Organisms, The (Skinner), 192
Benedict, Ruth, 241, 252
Benjamin, Lorna, 180
Bernheim, Hippolyte, 38, 39
Bewitchment, 232
Beyond Freedom and Dignity (Skinner), 193, 203, 204
Binswanger, Ludwig, 243, 244
Biological motives, 20–21
Blanchard, Kenneth, 208
Blumer, Herbert, 220
Bodily self, 136
Bois-Reymond, Emile du, 48
Brain
  phrenology and, 32, 33
  regnant processes in, 152
Branch Davidians, 76
Breuer, Josef, 48, 50
British empiricism, 187
Brucke, Ernst, 47, 48, 50
Burlingame, Dorothy, 268
Butler, Samuel, 28

California Psychological Inventory (CPI), 34, 35, 36
Cameron, Norman, 223
Cardinal dispositions, 134
Care, virtue of, 280
Careers
  classification system for, 291

personality characteristics and, 291–292
vocational type theory and, 31
women's issues and, 123–124
See also Work issues
Carson, Robert, 180
Castration anxiety, 58–59
Cathected objects, 150
Central dispositions, 134
Character
  development of problems with, 279
  neurotic styles and, 56–57
Charcot, Jean-Martin, 38–39, 48
Charismatic leaders, 76
Childhood, 84, 173–174, 249, 300–301
Childhood and Society (Erikson), 270, 273
Childrearing practices, 272
Chmura, Mark, 304
Chodorow, Nancy, 111
Cicero, 16
Circumplex, 181
Civilization and Its Discontents (Freud), 49, 51
Classical conditioning, 187–188, 190, 193–194
Claus, Carl, 47
Client-centered approach, 253
Client-Centered Therapy (Rogers), 252–253, 261
Clinton, Bill, 304, 308
Cognitive development, 171
Cognitive psychology, 261
Cognitive revolution, 165
Cognitive social learning theory, 195, 206–207
Cognitive therapy, 202
Cognitive type theory, 31
Collective unconscious, 87
Combat neuroses, 284–285
Common traits, 133
Communal identification, 58
Communion, 181
Comparative biology, 296
Competence, 277
Complementary roles, 231
Complexes, 150, 152–153

Future of an Illusion, The (Freud), 70

Galen, 28, 29–30
Gall, Franz Joseph, 32–33
Galton, Francis, 34, 295
Game playing, 300, 301–303
Gandhi, Mohandas, 271, 286
Gandhi's Truth (Erikson), 270
Gassner, Johann Joseph, 37
Gay, Peter, 45
Gender differences. See Sex differences
Generativity vs. Stagnation stage, 279–280
Genetics, behavior, 295, 296
Genital stage, 55
Genuine Remains (Butler), 28
German Ideology, The (Marx), 216
Gilligan, Carol, 111
Goffman, Erving, 215, 305
    impression management and, 220–222
    role theory and, 218, 220–222
Gough, Harrison, 35
Group living, 296
*Group Psychology and the Analysis of the
    Ego* (Freud), 50
Guilt, 275–276
Guntrip, Harry, 287

Hall, G. Stanley, 34, 49
Hall, Joseph, 28
Happiness, 308–309
Harris, Eric, 40
Hartley, David, 187
Hartmann, Heinz, 268, 269
Hathaway, S. R., 35
Hawthorne studies, 182
Hegel, G. W. F., 15
Helmholtz, Herman von, 48
Helplessness, learned, 201, 203
Hemingway, Ernest, 74–75
Heraclitus, 83
Hereditary Genius (Galton), 34, 295
Hero archetype, 91
Hershey, Lewis B., 179
Hierarchy of needs theory, 248, 251–252
Historical actuality, 286
History

    of learning theory, 186–196
    of personality psychology, 27–41
    of research on personality, 19
    of socioanalytic theory, 294–296
    of sociological approaches, 216–222
    See also Psychohistory
Hitler, Adolf, 278, 288–289
Hogan Personality Inventory, 35, 36
Holland, John, 30, 31, 291
Hope, 274
Horney, Karen, 22, 103–124, 167
    biographical sketch of, 103–106
    core problem for, 106–107
    evaluating theories of, 120, 123
    motivational theory of, 107, 109–110
    personality development theory of,
        110
    psychological adjustment theory of,
        113, 115, 117–118, 120
    self-knowledge and, 110, 112
    societal factors viewed by, 119, 120
    unconscious processes and, 112–113
    women's issues and, 108–109
    See also Female psychology
Hsu, F. L. K., 282
Humanistic psychology, 241–265
    biographical example of, 262–263
    core problem of, 250
    evaluation of, 260–261
    existentialism and, 242–246, 260
    medieval roots of, 246
    motivation and, 251–253
    peak experiences and, 256
    personality development and, 253–254
    practical application of, 264–265
    problems with, 261, 263–264
    psychological adjustment and, 257–258
    scientific psychology vs., 254
    self-actualization process and,
        252
    self-knowledge and, 255–256
    societal factors and, 259–260
    unconscious processes and, 256–256
Hume, David, 187
Hunter-gatherer societies, 299
"Hunters Across the Prairie" (Erikson), 282

importance of "fit" in, 24–25
See also Employees; Work issues
Johnson, Spencer, 208
Jones, Ernest, 45, 312
Jonestown massacre, 76
Journal of Humanistic Psychology, 263
Jung, Carl, 22, 77–102
   archetypes and, 79, 89–90, 93, 232
   biographical sketch of, 79–82
   core problem for, 82
   evaluating theories of, 97–99
   Freud's relationship with, 49, 51, 80–82
   motivational theory of, 83–84
   personality development theory of,
      84–87, 175–176
   psychological adjustment theory of,
      94–95
   self-knowledge and, 93
   societal factors viewed by, 95, 97
   unconscious processes and, 87,
      89–91, 93
Juvenile era, 173

Kandinsky, Wassily, 262–263
Kant, Immanuel, 29, 79
Kelly, George, 158–166, 305
   biographical sketch of, 158–159
   core problem for, 159–160
   evaluating theories of, 165–166
   motivational theory of, 162–163
   personal constructs theory, 160,
      215–216
   personality development theory of,
      163
   psychological adjustment theory of,
      164–165
   self-knowledge and, 163–164
   societal factors viewed by, 165
   system of corollaries of, 181–182
   unconscious processes and, 164
Kierkegaard, Soren, 242, 245
Kiesler, Donald, 180
Klebold, Dylan, 40
Koresh, David, 76

Labeling theory, 163

Lasswell, Harold, 167
Latency phase, 55, 60, 276
Latent complexes, 150
Latent content, 61
Law and order, 275
Law of Effect, 191
Law of Exercise, 191
Leadership
   charismatic, 76
   Freud's views on, 70, 72, 75–76
   needs characteristic of, 155
   nominal vs. effective, 309
   See also Authority
Learned helplessness, 201, 202, 203
Learning theory, 185–211
   core problem of, 196–197
   distinctive features of, 185–186
   evaluation of, 205–208
   historical overview of, 201
   motivation and, 197–198
   personality development and, 198–199
   practical applications of, 208, 210–212
   psychological adjustment and, 201, 203
   self-knowledge and, 199, 201
   societal factors and, 203–205
   unconscious processes and, 201
"Learning to Be Free" (Rogers), 264
Leary, Timothy, 180
"Legend of Adolf Hitler's Childhood, The"
   (Erikson), 288–289
Leonardo da Vinci, 286
Letters from Jenny (Allport), 144
Lewin, Kurt, 39
Libido
   Freud's theory of, 51
   Jung's theory of, 83
Liebault, Auguste, 38
Lifestyle, 114
Literary type theory, 28
Little Albert study, 190
Locke, John, 187
Loneliness, 306
Looking glass self, 218
Love
   intimacy stage and, 279
   need for belongingness and, 251

neurotic need for, 251
Ludwig, Carl, 48
Luther, Martin, 271, 286

Macrosociology, 218
Mahler, Margaret, 60
Malcolm X, 168–169
Management
    behavioral approach to, 207, 208,
        210–211
    women in positions of, 123–124
    See also Work issues
Man and His Symbols (Jung), 82
Mandalas, 94, 95
Manifest complexes, 150
Manifest content, 61
Marriage, 108
Marx, Karl, 216
Masculine protest, 114
Maslow, Abraham, 241
    biographical sketch of, 247–248
    evaluating the views of, 260–261,
        263–264
    hierarchy of needs theory of, 248,
        251–253
    motivational theory of, 251–253
    peak experiences and, 256–257
    self-actualization and, 251–252,
        257–259
Masterson, Jenny, 144–145
Maternal conflicts, 108–109
Maturity
    Allport's criteria for, 138–139
    Freud's definition of, 67
    socioanalytic view of, 310–311
    Sullivan's characteristics of, 179
May, Rollo, 242, 244
McAdams, Dan, 289
McClelland, David, 155
McDougall, William, 127, 130, 147, 295,
    301
McKinley, J. C., 35
Mead, George Herbert, 167, 215, 235–230
    role theory and, 218–220, 223
    self-knowledge and, 301
    symbolic interactionism and, 220

Mead, Margaret, 106, 282
Meaning
    happiness and, 310
    individuation and, 84
    need for, 244
Mein Kampf (Hitler), 288
Melville, Herman, 128
Mental health. See Psychological
    adjustment
Mesmer, Franz Anton, 37
Metaneeds, 252
Microsociology, 218
Milgram, Stanley, 52
Mill, John Stuart, 187
Miller, Geoffrey, 296
Miller, Neal, 201
Mind, Self, and Society (Mead), 218
Minnesota Multiphasic Personality Inventory
    (MMPI), 34, 35, 36
Mischel, Walter, 166, 305
Monogamy, 108
Montessori, Maria, 265
Moods, 306–307
Moral development, 165, 180
Morgan, Christiana, 146
Morris, Edmund, 226
Moses and Monotheism (Freud), 50, 75
"Mother-Baby" games, 302
Motivation, 20, 23
    Adler's theory of, 114–115
    Allport's theory of, 132–134
    Erikson's theory of, 272–273
    Freud's theory of, 51, 53, 71
    Horney's theory of, 107, 110
    humanistic view of, 215–253
    Jung's theory of, 83–84
    Kelly's theory of, 162–163
    learning theory of, 197–198
    Murray's theory of, 148–150
    socioanalytic view of, 225, 229
    sociological approach to, 225, 229
    Sullivan's theory of, 170, 182
Motivation and Personality (Maslow),
    151, 257
Multiform method of assessment, 146
Munsterberg, Hugo, 129

Murray, Henry, 127–128, 143, 145–147
    assessment centers and, 146, 154,
        155–156
    biographical sketch of, 143, 145–147
    core problem for, 147–148
    evaluating theories of, 154–155
    Jung's influence on, 143, 146, 151–152
    motivational theory of, 148–150
    personality development theory of,
        150–151
    psychological adjustment theory of,
        152–153
    self-knowledge and, 151
    societal factors viewed by, 153–154
    unconscious processes and, 151–152
Mutual mode, 243
Myers, Isabel, 86, 88
Myers-Briggs Type Indicator (MBTI), 31, 36,
    88, 89, 98, 102,
Myths, 94–95

Narrative psychology, 224
Needs
    intimacy, 173
    Maslow's hierarchy of, 248, 251–253
    Murray's concept of, 148–149, 150
    neurotic, 109, 113, 115, 117
Negative identity, 284, 285
Negative reinforcement, 197
Neill, A. S., 265
Neuropsychology, 296
Neurosis
    authority and, 50
    character and, 56–57
    ego development and, 260
    interactive strategies and, 117–118, 120
    needs indicative of, 108–109, 113,
        115, 117
Neurotic styles, 113–114
Newton, Isaac, 162
New Ways in Psychoanalysis (Horney), 106
Nietzsche, Frederich, 242–243, 252
Nofziger, Lynn, 228
Nominal leaders, 309
Nomothetic science, 133
Nonverbal cues, 142

Obedience, 52–53
Object relations theorists, 60
Obsessive-compulsive style, 56
Odbert, H. S., 141
Oedipus conflict, 55, 58–59, 276, 312
Office of Strategic Services (OSS), 146,
    155–156
Old age, 84–84
O'Neill, Tip, 228–229
One Minute Manager, The (Blanchard &
    Johnson), 208, 210–211
Ontogenesis, 299–301
Open approaches to education, 265
Operant conditioning, 191–193, 194, 195
Operant response, 193
Optimism, 260
Oral stage, 54, 273
Organ inferiority, 115
Organismic involvement, 231
Organismic valuing process, 253–255
Organization Man, The (Whyte), 250
Origin of Species (Darwin), 47, 294
Outline of Psychology (McDougall), 295

Pair bonding, 299
Paleontology, 296
Paranoid style, 56
Parataxic thinking, 171–172
Pattern and Growth in Personality (Allport),
    134
Pavlov, Ivan P., 29, 187–190, 194, 206,
    298
Peak experiences, 256–257
Penis envy, 59
Pepper, Stephen, 224
Persona archetype, 89–90, 232
Personal constructs theory, 160, 168
Personal dispositions, 133–134
Personal identity, 283
Personality
    assumptions about, 16
    career choice and, 291–292
    definitions of, 16–18, 129
    history of studies on, 19
    reputation and, 303–304